mosaics FOCUSING ON PARAGRAPHS IN CONTEXT

Kim Flachmann

Wendy Wilson
Fanshawe College

Melissa Mackey
Fanshawe College

CANADIAN EDITION

PEARSON

Prentice Hall

Toronto

Library and Archives Canada Cataloguing in Publication

Flachmann, Kim
    Mosaics : focusing on paragraphs in context / Kim Flachmann,
Wendy Wilson, Melissa Mackey.—Canadian ed.

Includes index.
ISBN 0-13-127559-3

    1. English language—Paragraphs. 2. English language—Rhetoric.
I. Wilson, Wendy, 1946– II. Mackey, Melissa, 1973– III. Title.

PE1439.F52 2006   808'.042   C2005-907857-X

ISBN 0-13-127559-3

Vice President, Editorial Director: Michael J. Young
Sponsoring Editor: Carolin Sweig
Marketing Manager: Leigh-Ann Graham
Marketing Coordinator: Shelley Pollock
Developmental Editor: Jennifer Murray
Production Editor: Avivah Wargon
Copy Editor: Judith Turnbull
Production Coordinator: Janis Raisen
Page Layout: Jansom
Art Director: Mary Opper
Interior Design: Gail Ferreira Ng-A-Kien
Cover Design: Michelle Bellemare
Cover Image: Masterfile

2 3 4 5   11 10 09 08 07

Printed and bound in the United States of America.

For Christopher

—K.F.

For Andrea, Mike, and Diana, my three best writing students.

—W.W.

For Emily Laura and Sarah Maree Mackey. When you get older,
I think you'll be happy to have an English professor for an aunt!

—M.M.

Brief Contents

CONTENTS

PREFACE

Experience tells us that students have the best chance of succeeding in college or university if they learn how to respond productively to the varying academic demands made on them throughout the curriculum. One extremely important part of this process is being able to analyze ideas and think critically about issues in many different subject areas. *Mosaics: Focusing on Paragraphs in Context* is the second in a series of three books that teach the basic skills essential to all good academic writing. This series illustrates how the companion skills of reading and writing are parts of a larger, interrelated process that moves back and forth through the tasks of prereading and reading, prewriting and writing, and revising and editing. In other words, the *Mosaics* series shows how these skills are integrated at every stage of the writing process.

THE *MOSAICS* SERIES

This Canadian edition of the *Mosaics* series consists of three books, each with a different emphasis—*Focusing on Essays, Focusing on Paragraphs in Context,* and *Focusing on Sentences in Context.* The first book highlights the composition of essays, the second book paragraph development, and the third sentence structure. Each book introduces the writing process as a unified whole and asks students to begin writing in the very first chapter. Each volume also moves from personal to more academic writing. The books differ in the length and level of their reading selections, the complexity of their writing assignments, the degree of difficulty of their revising and editing strategies, and the length and level of their student writing samples.

This entire three-book series is based on the following fundamental assumptions:

- Students build confidence in their ability to read and write by reading and writing.
- Students learn best from discovery and experimentation rather than from instruction and abstract discussions.
- Students need to discover and develop their personal writing process.
- Students learn both individually and collaboratively.
- Students profit from studying both professional and student writing.
- Students benefit most from assignments that integrate thinking, reading, and writing.

- Students learn how to revise their writing by following clear guidelines.
- Students learn grammar and usage rules by editing their own writing.
- Students must be able to transfer their writing skills to their other courses.
- Students must think critically and analytically to succeed in college or university.

HOW THIS BOOK WORKS

Mosaics: Focusing on Paragraphs in Context teaches students how to write effective paragraphs. For flexibility and easy reference, this book is divided into five parts:

Part I: The Writing Process
Part II: Writing Effective Paragraphs
Part III: Essays: Paragraphs in Context
Part IV: From Reading to Writing
Part V: Handbook

Part I: The Writing Process   All five chapters in Part I demonstrate the cyclical nature of the writing process. They begin with the logistics of getting ready to write and then move systematically through the interlocking stages of the process by following a student essay from prewriting to revising and editing. Part I ends with a quiz that students can take to identify their "Editing Quotient"—their strengths and weaknesses in grammar and mechanics.

Part II: Writing Effective Paragraphs   Part II, the heart of the instruction in this text, teaches students how to write paragraphs by introducing the rhetorical modes as patterns of development. It moves from personal writing to more academic types of writing: describing, narrating, illustrating, analyzing a process, comparing and contrasting, dividing and classifying, defining, analyzing causes and effects, and arguing. Within each chapter, students write their own paragraphs, read professional paragraphs, study the paragraphs of other students, and finally revise and edit the paragraph they wrote earlier in the chapter. By following specific guidelines, students learn how to produce a successful paragraph using each rhetorical mode.

Part III: Essays: Paragraphs in Context   The next section of this text helps students move from writing effective paragraphs to writing effective essays. It systematically illustrates the relationship between a paragraph and an essay. Then it explains the essay through both professional and student examples. Part III ends with a series of writing assignments and workshops designed to encourage students to write, revise, and edit an essay and then reflect on their own writing process.

Part IV: From Reading to Writing   Part IV of this text is a collection of readings arranged by rhetorical mode. Multiple rhetorical strategies are at work in most of these essays, but each is classified according to its primary rhetorical purpose. As a result, students can refer to particular essays in this part that demonstrate a rhetorical mode they are studying in Part II. In this way, students can actually see the features of each rhetorical mode at work in an extended piece of writing. Each professional essay is preceded by prereading activities that will help students focus on the topic at hand and then is followed by 10 questions that move students from literal to analytical thinking as they consider the essay's content, purpose, audience, and paragraph structure.

Part V: Handbook   Part V is a complete handbook, including exercises, that covers eight main categories: Sentences, Verbs, Pronouns, Modifiers, Punctuation, Mechanics, Effective Sentences, and Choosing the Right Word. These categories are coordinated with the Editing Checklist that appears periodically throughout this text. Each chapter starts with five self-test questions so that students can determine their strengths and weaknesses in a specific area. The chapters provide at least three types of practice after each grammar concept, moving the students systematically from identifying grammar concepts to writing their own sentences. Each unit ends with a practical "Editing Workshop" that asks students to use the skills they just learned as they work with another student to edit their own writing. Unit Tests—including practice with single sentences and paragraphs—complete each unit.

APPENDICES

The appendices will help students keep track of their progress in the various skills they are learning in this text. References to these appendices are interspersed throughout the book so that students know when to use them as they study the concepts in each chapter:

Appendix 1: Editing Peer Evaluation Form
Appendix 2: Revising Peer Evaluation Forms
Appendix 3: Revising Peer Evaluation Form for an Essay
Appendix 4: Editing Peer Evaluation Form for an Essay
Appendix 5: Editing Quotient Error Chart
Appendix 6: Error Log
Appendix 7: Spelling Log
Appendix 8: Test Yourself Answers (Handbook)

OVERALL GOAL

Ultimately, each book in the *Mosaics* series portrays writing as a way of thinking and processing information. One by one, these books encourage students to discover how the "mosaics" of their own writing process work together to form a coherent whole. By demonstrating the relationships among thinking, reading, and writing on progressively more difficult levels, these books promise to help prepare students for success throughout the curriculum.

UNIQUE FEATURES

Several unique and exciting features separate this book from other basic writing texts.

- It moves students systematically from personal to academic writing.
- It uses both student writing and professional writing as models.
- It demonstrates all aspects of the writing process through student writing.
- It integrates reading and writing throughout the text.
- It teaches revising and editing through student writing.
- It features culturally diverse reading selections that are of high interest to students.
- It includes many readings written by and about Canadians.
- It teaches rhetorical modes as patterns of thought.
- It helps students discover and develop their own writing process.
- It includes a complete handbook with exercises.
- It offers worksheets for students to chart their progress in reading and writing.

CANADIAN FEATURES

This textbook has been changed to reflect the needs of Canadian students. High-interest paragraphs and essays by Canadian authors such as Margaret Atwood, David Suzuki, Joan Clark, and Robert Fulford, among others, have been included. Examples throughout the text have been updated, and the grammar Handbook in Part V streamlined. At the same time, the integrity of the original text has been maintained. In the interests of keeping the book at a manageable size and providing electronic templates, some student material has been moved from the appendices to the Companion Website.

The Instructor's Resource Manual and Companion Website have also been updated to include the interests of Canadian students.

SUPPLEMENTS

To help both students and instructors get the most out of *Mosaics: Focusing on Paragraphs on Context*, we have provided both an Instructor's Resource Manual and a Companion Website.

The Instructor's Resource Manual (0-13-204293-2) provides over 500 pages of additional teaching strategies, collaborative activities, sample syllabi, chapter summaries, and two quizzes for each chapter. Instructors can download this supplement from a password-protected location on Pearson Education Canada's online catalogue. Simply search for the text, go to "Resources" in the left-hand menu, and click on "Instructors."

Contact your local sales representative for further information.

The **Companion Website, www.pearsoned.ca/flachmann/mosaics** offers students chapter objectives, quizzes, and internet activities, as well as further sample student essays.

ACKNOWLEDGMENTS

For the Canadian edition, we would like to thank all our supportive colleagues in the General Studies Division at Fanshawe College. We would also like to thank Carolin Sweig, sponsoring editor; Jennifer Murray, developmental editor; and Avivah Wargon, production editor, for all of their hard work and patience working with us on the *Mosaics* series.

The following individuals graciously gave up their time to provide constructive criticism of various drafts of the revisions of this book or of the first book in the *Mosaics* series. We are grateful to these people, as well as to a few who wish to remain anonymous, for their many useful comments and suggestions.

Natalie Anklesaria, Seneca College
Marlet Ashley, Kwantlen University College
Marie Brodie, Nova Scotia Community College
Patricia Campbell, Red Deer College
Lynn Clark-Jones, Northern Alberta Institute of Technology
Kathy Cocchio, Northern Alberta Institute of Technology
Calum Cunningham, Fanshawe College
Becky Halvorson, Capilano College
Chandra Hodgson, Humber College
Kristine Kerins, Camosun College
Sheila Lanthier O'Connor, Concordia University
Andrea Lovering, Georgian College
Helen Mendes, Kawntlen Univeristy College
Martin Reyto, George Brown College

Melanie Rubens, Seneca College
Lara Sauer, George Brown College
Vicky Simpson, Cape Breton University

Wendy Wilson and Melissa Mackey

I want to express my gratitude to my students, from whom I have learned so much about the writing process, about teaching, and about life itself, and to Cheryl Smith's classes, who tested various sections of the books and gave me good ideas for revising them over the past three years. Thanks finally to the students who contributed paragraphs and essays to this series: Josh Ellis, Jolene Christie, Mary Minor, Michael Tiede, and numerous others.

Finally, I owe a tremendous personal debt to the people who have lived with this project for the last two years; they are my closest companions and my best advisors: Michael, Christopher, and Laura Flachmann. To Michael, I owe additional thanks for the valuable support and feedback he has given me through the entire process of creating and revising this series.

Kim Flachmann

A Great Way to Learn and Instruct Online

The Pearson Education Canada Companion Website is easy to navigate and is organized to correspond to the chapters in this textbook. Whether you are a student in the classroom or a distance learner you will discover helpful resources for in-depth study and research that empower you in your quest for greater knowledge and maximize your potential for success in the course.

[www.pearsoned.ca/flachmann/mosaics]

PEARSON
Prentice Hall

Jump to... http://www.pearsoned.ca/flachmann/mosaics ⬍ Home Search Help Profile

Companion Website

Home >

Companion Website

Mosaics: Focusing on Paragraphs in Context, Canadian Edition, by Flachmann, Wilson, and Mackey

Student Resources

The modules in this section provide students with tools for learning course material. These modules include:

- Objectives
- Chapter Quiz
- Internet Activities
- Destinations
- Student Essays

In the quiz modules students can send answers to the grader and receive instant feedback on their progress through the Results Reporter. Coaching comments and references to the textbook may be available to ensure that students take advantage of all available resources to enhance their learning experience.

PART

I

THE WRITING PROCESS

What student's mind—what writer's mind—has not begun to write without knowing really where it will go, only to learn at the end where it meant to start?

—VICTOR KANTOR BURG

Part I of *Mosaics* is designed to build your confidence as a writer. In these five chapters, you will learn more about the writing process so that you can understand and take control of the unique way you write. As you mould the writing process into a series of stages and activities that will work for you, you will become more aware of your own strengths and weaknesses as a writer. You can then use this information throughout the text to establish your identity in the community of writers.

CHAPTER 1

GETTING STARTED

The simple act of using the written word to communicate makes a person a writer. Whether you use writing to make a grocery list, email a friend, do your history assignment, or write a report for your manager, you are part of a community of writers. In fact, you *are* a writer.

Any piece of writing more formal than a grocery list, however, is usually the result of a sequence of activities. On the surface, these activities may seem to have very little to do with the act of writing itself. But they make up what is called the *writing process,* and learning to use this process to help you communicate your ideas is what this book is all about.

YOUR PERSONAL WRITING RITUAL

Though all writers are different, some general principles apply to everyone—students and professional writers alike. Before you can begin the writing process, you need to set aside a time and place for your task, gather supplies, and think of yourself as a writer.

1. *Set aside a special time for writing, and plan to do nothing else during that time.* The dog's bath can wait until tomorrow, the kitchen appliances don't have to be scrubbed today, drawers can be cleaned and organized some other time, and the dirt on the car won't turn to concrete overnight. When you first get a writing task, a little procrastination is good because it gives your mind time to plan your approach to the assignment. The trick is to know when to quit procrastinating and get down to work.

2. *Find a comfortable place with few distractions.* In her famous essay *A Room of One's Own,* Virginia Woolf claims that all writers have a basic need for space, privacy, and time. You need to set up a place of your own that suits your needs as a writer, and it should be a place where you are not distracted or interrupted. Some people work best sitting in a straight chair at a desk, while others write in a big armchair or on a bed. The particular place doesn't matter, as long as you feel comfortable writing there.

   Even if you are lucky enough to have a private study area, you may find that you still need to make some adjustments. For example, you might want to turn off the ringer on your phone during the time you spend on your writing assignments. Or you may discover that tuning your radio to a jazz station helps you shut out noise from other parts of the house but doesn't distract you in the way that talk shows or rock music might. One student may write sitting in bed with her legs crossed, wearing jeans and a T-shirt; another may prefer sprawling on the floor in pyjamas. The point is this: Whatever your choices, you need to set up a working environment that is comfortable for you.

3. *Gather your supplies before you begin to write.* Who knows what great idea might escape while you search for a pen that works or a formatted disk! Some writers use a legal pad and a pencil to get started on a writing task, while others go straight to their computers. One of the main advantages of working on a computer is that once you type in your ideas, changing them or moving them around is easy. As a result, you are more likely to revise when you work on a computer and, therefore, you will probably turn in a better paper. Whatever equipment you choose, make sure it is ready at the time you have set aside to write.

4. *Think of yourself as a writer.* Once you have a time and place for writing and all the supplies you need, you are ready to discover your own writing process. Understanding your unique habits and rituals is extremely important to your growth as a writer. So in the course of recognizing yourself as a writer, take a moment now to record some of your own preferences when you write.

◆ *P r a c t i c e 1* Explain the rituals you instinctively follow as you prepare to write. Where do you write? At what time of day do you produce your best work? Do you like noise? Quiet? What other details describe your writing environment? What equipment do you use to write?

KEEPING A JOURNAL

The word *journal* means "a place for daily writing." Your journal is a place for you to record ideas, snatches of conversation, dreams, descriptions of people, pictures of places or objects—whatever catches your attention.

If you use a notebook for your journal, take some time to pick a size and colour that you really like. Some people choose spiral-bound notebooks; others prefer cloth-bound books or loose-leaf binders. You might even want a notebook divided into sections so that different types of entries can have their own location. The choice is yours—unless your instructor specifies a particular journal. Just remember that a journal should be a notebook you enjoy writing in and carrying with you.

Your journal might even be electronic. However, unless you have a laptop or hand-held computer, you won't have your electronic journal with you all the time. So you need to schedule time to write at your computer every day. If you use a hand-held computer, remember to download your entries to your main computer on a regular basis. Also be sure to back up computer journal entries on a disk and save your work fairly often so you don't lose anything in a power failure. You may also want to print hard copies of your journal entries to take with you to class.

To help improve your life as a writer, you will find a personal journal extremely valuable. As with any skill, the more you practise, the more you will improve. In addition, your journal is a collection of thoughts and topics for your writing assignments. In other words, your journal is a place to both generate and retrieve your ideas. Finally, writing can help you solve problems. Writing in your journal can help you discover what you think and feel about specific issues and lets you think through important choices you have to make.

You can use this textbook to help you establish the habit of journal writing. For example, in your journal you might answer the questions that accompany the instruction in Parts II and III of this text, the readings in Part IV, and the writing exercises in the handbook (Part V). You might also want to use your journal for prewriting or generating ideas on a specific topic. Keeping track of your journal is much easier than tracking down assorted scraps of paper when you need them.

Making at least one section of your journal private is also a good idea. Sometimes when you think on paper or let your imagination loose, you don't want to share the results with anyone, but those notes can be very important in finding a subject to write about or in developing a topic.

Everyone's journal entries will be different and will often depend on the instructor's objectives in a particular course. But some basic advice applies to all entries, whether you keep your journal on paper or on a computer.

1. Date your entries. (Jotting down the time is also useful so you can see when your best ideas occur.)
2. Record anything that comes to your mind, and follow your thoughts wherever they take you (unless your instructor gives you different directions).
3. Download or tape anything into your journal that stimulates your thinking or writing—cartoons, magazine ads, poems, pictures, advice columns, and pages from the Internet.
4. Think of your journal as someone to talk to—a friend who will keep your ideas safe and sound and won't talk back or argue with you.

◆ *P r a c t i c e   2*   Begin your own journal.

1. Buy a notebook that you like, and write in it.
2. Make at least two journal entries on your computer.
3. Which type of journal do you prefer—paper or electronic? Write an entry explaining your preference.

THE WRITING PROCESS

The writing process begins the minute you get a writing assignment. It involves all the activities you do, from choosing a topic to turning in a final draft. During this time, you will be thinking about your topic on both a subconscious and conscious level. Whether you are washing your car, reading in the library, preparing a meal, or writing a draft of your paper, you are going through your writing process. The main parts of the process are outlined here.

Prewriting

Prewriting refers to all activities that help you explore a subject, generate ideas about it, settle on a specific topic, establish a purpose, and analyze the audience for your essay. In Chapter 2, you will learn different strategies for accomplishing these goals before you actually begin to write a draft of your paragraph or essay. Your mission at this stage is to stimulate your thinking before and during the act of writing. Every time you think of a new idea at any time during the writing process, you are prewriting.

Writing

When you have lots of ideas to work with, you are ready to start writing. Writing involves expanding some of your best ideas, organizing your thoughts to reflect your purpose, and writing a first draft. To start on your draft, you may want to spread out your class notes, your journal entries, or various other prewriting notes so that you can start to string your ideas together into coherent sentences. This is the time to keep your thoughts flowing without worrying too much about grammar, punctuation, or spelling.

Revising

As you may already suspect, the process of writing is not finished with your first draft. You should always revise your work to make it stronger and better. Revising involves rethinking your content and organization so that your writing says exactly what you want it to. (Editing, the last step, focuses on correcting grammar and spelling.) Your main goal in revising is to make sure that the purpose of your essay is clear to your audience and that your main ideas are supported with details and examples. In addition, you should check that your organization is logical.

Editing

The final step in the writing process is editing. In this stage, you should read your paragraph or essay slowly and carefully to make sure no errors in grammar, punctuation, mechanics, or spelling have slipped into your draft. Such errors can distract your reader from the message you are trying to communicate or can cause communication to break down altogether. Editing gives you the chance to clean up your draft so that your writing is clear and precise.

Writing as a Cycle

Even though we talk about the stages of writing, writing is actually a cyclical process, which means that at any point you may loop in and out of other stages. The diagram on the next page shows how the stages of the writing process can overlap.

Once you start on a writing project, the stages of writing do not occur in any specific order. You may change a word (revise) in the very first sentence that you write and then think of another detail (prewrite) that you can add to your opening sentence and next cross out and rewrite a misspelled word (edit)—all in the first two minutes of your writing task. Although you may approach every writing project in a different way, we hope that as you move through Part I, you will establish a framework for your personal writing process and start to get comfortable as a writer working within that framework.

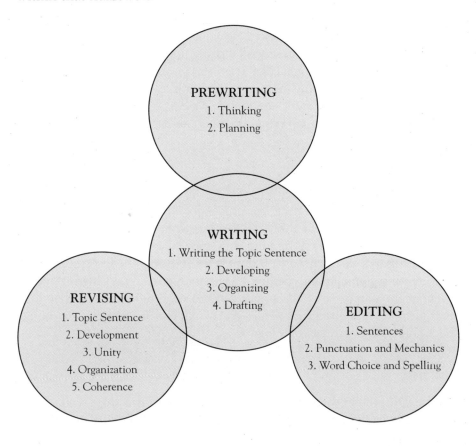

PREWRITING
1. Thinking
2. Planning

WRITING
1. Writing the Topic Sentence
2. Developing
3. Organizing
4. Drafting

REVISING
1. Topic Sentence
2. Development
3. Unity
4. Organization
5. Coherence

EDITING
1. Sentences
2. Punctuation and Mechanics
3. Word Choice and Spelling

◆ *P r a c t i c e   3*

1. Explain prewriting in your own words.

   _____

   _____

2. Describe your writing environment.

   _____

   _____

3. What does "writing" consist of?

   _____

   _____

4. What is the difference between revising and editing?

   _____

   _____

WRITING ASSIGNMENT

This first writing assignment is much like the writing tasks you will be responding to throughout this book. You'll be working on this assignment yourself over the next four chapters as you apply what you are learning about the writing process. At the same time, we will follow the work of a student named Travis Morehouse so you can see how he approaches and completes the same assignment. By the end of Chapter 5, you will have a feel for the entire writing process, which is essential to strengthening your identity as a writer.

 Write Your Own Paragraph

Think about a favourite place that you visit frequently. It could be somewhere that is peaceful, beautiful, or busy. It could be a restaurant, a park, or a place of employment or worship. Then describe this location for someone who has never been there. Explain to your readers the sights, sounds, tastes, smells, and textures that attract you to this spot.

PREWRITING

Many students are surprised that a number of steps in the writing process occur before the actual act of putting words on paper. These steps fall into the general category of **prewriting.** Prewriting activities help us do the following tasks:

- Explore a subject
- Generate ideas about the subject
- Settle on a specific topic
- Establish a purpose
- Analyze our audience

Let's begin this chapter by looking at activities that many writers use to stimulate their thinking as they approach a writing assignment. You will get a chance to try each one. Consider keeping your responses to these activities in a journal that you can refer to throughout the course.

THINKING

Thinking is always the initial stage of any writing project. It's a time to explore your topic and let your mind run free over the material you have to work with. We'll explore six activities that promise to stimulate your best thoughts: reading, freewriting, brainstorming, clustering, questioning, and discussing. You will see how Travis Morehouse uses each strategy and then have a chance to try out the strategy yourself.

Reading

Sometimes a good way to jump-start your thinking and your writing process is to surf the Web or read an article on your topic. If you take notes on sources as you read, you may find yourself spinning off into your own thoughts on the subject.

Travis's Reading   Travis read the following paragraph from an essay titled "Micanopy" by Bailey White. It stimulated his thoughts about his own favourite place, so he jotted several notes to himself in the margins.

Wow! She   But the reason I drive the two hundred miles year
must   after year is the bookstore. The building is tall, a
really   beautiful pink brick. The sign says,
like this
place!
                        O. Brisky
                         Books
                     Old Used Rare
                    Bought and Sold
                 Out of Print Search Service   *What is*
                                                        this?

I can   Even before you go inside, you can smell the old,
always   used, and rare books. On sunny days, Mr. Brisky
smell old   arranges a collection of books on a table on the side-
books.   walk. There are books in the windows and stacks of
                books on the floor just inside the entrance. From an
Name of   open back door the misty green light of Micanopy
town?   shines into the dust. Tendrils of wisteria have crept in   *Plants?*
                through the doorway and are stealthily making their
                way toward the religion and philosophy section.

Later, Travis made this entry in his journal.

> I really liked Bailey White's description of the
> bookstore. The first sentence shows how much she likes
> this place. She gives so many examples about why she
> drives two hundred miles just to go to this bookstore. I
> don't really have a place that I would drive that far to
> see. I wish I did! I wouldn't say a bookstore or library is
> my favourite place. I get too bored looking at so many
> books, but I do like feeling alone in such a big place. I
> guess my favourite place would just be out of the house.
> Far, far away where no one can find me. I love to be
> by myself, even though most of my friends don't
> understand this.

Your Reading   Read the following paragraph from "Magpies," an essay by Amy Tan (pages 196–199), and take notes in the margins as you read. Then, in your journal, write down any thoughts this paragraph stimulates.

> Sitting in this bed, I admired everything as if I were
> a princess. This room had a glass door that led to a

balcony. In front of the window door was a round table of the same wood as the bed. It too sat on carved lion's legs and was surrounded by four chairs. A servant had already put tea and sweet cakes on the table and was now lighting the houlu, a small stove for burning coal.

Freewriting

Writing about anything that comes to your mind is freewriting. You should write without stopping for five to ten minutes. Do not worry about grammar or spelling. If you get stuck, repeat an idea or start rhyming words. The mere act of writing makes writers think of other ideas. So just keep writing.

Travis's Freewriting   Travis had trouble freewriting, but he followed directions and just started in.

> Here I am in English class, and we're supposed to be freewriting. But I don't know what to write about—my mind is a complete blank. Blank blank blankety blank. I could write about my car. It's been burning oil like crazy. Wherever I drive, there's a trail of blue smoke. I have to put in a litre of oil every week or two! But I don't want to take it in because I don't have the money to get it fixed. The rest of my tuition payment is due. I need money coming in, not going out. But if I don't get my car fixed, I'm not going to be able to get to school. That would not be good. School ends up being an escape for me—from my family, from my friends, from my teachers. It's where my dreams are. I don't know what these dreams are yet, but I think they're at school. For the first time in my life I actually like school. Who would have thought?

Focused freewriting is the same procedure focused on a specific topic—either one your instructor gives you or one you choose. It is a systematic way of turning thoughts and impressions into words.

Travis's Focused Freewriting   Travis produced the following focused freewriting in his journal. He is trying to get his mind ready to write about his favourite place.

> I don't know what I consider to be my favourite place. I usually just get in my car and drive when I want to get away from things. I guess I can consider that ridge I sometimes go to as my favourite place. I do end up driving there when I just feel like I want to leave

everything behind. I like how I can see the city and the river from up high. I especially like to be there during sunsets because it is always so beautiful. I feel a peace that I can't seem to describe. Although no one would really understand anyway.

Your Freewriting   To start preparing for your own paragraph, try a focused freewriting assignment by writing in your journal about some of your favourite places.

Brainstorming

Like freewriting, brainstorming draws on free association—one thought naturally leads to another. But brainstorming is usually done in list form. You can brainstorm by yourself, with a friend, or with a group. Regardless of the method, list whatever comes into your mind on a topic—ideas, thoughts, examples, facts. As with freewriting, don't worry about grammar or spelling.

Travis's Brainstorming   Here is Travis's brainstorming on his favourite place:

> the ridge—high above the city
>
> can see the city
>
> the river—always has boats
>
> sometimes I can see cars
>
> the sunsets are really beautiful
>
> the city lights always look cool when it gets dark
>
> sometimes it can get really cold at night
>
> it's peaceful
>
> I can be alone
>
> I can think out my problems

Your Brainstorming   Brainstorm in your journal about a favourite place or several favourite places.

Clustering

Clustering is like brainstorming, but it has the advantage of showing how your thoughts are related. To cluster, take a sheet of blank paper, write a key word or phrase in the centre of the page, and draw a circle around it. Next, write down and circle any related ideas that come to mind. As you add ideas, draw lines to the thoughts they are related to. Try to keep going for two or three minutes. When you finish, you'll have a map of your ideas that can help you find your way to a good paragraph.

Travis's Cluster   Here is Travis's cluster:

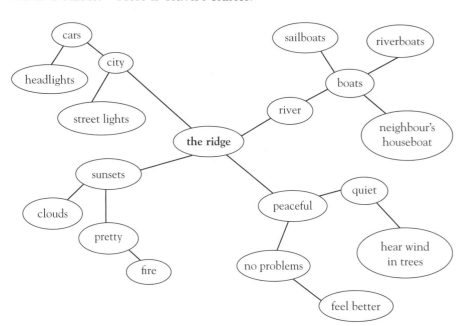

Your Cluster   Write "favourite place" in the middle of a piece of paper, circle it, and draw a cluster of your own personal associations with these words.

Questioning

Journalists use the questions known as the "five *W*s and one *H*"—Who? What? When? Where? Why? and How?—to check that they've included all the important information in a news story. You can use these same questions to generate ideas on a writing topic.

Travis's Questions   Here is how Travis used questioning to generate ideas on his topic:

Who?   I most enjoy being by myself up here, but I sometimes bring my friend Carlos because he thinks it's cool too.

What?   My favourite place that is really quiet and peaceful, the ridge that sits high above the city.

When?   My absolute favourite time to be here is when the sun goes down. The sun looks like it's on fire before it finally sets.

Where?   The ridge that's high above the city.

Why?   I can think up here. The beautiful sunset and the city and river help me clear my mind so I can solve problems.

How?   Just watching the boats and looking at the view make me feel better.

Your Questions   In your journal, answer these six questions about your favourite place: Who? What? When? Where? Why? How?

Discussing

Run your ideas by friends, classmates, and tutors. Often they'll have a perspective on your topic that will give you some entirely new ideas. Make sure you record your notes from these conversations so you don't lose the ideas.

Travis's Discussion   Here are Travis's notes from a conversation he had with his roommate about his favourite place:

> Because I have never spent much time thinking about the ridge, I am now trying to figure out why I enjoy this spot so much. When discussing the ridge with my roommate, Ralph, I remember that it's during sunsets when I feel most at peace. We discussed my love for the river and how the beauty of the place makes my problems disappear and how city lights shine after the sun goes down. I realize that this spot means more to me than I first thought. I want to tell my classmates about this place without sounding sentimental; I'm afraid that people will think I am too sensitive.

Your Discussion   Discuss your favourite place with someone, and record notes from your conversation in your journal.

◆ *P r a c t i c e   1 A*   Now that you have been introduced to several prewriting strategies, which is your favourite? Why do you like it best?

◆ *P r a c t i c e   1 B*   Using two prewriting strategies on one assignment is often a good idea. What is your second favourite prewriting strategy? Why do you like this strategy?

PLANNING

In this course, you'll be writing paragraphs—single paragraphs at first and paragraphs in essays later. A paragraph is a group of sentences on a single topic. The first line of each paragraph is indented to show that a new topic or subtopic is starting. Although paragraphs vary in length, typical paragraphs in student themes range from 50 to 250 words, averaging about 100 words.

Writing a paragraph takes planning. You need to make certain decisions about your subject, your purpose for writing, and your audience before you actually write, so that the task of writing is as smooth and stress-free as possible.

- *What is your subject (person, event, object, idea, etc.)?* A paragraph focuses on a single topic and includes related thoughts and details. Your first decision, therefore, is about your *subject:* What are you going to write about? Sometimes your topic is given to you—for example, when your sociology instructor assigns a paper on drug abuse among teenagers. But at other times, you choose your own topic. In such cases, choosing a subject that interests you is the best strategy. You will have more to say, and you will enjoy writing much more if you find your topic appealing.

- *What is your purpose?* Your *purpose* is your reason for writing a paragraph. Your purpose could be to explore your feelings on a topic (*to do personal writing*), to tell a friend about something funny that happened to you (*to entertain*), to explain something or share information (*to inform*), or to convince others of your position on a controversial issue (*to persuade*). Whatever your purpose, deciding on it in advance makes writing your paragraph much easier.

- *Who is your audience?* Your *audience* consists of the people for whom your message is intended. The more you know about your audience, the more likely you are to accomplish your purpose. The audience for your writing in college is usually your instructor, who represents what is called a "general audience"—people with an average amount of knowledge on most subjects. A general audience is the group to aim for in all your writing unless you are given other directions.

◆ **P r a c t i c e   2**   Identify the subject, purpose, and audience of each of the following paragraphs.

1. My best friend just got arrested for rioting. Until yesterday, she was a great student with an unblemished record, and now she will be spending school time in court trying to keep out of jail. I don't know why she did it; she says she got caught up in the energy of the crowd. That just sounds like an excuse to me. She knew she was doing something wrong, she knew she was hurting business owners, and she did it anyway. I know she'll be punished for what she did and that will be humiliating enough, but I don't think she realizes her parents, friends, and teachers will now see her as someone who has the potential for getting into trouble.

   Subject: _____

   Purpose: _____

   Audience: _____

2. The press is about finding the truth and telling it to the people. In pursuit of that, I am making a case for the broadest possible freedom of the press. However, with that great gift comes great responsibility. The press—print and electronic—has the power to inform, but that

implies the power to distort. The press can lead our society toward a more mature and discriminating understanding of the process by which we choose our leaders, make our rules, and construct our values, or it can encourage people to despise our systems and avoid participating in them. The press can teach our children a taste for violence, encourage a fascination with perversity and inflicted pain, or it can show them a beauty they have not known. The press can make us wiser, fuller, surer, and sweeter than we are. (MARIO CUOMO, "Freedom of the Press Must Be Unlimited")

Subject: _____

Purpose: _____

Audience: _____

3. My friends say that when I get in my car, I become blind to my surroundings. I have driven next to friends and not seen them, have been waiting at stoplights next to friends and not noticed them, and have passed friends on a small two-lane road and not known it. I tell them it's because I am very engrossed in my driving; I take driving a vehicle very seriously. Actually, though, I am usually daydreaming about where I wish I could be going.

Subject: _____

Purpose: _____

Audience: _____

Travis's Plans   Travis made the following decisions before beginning to write about his favourite place:

Subject: the peacefulness of the ridge

Purpose: personal—to reflect on the characteristics of my favourite place

Audience: general—I want people who read this to imagine a similar place where they can think about their problems

Your Plans   Identify the subject, purpose, and audience of the paragraph you will write on your favourite place.

Subject: _____

Purpose: _____

Audience: _____

CHAPTER 3

WRITING

Writing is made up of several steps that lead you to your first draft. At this point, you have been given a topic (a favourite place) and worked through various prewriting techniques with that subject. You have also generated a number of ideas that you can use in a paragraph and decided on a subject, purpose, and audience. In this chapter, you will first learn how to write a topic sentence. Next, you will add some specific, concrete details to your notes from prewriting activities and choose a method of organization for your paragraph. Finally, you will write the first draft of your paragraph, which you will then revise and edit in Chapters 4 and 5. Again, you will be writing alongside Travis as he goes through the writing process with you.

WRITING THE TOPIC SENTENCE

The decisions you made in Chapter 2 about subject, purpose, and audience will lead you to your topic sentence. The **topic sentence** of a paragraph is its controlling idea. A typical paragraph consists of a topic sentence and details that expand on the topic sentence. Although a topic sentence can appear as the first or last sentence of its paragraph, it functions best as the first sentence. Beginning a paragraph with the topic sentence gives direction to the paragraph and provides a kind of road map for the reader.

A topic sentence has two parts—a topic and a statement about that topic. The topic should be limited enough that it can be developed in the space of a paragraph.

Topic	Limited Topic	Statement
Writing	In-class writing	is difficult but is good practice for a job.
Voting	Voting in Canada	is a right of citizenship.
Sports	Participation in sports	makes people well-rounded.
Anger	Road rage	seems to me like a waste of energy.

◆ *P r a c t i c e   **1 A***   Limit the following topics. Then develop them into statements that could be topic sentences.

Topic	Limited Topic	Statement
1. Weekends	_____	_____
2. Work	_____	_____
3. Restaurants	_____	_____
4. Reading	_____	_____
5. Winter	_____	_____

◆ *P r a c t i c e   **1 B***   Complete the following topic sentences. Make sure they are general enough to be developed into a paragraph but not too broad.

1. Automobile accidents _____.

2. _____ is my favourite movie.

3. Smoking _____.

4. Teen pregnancies _____.

5. _____ must be brought under control in Canada.

◆ *P r a c t i c e   **1 C***   Write topic sentences for the following paragraphs.

1. _____

When I come home from school, Rusty is always the first one to greet me. He usually jumps on me and knocks me down, but I am used to this. After we wrestle on the ground, he follows me to my room and sits by my feet while I do homework. Every once in a while he'll nudge my hand so I will pet him. When I go to bed, Rusty always sleeps with me at night, which is nice because I can snuggle up to his fur and know that I am safe.

2. _____

First, you must undergo an intensive scuba-diving class that includes a lot of reading and calculating. Next, you must practise scuba skills in a pool so you can learn how to react if, for instance, your breathing regulator comes out of your mouth underwater. Then you have four checkout dives in the ocean. Finally, after six weeks of preparation, you'll be a certified scuba diver.

3. _____

It will be two storeys and will be painted blue. Inside it will have at least four bedrooms and an office for me to work. It will have a grand kitchen and enough room to entertain all my friends and co-workers. A pool would be nice, with a lush backyard for my dogs to get lost in. And I hope that it will be close to my mom and dad's house.

Travis's Topic Sentence   Travis writes a topic sentence that he thinks represents his whole paragraph. It introduces a ridge in his hometown.

Limited Topic	Statement
A high, wooded ridge	overlooks my hometown.

Your Topic Sentence   Write a topic sentence here that can serve as the controlling idea for your paragraph.

Limited Topic	Statement
_____	_____

DEVELOPING

After you have written a topic sentence, you are ready to develop the specific details that will make up the bulk of your paragraph. Later in this text, you will learn about different methods of developing your ideas, such as describing, using examples, comparing and contrasting, and defining. For now, we are simply going to practise generating concrete supporting details and examples that are directly related to a specific topic. Concrete words refer to anything you can see, hear, touch, smell, or taste, like *trees, boats, water, friends, fire alarm,* and *fresh bread.* They make writing come alive because they help us picture what the writer is discussing.

Practice 2   For each of the following topic sentences, list five details and/or examples to develop them.

1. If I win the lottery, I will be the envy of all my friends.

_____

_____

_____

_____

_____

2. People can't always count on their relatives.

   _____

   _____

   _____

   _____

   _____

3. My favourite pastime is fun as well as challenging.

   _____

   _____

   _____

   _____

   _____

Travis's Development   To come up with concrete details and examples that would support his topic sentence, Travis goes back to the questions he used during his planning stage (five *W*'s and one *H*) and adds these details.

Who?	I like to be by myself
What?	rowboats, sailboats, motorboats, freighters
	I like the sailboats best because I love to sail
	car lights outlining the streets in the distance
When?	sunset—pink and purple
	light at dusk; moonlight
	headlights streaming through the darkness
Where?	outside the city
	above the city
	people in the city don't know I am watching
Why?	the scent of honeysuckle on a hot summer day
	the smell of the earth
	birds building nests, scolding other birds to keep them away
	traffic noises, wind, rain, thunder, lightning
	problems fade away
How?	peaceful, quiet
	I can think out my problems

Your Development   Choose one of the prewriting activities you learned in Chapter 2, and use it to generate more specific details and examples about your topic sentence.

ORGANIZING

At this point, you are moving along quite well in the writing process. You were given a topic for your paragraph (a favourite place). You have determined your subject, purpose, and audience, and you have written your topic sentence. You have also thought of details, examples, and facts to develop your topic sentence. Now you are ready to organize your ideas. What should come first? What next? Would one way of organizing your ideas accomplish your purpose better than another?

Most paragraphs are organized in one of five ways:

1. General to particular
2. Particular to general
3. Chronologically (by time)
4. Spatially (by physical arrangement)
5. One extreme to another

Let's look at these methods of organization one by one.

General to Particular

The most common method of organizing details in a paragraph is to begin with a general statement and then offer particular details to prove or explain that topic sentence. The general-to-particular paragraph looks like this, although the number of details will vary:

Topic Sentence
    Detail
    Detail
    Detail

Here is a paragraph organized from general to particular:

Over the last two years, I have become an adventurous person because of my friend Taylor. When I met Taylor, she had just signed up for a rock-climbing class, and it sounded so interesting that I joined too. We loved climbing the amazingly tall rocks so much that we decided to try skydiving. We both jumped out of a plane attached to a qualified instructor; it was incredible. In fact, we've been back four times. Now we are trying our hands at exploring the ocean and are in the middle of scuba-diving lessons. By the time we are certified, we'll be off on a two-week vacation to South America, where we can participate in all three exciting sports.

◆ *Practice 3*   Write a paragraph organized from general to particular that begins with this sentence: "Several people I know have broken bad habits."

Particular to General

Occasionally, the reverse order of particular to general is the most effective way to organize a paragraph. In this case, examples or details start the paragraph and lead up to the topic sentence, which appears at the end of the paragraph. This type of organization is particularly effective if you suspect that your reader might not agree with the final point you are going to make or you need to lead your reader to your opinion slowly and carefully. A particular-to-general paragraph looks like this, although the number of details may vary:

> Detail
> Detail
> Detail
> Topic Sentence

Here is an example of particular-to-general organization:

> Two sunny-side-up eggs, the whites rimmed with ruffled edges, lay in the middle of the plate. Specks of red pimento and green pepper peeked out of a heap of perfectly diced hash brown potatoes. Alongside lay strips of crispy, crinkly, maple-flavoured bacon. A tall glass of ice-cold orange juice stood to my left. A big mug of steaming coffee was at my right. Then the biggest blueberry muffin in the universe was delivered straight from the oven, its aroma curling up to my nose. I broke it open and spread it with real butter. Nobody makes breakfast like my mom!

◆ *Practice 4*   Write a paragraph organized from particular to general that ends with this sentence: "Some people put their free time to good use."

Chronological Order

When you organize details chronologically in a paragraph, you are arranging them according to the passage of time—in other words, in the order in which they occurred. Most of the time when you tell a story or explain how to do something, you use chronological order. Paragraphs organized chronologically use such signal words as *first, then, next,* and *finally.*

> Topic Sentence
> First
> Then
> Next
> Finally

Here is an example of a paragraph organized in chronological order:

Paper training is an easy way to housebreak a puppy. <u>First</u>, locate a box that is low enough for the puppy to climb in and out of easily. <u>Then</u>, line the box with newspapers and place it in an area that is always available to the puppy. <u>Next</u>, place the puppy in the box at regular intervals. <u>As soon as</u> the puppy begins to understand what is required, scold him or her for making mistakes. <u>Finally</u>, praise the puppy when he or she uses the box properly, and you will soon have a well-trained puppy.

◆ *P r a c t i c e   5*   Write a topic sentence for the following group of sentences. Then organize the sentences into a paragraph using chronological order. Add words, phrases, or sentences as necessary to smooth out the paragraph.

Topic Sentence: _____

Add the colour of your choice to the melted wax.

Drop a wick in the melted wax.

First, melt some paraffin in a saucepan.

Put the mould in the refrigerator overnight. (This way, the wax will contract and will be easy to get out of the mould the next day.)

Finally, take the candle out of the mould and admire your creation.

Pour the melted wax in a candle mould of any shape.

Spatial Order

Another method of arranging details is by their relationship to each other in space. You might describe someone's outfit, for example, *from head to toe* or recount your summer travels across the country *from the east coast to the west coast*. Beginning at one point and moving detail by detail around a specific area is the simplest way of organizing by space. This method uses signal words such as *here, there, next, across,* and *beyond* to help the reader move through the paragraph smoothly and efficiently.

Topic Sentence
  Here
  There
  Next
  Across
  Beyond

Here is an example of a paragraph that uses spatial organization:

The prison was ringing with angry men wanting attention. <u>In the first cell</u> was a small prickly man who was yelling the loudest. He was banging a cup on the bars to signal that he needed something to drink. <u>The next cell</u> held two men who were trying to get their energy up to yell but couldn't seem to make their vocal cords work. The guard was grateful for this small favour. <u>Across the room</u>, a ferocious-looking man waving a newspaper was in the third cell. He was citing a passage from the paper and demanding his rights. <u>Opposite the first cell</u> was a generally quiet man who was reciting the names of people. All the prisoners in this particular block were gearing up for quite a day.

◀ **P r a c t i c e 6**   Write a topic sentence for the following group of sentences. Then write a paragraph putting the sentences in spatial order. Add words, phrases, or sentences as necessary to smooth out the paragraph.

Topic Sentence: _____

Actually, the plant should separate the bed from the door.

I'll begin by putting my bed against the west wall in the north corner of the room.

I would like my floor plant to be next to the head of my bed.

My bureau fits perfectly in the southeast corner of the room.

The desk will be best in the southwest corner of the room where the window is.

The entire east wall is covered with closets.

My bookcase will go between the bed and the desk (on the west wall).

One Extreme to Another

Sometimes the best way to organize a paragraph is from one extreme to another: from most important to least important, from most troublesome to least troublesome, from most serious to least serious, from most humorous to least humorous, and so on. (Of course, you can also move from least to most.) Use whatever extremes make sense for your topic. For example, you might describe the courses you are taking this term from most important to least important in terms of a career. On returning from a trip, you might talk about the places you visited from least interesting to most interesting. Arranging your ideas from one extreme to another has one distinct advantage over the other four approaches—it is the most flexible. When no other method of organization works, you can always organize details from one extreme to the other. Words such as *most, next most, somewhat,* and *least* signal transitions in this type of paragraph.

Topic Sentence
  Most
  Next most
  Somewhat
  Least

Here is an example of organization that moves from one extreme to the other:

> I like some of my extracurricular activities better than others. My <u>favourite</u> is dance. I take classes in jazz, tap, and ballet, and I'm anxious to get home on the days I go to the dance studio. My <u>next favourite</u> activity is track. During track season, my schedule is tight, but I really look forward to working out every day. Although no one would believe it, my <u>next favourite</u> activity is shopping for school supplies. I love going to the big office supply stores and getting lost for 30 minutes or so. It is really like going into another world. When I emerge, I have some supplies that will make my life as a student easier. My <u>least favourite</u> activity is work. I work part time delivering food for a restaurant at night. No matter when I deliver the food, it is too late or too cold or too hot. No one is satisfied. That is why this is my <u>least favourite</u> task.

◆ ***Practice 7***   Write a topic sentence for the following group of sentences. Then write a paragraph arranging the sentences from one extreme to another. Add words, phrases, and sentences as necessary to smooth out the paragraph. Also, label your system of classification: from most _____ to least _____ or from least _____ to most _____.

Topic Sentence: _____

I am failing math.
I still do not understand when to use semicolons in my writing.
My English instructor says my style of writing is loose.
I am barely passing music theory.
I have cut my philosophy class twice.
My tennis coach is mad at me.
I have not talked to my family in two weeks.
I have more homework than I could do in my lifetime.
I hardly ever have time to sleep.

Travis's Organization   Travis decides to organize his paragraph from one extreme to another—from his most favourite view to his least favourite view from the ridge. He first wants to introduce the ridge that sits over his hometown. Then he plans to describe his favourite views from this isolated place (the river with its boats, the beautiful sunset, and finally the city at night). He thinks the following order might work. He lists as many concrete details as he can under each view.

General:	A high, wooded ridge is in my hometown.
Most Favourite View:	I love the river.
Specific Details:	I like the sailboats because I love to sail.
	I like to see different kinds of boats—rowboats, sailboats, motorboats, freighters
Next Favourite View:	sunset—beautiful
Specific Details:	at dusk; moonlight
	clouds from pink to purple to red
	sun like fire
Third Favourite View:	I like seeing the whole city.
Specific Details:	headlights streaming through the darkness
	lighting the streets
	traffic noises, wind, rain, thunder, lightning
Concluding Thoughts:	I like to be by myself.
Specific Details:	peaceful, quiet
	I can think out my problems.
	problems fade away

Does the method of organization that Travis has chosen suit his topic? Would any other method of organization work as well?

Your Organization   What method of organization will work best for your ideas about your favourite place? Why do you think this method will be best?

DRAFTING

Drafting is putting your thoughts on paper. Having completed lots of prewriting activities, you're ready to write a working draft of your paragraph in complete sentences—no more lists and circles. The prewriting phase of this process has helped you generate lots of ideas, observations, and details for your paragraph. If you let these notes lead you to related ideas, you will have plenty of material to work with. At this stage, don't worry too much about grammar or spelling; you'll deal with those particulars when you edit your writing.

Travis's First Draft   Here is Travis's first draft, the result of his thinking, planning, developing, and organizing. (We'll look at editing errors at the next stage.)

A high, wooded ridge overlooks my hometown.
I can sit up there and see the river, the sunset, and the
city. The sun shines like fire, and then the sun is gone
behind the ridge. I love the river best, I can always see
the river. I watch different kinds of boats on the river. I
see rowboats, sailboats, motorboats, and freighters.
I have always liked to sail. My next favourite view is the
sunset. Some nights the sunset is really beautiful. There
are huge clouds when the sun goes down behind them.
When it gets dark. I can see the headlights of the cars
moving through the city streets. I bet people don't realize
they're being watched. The headlights follow the street
lights. When I am up high above the city, I get lost in my
dreams. All my troubles melt away. I just look around
this place, think about this place's beauty, and feel
good—automatically.

Your First Draft   Write a draft of your thoughts on your favourite place.

_____

_____

_____

_____

_____

_____

_____

_____

_____

REVISING

As you know, the writing process does not end with your first draft. **Revising** means "seeing again," and that is exactly what you should try to do when you revise—see your writing again from as many different angles as possible.

More specifically, revising your writing means working with it so that it says exactly what you mean in the most effective way. Revision involves both *content* (what you are trying to say) and *form* (how you deliver your message). Having a friend or tutor read your paper before you revise it is a good idea so that you can see if you are communicating clearly.

Revising content means working with your words until they express your ideas as accurately and completely as possible. Revising form consists of working with the organization of your writing. When you revise, you should look closely at five basic elements of your paragraph, listed in the following checklist.

REVISING CHECKLIST ✔

TOPIC SENTENCE
✔ Does the topic sentence convey the paragraph's controlling idea?

✔ Does the topic sentence appear as the first or last sentence of the paragraph?

DEVELOPMENT
✔ Does the paragraph contain *specific* details that support the topic sentence?

✔ Does the paragraph include *enough* details to explain the topic sentence fully?

UNITY
✔ Do all the sentences in the paragraph support the topic sentence?

ORGANIZATION
✔ Is the paragraph organized logically?

COHERENCE
✔ Do the sentences move smoothly and logically from one to the next?

Let's look at these revision strategies one by one.

Topic Sentence

> ✔ Does the topic sentence convey the paragraph's controlling idea?
>
> ✔ Does the topic sentence appear as the first or last sentence of the paragraph?

As you learned in Chapter 3, every paragraph has a topic sentence that states its controlling idea. This sentence gives direction to the rest of the paragraph. It consists of both a limited topic and a statement about that topic. Generally, the topic sentence is the first sentence in a paragraph, but occasionally it is the last sentence, as in particular-to-general order.

◆ *P r a c t i c e   1 A*   Revise the underlined topic sentences so that they introduce all the details and ideas in their paragraphs.

1. I have many friends. I know that if I talk to Sean about a problem, he won't repeat it to anyone. He's also great to talk to because he never really tells me what I should do. Instead, he gives me what he thinks are all of my options and then helps me decide what to do. Karen, on the other hand, is a wonderful person, and I love to spend time with her. But I know she has trouble keeping a secret. She is great to talk to about small problems (things I don't care if anyone else knows about), but not the big problems. These friends mean a lot to me.

   Revised Topic Sentence: _____

   _____

2. I really enjoy watching suspense films because I am constantly afraid of what may happen next. Then I like the action movies. These are great because they move so fast and they usually have the best special effects. I hate it when they throw in love stories, though. This just takes away from the real action. My least favourite are the romantic love stories. I can't stand to watch people for over two hours going through near-misses or traumatic problems. I know they are going to end up together in the end, so spare me the time to get there! Overall, going to movies is a lot of fun.

   Revised Topic Sentence: _____

   _____

3. Buying a car is not an enjoyable experience. First, the buyers have to decide on whether they want a new car or a used car. Some people want a new car because they know they won't have to worry about it

breaking down for a while and they would have a longer warranty. Others want the price break a used car brings, but they don't know the people selling the cars, and they are afraid of getting ripped off. A good compromise might be to buy a used car from a reputable car dealership. This way the buyer gets the best of both worlds.

Revised Topic Sentence: _____

_____

◆ ***Practice 1B***   Write a topic sentence for each of the following paragraphs.

1. _____

I always have to put my sweats on and tie back my hair. I then sit on the couch and watch TV, all the while looking at my study guide and feeling guilty that I'm not putting more energy into it. After about a half hour, I realize I am going to get a bad grade on my test if I keep up this behaviour, so I turn the TV off, get comfortable, and start studying hard. If I go through this routine, then I know I will have a good study session and will get a good grade on a test.

2. _____

Yet she goes with us every year. She complains about sleeping in a tent, cooking over an open fire, and not having a clean bathroom for a week. Aunt Rita always ends up having fun, but she hates to do so much extra work. We love to joke with her and tease her about being a "city slicker." Every year she says she will never go camping again, but we always make sure she comes along. I guess this has turned into a family ritual, and I'm glad. I always enjoy her company—especially when she complains.

3. _____

Even though my roommate has her own room, she leaves clothes all over the place. I've found jeans on the couch, sweaters in the kitchen, and underwear in the bathroom. I once peeked into her room, which was so cluttered I couldn't even see her carpet. When she cooks, she leaves pots, pans, and dishes (all dirty and caked with food) all over the place.

Travis's Revision   When Travis looks back at his topic sentence in Chapter 3, he realizes it does not accurately introduce what he talks about in his paragraph. His topic sentence only tells readers that a ridge overlooks his hometown, not that this ridge is his favourite place:

Topic Sentence: A high, wooded ridge overlooks my hometown.

He decides to expand his topic sentence so that it more accurately introduces the details that will follow in his paragraph:

> **Revised Topic Sentence:**   A high, wooded ridge **that** overlooks my hometown **is my favourite place.**

He feels that this topic sentence introduces his favourite place and will let him talk about the river, the sunset, and the city.

Your Revision   With these guidelines in mind, revise your topic sentence.

Your Topic Sentence: _____

Your Revised Topic Sentence: _____

_____

Development

✔ Does the paragraph contain *specific* details that support the topic sentence?

✔ Does the paragraph include *enough* details to explain the topic sentence fully?

Details are the building blocks that you combine to construct a paragraph. The details in your paragraph should be as specific as possible, and you need to provide enough details to support your topic sentence. If you keep both of these guidelines in mind, you will develop your paragraphs specifically and adequately.

Can you recognize details that are more specific than other details? This is a major part of development. Look at the following details, and see how they move from general to specific and from abstract to concrete. As you learned in Chapter 3, concrete words refer to items you can see, hear, touch, smell, or taste—as opposed to abstract words, which refer to ideas and concepts, like *hunger* and *happiness*.

transportation (general, abstract)
　　vehicle
　　　　　car
　　　　　　　Dodge
　　　　　　　　　Dodge Durango
　　　　　　　　　　　red Dodge Durango
　　　　　　　　　　　　　red Dodge Durango
　　　　　　　　　　　　　with four-wheel drive
　　　　　　　　　　　　　and black interior
　　　　　　　　　　　　　(specific, concrete)

nutrition (general, abstract)
> food
>> meat
>>> beef
>>>> tri-tip
>>>>> tri-tip marinated in sauce
>>>>>> tri-tip marinated in
>>>>>> Aunt Bertha's homemade
>>>>>> barbecue sauce
>>>>>> (specific, concrete)

◆ *P r a c t i c e   2 A*   Underline the most specific word or phrase in each group.

1. street, small road, Westwind Avenue, city, neighbourhood
2. household, chores, weekend, rag, employment
3. grade point average, science major, chemistry, sulfuric acid, science lab
4. landscaping, address, plant, garden, city planning
5. mountains, British Columbia, ski resort, Dave Murray Downhill, a ski resort in Whistler

◆ *P r a c t i c e   2 B*   Fill in the blanks so that each sequence moves from the general and abstract to the specific and concrete.

1. homework

   _____

   _____

   _____

2. dog

   _____

   _____

   _____

3. trouble

   _____

   _____

   _____

4. car

_____

_____

_____

Travis's Revision   When Travis looks at his first draft, he realizes that he can make his details much more specific and concrete. Here are three sentences that he revises (with concrete details in bold type):

Revised: I can sit up there and see the river **with its many ripples,** the **colourful** sunset, and the city **with lots of tall buildings.**

Revised: There are huge clouds **that change from pink to purple to red** when the sun goes down behind them.

Revised: ~~All my troubles~~ **Homework and family problems** melt away.

In addition to providing specific, concrete details, you need to furnish enough details to support the main idea of each paragraph. Without enough details, the main idea of a paragraph will not be adequately developed and may be misunderstood.

◆ *P r a c t i c e   3 A*   List three details that could support each of the following sentences.

1. Some people have funny hobbies.

_____

_____

_____

2. My paycheque never lasts as long as it should.

_____

_____

_____

3. Exercising is important for people of all ages.

_____

_____

_____

◆ *Practice 3B* Develop the following topic sentences with enough specific details.

1. Advertising surrounds us every day all day long.

_____

_____

_____

2. Most people use their sense of right and wrong to make major decisions.

_____

_____

_____

3. College life can be frustrating.

_____

_____

_____

Travis's Revision Travis's paragraph needs *more* details and *more specific* details to help it communicate its message. Travis accomplishes this by adding more details about the river, the sunset, the city, and his feelings. He talks about how the street lights guide the cars, he explains how the boats look like toys, he compares the colours in the clouds to a kaleidoscope and a colour wheel, and he talks about time stopping when he is on the ridge.

General statement   A high, wooded ridge **that** overlooks my hometown **is my favourite place.** I can sit up there and see the river **with its many ripples,** the **colourful** sunset, and the city **with lots of tall buildings.** The sun shines like fire, and then the sun is gone behind the ridge. I love the river best, I can always see the river. I watch different kinds of boats on the river. I see rowboats, sailboats, motorboats, and freighters. **The boats look like toys because I am up so high.** I have always liked to sail. My next favourite view is the sunset. Some nights the sunset is really beautiful. There are huge clouds **that change from pink to purple to red when the sun goes down behind them. Sometimes I think of a kaleidoscope, and other times I think of**

Specific details

Specific comparison

Specific details

a colour wheel that spins in slow motion. When it gets dark. I can see the headlights of the cars moving through the city streets. I bet people don't realize they're being watched. The **bright** head-lights follow the street lights **as if the street lights are showing the cars where to go.** When I am up *More details* high above the city, I get lost in my dreams, **and time doesn't exist. Homework and family problems** melt away. I just look around this place, think about this place's beauty, and feel good—automatically.

Concrete details

Specific comparison

Concrete details

Your Revision   Add more details to your paragraph, making your explanations and descriptions as concrete and specific as possible.

Unity

> ✔ Do all the sentences in the paragraph support the topic sentence?

A paragraph has unity when it discusses the one idea that is introduced in the topic sentence. All other sentences in a paragraph expand on this controlling idea and relate to it in some way. Information that is not about the main idea is considered irrelevant and does not belong in the paragraph.

◀ *P r a c t i c e   4 A*   Cross out the three irrelevant sentences in the following paragraph.

Reading helps bring back memories from our own lives. I never liked to read until I had Ms. Fischer. If we are reading about the thrill of Gretzky's record in goals scored, we might remember a great sports event in our lives. I never liked sports, but my mom made me play soccer. If we are reading about Jules Verne traveling around the world, memories of our favourite trips might come to the surface of our minds. I liked Europe, but all I wanted to do was go home. I was also missing my girlfriend. Reading is a wonderful way to lose ourselves in the lives of others while reliving some important moments in our own lives.

◀ *P r a c t i c e   4 B*   Cross out the three irrelevant sentences in the following paragraph.

Your body has a three-stage reaction to stress: (1) alarm, (2) resistance, and (3) exhaustion. In the alarm stage, your body recognizes the presence of stress and, through a release of hormones from the endocrine glands, prepares for fight or flight. I've been there; I have felt the fight feeling before. In the resistance stage, your body repairs any damage caused by the stress. Repairing must be difficult for the body, but it has to be done. If the stress does not go away, however, the body cannot repair the damage and must remain alert. This plunges you into the third stage—exhaustion. If this state continues long enough, you may develop one of the diseases of stress. I'll bet these diseases are difficult to diagnose and cure, but I don't know for sure. The best idea would be to learn how to deal with stress of all kinds and use it to your benefit.

Travis's Revision   Travis sees now that some of his sentences do not fit into his paragraph. In his case, the comments about his love for sailing and about people not knowing they are being watched do not support his topic sentence, the first sentence in his paragraph. If these details were dropped, the revised paragraph would look like this:

> A high, wooded ridge that overlooks my hometown is my favourite place. I can sit up there and see the river with its many ripples, the colourful sunset, and the city with lots of tall buildings. The sun shines like fire, and then the sun is gone behind the ridge. I love the river best, I can always see the river. I watch different kinds of boats on the river. I see rowboats, sailboats, motorboats, and freighters. The boats look like toys because I am up so high. ~~I have always liked to sail.~~ My next favourite view is the sunset. Some nights the sunset is really beautiful. There are huge clouds that change from pink to purple to red when the sun goes down behind them. Sometimes I think of a kaleidoscope, and other times I think of a colour wheel that spins in slow motion. When it gets dark. I can see the headlights of the cars moving through the city streets. ~~I bet people don't realize they're being watched.~~ The bright headlights follow the street lights as if the street lights are showing the cars where to go. When I am up high above the city, I get lost in my dreams, and time doesn't exist. Homework and family problems melt away. I just look around this place, think about this place's beauty, and feel good—automatically.

Your Revision   Read your paragraph carefully, and cross out any irrelevant sentences or ideas.

Organization

> ✔ Is the paragraph organized logically?

In Chapter 3, you learned five ways to organize your paragraphs:

1. General to particular
2. Particular to general
3. Chronologically (by time)
4. Spatially (by physical arrangement)
5. One extreme to another

You might want to review pages 20–25 for an explanation of each of these methods.

The method that you choose depends to a great extent on your topic and your purpose. What are you trying to accomplish? What order will help you deliver your message as effectively and efficiently as possible?

Practice 5A   Reorganize the following sentences so that they are in a logical order. Then identify your method of organization.

> This is convenient because it's at the beginning of the Promenade Queen Elizabeth.
>
> Hours later, I walk back to my car and think of the day I can return.
>
> I always eat at my favourite Mexican restaurant first.
>
> Whenever I visit Ottawa, my hometown, I always walk along the Rideau Canal.
>
> I usually end my journey near a road that will lead me to Parliament Hill.
>
> I always park at the end near Lansdowne Park.
>
> I then walk down the streets, stopping in all of the unique shops.
>
> I always stop here because of the wonderful historical buildings.
>
> This way I can spend hours just walking along the beautiful Promenade and stopping in my favourite places.

Method of Organization: _____

Practice 5B   Reorganize the sentences in the following paragraph so that they are in a logical order. Then label your method of organization.

> I know that I have about a metre when I get out of bed before I run into the dresser. It is especially bad at night, when I don't have my contacts in and I have to get from my bed to the bathroom. My sight is so bad that I can't even see a metre in front of me without my contacts. From the doorway, I then go left and walk three steps to the bathroom. From the dresser, if I turn right, I have to walk five steps to get to the doorway of my room. If I reverse my steps and count backwards, I can usually make it to and from the bathroom without breaking a toe or crashing into a wall.

Method of Organization: _____

Travis's Revision   In Chapter 3, Travis decided that the best way to organize his paragraph was from most favourite to least favourite. But now he needs to make sure that every detail is in the right place. He notices a sentence about the sunset that is out of order, so he moves the sentence to the part of the paragraph that focuses on the sunset.

A high, wooded ridge that overlooks my home-town is my favourite place. I can sit up there and see the river with its many ripples, the colourful sunset, and the city with lots of tall buildings. ~~The sun shines like fire, and then the sun is gone behind the ridge.~~ I love the river best, I can always see the river. I watch different kinds of boats on the river. I see rowboats, sailboats, motorboats, and freighters. The boats look like toys because I am up so high. My next favourite view is the sunset. Some nights the sunset is really beautiful. There are huge clouds that change from pink to purple to red when the sun goes down behind them. Sometimes I think of a kaleidoscope, and other times I think of a colour wheel that spins in slow motion. **The sun shines like fire, and then the sun is gone behind the ridge.** When it gets dark. I can see the headlights of the cars moving through the city streets. The bright headlights follow the street lights as if the street lights are showing the cars where to go. When I am up high above the city, I get lost in my dreams, and time doesn't exist. Homework and family problems melt away. I just look around this place, think about this place's beauty, and feel good—automatically.

Your Revision   Double-check the method of organization you chose in Chapter 3, and make sure each of your details is in its proper place.

Coherence

> ✔ Do the sentences in the paragraph move smoothly and logically from one to the next?

A well-written paragraph is coherent—that is, its parts *cohere*, or stick together. The paragraph is smooth, not choppy, and readers move logically from one thought to the next, seeing a clear relationship between the ideas. Here are four different strategies that writers use to help readers follow their train of thought: *transitions*, *repeated words*, *synonyms*, and *pronouns*.

Transitions

Transitional words and phrases are like bridges or links between thoughts. They show your readers how one idea is related to another or when you are moving to a new point. Good use of transitions makes your writing smooth rather than choppy.

Choppy: I watch different kinds of boats on the river. I see row-boats, sailboats, motorboats, and freighters.

Smooth: I watch different kinds of boats on the river. **For instance,** I see rowboats, sailboats, motorboats, and freighters.

Transitions have very specific meanings, so you should take care to use the most logical one.

Confusing: I watch different kinds of boats on the water. **Besides,** I see rowboats, sailboats, motorboats, and freighters.

Here is a list of some common transitional words and phrases that will make your writing more coherent. They are classified by meaning.

Some Common Transitions

Addition:	*moreover, further, furthermore, besides, and, and then, likewise, also, nor, too, again, in addition, next, first, second, third, finally, last*
Comparison:	*similarly, likewise, in like manner*
Contrast:	*but, yet, and yet, however, still, nevertheless, on the other hand, on the contrary, after all, in contrast, at the same time, otherwise*
Emphasis:	*in fact, indeed, to tell the truth, in any event, after all, actually, of course*
Example:	*for example, for instance, in this case*
Place:	*here, there, beyond, nearby, opposite, adjacent to, near*
Purpose:	*to this end, for this purpose, with this objective*
Result:	*hence, therefore, accordingly, consequently, thus, as a result, then, so*
Summary:	*to conclude, to sum up, to summarize, in brief, on the whole, in sum, in short, as I have said, in other words, that is*
Time:	*meanwhile, at length, immediately, soon, after a few days, now, in the meantime, afterwards, later, then, sometimes, (at) other times, still*

See page 314 in the Handbook (Part V) for more information on transitions.

◆ *Practice 6A* Fill in the blanks in the following paragraph with logical transitions.

People should spay or neuter their animals so that we don't end up with kittens and puppies that no one wants. _____, a family might have a male cat that they let roam the neighbourhood, and this cat might get a female cat pregnant. _____ who will care for the new kittens? Some people give them away or take them to a neighbourhood SPCA. Some people, _____, just let the kittens roam free, hoping someone will take care of them. This irresponsible action causes more problems, _____.

◆ **Practice 6B**   Rewrite the following paragraph, adding at least three transitions to make it more coherent.

> Growing up, my brother, sister, and I always looked forward to the summer Saturdays that our dad took us water-skiing. We often prepared the night before for our outing the next day. We would get our day-bags packed and our clothes ready to put on. We would pack a lunch big enough for all of us. We would make sure we had plenty of pop for the entire day. We loved spending the whole day with him. We hated that time went so fast. When he would drop us back at home, we would anxiously wait for the next Saturday to come.

Repeated Words

Repeating key words also helps bind the sentences of a paragraph together and guide readers through its ideas. At the same time, too much repetition becomes boring.

> **Effective Repetition:**   Sometimes **I think of** a kaleidoscope, and other times **I think of** a colour wheel that spins in slow motion.

◆ **Practice 7A**   Underline the four effective repeated words in the following paragraph.

> I worked in a law firm during my first summer break from university because I wanted to discover if a legal career was really for me. The law firm I worked in was very large, and many of the lawyers specialized in criminal law. I learned quite a lot about tricky defence strategies at this law firm, and I decided that if I did pursue a law degree, I would become a prosecutor, not a defender. Actually working in a law firm was a great way to learn more about the legal profession.

◆ **Practice 7B**   Add five repeated words where appropriate to clarify and smooth out the following paragraph.

> My friend Bojan is a TV addict. He watches it for over 10 hours every day, and he never gets his homework finished. He doesn't

understand that his instructors won't let him turn in his work late, so he watches it whenever he's home. The shows he watches on it are usually pretty boring; they don't require thought when he watches them. But he loves to sit there and watch it anyway. I hope he'll learn soon that watching it instead of doing other things can only lead to nowhere.

Synonyms

Next, using *synonyms* can link your sentences and help you avoid needless repetition. Synonyms are words that have identical or similar meanings. They can add variety and interest to your writing. A thesaurus, or book of synonyms, can help you locate the best replacements for specific words.

In the following example from Travis's paragraph, Travis uses *town* in place of one of his references to *city*.

Original Reference: When I am up high above the **city,** I get lost
in my dreams, and time doesn't exist.

Synonym: When I am up high above the **town,** I get lost
in my dreams, and time doesn't exist.

◆ *Practice 8A* Underline at least four synonyms that refer to cooking in the following paragraph.

I have loved to cook since I was 12 years old. My mother taught me everything I know. I especially love to cook for my dad because he is what we call "cooking challenged." When he cooks, he thinks microwaving is the only way to go, and even then he overcooks or burns the food. He kids me for cooking from scratch and using traditional methods because he firmly believes there's only one way to cook. I broil; he microwaves. I roast; he microwaves. I barbecue; he microwaves. But he always praises me for my culinary ability because in the end, he knows I will someday be a famous chef.

◆ *Practice 8B* Replace two references to *professor* with synonyms in the following paragraph.

I have discovered that one key to making good grades is to get a good professor. A good professor can encourage me to do my best and can make learning fun. I find that I do better for professors who don't just lecture the entire time but let us interact with one another in some way. Professors with a sense of humour also encourage me to perform better. They actually make me look forward to coming to their classes. The good professors simply help me earn a good grade.

Pronouns

The final way to link your sentences is with *pronouns*. When appropriate, you can replace specific words with pronouns. Not only do pronouns link your ideas, but they also keep your writing moving at a fairly fast pace.

Travis uses a pronoun to get rid of a repetition of the word *boats*.

Repetition:	I watch different kinds of boats on the river. For instance, I see rowboats, sailboats, motorboats, and freighters. **The boats** look like toys because I am up so high.
Pronoun:	I watch different kinds of boats on the river. For instance, I see rowboats, sailboats, motorboats, and freighters. ~~**The boats**~~ **They** look like toys because I am up so high.

For more information on pronouns, see pages 275–277 in the Handbook (Part V).

Practice 9A   Underline the 14 pronouns in the following paragraph.

When I was preparing for my wedding, I relied a lot on my best friend, Tanya. She helped me pick out my dress, decide on the flowers, and book the banquet hall. They all were the perfect choices for me. Tanya worked in a craft store, so she was able to help me decorate the hall for a reasonably cheap price. Throwing a wedding is a huge event, and Tanya was a great friend throughout the process. I couldn't have done it without her.

Practice 9B   Add five pronouns where appropriate in the following paragraph.

Tom, Sandy, and I have been friends for life. Tom, Sandy, and I met in third grade when we all tried to survive the neighbourhood bully on our walks home. Tom, Sandy, and I went through high school together and are now attending the same college. Tom, Sandy, and my college are two hours from our hometown. So, Tom, Sandy, and I share an apartment. Our apartment is very nice, and our apartment is always clean. I hope that Tom, Sandy, and I will always remain good friends.

Travis's Revision   When Travis checks his paragraph for coherence, he decides his writing can use some improvement. So he makes revisions that help bind his sentences together and show the relationships between his ideas.

Here is Travis's paragraph with transitions, repeated words, synonyms, and pronouns highlighted.

A high, wooded ridge that overlooks my home-town is my favourite place. I can sit up ~~there~~ **on the ridge** and see the river with its many ripples, the colourful sunset, and the city with lots of tall build-ings. I love the river best, I can always see ~~the river~~ **it** from the ridge. I watch different kinds of boats on the ~~river~~ **water. For instance,** I see rowboats, sailboats, motorboats, and freighters. ~~The boats~~ **They** look like toys because I am up so high. My next favourite view is **the sunset.** Some nights **the sunset** is really beauti-ful. There are huge clouds that change from pink to purple to red when the sun goes down behind them. **Sometimes I think of** a kaleidoscope, and **other times I think of** a colour wheel that spins in slow motion. The sun shines like fire, and then ~~the sun~~ **it** is gone behind the ridge. **Finally,** when it gets dark. I can see the headlights of the cars moving through the city streets. The bright headlights follow the street lights as if the street lights are showing the cars where to go. When I am up ~~high~~ **on the ridge** above the ~~city~~ **town,** I get lost in my dreams, and time doesn't exist. **On the whole,** homework and family problems melt away. I just look around this place, think about ~~this place's~~ **its** beauty, and feel good—automatically.

repetition

pronoun

synonym

repetition

transition
repetition

transition

repetition

transition

repetition
transition
pronoun

transition

pronoun

synonym

pronoun

Transitions   In addition to *for instance*, *sometimes*, and *other times*, Travis added two more transitions to his paragraph. What are they?

_____

List the meaning of all five transitions in Travis's paragraph:

1. Transition: _____   Meaning: _____

2. Transition: _____   Meaning: _____

3. Transition: _____   Meaning: _____

4. Transition: _____   Meaning: _____

5. Transition: _____   Meaning: _____

Repeated Words   When Travis checked his paragraph for repeated key words, he thought he needed to refer directly to the ridge more often. So he revised some of his sentences. How many new references to the ridge did he add?

_____

Synonyms   When Travis looked at his paragraph again, he found another opportunity to use a synonym to link his ideas more clearly. Besides the addition of *town* for *city*, what other synonym does Travis use in his revision?

_____ for _____

Pronouns   Finally, in addition to substituting *they* for *boats*, Travis found three more places to use pronouns to bind his paragraph together. Where are these places in his paragraph?

_____ for _____

_____ for _____

_____ for _____

Your Revision   Now it's time to make your essay more coherent.

Transitions   Check the transitions in your paragraph. Do you use enough transitions so that your paragraph moves smoothly and logically from one idea to the next? Do you use your transitions correctly?

Repeated Words   Look at your paragraph to see when you might want to repeat a key word. Then revise your paragraph accordingly.

Synonyms   Look for places in your paragraph where you might add synonyms to link your sentences. Use a thesaurus in book form or on your computer if you need help.

Pronouns   Check your paragraph for opportunities to use pronouns. Add appropriate pronouns.

Travis's Revised Paragraph   After revising his topic sentence, his development, his unity, his organization, and his coherence, Travis produced the following revised paragraph. All of his revisions are in bold type.

A high, wooded ridge **that** overlooks my hometown **is my favourite place.** I can sit up ~~there~~ on the ridge and see the river **with its many ripples,** the **colourful** sunset, and the city **with lots of tall buildings.** ~~The sun shines like fire, and then the sun is gone behind the ridge.~~ I love the river best, I can always see ~~the river~~ it from **the ridge.** I watch different kinds of boats on the **river** ~~water.~~ **For instance,** I see rowboats, sailboats, motorboats, and freighters. ~~The boats~~ **They** look like toys because I am up so high. ~~I have always liked to sail.~~ My next favourite view is the sunset. Some nights the sunset is really beautiful. There are huge clouds **that change from pink to purple to red** when the sun goes down behind them. **Sometimes I think of a kaleidoscope, and other times I think of a colour wheel that spins in slow motion. The sun shines like fire, and then** ~~the sun~~ **it is gone behind the ridge. Finally,** when it gets dark. I can see the headlights of the cars moving through the city streets. ~~I bet people don't realize they're being watched.~~ The **bright** headlights follow the street lights **as if the street lights are showing the cars where to go.** When I am up ~~high~~ **on the ridge** above the ~~city~~ **town,** I get lost in my dreams, **and time doesn't exist. On the whole,** ~~All my troubles~~ homework **and family problems** melt away. I just look around this place, think about ~~this place's~~ **its** beauty, and feel good—automatically.

Your Revised Paragraph   Now that you have applied all the revision strategies to your own writing, write your revised paragraph here.

_____

_____

_____

_____

_____

_____

_____

CHAPTER 5

EDITING

After you have revised your paragraph, you are ready to edit it. **Editing** involves checking your grammar, punctuation, mechanics, and spelling to be sure that your writing is free of errors. Grammar, punctuation, mechanics, and spelling are as important to communicating clearly as well-chosen words. They help your reader navigate through your writing. Nothing confuses readers more than editing errors. These errors attract the readers' attention and can distract them from what you are saying.

For easy reference, we have divided the editing strategies into three large categories in the following checklist: sentences, punctuation and mechanics, and word choice and spelling. This checklist doesn't cover all the grammar and usage problems you may find in your writing, but it focuses on some of the main mistakes college and university students frequently make.

EDITING CHECKLIST ✔

SENTENCES
✔ Does each sentence have a main subject and verb?
✔ Do all subjects and verbs agree?
✔ Do all pronouns agree with their nouns?
✔ Are modifiers as close as possible to the words they modify?

PUNCTUATION AND MECHANICS
✔ Are sentences punctuated correctly?
✔ Are words capitalized properly?

WORD CHOICE AND SPELLING
✔ Are words used correctly?
✔ Are words spelled correctly?

YOUR EQ (EDITING QUOTIENT)

You might want to start the editing stage by finding your EQ (editing quotient). Knowing this information will help you look for specific errors in your writing and make your editing more efficient.

To determine your EQ, read the paragraphs in Practice 1, identifying each error you find from the following list. Then score your answers in Practice 2, and see if your errors form any pattern by charting them in Appendix 5.

◆ *P r a c t i c e   1*   **EQ Test** In the following paragraphs, underline the errors you find, and label them a, b, c, and so on. Then list them on the lines below the paragraph. The number of lines corresponds to the number of errors in the paragraph.

The possible errors are listed here:

abbreviation	end punctuation	pronoun agreement
capitalization	fragment	run-on sentences
comma	modifier	spelling
confused word	number	subject-verb agreement
		verb form

1. A lot of teenage girls are influenced by what they see in the movies and on TV. Some of the actresses are so thin that rumours begin about their various eating disorders. Which they all deny. Sometimes actresses don't get roles because they are "too heavy." Even though these actresses are at their ideal weight. The message Hollywood sends is that ultra-thin is best young girls take this message to heart. Hollywood provides physical role models for all of society these role models are not always good to follow.

   (a.) _____

   (b.) _____

   (c.) _____

   (d.) _____

2. Bilingual education is a problem in Ontario. Some people have pressured their MPPs to eliminate such programs, the majority believe bilingual programs must be present in every school. In order for second-language learners to learn. Surely a happy medium exist somewhere between expensive programs and total elimination. Perhaps the solution lies in finding a program. To accommodate both students and taxpayers.

   (a.) _____

   (b.) _____

(c.) _____

(d.) _____

(e.) _____

3. Pesticide use on fruits and vegetables has ran into trouble because it is often misunderstood. The government places strict regulations on chemical use in fields, each chemical must be tested and approved for each crop it is used for. Often pesticides degrade within twenty-four hours when exposed to sunlight. Strict rules apply to the application of a chemical, the re-entry time for workers, and the time that must lapse before harvesting the fruits and vegetables. Hefty fines imposed on violators of proper pesticide use. People who have swore off nonorganic foods need to become better informed about the rules and regulations regarding pesticides.

(a.) _____

(b.) _____

(c.) _____

(d.) _____

(e.) _____

4. Political campaigns have become difficult to watch because of the constant intrusion into candidates' personal lives. What starts out as a clean campaign quickly turns dirty. When one candidate exposes a secret about their opponent's past. From that point on, a candidate is explaining and apologizing for their past, and quite often they launch an attack of their own. Just once a clean political campaign would be nice to see the public would not know what to do.

(a.) _____

(b.) _____

(c.) _____

(d.) _____

(e.) _____

(f.) _____

5. Many people do not understand how severely allergies can affect someone. Most people think that a runny nose and a little sneezing are no big deal allergies can cause severe headaches, asthma, rashes, and sometimes death. Suffering from severe allergies, days can really be miserable. Sometimes people must take daily medications

so they can live a normal life, which may include steroids. But people with bad allergies live in constant fear that they'll eat, be stung by, or be prescribed something that might kill them, allergies can be very hard on people.

(a.) _____

(b.) _____

(c.) _____

(d.) _____

6. Violence on television is influencing Canada's youth. Teenagers whose daily lives involve watching violent tv shows have killed people. Parents need to monitor what their children watch. In order to guarantee the children don't see, and become desensitized by too much violence. Censoring violent television shows will not help those children who are unsupervised, parents must take control of what their children watch?

(a.) _____

(b.) _____

(c.) _____

(d.) _____

(e.) _____

7. 17 college students were needlessly killed last Friday night because they ignored the law. A group of students held a party in an abandoned warehouse that had "CONDEMNED" signs all over the place the students ignored the warnings. At about 1:00 a.m., a fire broke out, because most of the exits were blocked off, some students did not get out alive. Fire chief Mary Thomas of the local fire department said that it was a horrible tragedy. Maybe now people will understand. The seriousness of the signs.

(a.) _____

(b.) _____

(c.) _____

(d.) _____

(e.) _____

8. Genetic research has made some great, although scary, advances in the past decade. Agriculture is bennefitting from genetically altered crops. That are comprised of insect-resistant and disese-resistant

plants. Yet now genetic research is capable of cloning an animal, it is probably capable of cloning human life. At what point does science go to far?

(a.) _____

(b.) _____

(c.) _____

(d.) _____

(e.) _____

9. Studies have proved that children who listen to Classical music when they are young are more likely to be better students later in life. Beethoven and Mozart can stimulate young brains and open there minds for further learning, classical music has been proved to produce students who yearn for more knowledge. Researchers have even stated that listening to classical music while studying create an environment for retaining more information. Than an environment with no music. If children are brought up with classical music in their lives it could become a lifelong, beneficial habit.

(a.) _____

(b.) _____

(c.) _____

(d.) _____

(e.) _____

(f.) _____

10. People who are thinking about owning a dog need to understand all that is involved in the care. First of all. Dogs must be taken to the vet for a series of shots the animal should also be spayed or neutered. Proper food and medicines must be purchased. As well as toys and treats. People must also invest alot of their time in the animal. A dog is perceptive, and responds to the way they are treated. Anything less than full health care and quality time is simply unfair to the dog.

(a.) _____

(b.) _____

(c.) _____

(d.) _____

(e.) _____

(f.) _____

◆ *P r a c t i c e 2* **EQ Answers** Score your answers in Practice 1 using the following answer key. Then chart your errors in Appendix 5.

1. A lot of teenage girls are influenced by what they see in the movies and on TV. Some of the actresses are so thin that rumours begin about their various eating disorders. ⓐUnderline{Which they all deny}. Sometimes actresses don't get roles because they are "too heavy." ⓑUnderline{Even though these actresses are at their ideal weight}. ⓒUnderline{The message Hollywood sends is that ultra-thin is best young girls take this message to heart}. ⓓUnderline{Hollywood provides physical role models for all of society these role models are not always good to follow}.

   (a.) *fragment*

   (b.) *fragment*

   (c.) *run-on sentences or end punctuation*

   (d.) *run-on sentences or end punctuation*

2. Bilingual education is a problem in Ontario. ⓐUnderline{Some people have pressured their MPPs to eliminate such programs,} ⓑUnderline{the majority believe bilingual programs must be present in every school.} ⓒUnderline{In order for second-language learners to learn.} Surely a happy ⓓUnderline{medium exist} somewhere between expensive programs and total elimination. Perhaps the solution lies in finding a program. ⓔUnderline{To accommodate both students and taxpayers.}

   (a.) *run-on sentences or end punctuation*

   (b.) *subject-verb agreement*

   (c.) *fragment*

   (d.) *subject-verb agreement*

   (e.) *fragment*

3. Pesticide use on fruits and vegetables ⓐUnderline{has ran} into trouble because it is often misunderstood. ⓑUnderline{The government places strict regulations on chemical use in fields, each chemical must be tested and approved for each crop it is used for}. Often pesticides degrade within ⓒUnderline{twenty-four} hours when exposed to sunlight. Strict rules apply to the application of a chemical, the re-entry time for workers, and the time that must lapse before harvesting the fruits and vegetables. ⓓUnderline{Hefty fines imposed on violators of proper pesticide use}. People who ⓔUnderline{have swore} off nonorganic foods need to become better informed about the rules and regulations regarding pesticides.

   (a.) *verb form*

(b.)   _run-on sentences or end punctuation_

(c.)   _number_

(d.)   _fragment_

(e.)   _verb form_

4. Political campaigns have become difficult to watch because of the constant intrusion into candidates' personal lives. What starts out as a clean campaign quickly turns dirty. ⁽ᵃ⁾<u>When one candidate exposes a secret about</u>⁽ᵇ⁾<u>their</u> opponent's past. From that point on, a candidate is explaining and apologizing for ⁽ᶜ⁾<u>their</u> past, and quite often ⁽ᵈ⁾<u>they</u> launch an attack of ⁽ᵉ⁾<u>their</u> own. ⁽ᶠ⁾<u>Just once a clean political campaign would be nice to see the public would not know what to do.</u>

(a.)   _fragment_

(b.)   _pronoun agreement_

(c.)   _pronoun agreement_

(d.)   _pronoun agreement_

(e.)   _pronoun agreement_

(f.)   _run-on sentences or end punctuation_

5. Many people do not understand how severely allergies can affect someone. ⁽ᵃ⁾<u>Most people think that a runny nose and a little sneezing are no big deal allergies can cause severe headaches, asthma, rashes, and sometimes death.</u> ⁽ᵇ⁾<u>Suffering from severe allergies,</u> days can really be miserable. Sometimes people must take daily medications so they can live a normal life, ⁽ᶜ⁾<u>which may include steroids.</u> ⁽ᵈ⁾<u>But people with bad allergies live in constant fear that they'll eat, be stung by, or be prescribed something that might kill them, allergies can be very hard on people.</u>

(a.)   _run-on sentences or end punctuation_

(b.)   _modifier_

(c.)   _modifier_

(d.)   _run-on sentences or end punctuation_

6. Violence on television is influencing Canada's youth. Teenagers whose daily lives involve watching violent ⁽ᵃ⁾<u>tv</u> shows have killed people. Parents need to monitor what their children watch. ⁽ᵇ⁾<u>In order to guarantee the children don't see,</u>⁽ᶜ⁾<u>and become desensitized by too much violence.</u> ⁽ᵈ⁾<u>Censoring violent television shows will not</u>

help those children who are unsupervised, parents must take control of what their children watch?[c]

(a.) *capitalization* _____

(b.) *fragment* _____

(c.) *comma* _____

(d.) *run-on sentences or end punctuation* _____

(e.) *end punctuation* _____

7. [a]17 college students were needlessly killed last Friday night because they ignored the law.[b]A group of students held a party in an abandoned warehouse that had "CONDEMNED" signs all over the place the students ignored the warnings.[c]At about 1:00 a.m., a fire broke out, because most of the exits were blocked off, some students did not get out alive.[d]Fire chief Mary Thomas of the local fire department said that it was a horrible tragedy. Maybe now people will understand.[e]The seriousness of the signs.

(a.) *number* _____

(b.) *run-on sentences or end punctuation* _____

(c.) *run-on sentences or end punctuation* _____

(d.) *abbreviation* _____

(e.) *fragment* _____

8. Genetic research has made some great, although scary, advances in the past decade. Agriculture is[a]bennefitting from genetically altered crops.[b]That are comprised of insect-resistant and[c]disese-resistant plants.[d]Yet now genetic research is capable of cloning an animal, it is probably capable of cloning human life. At what point does science go[e]to far?

(a.) *spelling* _____

(b.) *fragment* _____

(c.) *spelling* _____

(d.) *run-on sentences or end punctuation* _____

(e.) *confused word* _____

9. Studies have proved that children who listen to[a]Classical music when they are young are more likely to be better students later in life.[b]Beethoven and Mozart can stimulate young brains and open [c]there minds for further learning, classical music has been proved

to produce students who yearn for more knowledge. Researchers have even stated that ^(d)<u>listening</u> to classical music while studying <u>create</u> an environment for retaining more information. ^(e)<u>Than an environment with no music.</u> If children are brought up with classical music in their lives^(f) it could become a lifelong, beneficial habit.

   (a.)   capitalization

   (b.)   run-on sentences or end punctuation

   (c.)   confused word

   (d.)   subject-verb agreement

   (e.)   fragment

   (f.)   comma

10. People who are thinking about owning a dog need to understand all that is involved in the care.^(a)<u>First of all.</u>^(b)<u>Dogs must be taken to the vet for a series of shots the animal should also be spayed or neutered.</u> Proper food and medicines must be purchased.^(c)<u>As well as toys and treats.</u> People must also invest ^(d)<u>alot</u> of their time in the animal. A dog is perceptive,^(e) and responds to the way^(f)<u>they</u> are treated. Anything less than full health care and quality time is simply unfair to the dog.

   (a.)   fragment

   (b.)   run-on sentences or end punctuation

   (c.)   fragment

   (d.)   spelling

   (e.)   comma

   (f.)   pronoun agreement

◄ *P r a c t i c e 3* **Finding Your EQ** Turn to Appendix 5, and chart the errors you didn't identify in Practice 1. Then place your errors on the second EQ chart, and see what pattern they form.

HOW TO EDIT

Editing is a two-part job: First, you must locate the errors. Then you must know how to correct them.

Finding Your Errors

Since you can't correct errors until you find them, a major part of editing is proofreading. *Proofreading* is reading to catch grammar, punctuation, mechanics, and spelling errors. If you do not proofread carefully, you will not be able to make the changes that will improve your writing.

One good idea is to read your paragraphs backwards, starting with the last sentence first, so you can concentrate on your sentences. Another technique is to keep an Error Log, in which you list the mistakes you commonly make. An Error Log is provided for you in Appendix 6. To use this log in proofreading, read your paper for one type of error at a time. For example, if you often write fragments, you should read your paper once just to catch fragments. Then read it again to find a second type of error. Asking a friend or tutor to read your writing is always a good idea because you might be missing some errors in your writing that another reader will see. When others read your writing, they might want to use the editing symbols on the inside back cover to label your errors. Then the page references on this chart will guide you to corrections for your errors. You can also use the grammar- or spell-check on your computer, which will point out possible grammar or spelling errors and make suggestions for correcting them.

Correcting Your Errors

After you find your errors, you need to correct them. To guide you through this phase, a handbook appears in Part V of this text. You can also refer to the list of correction symbols (inside front cover) that your instructor might use on your papers.

As you proofread, you should record in your Error Log the corrections you make in your writing. This log can then help you get control of these errors. If you record your corrections each time you find errors, you will eventually learn the grammar concepts that are confusing to you.

Finally, you should use the Editing Checklist at the beginning of this chapter to help you edit your writing. As you attempt to answer each one of the questions on this checklist, look up the grammar items in Part V and make your corrections.

◤ *P r a c t i c e 4* **Using the Handbook** Using the Handbook in Part V, list the page number where you can learn to correct each error you found in Practice 1. This will help you start to use the Handbook as a reference guide.

abbreviation   page _____

capitalization   page _____

comma   page _____

confused word   page _____

end punctuation   page _____

fragment   page _____

modifier   page _____

number	page _____
pronoun agreement	page _____
run-on sentences	page _____
spelling	page _____
subject-verb agreement	page _____
verb form	page _____

◄ *P r a c t i c e   5*   **Using the Error Log and the Spelling Log** Turn to Appendixes 6 and 7, and start an Error Log and a Spelling Log of your own with the errors you didn't identify in Practice 1. For each error, write out the mistake, the Handbook reference, and your correction.

◄ *P r a c t i c e   6*   **Using the Editing Checklist** Use the Editing Checklist at the beginning of this chapter to edit two of the paragraphs from Practice 1. Rewrite the entire paragraphs.

Travis's Editing   When Travis proofreads his paper for grammar, punctuation, mechanics, and spelling, he finds two errors that he looks up in Part V and corrects. The first error is a run-on sentence:

> **Run-On:**   I love the river best, I can always see it from the ridge.

Travis realizes that this sentence has too many subjects and verbs without any linking words or end punctuation between them. He looks up "run-on" on page 310 of Part V and corrects the error by putting a comma and a coordinating conjunction (*and*) between the two sentences.

> **Correction:**   I love the river best, **and** I can always see it from the ridge.

He also finds a sentence that doesn't sound complete—it is not a sentence but a fragment:

> **Fragment:**   Finally, when it gets dark.

When he looks up the problem in Part V (page 297), he learns that a fragment is easily corrected by connecting it to another sentence.

> **Correction:**   Finally, when it gets dark**/,** I can see the headlights of the cars below me moving through the city streets.

Travis's Edited Draft   Both of these errors are corrected here in Travis's edited draft.

A high, wooded ridge that overlooks my hometown is my favourite place. I can sit up on the ridge and see the river with its many ripples, the colourful sunset, and the city with lots of tall buildings. I love the river best, **and I** can always see it from the ridge. I watch different kinds of boats on the water. For instance, I see rowboats, sailboats, motorboats, and freighters. They look like toys because I am up so high. My next favourite view is the sunset. Some nights the sunset is really beautiful. There are huge clouds that change from pink to purple to red when the sun goes down behind them. Sometimes I think of a kaleidoscope, and other times I think of a colour wheel that spins in slow motion. The sun shines like fire, and then it is gone behind the ridge. Finally, when it gets dark**/,** I can see the headlights of the cars moving through the city streets. The bright headlights follow the street lights as if the street lights are showing the cars where to go. When I am up on the ridge above the town, I get lost in my dreams, and time doesn't exist. On the whole, homework and family problems melt away. I just look around this place, think about its beauty, and feel good—automatically.

Your Editing   Proofread your paragraph carefully to find errors. Then use at least two of the methods from this chapter to help you correct any errors you made in your paragraph. Record your errors and their corrections here.

_____

_____

_____

_____

_____

_____

_____

Your Edited Draft   Now write out a corrected draft of your paragraph.

_____

_____

_____

_____

_____

_____

_____

_____

_____

_____

_____

REVIEW OF THE WRITING PROCESS

Clues for Review

◆ The **writing process** is a series of cyclical tasks that involves prewriting, writing, revising, and editing.

◆ **Prewriting** consists of generating ideas and planning your paragraph.

Thinking: Reading, freewriting, brainstorming, clustering, questioning, discussing

Planning: Deciding on a subject, purpose, and audience

◆ **Writing** includes writing a topic sentence, developing your ideas, organizing your paragraph, and writing a draft.

Writing a topic sentence: A limited topic and a statement about that topic

Developing: Making details more specific; adding details and examples

Organizing: General to particular, particular to general, chronological, spatial, one extreme to another

Drafting: Writing a first draft

◆ **Revising** means "seeing again" and working with organization and development.

◆ **Editing** involves proofreading and correcting your grammar, punctuation, mechanics, and spelling errors.

◆ Review Practice 1

1. What are the four main parts of the writing process?

   _____

2. What is your favourite prewriting activity? Why is it your favourite?

   _____

3. What individual activities do you find yourself doing to start on a writing project?

   _____

4. Where do you usually do your academic writing? Do you write your first draft on a computer? What time of day do you do your best writing?

   _____

5. Do you usually let a tutor or friend look at your draft before you revise it?

   _____

6. What is the difference between revising and editing?

   _____

   _____

7. What are the three main categories of editing?

   _____

   _____

8. Explain editing.

   _____

9. What are the two main phases of editing?

   _____

10. Do you try to get someone to read your writing before you turn it in? Explain your answer.

    _____

    _____

◈ *Review Practice 2*   Develop each of the following topics into topic sentences, limiting them as much as possible. Then, by following the guidelines furnished in Part I, develop one topic sentence into a paragraph.

1. My English class
2. National politics
3. My favourite pastime
4. Families
5. On the way to school
6. When students relax
7. My dream job
8. The best stereo system
9. What supervisors should never do
10. The clothes I wear to school

◈ *Review Practice 3*   Revise the paragraph you wrote for Review Practice 2, using the checklist on page 27.

◈ *Review Practice 4*   Edit the paragraph you wrote for Review Practice 2, using the checklist on page 46.

II

WRITING EFFECTIVE PARAGRAPHS

Get to the point as directly as you can;
never use a big word if a little one will do.

—EMILY CARR

Part II of *Mosaics* will help you write effective paragraphs. These nine chapters will teach you how to use each rhetorical mode to bring out your best writing. First, each chapter provides you with specific guidelines to follow for writing in a particular mode. Then the chapter shows you how to apply those guidelines to three paragraphs—two written by professional writers and one by a student writer. Finally, the chapter takes you through the stages of revising and editing, showing you how to systematically improve your drafts with each of these strategies.

CHAPTER 6

DESCRIBING

You can observe a lot just by watching.

—YOGI BERRA

We all use description every day of our lives when we tell others about

The noisy home we grew up in
The locker-room smell that lingers in a hockey bag
The sour taste of a lemon
The smoothness of a snake's skin
The beauty of a special sunset
A sudden clap of thunder in the middle of a quiet night

Whatever you do, description is a large part of your daily thought and language. Your friends might ask what kind of CD player you just bought for your car; your parents may want to know what your duties will be in your new job; your supervisor might need a description of the project you just completed. You really can't communicate effectively without being able to describe people, places, objects, and activities for different audiences.

Description paints a picture in words to help a reader visualize something you have seen or heard or done. Writing about some early memories, Mike Rose describes "a peculiar mix" of elements in his life. What memories do you have of your younger years? Do they form any distinct pattern?

> I have many particular memories of this time, but in general these early years seem a peculiar mix of physical warmth and barrenness: a gnarled lemon tree, thin rugs, a dirt alley, concrete in the sun. My uncles visited a few times, and we went to the beach or to orange groves. The return home, however, left the waves and spray, the thick leaves, and split pulp far in the distance. I was aware of my parents watching their money and got the sense from their conversations that things could quickly take a turn for the worse. I started taping pennies to the bottom of a shelf in the kitchen.

Before continuing in this chapter, take a moment to record some of your own memories. Save your work because you will use it later in the chapter.

WRITE YOUR OWN DESCRIPTION

What are some of your most vivid memories from childhood? Do any of them form a single impression when you think about them? Write a paragraph describing your clearest recollection.

HOW TO WRITE A DESCRIPTION PARAGRAPH

Describing is a very natural process that we all do simply and freely without any complex directions. But have you noticed that some people seem to describe events and objects more clearly than other people do? When they tell you what they saw or did, you feel as though you were there too. You can improve your description skills by following a few simple guidelines:

1. ***Decide on a dominant impression—the feeling or mood you are trying to communicate.*** Do you want your reader to feel sorry for you, to sense the excitement of an amazing fireworks display, or to share your disappointment in a bad restaurant? Choosing a dominant impression will give your description focus and unity. You can't possibly write down everything you observe about a person, place, incident, or object. The result would be a long, confusing, and probably boring list. But if you first decide on a dominant impression for your description, you can then choose which details will best convey that impression.

   The dominant impression Rose conveys about his childhood is its strange mix of "warmth and barrenness [emptiness]." This dominant impression gives his paragraph focus and helps him choose the details that will communicate this feeling most effectively.

2. ***Draw on your five senses to write a good description.*** If you use all your senses, your readers will be able to see, hear, smell, taste, or touch what you are describing as if they were there with you having the same experience. The more senses you draw on, the more interesting your description will be.

   Look again at Rose's description. He uses his sense of touch when he talks about "physical warmth and barrenness" and refers to "concrete in the sun." He draws on sight when he mentions "a gnarled lemon tree, thin rugs, a dirt alley." "The waves and spray, the thick leaves, and split pulp" draw on our senses of touch and sight. His paragraph is vivid because of all the specific sensory details he furnishes.

3. ***When you describe, try to*** show ***rather than*** tell ***your readers what you want them to know.*** You can tell someone you bought a "great new car." But if you say you bought a "sleek, new black Blazer with four-wheel drive, a tan interior, custom wheels, and an awesome stereo," you're *showing* your readers why you are so excited about your purchase.

If Rose had simply stopped after stating his dominant impression (that he felt a combination of physical warmth and barrenness in his early childhood), he would be *telling* his readers how he felt. Instead, he *shows* them: The sensory details he cites demonstrate his main point, and the statement "I started taping pennies to the bottom of a shelf in the kitchen" shows us that the feeling of "barrenness" had even seeped into the family finances.

4. ***Organize your description so that your readers can easily follow it.*** Most descriptions are organized from general to particular (from main idea to details), from particular to general (from details to main idea), or spatially (from top to bottom, left to right, inside to outside, and so on). These patterns are all easy for readers to follow.

Mike Rose organizes his paragraph from general to particular. He starts with the main idea that his childhood was a mixture of "physical warmth and barrenness" and then explains this idea with specific details of both the love and good times (warmth) along with the poverty and insecurity (barrenness) he experienced. In his paragraph, the idea of "warmth" is represented by references to "concrete in the sun," his uncle's visits, trips to the beach, outings to the orange groves, and home. He characterizes the barrenness of his childhood with such details as "a gnarled lemon tree, thin rugs, a dirty alley"; "parents watching their money"; and "pennies [taped] to the bottom of a shelf in the kitchen." The choice and order of these details make Rose's topic sentence come alive.

DISCOVERING HOW DESCRIPTION WORKS

Let's look at two other descriptions. In a paragraph taken from an essay on gambling in Canada, author Janice Kennedy writes about the many ways Canadians are finding to gamble away their money. As you read this paragraph, ask yourself what dominant impression Kennedy is trying to communicate to her readers.

We buy lottery tickets. We flip coins. We bet on the ponies, live and on-screen. We lay down our hard-earned cash on surefire outcomes, from prize-fights to football games. We fill the bingo halls. We press the button and pull the levers of slot and video machines till our eyes are sore and our brains are buzzing. We play poker, blackjack, faro. We roll the dice for craps and watch the roulette wheel spin, heart stopped. Day after day, we put our money where our big mouths are, with the result that we are now gambling on a scale never before seen in human history.

1. The entire paragraph creates a certain mood. What is the dominant impression that Kennedy communicates?

_____

2. In this particular passage, Kennedy uses mainly visual descriptions, but there is also a sense of tension, of busyness. What details does the author use to convey this sense?

_____

_____

_____

3. Kennedy works hard in this paragraph to show rather than tell. She wants to make a point but lets the description make it for her. What descriptions *show* us the truth of the conclusion that the author makes in the final sentence?

_____

_____

_____

4. What impression or feeling does the author convey with the constant use of "we" at the start of every sentence except the final one?

_____

_____

_____

5. How does Kennedy organize the details in her paragraph? List some of the details in the order they appear. Then identify her method of organization: general to particular, particular to general, or spatial.

_____   _____

_____   _____

_____   _____

_____   _____

_____   _____

Method of organization: _____

In the next example, an excerpt from "American Horse," author Louise Erdrich describes the house where a poor family lived. See if you can picture this place as she describes it.

They could see the house was empty at first glance. It was only one rectangular room with whitewashed walls and a little gas stove in the middle. They had already come through the cooking lean-to with the other stove and washstand potatoes and a package of turkey necks. Vicki Koob noted that in her perfect-bound notebook. The beds along the walls of the big room were covered with quilts that Albertine's mother, Sophie, had made from bits of old wool coats and pants that the Sisters sold in bundles at the mission. There was no one hiding beneath the beds. No one was under the little aluminum dinette table covered with a green oilcloth or the soft brown wood chairs tucked up to it. One wall of the big room was filled with neatly stacked crates of things—old tools and springs and small half-dismantled appliances. Five or six television sets were stacked against the wall. Their control panels spewed colored wires, and at least one was cracked all the way across. Only the topmost set, with coat-hanger antenna angled sensitively to catch the bounding signals around Little Shell, looked like it could possibly work.

1. What dominant impression do you think Erdrich creates in this paragraph?

   _____

2. Erdrich describes the house she is visiting mainly through the sense of seeing, with one reference to touching. Record one example of each of these senses from this paragraph.

   Seeing: _____

   _____

   Touching: _____

3. Like Kennedy, Erdrich *shows* rather than *tells* us what this house looks like. List three details that go beyond telling to *showing*.

   _____

   _____

   _____

4. How does Erdrich organize the details in her paragraph? List some of her details in the order they appear. Then identify her method of organization: general to particular, particular to general, or spatial.

   _____   _____

   _____   _____

   _____   _____

_____   _____

_____   _____

_____   _____

Method of organization: _____

REVISING AND EDITING A STUDENT PARAGRAPH

Here is a descriptive paragraph written by Joe Simmons, a college student. As you read it, figure out what dominant impression Joe is trying to communicate, and think of ways he might convey this impression more fully.

¹I started college. ²I decided to redecorate my room. ³It is now one of my favourite places in the world. ⁴But it used to remind me of a damp cave with no light. ⁵The room had no personality at all. ⁶Now the walls is loaded with posters of my favourite mottoes. ⁷And musical groups. ⁸The bed came from Goodwill Industries and is made of black wrought iron. ⁹The space at an angle to my bed is a window covered by some wild curtains of blue, green, silver, and lavender that my grandma made. ¹⁰My antique desk with a roll-top is against the wall opposite my bed the top of it is always buried with everything but school work. ¹¹Some incense sits on a small table next to my door. ¹²My door is usually closed so I can get some peace and quiet. ¹³I love the silent times behind my door. ¹⁴When no one can get to me.

This paragraph is Joe's first draft, which now needs to be revised and edited. First, apply the Revising Checklist below to the content of Joe's draft. When you are satisfied that his ideas are fully developed and well organized, use the Editing Checklist on page 70 to correct his grammar and mechanics errors. Answer the questions after each checklist. Then write your suggested changes directly on Joe's draft.

REVISING CHECKLIST ✔

TOPIC SENTENCE

✔ Does the topic sentence convey the paragraph's controlling idea?

✔ Does the topic sentence appear as the first or last sentence of the paragraph?

DEVELOPMENT

✔ Does the paragraph contain *specific* details that support the topic sentence?

✔ Does the paragraph include *enough* details to explain the topic sentence fully?

UNITY
✔ Do all the sentences in the paragraph support the topic sentence?

ORGANIZATION
✔ Is the paragraph organized logically?

COHERENCE
✔ Do the sentences move smoothly and logically from one to the next?

Topic Sentence

1. What dominant impression does Joe communicate in his paragraph?

   _____

2. Put brackets around Joe's topic sentence. Does it convey Joe's dominant impression?

   _____

3. Rewrite the topic sentence if necessary to introduce all the ideas in Joe's paragraph.

   _____

Development

1. Does the paragraph draw on all five senses? Record three details from Joe's paragraph that come from three different senses. Label each example with the sense related to it.

Sense	Detail
_____	_____
_____	_____
_____	_____

2. Does Joe's paragraph *show* rather than *tell* readers what they need to know?

   _____

Give three examples.

_____

_____

_____

3. Add another detail to Joe's paragraph.
4. Add one simile to Joe's paragraph. (Reminder: A simile is a comparison between two unlike items using *like* or *as*.)

Unity

1. Read each of Joe's sentences with his topic sentence (revised, if necessary) in mind.
2. Drop or rewrite any of his sentences that are not directly related to his topic sentence.

Organization

1. Read Joe's paragraph again to see if all the sentences are arranged logically.
2. List some of his details in the order they appear. Then identify his method of organization: general to particular, particular to general, or spatial.

_____   _____

_____   _____

_____   _____

Method of organization: _____

Coherence

1. Circle three transitions Joe uses.
2. Explain how one of these makes Joe's paragraph easier to read.

For a list of transitions, see page 38.

_____

Now rewrite Joe's paragraph with your revisions.

> **EDITING** CHECKLIST ✔
>
> ### SENTENCES
> ✔ Does each sentence have a main subject and verb?
> ✔ Do all subjects and verbs agree?
> ✔ Do all pronouns agree with their nouns?
> ✔ Are modifiers as close as possible to the words they modify?
>
> ### PUNCTUATION AND MECHANICS
> ✔ Are sentences punctuated correctly?
> ✔ Are words capitalized properly?
>
> ### WORD CHOICE AND SPELLING
> ✔ Are words used correctly?
> ✔ Are words spelled correctly?

Sentences

Subjects and Verbs

For help with subjects and verbs, see Chapter 30.

1. Underline the subjects once and verbs twice in your revision of Joe's paragraph. Remember that sentences can have more than one subject-verb set.

2. Does each of the sentences have at least one subject and verb that can stand alone?

_____

For help with fragments, see Chapter 31.

3. Did you find and correct Joe's two fragments? If not, find and correct them now.

For help with run-ons, see Chapter 32.

4. Did you find and correct Joe's run-on sentence? If not, find and correct it now.

Subject-Verb Agreement

For help with subject-verb agreement, see Chapter 34.

1. Read aloud the subjects and verbs you underlined in your revision of Joe's paragraph.

2. Did you find and correct the subject and verb that do not agree? If not, find and correct them now.

Pronoun Agreement

For help with pronoun agreement, see Chapter 38.

1. Find any pronouns in your revision of Joe's paragraph that do not agree with their nouns.

2. Correct any pronouns that do not agree with their nouns.

Modifier Errors

1. Find any modifiers in your revision of Joe's paragraph that are not as close as possible to the words they modify.

2. Rewrite sentences if necessary so that modifiers are as close as possible to the words they modify.

For help with modifier errors, see Chapter 41.

Punctuation and Mechanics

Punctuation

1. Read your revision of Joe's paragraph for any errors in punctuation.

2. Find the two fragments and one run-on sentence you revised, and make sure they are punctuated correctly.

For help with punctuation, see Chapters 42–45.

Mechanics

1. Read your revision of Joe's paragraph for any errors in capitalization.

2. Be sure to check Joe's capitalization in the fragments and run-on sentence you revised.

For help with capitalization, see Chapter 46.

Word Choice and Spelling

Word Choice

1. Find any words used incorrectly in your revision of Joe's paragraph.

2. Correct any errors you find.

For help with confused words, see Chapter 52.

Spelling

1. Use spell-check and a dictionary to check the spelling in your revision of Joe's paragraph.

2. Correct any misspelled words.

For help with spelling, see Chapter 53.

Now rewrite Joe's paragraph again with your editing corrections.

REVISING AND EDITING YOUR OWN PARAGRAPH

Returning to the description paragraph you wrote earlier in this chapter, revise and edit your own writing. The checklists above will help you apply what you have learned to your own paragraph.

PRACTISING DESCRIPTION

Reading Suggestions

In Chapter 21, you will find two essays that follow the guidelines for writing description that you studied in this chapter: "Magpies" by Amy Tan and "The Films Stink More than the Greasy Audience" by Russell Smith. You might want to read these selections before writing another description. As you read, notice how the writers pull you into each experience through sensory details.

Writing Workshop

Guidelines for Writing a Description Paragraph

1. Decide on a dominant impression—the feeling or mood you are trying to communicate.
2. Draw on your five senses to write a good description.
3. When you describe, try to *show* rather than *tell* your readers what you want them to know.
4. Organize your description so that your readers can easily follow it.

1. Place yourself in this scene, and describe it in as much detail as possible. Imagine that you can see, hear, smell, taste, and touch everything in this picture. What are your sensations? How do you feel? Before you begin to write, be sure you decide what dominant impression you want to convey. Then choose your details carefully.

2. Starting university or college is an important decision for students and everyone associated with them—parents, children, friends, relatives, even the household pets. Describe a person who was helpful with your decision to continue your education. Be sure you decide on a dominant impression before you begin to write.

3. You have been asked to write a short statement for your psychology class on the study environment that is best for you. Describe this environment. Where do you study? What sounds do you hear? What do you eat or drink as you study? What do you wear? Help your readers picture your study environment so that they feel they are actually there. Be sure you decide on a dominant impression before you begin to write.

4. Create your own description assignment (with the help of your instructor), and write a response to it.

Revising Workshop

Small-Group Activity (5–10 minutes per writer)   Working in groups of three or four, each person should read his or her description paragraph to the other members of the group. Those listening should record their reactions on a copy of the Peer Evaluation Form in Appendix 2A. After your group goes through this process, give your evaluation forms to the appropriate writers so that each writer has two or three peer comment sheets for revising.

Paired Activity (5 minutes per writer)   Using the completed Peer Evaluation Forms, work in pairs to decide what you should revise in your paragraphs. If time allows, rewrite some of your sentences and have your partner check them.

Individual Activity   Rewrite your paragraph, using the revising feedback you received from other students.

Editing Workshop

Paired Activity (5–10 minutes per writer)   Exchange papers with a classmate, and use the Editing Peer Evaluation Form in Appendix 1 to identify as many grammar, punctuation, mechanics, and spelling errors as you can. If time allows, correct some of your errors and have your partner check them. Record your grammar, punctuation, and mechanics errors in the Error Log (Appendix 6) and your spelling errors in the Spelling Log (Appendix 7).

Individual Activity   Rewrite your paragraph again, using the editing feedback you received from other students.

Reflecting on Your Writing

When you have completed your own paragraph, answer these five questions:

1. What was most difficult about this assignment?
2. What was easiest?
3. What did you learn about description by completing this assignment?
4. What do you think are the strengths of your description? What are its weaknesses?
5. What did you learn from this assignment about your own writing process—about preparing to write, about writing the first draft, about revising, and about editing?

CHAPTER 7

NARRATING

> There is only one trait that marks the writer. He is always watching. It's a trick of mind and he is born with it.
>
> —MORLEY CALLAGHAN

Although you may not realize it, you are already very good at narrating. Think of the times you told someone about something that happened to you:

The traffic jam on the way to school today
The conversation you had at the gym last night
The funny experience at the mall
Your favourite vacation as a child

Narrating is storytelling. Whenever you tell someone about something that happened to you—your senior prom, a job interview, an argument with your spouse, a terrific (or terrible) date—you are narrating. We probably rely more on narration than on any other rhetorical mode. Even jokes depend on our ability to tell a story.

Narration is a powerful way of focusing other people's attention on the thoughts you want to share with them. Because narration is often based on personal experience, it also teaches us about life. Russell Baker, a newspaper writer and the author of an award-winning autobiography titled *Growing Up,* recalls the "sweet times" in his house when he was a young child. Can you think of an event that taught you something important about life? What was the event? What did you learn?

The summer I was four years old my mother bought me my first book and started to teach me to read. One night at bedtime she and my father stretched out on the blanket for sleep, but before dousing the lamp my father wanted to see how I was progressing with the written word.

They placed me between them with the open book. I knew a few words, but under pressure to perform forgot everything. It was beginner material: "cat," "rat," "boy," "girl," "the." I didn't recognize a word.

My mother was disappointed that I could do nothing but stare stupidly at the printed page. My father saved my pride. "Have a little patience with him," he said. Taking the book in hand, he moved me close against him and rubbed his cheek against mine. "Now," he said, pointing to a word, "you know that word, don't you?"

I did indeed. "The," I said.

"You're a smart boy. I bet you know this one too."

"Boy," I said.

When I read most of the sentence without too much help, he said to my mother, "You're doing good with him. Maybe we ought to send him to college." Pleased, my mother reached across me and kissed him on the cheek. Smiling down at me, he said, "You want to go to college?" They both laughed a little at this. Maybe he liked the extravagance of the idea as much as she did. Then he turned off the kerosene lamp. That night they let me sleep between them.

Before continuing in this chapter, take a moment to record a story of your own. Save your work because you will use it later in the chapter.

 WRITE YOUR OWN NARRATION

What are some events in your life that have taught you important lessons? Does one event stand out in your mind? What lesson did it teach you? Write a paragraph telling the students in your class about this event.

HOW TO WRITE A NARRATION PARAGRAPH

To write a narration paragraph, you simply tell a story with a point to it. It doesn't have to be a heart-stopping adventure or a romantic episode with a happy ending. Just draw on what you know, as the quotation that opened this chapter suggests. Choose an event that matters to you, and give your readers a sense of that event's significance. Here are some guidelines to help you make your narrative interesting.

1. ***Make sure your story has a point.*** Before you begin to write, decide what the main point of your story is. What is your purpose for writing the narrative? We have all heard stories that seem to go on forever with no apparent point. Such unfocused narratives become boring very quickly.

   In the excerpt you just read, Russell Baker captures the pride he and his parents felt as he showed off his new reading skills. All the details in the story build up to this main point.

2. ***Use the five W's and one H to construct your story.*** The five *W*'s and one *H* are the questions *Who? What? When? Where? Why?* and *How?* These are the questions journalists use to make sure they cover all the basic information in a news story. Though you may not be a journalist, these questions can help you come up with details and ideas for a well-developed narrative paragraph.

When you review Baker's story, you can see that he might have used the reporter's questions to guide his writing: Who is present? What is each person doing? When is this scene taking place? Where are they? Why is Baker proud of himself? How do we know this was a memorable event for Baker? Baker covers the answers to all these questions in this brief narrative.

3. ***Use vivid descriptive details to develop your story.*** The more specific your details, the more vivid your story becomes because your readers will actually be able to picture the scenes. These descriptive details should fill in the ideas you generated with the six journalistic questions.

    Look again at Baker's story. From this narrative, we know that Baker is four years old; we know it is bedtime; we know Baker is between his parents in bed; we know he is reading his first book, which is full of words like "cat," "rat," "boy," "girl," and "the"; we know his father encouraged him by rubbing his cheek against Baker's; we know Baker finally read the words "the" and "boy"; we know his parents were pleased enough to let him sleep between them that night. These descriptive details help readers participate in Baker's narrative.

4. ***Organize your narration so that your readers can easily follow it.*** Most narratives are organized chronologically, according to a time sequence. Begin your paragraph with a topic sentence, and then arrange your details in the order they happened: First this happened, then that, and next something else. Help your reader follow your narrative by using good transitions—words like *first, second, then, next,* and *finally.* Good transitions also make your narrative smooth rather than choppy.

    Russell Baker organizes his narrative chronologically. It moves through time from one incident to the next. Baker begins by explaining that his mom was teaching him how to read when he was four years old, continues by relating how he was going to show his father his progress, and finishes by implying how happy he was that his parents were so proud of him. Because it follows a single time sequence and does not jump around, this paragraph is easy to follow.

DISCOVERING HOW NARRATION WORKS

Let's consider two more narration paragraphs. In the first example, Brent Staples, the author of the autobiography *Parallel Time: Growing Up in Black and White*, relates an event that happened in his English class. What do you think Staples's main point is?

> [Miss Riley] had a talent for reaching us. One day while reading to us, she came across the word "rhubarb" and was stunned to find that none of us had ever tasted it. Her eyes flashed in amazement; you could see a novel solution taking shape. Later that week, she came to class with a tray of rhubarb pielets, one for each of us. As the tray went around the room, she held aloft a stalk of rhubarb and talked about its origins. We bit into the pies in unison. "Taste how it's sweet and tangy at the same time," she said. She watched intently, as though tasting the pie through our mouths.

1. All the details in Staples's paragraph lead to one main point. What is that point?

   _____

2. Staples covers all the journalist's questions. Record at least one detail the author uses in response to each question.

   Who? _____

   What? _____

   When? _____

   Where? _____

   Why? _____

   How? _____

3. Staples uses vivid descriptive details to develop his brief story. In your opinion, which two details are most vivid? What makes them so vivid?

   _____

   _____

   _____

4. How does Staples organize the details in this paragraph? List some of his details in the order they appear. Then identify his method of organization.

   _____   _____

   _____   _____

   _____   _____

   Method of organization: _____

   The next paragraph is from an article titled "Romancing the Game" by Jemal Hamilton. In it, Hamilton recalls playing card games with his grandfather and describes how his grandfather tried to teach him the importance of betting to the game of poker. If you have played Texas hold 'em you will recognize the lessons the grandfather is trying to teach.

   While I may be new to poker, cards have always given me a rush. At age 7, my grandfather and I played gin rummy in his bedroom. He'd let me deal—which always made me feel tough—and give me sips of his Molson Golden while chiding me for my ridiculous attempts at cheating. He told me to never chase cards. I often begged him to play poker with me—five card stud was big in the westerns I was watching—but he wouldn't do it. "To play poker you need money," he'd say, "because to play poker you need to bet." I did get him to play once, for matches, but after my second nonsense raise he refused to play again. What he was trying to teach me is that poker is about serious stuff: money, self-control, nerve—things a man needs to learn.

1. What is the main point that the writer is making in this paragraph?

    _____

2. Hamilton covers all the journalist's questions in this paragraph. Record at least one detail he uses in response to each question.

    Who? _____

    What? _____

    When? _____

    Where? _____

    Why? _____

    How? _____

3. Hamilton uses vivid descriptive details to develop his brief story. In your opinion, which two details are the most vivid? Why are they vivid?

    _____

    _____

4. How does Hamilton organize the details in this paragraph? List some of his details in the order they appear. Then identify his method of organization.

    _____   _____

    _____   _____

    _____   _____

    _____   _____

    _____   _____

    Method of organization: _____

REVISING AND EDITING A STUDENT PARAGRAPH

The following is a narrative paragraph written by a student named Robert Martinez. As you read his paragraph, try to figure out his main point.

[1]We started our vacation early in the morning fishing for bass. [2]We had gone to the lake so many times with our dads, and now we were there all by ourselves. [3]Boy, this was a great feeling? [4]We settled back. [5]And waited for those nibbles on my line. [6]The first sign of trouble came when the conservation officer's boat started heading toward us. [7]Suddenly, I remembered fishing licences, a detail our dads always took care of for us. [8]We were worried, but we didn't think that anything really bad would happen. [9]Except for once when I got caught cheating on a science test, I had never been in trouble before. [10]But we have several friends who get in trouble all the time. [11]The conservation officer looked serious. [12]Can you imagine our surprise when he told us we really were in trouble. [13]We were under arrest. [14]Suddenly, we weren't so excited about being on our own.

This paragraph is Robert's first draft, which now needs to be revised and edited. First, apply the Revising Checklist below to the content of Robert's draft. When you are satisfied that his ideas are fully developed and well organized, use the Editing Checklist on page 81 to correct his grammar and mechanics errors. Answer the questions after each checklist. Then write your suggested changes directly on Robert's draft.

REVISING CHECKLIST ✔

TOPIC SENTENCE
✔ Does the topic sentence convey the paragraph's controlling idea?
✔ Does the topic sentence appear as the first or last sentence of the paragraph?

DEVELOPMENT
✔ Does the paragraph contain *specific* details that support the topic sentence?
✔ Does the paragraph include *enough* details to explain the topic sentence fully!

UNITY
✔ Do all the sentences in the paragraph support the topic sentence?

ORGANIZATION
✔ Is the paragraph organized logically?

COHERENCE
✔ Do the sentences move smoothly and logically from one to the next?

Topic Sentence

1. What is Robert's main point in his paragraph?

    _____

2. Put brackets around Robert's topic sentence. Does it convey Robert's main point?

    _____

3. Rewrite the topic sentence if necessary to introduce all the ideas in his paragraph.

    _____

    _____

Development

1. Does the paragraph answer all the journalist's questions? Record at least one detail Robert uses in response to each question.

    Who? _____

    What? _____

    When? _____

    Where? _____

    Why? _____

    How? _____

2. Add two new details to Robert's paragraph that support his main idea.

Unity

1. Read each of Robert's sentences with his topic sentence (revised, if necessary) in mind.
2. Cross out the two sentences not directly related to Robert's topic sentence.

Organization

1. Read Robert's paragraph again to see if all the sentences are arranged logically.

2. List the word clues in Robert's paragraph that tell you how it is organized. Then identify his method of organization.

_____   _____

_____   _____

Method of organization: _____

Coherence

1. Circle two words or phrases Robert repeats.
2. Explain how one of these makes Robert's paragraph easier to read.

_____

Now rewrite Robert's paragraph with your revisions.

EDITING CHECKLIST ✔

SENTENCES
✔ Does each sentence have a main subject and verb?
✔ Do all subjects and verbs agree?
✔ Do all pronouns agree with their nouns?
✔ Are modifiers as close as possible to the words they modify?

PUNCTUATION AND MECHANICS
✔ Are sentences punctuated correctly?
✔ Are words capitalized properly?

WORD CHOICE AND SPELLING
✔ Are words used correctly?
✔ Are words spelled correctly?

Sentences

Subjects and Verbs

1. Underline the subjects once and verbs twice in your revision of Robert's paragraph. Remember that sentences can have more than one subject-verb set.
2. Does each of the sentences have at least one subject and verb that can stand alone?

For help with subjects and verbs, see Chapter 30.

_____

3. Did you find and correct Robert's fragment? If not, find and correct it now.

For help with fragments, see Chapter 31.

Subject-Verb Agreement

For help with subject-verb agreement, see Chapter 34.

1. Read aloud the subjects and verbs you underlined in your revision of Robert's paragraph.
2. Correct any subjects and verbs that do not agree.

Pronoun Agreement

For help with pronoun agreement, see Chapter 38.

1. Find any pronouns in your revision of Robert's paragraph that do not agree with their nouns.
2. Did you find and correct the pronoun that does not agree with its noun? If not, find and correct it now.

Modifier Errors

For help with modifier errors, see Chapter 41.

1. Find any modifiers in your revision of Robert's paragraph that are not as close as possible to the words they modify.
2. Rewrite sentences if necessary so that modifiers are as close as possible to the words they modify.

Punctuation and Mechanics

Punctuation

For help with punctuation, see Chapters 42–45.

1. Read your revision of Robert's paragraph for any errors in punctuation.
2. Find the fragment you revised, and make sure it is punctuated correctly.
3. Did you find and correct his other two punctuation errors? If not, find and correct them now.

Mechanics

For help with capitalization, see Chapter 46.

1. Read your revision of Robert's paragraph for any errors in capitalization.
2. Be sure to check Robert's capitalization in the fragment you revised.

Word Choice and Spelling

Word Choice

For help with confused words, see Chapter 52.

1. Find any words used incorrectly in your revision of Robert's paragraph.
2. Correct any errors you find.

Spelling

For help with spelling, see Chapter 53.

1. Use spell-check and a dictionary to check the spelling in your revision of Robert's paragraph.
2. Correct any misspelled words.

Now rewrite Robert's paragraph again with your editing corrections.

REVISING AND EDITING YOUR OWN PARAGRAPH

Returning to the narration paragraph you wrote earlier in this chapter, revise and edit your own writing. The checklists above will help you apply what you have learned to your own paragraph.

PRACTISING NARRATION

Reading Suggestions

In Chapter 22, you will find two narrative essays that follow the guidelines you studied in this chapter: "How Do I Look?" by Joan Clark and "I Was a Teenage Hijabi Hockey Player" by Sheema Khan. You might want to read these selections before writing another narration. As you read, notice how the writers cover the journalistic questions and use vivid descriptive details to pull you into their narratives, making the significance of the essays all the more meaningful.

Writing Workshop

Guidelines for Writing a Narration Paragraph

1. Make sure your story has a point.
2. Use the five *W*'s and one *H* to construct your story.
3. Use vivid descriptive details to develop your story.
4. Organize your narration so that your readers can easily follow it.

1. Place yourself in this scene, and write a narrative about what is happening. How did you get here? Why are you here? Where are you going? Be sure to decide on a main point before you begin to write.

2. We have all had experiences that began as carefree adventures and ended up as misadventures. Imagine that a national magazine is asking for honest stories about experiences that turned bad unexpectedly. The winning story will be published, and the author will win $200. You decide to enter the competition. The directions are to explain an experience in such a way that you reveal your feelings about this activity. Be sure to decide on a main point before you begin to write.

3. Your high school's alumni newsletter has asked you to explain an episode that influenced the values you hold today. Recall an event that influenced the kind of person you are today. First, identify one of your core values, such as honesty, hard work, a strong sense of responsibility, independence, or patience. Then think back to what happened to give you this particular value, and write a paragraph telling the story about that value. The purpose of this narrative is to give current high school students some sense of how values might form in their own lives. Where can they look? How do values develop? Be sure to decide on a main point before you begin to write.

4. Create your own narration assignment (with the help of your instructor), and write a response to it.

Revising Workshop

Small-Group Activity (5–10 minutes per writer) Working in groups of three or four, each person should read his or her narrative paragraph to the other members of the group. Those listening should record their reactions on a copy of the Peer Evaluation Form in Appendix 2B. After your group goes through this process, give your evaluation forms to the appropriate writers so that each writer has two or three peer comment sheets for revising.

Paired Activity (5 minutes per writer) Using the completed Peer Evaluation Forms, work in pairs to decide what you should revise in your paragraphs. If time allows, rewrite some of your sentences and have your partner check them.

Individual Activity Rewrite your paragraph, using the revising feedback you received from other students.

Editing Workshop

Paired Activity (5–10 minutes per writer) Exchange papers with a classmate, and use the Editing Peer Evaluation Form in Appendix 1 to identify as many grammar, punctuation, mechanics, and spelling errors as you can. If time allows, correct some of your errors and have your partner check them. Record your grammar, punctuation, and mechanics errors in the Error Log (Appendix 6) and your spelling errors in the Spelling Log (Appendix 7).

Individual Activity Rewrite your paragraph again using the editing feedback you received from other students.

Reflecting on Your Writing

When you have completed your own paragraph, answer these five questions:

1. What was most difficult about this assignment?
2. What was easiest?
3. What did you learn about narration by completing this assignment?
4. What do you think are the strengths of your narration paragraph? What are its weaknesses?
5. What did you learn from this assignment about your own writing process—about preparing to write, about writing the first draft, about revising, and about editing?

CHAPTER **8**

ILLUSTRATING

All that can be asked of a writer, the best he can offer you, is his own special window on reality.

—MORDECAI RICHLER

Think of the many times you have said to someone, "What do you mean? Can you give me an example?" We use examples every day to make a point.

Point: There are a lot of fundraising drives for cancer research in Canada.

Example: The Run for the Cure raises money for breast cancer research.

Point: Vancouver is an exciting city.

Example: Crossing the Lion's Gate Bridge is a thrill, and the people and cable cars going up Grouse Mountain are always in motion.

Illustrating is simply giving examples to make a point. In other words, examples or "illustrations" are specific instances that explain a general statement. Examples come very naturally in daily conversation. You might say, for instance, that professional athletes train hard and long to maintain their skills and then give a couple of examples to prove your point: Maureen Drake trains six to eight hours a day all year long, Mike Weir spends five hours a day at the driving range, and Mario Lemieux practised on the ice seven days a week.

You can draw examples from your experience, your observations, and your reading. Well-chosen examples supply concrete detail to support abstract ideas such as courage, embarrassment, understanding, love, and boredom. For example, you can *tell* your reader that you were bored ("I was bored"), or you can *show* how bored you were by giving an example ("I was so bored that I read the cereal box"). Similarly, you can make a generalization ("I like sweets") more interesting by furnishing specifics ("I love chocolate").

For his article "It's Such a Pleasure to Learn," Wallace Terry interviewed a 100-year-old man named John Morton-Finney. In his topic sentence, Terry uses the general term *special* to describe Morton-Finney. In the rest of the paragraph, he uses specific examples to support this statement. Who are some special people in your life?

> John Morton-Finney is a very special old man. Born the son of a former slave, he served in World War I, became fluent in six foreign languages, earned 11 degrees, taught school until he was 81, and still practices law. His thirst for learning has never abated. In his 60s, he started college all over again, earning his fourth bachelor's degree at 75. Today he attends law-school seminars with the wide-eyed eagerness of a freshman.

Before continuing in this chapter, take a moment to write your own paragraph using examples. Save your work because you will use it later in the chapter.

 WRITE YOUR OWN ILLUSTRATION

Who is a very special person in your life? Why is this person so special? Write a paragraph that starts with a general statement about your special person and includes specific examples to support your claim.

HOW TO WRITE AN ILLUSTRATION PARAGRAPH

To write an illustration paragraph, you use examples to support a point you want to make. Although good examples come in a variety of forms, they often draw on description. For example, if you say that someone is a good cook, you might give the following examples, all of which draw on description: His chicken pot pie has huge chunks of chicken and carrots and the flakiest crust ever; he makes a really crunchy cole slaw; and the sweet, nutty smell of his cinnamon rolls makes you want to eat breakfast three times a day. Furnishing examples usually just means following your instincts, but the guidelines here will help you write a paragraph that uses examples in clear and interesting ways.

1. *State your main point in your first sentence.* Before you begin to write, think about the main point you want to make. Then choose your words as carefully as possible to express that idea as the topic sentence of your paragraph. This should be your first sentence. In the rest of your paragraph, you will explain this main point through the examples you furnish.

   In the sample paragraph at the beginning of this chapter, Terry expresses his main point in his first sentence: *John Morton-Finney is a very special old man*. He introduces this idea as the focus of the paragraph and then sets out to expand on it.

2. *Choose examples that focus on the point you want to make.* The examples themselves serve as your explanation of the paragraph's main point. They help you prove that your main point is true, and they should all be directly related to your main point. As in a well-written

descriptive paragraph, good examples *show* rather than *tell* the readers what the author is trying to say.

In his paragraph, Terry provides examples from Morton-Finney's life that *show* why he is special. All of the examples in the paragraph focus on this single point: Morton-Finney's specialness. This clear focus makes this paragraph coherent and unified.

3. *Use a sufficient number of examples to make your point.* How many examples are enough? That depends on the point you are trying to make. Usually, two or three short examples are sufficient, although sometimes one extended example is the best choice.

Wallace Terry offers eight examples to demonstrate how special Morton-Finney's life really was: son of a slave, World War I veteran, six foreign languages, 11 degrees, teacher until 81, law practice, fourth bachelor's degree at 75, law seminars. He wants to make sure his readers have no doubts whatsoever about the truth of his main point.

4. *Organize your illustrations so that your readers can easily follow along.* Most illustration paragraphs are organized from general to particular—in other words, a general statement is followed by examples. The examples should also be organized in some logical way—chronologically, spatially, or by extremes (most to least or least to most).

Terry organizes his paragraph from general to particular and presents two different sets of examples chronologically. The first six examples name some extraordinary feats in Morton-Finney's life: son of a slave, World War I, six languages, 11 degrees, teaching until 81, practising law at age 100. Two more chronological examples demonstrate his thirst for learning: his fourth bachelor's degree at age 75 and his law seminars. Terry's method of organizing these illustrations allows us to follow his train of thought easily.

DISCOVERING HOW ILLUSTRATION WORKS

Let's look at two more example paragraphs. The first is by Roberto Verí, from an essay called "In Praise of the Mullet." In this paragraph, Verí uses examples to support his topic, which is that the NHL could make money if they considered not only selling heritage jerseys but also bringing back "hockey hair." How many examples does he use?

But alas, it [marketing strategies] could be all for naught unless we pay serious attention to the ever-decreasing number of bad hairstyles in professional hockey. Goals come and go. Uniforms too. Stats become trivial. But no one forgets what Darryl Sittler looked like in the '70s. Hockey hair is the paragon of the game's culture and the epitome of a player's style: a reflection of ambition, confidence and self-esteem. A relatively recent development in the history of the sport, it came about with the mainstream acceptance of "men's hairstyling" in the 1960s, coinciding with the expansion of the NHL. Pop music and the sexual revolution filtered into hockey. Tim Horton's brush cut morphed into a style similar to that of Monkees guitarist

Mike Nesmith. The Habs' Jacques Laperriere soon followed suit. Even sport elder Gump Worsley adjusted his sideburn length to match his younger counterpart, Ranger goalie Ed Giacomin. The tyranny of Brylcreem was overthrown in a bloodless coup, and the fad even spilled into politics. Photos of Pierre Elliott Trudeau as a newlywed in 1971 confirm that at no other time in our history did hockey players' hairstyles so closely resemble that of a sitting Prime Minister—or his wife's.

1. What main idea do you think Verí is trying to communicate in this paragraph?

   _____

2. How does each of Verí's examples explain his main point? List the three main examples he furnishes, and explain how they are related to his topic.

   Example 1: _____

   Example 2: _____

   Example 3: _____

3. Does Verí include enough examples to make his point? Explain your answer.

   _____

   _____

4. How are the examples in Verí's paragraph arranged? Look at your list of examples in response to question 2 to help you answer this question. Then identify Verí's method of organization.

   Method of organization: _____

The next paragraph, from "A Century of Women" by Lynn Peters Alder, also uses examples to prove its point. As you read this paragraph, try to put Alder's main point in your own words.

What a century for women. In countries around the world, women have overturned several millennia's worth of second-class citizenship to participate at nearly all levels of society. We have won the right to vote, own property, make our own decisions about sexual orientation, marriage, motherhood, and custody of our children. Should we choose to marry, we can keep our own names and legal identities. We can pursue higher education, have our own credit, earn and control our own money. We have access to most jobs, are rapidly establishing our own businesses, and are being elected to political office in ever-increasing numbers. We have established our right to sexual pleasure and reproductive freedom.

1. What main idea do you think Alder is trying to communicate?

   _____

2. Alder groups her examples in five different sentences. How does each sentence illustrate her main idea?

   "won the right" _____

   "choose to marry" _____

   _____

   money _____

   _____

   jobs _____

   sexual freedom _____

3. Does Alder use enough examples to make her point? Explain your answer.

   _____

   _____

4. How does Alder organize her examples: chronologically or spatially? Do you think this method is the best choice? Why or why not?

   _____

   _____

REVISING AND EDITING A STUDENT PARAGRAPH

The following is a paragraph written by Amanda Bliss, a freshman in college. As you read her paragraph, try to figure out her main point.

[1]When I was growing up I never understood the holidays. [2]My mom always wanted everyone to get along all year long. [3]The tension begins about a week before Thanksgiving she starts bringing a ton of strange foods into the house. [4]We had evergreen wreaths on every door, evergreen candle holders, evergreen tablecloths with matching napkins, and evergreen baskets with pine cones. [5]At about the same time the strange foods come into the house, she decides that every

room in the house needs decorations of some sort. [6]One year their was so much stuff that smelled like cinnamon in our house that I dreamed to often about working in a spice factory. [7]During another year, Mom decided that are entire house should smell like evergreen, and look like a pine forest. [8]Mom had finally gone off the deep end, who is usually a stable person.

This paragraph is Amanda's first draft, which now needs to be revised and edited. First, apply the Revising Checklist below to the content of Amanda's draft. When you are satisfied that her ideas are fully developed and well organized, use the Editing Checklist on page 93 to correct her grammar and mechanics errors. Answer the questions after each checklist. Then write your suggested changes directly on Amanda's draft.

REVISING CHECKLIST ✔

TOPIC SENTENCE
- ✔ Does the topic sentence convey the paragraph's controlling idea?
- ✔ Does the topic sentence appear as the first or last sentence of the paragraph?

DEVELOPMENT
- ✔ Does the paragraph contain *specific* details that support the topic sentence?
- ✔ Does the paragraph include *enough* details to explain the topic sentence fully?

UNITY
- ✔ Do all the sentences in the paragraph support the topic sentence?

ORGANIZATION
- ✔ Is the paragraph organized logically?

COHERENCE
- ✔ Do the sentences move smoothly and logically from one to the next?

Topic Sentence

1. What is Amanda's main idea in this paragraph?

_____

2. Put brackets around Amanda's topic sentence. Does it convey Amanda's main idea?

_____

3. Rewrite the topic sentence if necessary to introduce all the ideas in her paragraph.

_____

_____

Development

1. Are Amanda's examples specific enough?

_____

Add another more specific detail to an example in her paragraph.

2. Does she give enough examples to make her point?

_____

Add at least one new example to Amanda's paragraph to strengthen her topic sentence.

Unity

1. Read each of Amanda's sentences with her topic sentence (revised, if necessary) in mind.
2. Cross out the one sentence that does not relate to Amanda's topic sentence.

Organization

1. Read Amanda's paragraph again to see if all the sentences are arranged logically.
2. List some of her examples in the order they appear. Then identify her method of organization.

_____   _____

_____   _____

_____   _____

_____   _____

_____   _____

_____   _____

Method of organization: _____

3. Move the one sentence that is out of place in Amanda's paragraph.

Coherence

1. Circle three transitions, repetitions, synonyms, or pronouns Amanda uses.

2. Explain how one of these makes Amanda's paragraph easier to read.

For a list of transitions, see page 38.

For a list of pronouns, see page 276.

_____

_____

Now rewrite Amanda's paragraph with your revisions.

EDITING CHECKLIST ✔

SENTENCES

✔ Does each sentence have a main subject and verb?

✔ Do all subjects and verbs agree?

✔ Do all pronouns agree with their nouns?

✔ Are modifiers as close as possible to the words they modify?

PUNCTUATION AND MECHANICS

✔ Are sentences punctuated correctly?

✔ Are words capitalized properly?

WORD CHOICE AND SPELLING

✔ Are words used correctly?

✔ Are words spelled correctly?

Sentences

Subjects and Verbs

For help with subjects and verbs, see Chapter 30.

1. Underline the subjects once and verbs twice in your revision of Amanda's paragraph. Remember that sentences can have more than one subject-verb set.

2. Does each of the sentences have at least one subject and verb that can stand alone?

_____

3. Did you find and correct Amanda's run-on sentence? If not, find and correct it now.

For help with run-ons, see Chapter 32.

Subject-Verb Agreement

1. Read aloud the subjects and verbs you underlined in your revision of Amanda's paragraph.

For help with subject-verb agreement, see Chapter 34.

2. Correct any subjects and verbs that do not agree.

Pronoun Agreement

For help with pronoun agreement, see Chapter 38.

1. Find any pronouns in your revision of Amanda's paragraph that do not agree with their nouns.

2. Correct any pronouns that do not agree with their nouns.

Modifier Errors

For help with modifier errors, see Chapter 41.

1. Find any modifiers in your revision of Amanda's paragraph that are not as close as possible to the words they modify.

2. Did you find and correct her misplaced modifier? If not, find and correct it now.

Punctuation and Mechanics

Punctuation

For help with punctuation, see Chapters 42–45.

1. Read your revision of Amanda's paragraph for any errors in punctuation.

2. Find the run-on sentence you revised, and make sure it is punctuated correctly.

3. Did you find and correct her two comma errors? If not, find and correct them now.

Mechanics

For help with capitalization, see Chapter 46.

1. Read your revision of Amanda's paragraph for any errors in capitalization.

2. Be sure to check Amanda's capitalization in the run-on sentence you revised.

Word Choice and Spelling

Word Choice

For help with confused words, see Chapter 52.

1. Find any words used incorrectly in your revision of Amanda's paragraph.

2. Did you find and correct her three confused words? If not, find and correct them now.

Spelling

For help with spelling, see Chapter 53.

1. Use spell-check and a dictionary to check the spelling in your revision of Amanda's paragraph.

2. Correct any misspelled words.

Now rewrite Amanda's paragraph again with your editing corrections.

REVISING AND EDITING YOUR OWN PARAGRAPH

Returning to the illustration paragraph you wrote earlier in this chapter, revise and edit your own writing. The above checklist will help you apply what you have learned to your own writing.

PRACTISING ILLUSTRATION

Reading Suggestions

In Chapter 23, you will find two essays that use examples to make their point: "It's Not Me, It's You ... and You're Weird" by Leah McLaren and "Goin' Down the Road" by Jonathon Gatehouse. You might want to read these selections before writing another illustration. As you read, notice how the writers use examples to support and advance their ideas.

Writing Workshop

Guidelines for Writing an Illustration Paragraph

1. State your main point in your first sentence.
2. Choose examples that focus on the point you want to make.
3. Use a sufficient number of examples to make your point.
4. Organize your illustration so that your readers can easily follow along.

1. Identify a theme in this picture. Explain what you think this picture says about the theme.
2. Share with your classmates an opinion you have about communication and technology. Use examples to explain yourself.

3. Use examples or illustrations to explain how technology has made your life easier or harder. Is being able to be contacted 24 hours a day a good thing? Use examples to explain.

4. Create your own illustration assignment (with the help of your instructor) and write a response to it.

Revising Workshop

Small-Group Activity (5–10 minutes per writer)   Working in groups of three or four, each person should read his or her illustration paragraph to the other members of the group. Those listening should record their reactions on a copy of the Peer Evaluation Form in Appendix 2C. After your group goes through this process, give your evaluation forms to the appropriate writers so that each writer has two or three peer comment sheets for revising.

Paired Activity (5 minutes per writer)   Using the completed Peer Evaluation Forms, work in pairs to decide what you should revise in your paragraphs. If time allows, rewrite some of your sentences and have your partner check them.

Individual Activity   Rewrite your paragraph, using the revising feedback you received from other students.

Editing Workshop

Paired Activity (5–10 minutes per writer)   Exchange papers with a classmate, and use the Editing Peer Evaluation Form in Appendix 1 to identify as many grammar, punctuation, mechanics, and spelling errors as you can. If time allows, correct some of your errors and have your partner check them. Record your grammar, punctuation, and mechanics errors in the Error Log (Appendix 6) and your spelling errors in the Spelling Log (Appendix 7).

Individual Activity   Rewrite your paragraph again, using the editing feedback you received from other students.

Reflecting on Your Writing

When you have completed your own essay, answer these five questions:

1. What was most difficult about this assignment?

2. What was easiest?

3. What did you learn about using illustrations by completing this assignment?

4. What do you think are the strengths of your illustration paragraph? What are its weaknesses?

5. What did you learn from this assignment about your own writing process—about preparing to write, about writing the first draft, about revising, and about editing?

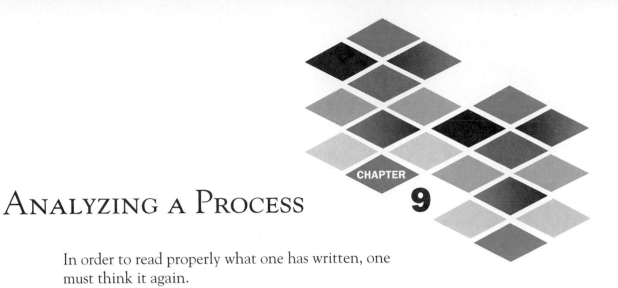

ANALYZING A PROCESS

In order to read properly what one has written, one
must think it again.

—JULES RENARD

Just visit any bookstore to find out how much we depend on process
analysis in our daily lives. Books with such titles as the following have been
on the best-seller lists for years.

How to Dress for Success
I Dare You! How to Stay Young Forever
How the West Was Won
How to Win Friends and Influence People
Boom, Bust and Echo: How to Profit from the Coming Demographic Shift

When we **analyze a process,** we explain how to do something or how something happened. Process analysis involves explaining an activity or event
according to what comes first, second, and so forth. Think about how often
you try to explain something. If you want to teach someone how to snow-
board, if you're late for a class or for your job, if someone doesn't understand
how a car engine works, what is the first thing you say? "Let me explain."

In "Playing to Win: Do You Think Like a Champ?" Coach Mike Shanahan
of Super Bowl fame explains how to be a winner—on the field and in life. In
other words, the author is analyzing a process. You have been reading how-to
process analysis all your life in the form of instruction manuals, recipes, and
directions for assembling products. In this paragraph, Shanahan provides an
excellent example of how-to analysis. What activities can you analyze? In
what areas can you give people advice?

It's easy to become a winner if you're simply willing to learn from those
who have been winners themselves. Find out who has had the most success
at what they do. Watch their technique. Observe their methods. Study their
behavior. By finding the best people in your industry, you'll learn what their
routines are, the mistakes they made along the way, and the various scenar-
ios they're forced to confront on a day-to-day basis. Then not only can you
imitate their habits, but you can also imitate their results. It can be that easy.

Before continuing in this chapter, take a moment to write your own process analysis. Save your work because you will use it later in this chapter.

 WRITE YOUR OWN PROCESS ANALYSIS

Think of an activity that you enjoy or that you do well. Consider all the steps involved in this activity. Then write directions for someone else to follow. (Some possible topics are how to change a tire, make a bed, get money from an ATM, keep a young child entertained, play pickup basketball, make chocolate chip cookies, change the oil in a car, relax after a stressful day, plan a surprise party, give a manicure, or cheer up a friend.)

HOW TO WRITE A PROCESS ANALYSIS PARAGRAPH

Most process analysis writing falls into one of two categories. The first type tells *how to do something,* such as change a tire, write an essay, or program a VCR. The second type clarifies *how something happened* or *how something works,* such as how the War of 1812 started, how Bill Gates became a billionaire, how glasnost changed the Soviet Union, how a cell phone functions, or how the heart pumps blood.

Explaining a process is often much easier in speech than in writing. Think about the last time you gave someone directions to get someplace. Your listener probably interrupted a couple of times to ask you to clarify what you meant. ("If I pass Randall Road, have I gone too far?") Or perhaps you saw a confused look on the person's face, so you knew you had to re-explain or add information. ("Don't worry, you can count stoplights. Elm Street is the fifth stoplight.") In a conversation, you can rely not only on your words to communicate but also on the tone of your voice, the expression on your face, and the movements of your hands and body.

When you write, however, you don't have face-to-face contact, so your listener can't ask what you mean, and you don't have the chance to add information or clear up confusion along the way. You must therefore furnish all the steps in the exact order in which they must occur. Your job will be much easier if you follow the guidelines listed here.

1. ***State in the topic sentence what the reader should be able to do or understand by the end of the paragraph.*** The topic sentence should give your readers a road map for what's to follow. They need to know where they're headed from the beginning of the paragraph. For example, a person giving directions might start by saying, "It's easy to get to Jeff's house from here." That introduces the task. You also want to try to make your topic sentence as interesting as possible. Look at the difference in these topic sentences for a paragraph about making a cup of coffee:

Topic Sentence 1:   I am going to tell you how to make a really good cup of coffee.

Topic Sentence 2:   Everyone can make coffee, but I have a
secret for making the best cup of coffee
you will ever taste.

Mike Shanahan's topic sentence says exactly what the readers will learn when they read his paragraph—how to become a winner. The rest of his paragraph explains how to achieve a winning edge.

2. ***Explain the rest of the process in the remainder of the paragraph.*** By the end of a "how-to" paragraph, your readers should be able to perform the activity you are analyzing. In the "how-something-works" paragraph, the readers should be able to operate the device being discussed. And in the "how-something-happened" paragraph, the readers should understand more about a particular event.

The success of a process analysis paragraph depends to a great extent on how well you know your audience. Since you are giving them complete directions, you need to understand how much they already know about a process. Knowing your audience also helps you decide how much detail you need to include and which terms to define.

Shanahan's paragraph tells us how to be a winner in four easy steps:

a. Find out who has had the most success at what they do.
b. Watch their technique.
c. Observe their methods.
d. Study their behaviour.

He even tells us the results we can expect after following these steps.

3. ***Organize your material in chronological order.*** Your readers need to know what happens first, second, and so on in order to perform a task or understand a device or an event. This is why transitions such as *first*, *second*, and *then* are very common in process paragraphs. Most process analysis paragraphs are organized chronologically (according to a time sequence), with the explanation starting at one point and progressing step by step through the process, directions, or event.

Explaining every step of a process is very important. Suppose, for example, that you see these directions for preparing a frozen pizza:

Preheat the oven to 425 degrees. If you like a crisp crust, put the pizza directly on the oven rack. If you prefer a soft crust, put the pizza on a cookie sheet. Bake for 20 minutes. Remove from the oven and enjoy.

Do you have all the information you need here to prepare a frozen pizza? What about the wrapping paper and the cardboard that just caught fire in the oven? The step after "Preheat the oven" should be "Remove all wrapping paper and cardboard from the pizza."

The guidelines in Shanahan's paragraph are in a loose chronological order. They move from identifying winners to studying their behaviour. Shanahan uses no transitions with his guidelines. He simply writes them as commands. Near the end of his paragraph, he uses the word "then" to lead his readers into the final two sentences.

DISCOVERING HOW PROCESS ANALYSIS WORKS

Having examined the "how-to-do-something" process analysis, we're now going to look at the second type of process analysis with a paragraph about how something works. The key to writing this form of process analysis is understanding your topic. If you're unclear about some part of the process, your reader will end up confused about it too. The first example here explains how a copying machine works. See if you can understand the details well enough to explain the process to someone else.

Static electricity enables a photocopier to produce almost instant copies of documents. At the heart of the machine is a metal drum that is given a negative charge at the beginning of the copying cycle. The optical system then projects an image of the document on the drum. The electric charge disappears where light strikes the metal surface, so only dark parts of the image remain charged. Positively charged particles of toner powder are then applied to the drum. The charged parts of the drum attract the dark powder, which is then transferred to a piece of paper. A heater seals the powder to the paper, and a warm copy of the document emerges from the photocopier.

1. What process does this paragraph explain? Which sentence gives you this information?

   _____

2. Explain the process in your own words.

   _____

   _____

   _____

3. Is the information about this process in chronological order? What word clues tell you the author's method of organization?

   _____

The next example explains how something happened. This type of process analysis gives readers background information and details to help them understand an event or a current situation. As with other types of process analysis, this type is organized chronologically because it consists of many steps or events that occurred one after the other. The following paragraph, about Post-it Notes™, is a good example of this type of analysis. See if you can follow the steps in this analysis.

Post-it Notes™ were spawned by an accidental discovery in a laboratory in St. Paul, Minnesota, where research was being conducted into extra-strong glue in 1968. One series of experiments produced an adhesive that was so lacking in sticking power that the company, 3M, dismissed it as useless. However, one of its employees, a chemist named Art Fry, sang in a choir and came up with the idea of using the new glue to make bookmarks for his hymnal that could be removed when they were no longer needed without damaging the page. Fry tried to persuade the firm that it was throwing away a discovery that could have worldwide uses. But it was an uphill battle. Finally, in 1980, 3M began selling pads of note tags with a strip of the weak adhesive along one edge for use in offices. Not only were they removable, but they could be restuck somewhere else. Today, it's hard to imagine life without them!

1. What is the purpose of this paragraph? State it in your own words.

   _____

   _____

2. Do you understand how Post-it Notes™ were discovered? Explain the main facts about this discovery.

   _____

   _____

   _____

   _____

3. If you didn't understand the process, what else do you need to know?

   _____

   _____

4. Are the details in the paragraph organized chronologically? Is this order effective for what the author is explaining? Why or why not?

   _____

   _____

   _____

REVISING AND EDITING A STUDENT PARAGRAPH

The following is a process analysis paragraph written by Victor Cantanzaro, a student. As you read it, notice when his paragraph tells you what he is explaining.

¹You will be surprised to find out how furniture goes from the store to your door. ²First of all, most furniture stores hire independent trucking agencies to deliver their orders. ³These delivery services

have to schedule their days very tightly so they can get as much furniture delivered per day as possible. [4]Customers don't understand this
idea. [5]They go on errands and make life very difficult for the delivery
service. [6]Why can't they wait patiently for their furniture when they
know it's coming? [7]Then the driver's deliver the furniture in the
order set by the computer. [8]The drivers from the delivery service has
to pick up the furniture at the furniture stores in reverse order so that
the pieces of furniture they're going to deliver first is at the end of the
truck. [9]The drivers always call the customers once the days schedule
is set. [10]The weather outlook is a major part of packing the truck,
because the furniture has to be covered with plastic, foam, or paper.
[11]Depending on the conditions outside. [12]The worst situation is customers who decide when the delivery truck arrives. [13]That they don't
want the furniture after all.

This paragraph is Victor's first draft, which now needs to be revised and
edited. First, apply the Revising Checklist below to the content of Victor's
draft. When you are satisfied that his ideas are fully developed and well
organized, use the Editing Checklist on page 104 to correct his grammar and
mechanics errors. Answer the questions after each checklist. Then write
your suggested changes directly on Victor's draft.

REVISING CHECKLIST ✔

TOPIC SENTENCE
- ✔ Does the topic sentence convey the paragraph's controlling idea?
- ✔ Does the topic sentence appear as the first or last sentence of the
  paragraph?

DEVELOPMENT
- ✔ Does the paragraph contain *specific* details that support the topic
  sentence?
- ✔ Does the paragraph include *enough* details to explain the topic sentence fully?

UNITY
- ✔ Do all the sentences in the paragraph support the topic sentence?

ORGANIZATION
- ✔ Is the paragraph organized logically?

COHERENCE
- ✔ Do the sentences move smoothly and logically from one to the next?

Topic Sentence

1. What is Victor's purpose in this paragraph?

   _____

2. Put brackets around Victor's topic sentence. Does it state his purpose?

   _____

3. Write an alternative topic sentence.

   _____

   _____

Development

1. Do Victor's details explain the process of delivering furniture step by step?

   _____

2. Where do you need more information?

   _____

3. What new details can you add to Victor's paragraph to make his steps clearer?

   _____

Unity

1. Read each of Victor's sentences with his topic sentence (revised, if necessary) in mind.
2. Cross out the three sentences not directly related to Victor's topic sentence.

Organization

1. Read Victor's paragraph again to see if all the sentences are arranged logically.
2. List the general steps covered in this paragraph.

   _____   _____

   _____   _____

   _____   _____

3. Circle in item 2 the one step that is out of order.

4. Renumber the sentences in chronological order.

Coherence

For a list of transitions, see page 38.

1. Circle three transitions Victor uses.

2. Explain how one of these makes Victor's paragraph easier to read.

_____

_____

Now rewrite Victor's paragraph with your revisions.

EDITING CHECKLIST ✔

SENTENCES

✔ Does each sentence have a main subject and verb?

✔ Do all subjects and verbs agree?

✔ Do all pronouns agree with their nouns?

✔ Are modifiers as close as possible to the words they modify?

PUNCTUATION AND MECHANICS

✔ Are sentences punctuated correctly?

✔ Are words capitalized properly?

WORD CHOICE AND SPELLING

✔ Are words used correctly?

✔ Are words spelled correctly?

Sentences

Subjects and Verbs

For help with subjects and verbs, see Chapter 30.

1. Underline the subjects once and verbs twice in your revision of Victor's paragraph. Remember that sentences can have more than one subject-verb set.

2. Does each of Victor's sentences have at least one subject and verb that can stand alone?

_____

For help with fragments, see Chapter 31.

3. Did you find and correct the two fragments in Victor's first draft? If not, find and correct them now.

Subject-Verb Agreement

1. Read aloud the subjects and verbs you underlined in your revision of Victor's paragraph.

2. Did you find and correct the two subjects and verbs that do not agree? If not, find and correct them now.

For help with subject-verb agreement, see Chapter 34.

Pronoun Agreement

1. Find any pronouns in your revision of Victor's paragraph that do not agree with their nouns.

2. Correct any pronouns that do not agree with their nouns.

For help with pronoun agreement, see Chapter 38.

Modifier Errors

1. Find any modifiers in your revision of Victor's paragraph that are not as close as possible to the words they modify.

2. Rewrite sentences if necessary so that the modifiers are as close as possible to the words they modify.

For help with modifier errors, see Chapter 41.

Punctuation and Mechanics

Punctuation

1. Read your revision of Victor's paragraph for any errors in punctuation.

2. Find the two fragments you revised, and make sure they are punctuated correctly.

3. Did you find and correct Victor's two apostrophe errors? If not, find and correct them now.

For help with punctuation, see Chapters 42–45.

Mechanics

1. Read your revision of Victor's paragraph for any errors in capitalization.

2. Be sure to check Victor's capitalization in the fragments you revised.

For help with capitalization, see Chapter 46.

Word Choice and Spelling

Word Choice

1. Find any words used incorrectly in your revision of Victor's paragraph.

2. Correct any errors you find.

For help with confused words, see Chapter 52.

Spelling

1. Use spell-check and a dictionary to check the spelling in your revision of Victor's paragraph.

2. Correct any misspelled words.

For help with spelling, see Chapter 53.

Now rewrite Victor's paragraph again with your editing corrections.

REVISING AND EDITING YOUR OWN PARAGRAPH

Returning to the process analysis paragraph you wrote earlier in this chapter, revise and edit your own writing. The checklists above will help you apply what you have learned to your own paragraph.

PRACTISING PROCESS ANALYSIS

Reading Suggestions

In Chapter 24, you will find two essays that illustrate the guidelines you have studied in this chapter. "A Financial Plan for New Graduates with Loans" by James Daw suggests effective ways to manage money and live debt-free, and "How We Kept the Farm" by Eugene Warwaruk explains how a family struggled to keep their land. You might want to read these selections before writing another process analysis. As you read, notice how the writers explain every step of the process carefully and completely.

Writing Workshop

Guidelines for Writing a Process Analysis Paragraph

1. State in the topic sentence what the reader should be able to do or understand by the end of the paragraph.
2. Explain the rest of the process in the remainder of the paragraph.
3. Organize your material in chronological order.

1. Place yourself in the scene on the previous page, and write a process analysis paragraph explaining the background, an event leading up to the picture, or an activity in the photograph. Be sure your explanation covers all steps or stages of the process you are discussing. Be sure that your topic sentence tells what the reader should know by the end of the paragraph.

2. Tell your classmates about a sport or hobby that you enjoy. Include what it takes to get started in this activity and what the satisfactions are. For example, how would a person get started playing the guitar, playing online games, or snowboarding? And what could it lead to?

3. Your college or university newspaper is running a special edition on study habits, and the editor has asked you to write an article explaining how you manage all the demands on your time, including studying, socializing, working, and keeping family obligations. Prepare your explanation for the next edition of the paper.

4. Create your own process analysis assignment (with the help of your instructor), and write a response to it.

Revising Workshop

Small-Group Activity (5–10 minutes per writer)   Working in groups of three or four, each person should read his or her process analysis to the other members of the group. Those listening should record their reactions on a copy of the Peer Evaluation Form in Appendix 2D. After your group goes through this process, give your evaluation forms to the appropriate writers so that each writer has two or three peer comment sheets for revising.

Paired Activity (5 minutes per writer)   Using the completed Peer Evaluation Forms as guides, work in pairs to decide what you should revise in your paragraphs. If time allows, rewrite some of your sentences and have your partner check them.

Individual Activity   Rewrite your paragraph, using the revising feedback you received from other students.

Editing Workshop

Paired Activity (5–10 minutes per writer)   Exchange papers with a classmate, and use the Editing Peer Evaluation Form in Appendix 1 to identify as many grammar, punctuation, mechanics, and spelling errors as you can. If time allows, correct some of your errors and have your partner check them. Record your grammar, punctuation, and mechanics errors in the Error Log (Appendix 6) and your spelling errors in the Spelling Log (Appendix 7).

Individual Activity   Rewrite your paragraph again using the editing feedback you received from other students.

Reflecting on Your Writing

When you have completed your own essay, answer these five questions:

1. What was most difficult about this assignment?
2. What was easiest?
3. What did you learn about process analysis by completing this assignment?
4. What do you think are the strengths of your process analysis? What are its weaknesses?
5. What did you learn from this assignment about your own writing process—about preparing to write, about writing the first draft, about revising, and about editing?

COMPARING AND CONTRASTING

All good writing is swimming under water and
holding your breath.

—F. Scott Fitzgerald

We rely on comparison and contrast to make many decisions—both big
and small—that affect our lives every day:

What to have for breakfast
Where to go on vacation
Which college to attend
Which person to marry

Actually, you are comparing and contrasting constantly. In fact, comparison
and contrast are at the heart of our competitive society. When we are children, we compare our toys with our friends' toys and what we wear with how
the in-group dresses. As we grow up, we learn that colleges and universities
award scholarships and coaches put together athletic teams by comparing
our abilities with other students' abilities. Even after graduation, comparison and contrast are essential elements in our social and professional lives.

Comparison and contrast allow us to understand one subject by putting
it next to another. **Comparing** involves discovering similarities; **contrasting**
is based on finding differences. But comparison and contrast are generally
considered part of the same process. As a result, the word *compare* is often
used to refer to both techniques.

In the following paragraph, Shannon Brownlee uses humour to compare
and contrast the behaviour of preteens and teenagers. As you read, see if you
can figure out Brownlee's purpose.

One day, your child is a beautiful, charming 12-year-old, a kid who pops
out of bed full of good cheer, clears the table without being asked, and brings
home good grades from school. The next day, your child bursts into tears

when you ask for the salt and listens to electronic music at maximum volume for hours on end. Chores? Forget it. Homework? There's little time, after talking to friends on the phone for five hours every night. Mornings? Your bluebird of happiness is flown, replaced by a groaning lump that can scarcely be roused for school. In short, your home is now inhabited by a teenager.

Before continuing in this chapter, take a moment to write a comparison/contrast paragraph of your own. Save your work because you will use it later in this chapter.

 WRITE YOUR OWN COMPARISON/CONTRAST

Think of two individuals you know, such as two friends, two dates, two grandmothers, or two co-workers. How are they similar? How are they different? Write a paragraph comparing or contrasting these two people.

HOW TO WRITE A COMPARISON/CONTRAST PARAGRAPH

To write a good comparison/contrast paragraph, you need to focus on items that will lead to a specific point. The following guidelines will help you write a comparison/contrast paragraph.

1. *State the point you want to make with your comparison in your topic sentence.* All good comparisons have a point. You might be using comparison and contrast to reveal a team's strengths and weaknesses. Or you might be trying to find the best stereo system or the most durable camera. Whatever your purpose, the items you are comparing or contrasting should be stated clearly in your topic sentence along with your main point.

   In Shannon Brownlee's paragraph, Brownlee explains the normal transition from preteen to teenager. She does this by comparing the pleasant preteen behavior with that of the difficult teenager. The author saves her main idea for the last sentence, which ties together the entire paragraph.

2. *Choose items to compare and contrast that will make your point most effectively.* To write a successful comparison, you need to choose items from the same category. For example, you can compare two movies to make a point, but it would be difficult to compare a movie with a swimming pool and come to any sensible conclusion.

   When you choose two items to compare, you might want to brainstorm a list of similarities and differences to see what patterns emerge. A common characteristic in this list will give your paragraph a focus. Brownlee's brainstorming might have looked something like the following:

Preteenager	Teenager
cheerful	sullen
communicates with parents	avoids parents, talks with friends
loves school	hates school, won't do homework
no emotional problems	bursts into tears without warning
responsible at home	avoids chores at home
looks forward to getting up	hates to get out of bed

3. ***Organize your paragraph either by topics or by points of comparison.***
   When you are ready to write, you have to decide whether to organize your ideas by topics or by points of comparison. Both methods are effective.
   Brownlee's paragraph is organized by topic—preteens and teens. First she talks about topic A, preteens; then she deals with topic B, teens. The result is a paragraph with the pattern AAAA, BBBB:

Topic by Topic

A	Preteen emotions
A	Preteen chores
A	Preteen homework
A	Preteen mornings
B	Teen emotions
B	Teen chores
B	Teen homework
B	Teen mornings

Brownlee could just as easily have organized her paragraph by points of comparison—emotions, chores, homework, and mornings. In this case, her outline would fall into the pattern AB, AB, AB, AB:

Point by Point

Emotions	A	Preteen emotions
	B	Teen emotions
Chores	A	Preteen chores
	B	Teen chores
Homework	A	Preteen homework
	B	Teen homework
Mornings	A	Preteen mornings
	B	Teen mornings

Notice that Brownlee discusses the same four qualities in both the topical pattern (AAAA, BBBB) and the point-by-point pattern (AB, AB, AB, AB). If you mention one topic for one group, you should mention it for the other group. Also, in both patterns, the qualities should always be discussed in the same order. If emotions are first for one topic, they should be first for the second topic as well. Following the same order makes your comparison easy for your reader to follow.

DISCOVERING HOW COMPARISON AND CONTRAST WORK

Looking at two more comparison/contrast examples will help you understand your options for developing this type of paragraph. First, Marie Winn compares reading and television. See if you can figure out her main points.

Children's feelings of power and competence are nourished by [a] feature of the reading experience that does not obtain for television: the non-mechanical, easily accessible, and easily transportable nature of reading matter. Children can always count on a book for pleasure, though the television set may break down at a crucial moment. They may take a book with them wherever they go, to their room, to the park, to their friend's house, to school to read under the desk: they can *control* their use of books and reading materials. The television set is stuck in a certain place; it cannot be moved easily. It certainly cannot be casually transported from place to place by a child. Children must not only watch television wherever the set is located, but they must watch certain programs at certain times and are powerless to change what comes out of the set and when it comes out.

1. What is Winn's main idea in this paragraph?

   _____

   _____

2. What exactly is Winn comparing or contrasting in this paragraph? List her main points under the topics below.

Books	**Television**
_____	_____
_____	_____
_____	_____

3. Does Winn organize her paragraph by topics or by points of comparison?

_____

The next example, by Deborah Tannen, compares and contrasts the behaviour of groups of boys and girls when they are young. What is the main idea the author is trying to convey in this comparison?

> Anthropologists Daniel Maltz and Ruth Borker point out that boys and girls socialize differently. Little girls tend to play in small groups or, even more common, in pairs. Their social life usually centers around a best friend, and friendships are made, maintained, and broken by talk—especially "secrets." If a little girl tells her friend's secret to another little girl, she may find herself with a new best friend. The secrets themselves may or may not be important, but the fact of telling them is all-important. It's hard for newcomers to get into these tight groups, but anyone who is admitted is treated as an equal. Girls like to play cooperatively; if they can't cooperate, the group breaks up.
>
> Little boys tend to play in larger groups, often outdoors, and they spend more time doing things than talking. It's easy for boys to get into the group, but not everyone is accepted as an equal. Once in the group, boys must jockey for their status in it. One of the most important ways they do this is through talk: verbal display such as telling stories and jokes, challenging and sidetracking the verbal displays of other boys, and withstanding other boys' challenges in order to maintain their own story—and status. Their talk is often competitive talk about who is best at what.

1. Although this excerpt is two paragraphs, they share a single topic sentence. What is their topic sentence?

_____

2. What exactly is Tannen comparing or contrasting in this paragraph? List some of her main points under the topics below.

Girls	**Boys**
_____	_____
_____	_____
_____	_____
_____	_____

3. Does Tannen organize her paragraphs by topics or by points of comparison?

_____

REVISING AND EDITING A STUDENT PARAGRAPH

The following is a comparison/contrast paragraph written by Nathalie Johnson, a post-secondary student. Her comparison identifies some real differences between two teachers. As you read, see if this comparison is clear to you.

[1]Ms. Tramel, my art teacher, and Mr. Morgan, my physics teacher, have two different approaches to their students. [2]Students eventually find out that even though Mr. Morgan doesn't smile much, he cares more about the students than they initially think he does. [3]When a student first meets Ms. Tramel, they think she is an easy teacher because she is so friendly. [4]Ms. Tramel encourages students to work hard on their own Mr. Morgan helps students study by giving them study questions and working with them outside of class. [5]I couldn't believe I got an A from Mr. Morgan. [6]He always helped me outside of class. [7]They both like their students a lot; however, Mr. Morgan doesn't smile as much as Ms. Tramel. [8]A student learns very quickly that both of these teachers will be there for them no matter what; even though the teachers express themselves in different ways.

This paragraph is Nathalie's first draft, which now needs to be revised and edited. First, apply the Revising Checklist that follows to the content of Nathalie's draft. When you are satisfied that her ideas are fully developed and well organized, use the Editing Checklist on page 116 to correct her grammar and mechanics errors. Answer the questions after each checklist; then write your suggested changes directly on Nathalie's draft.

REVISING CHECKLIST ✔

Topic Sentence
✔ Does the topic sentence convey the paragraph's controlling idea?
✔ Does the topic sentence appear as the first or last sentence of the paragraph?

Development
✔ Does the paragraph contain *specific* details that support the topic sentence?
✔ Does the paragraph include *enough* details to explain the topic sentence fully?

Unity
✔ Do all the sentences in the paragraph support the topic sentence?

Organization
✔ Is the paragraph organized logically?

Coherence
✔ Do the sentences move smoothly and logically from one to the next?

Topic Sentence

1. What is the main point of Nathalie's paragraph?

    _____

2. Put brackets around Nathalie's topic sentence. Does it introduce her main point?

    _____

3. Write an alternative topic sentence.

    _____

    _____

Development

1. Does Nathalie compare the same qualities in both teachers?

    _____

2. Where do you need more information?

    _____

3. What specific details can you add to Nathalie's paragraph to make her comparison more effective?

    _____

    _____

Unity

1. Read each of Nathalie's sentences with her topic sentence (revised, if necessary) in mind.
2. Cross out the two sentences not directly related to Nathalie's topic sentence.

Organization

1. Read Nathalie's paragraph again to see if all the sentences are arranged logically.
2. List some of the points Nathalie compares and contrasts in her paragraph in the order they appear.

<table>
<tr><td align="center">**Ms. Tramel**</td><td align="center">**Mr. Morgan**</td></tr>
</table>

_____	_____
_____	_____
_____	_____
_____	_____

3. Is the paragraph organized by topics or by points of comparison?

    _____

4. Move the one sentence that is out of order.

Coherence

1. Circle all of Nathalie's references to "teacher" or "teachers."
2. Change two of these words to synonyms.

    Now rewrite Nathalie's paragraph with your revisions.

EDITING CHECKLIST ✔

SENTENCES
- ✔ Does each sentence have a main subject and verb?
- ✔ Do all subjects and verbs agree?
- ✔ Do all pronouns agree with their nouns?
- ✔ Are modifiers as close as possible to the words they modify?

PUNCTUATION AND MECHANICS
- ✔ Are sentences punctuated correctly?
- ✔ Are words capitalized properly?

WORD CHOICE AND SPELLING
- ✔ Are words used correctly?
- ✔ Are words spelled correctly?

Sentences

Subjects and Verbs

For help with subjects and verbs, see Chapter 30.

1. Underline Nathalie's subjects once and verbs twice. Remember that sentences can have more than one subject-verb set.

2. Does each of Nathalie's sentences have at least one subject and verb that can stand alone?

_____

3. Did you find and correct Nathalie's run-on sentence? If not, find and correct it now.

For help with run-ons, see Chapter 32.

Subject-Verb Agreement

1. Read aloud the subjects and verbs you underlined in your revision of Nathalie's paragraph.
2. Correct any subjects and verbs that do not agree.

For help with subject-verb agreement, see Chapter 34.

Pronoun Agreement

1. Find any pronouns in your revision of Nathalie's paragraph that do not agree with their nouns.
2. Did you find and correct the two pronouns that do not agree with their nouns? If not, find and correct them now.

For help with pronoun agreement, see Chapter 38.

Modifier Errors

1. Find any modifiers in your revision of Nathalie's paragraph that are not as close as possible to the words they modify.
2. Rewrite sentences if necessary so that modifiers are as close as possible to the words they modify.

For help with modifier errors, see Chapter 41.

Punctuation and Mechanics

Punctuation

1. Read your revision of Nathalie's paragraph for any errors in punctuation.
2. Find the run-on sentence you revised, and make sure it is punctuated correctly.
3. Did you find and correct Nathalie's semicolon error? If not, find and correct it now.

For help with punctuation, see Chapters 42–45.

Mechanics

1. Read your revision of Nathalie's paragraph for any errors in capitalization.
2. Be sure to check Nathalie's capitalization in the run-on sentence you revised.

For help with capitalization, see Chapter 46.

Word Choice and Spelling

Word Choice

For help with confused words, see Chapter 52.

1. Find any words used incorrectly in your revision of Nathalie's paragraph.
2. Correct any errors you find.

Spelling

For help with spelling, see Chapter 53.

1. Use spell-check and a dictionary to check the spelling in your revision of Nathalie's paragraph.
2. Correct any misspelled words.

Now rewrite Nathalie's paragraph again with your editing corrections.

 **REVISING AND EDITING YOUR OWN PARAGRAPH**

Returning to the comparison/contrast paragraph you wrote earlier in this chapter, revise and edit your own writing. The checklists above will help you apply what you have learned to your own paragraph.

PRACTISING COMPARISON AND CONTRAST

Reading Suggestions

In Chapter 25, you will find two essays that follow the guidelines you have studied in this chapter. "London in My Life" by David Suzuki and "From Wretched Ugliness to Glamour Doll-dom" by Zebedee Nungak both compare the past with the present. Suzuki writes from an environmental perspective on the city of London when he was a child and in the present; Nungak writes about attitudes toward beauty in the past and now. You might want to read these selections before writing another comparison/contrast assignment. As you read, notice how the writers make their points through well-thought-out, detailed comparisons and contrasts.

Writing Workshop

Guidelines for Writing a Comparison/Contrast Paragraph

1. State the point you want to make with your comparison in your topic sentence.
2. Choose items to compare and contrast that will make your point most effectively.
3. Organize your paragraph either by topics or by points of comparison.

1. Explain the similarities and differences between these pictures. How can one place be so different and yet the same?

2. Discuss the similarities and differences between your high school life and your college or university life. Are your classes more difficult? Do you still socialize with your friends from high school? Are you treated differently by your parents, school officials, or old classmates? Have your expectations of yourself changed? Do you now have to juggle school and work?

3. You have been hired by your local newspaper to compare and contrast various aspects of daily life. For example, you might compare two musical groups, good drivers versus bad drivers, two malls, or two kinds of pets. Decide on the point you want to make before you begin writing.

4. Create your own comparison/contrast assignment (with the help of your instructor), and write a response to it.

Revising Workshop

Small-Group Activity (5–10 minutes per writer) Working in groups of three or four, each person should read his or her comparison/contrast paragraph to the other members of the group. Those listening should record their reactions on a copy of the Peer Evaluation Form in Appendix 2E. After your group goes through this process, give your evaluation forms to the appropriate writers so that each writer has two or three peer comment sheets for revising.

Paired Activity (5 minutes per writer) Using the completed Peer Evaluation Forms, work in pairs to decide what you should revise in your paragraph. If time allows, rewrite some of your sentences and have your partner check them.

Individual Activity Rewrite your paragraph, using the revising feedback you received from other students.

Editing Workshop

Paired Activity (5–10 minutes per writer)   Exchange papers with a class-mate, and use the Editing Peer Evaluation Form in Appendix 1 to identify as many grammar, punctuation, mechanics, and spelling errors as you can. If time allows, correct some of your errors and have your partner check them. Record your grammar, punctuation, and mechanics errors in the Error Log (Appendix 6) and your spelling errors in the Spelling Log (Appendix 7).

Individual Activity   Rewrite your paragraph again using the editing feed-back you received from other students.

Reflecting on Your Writing

When you have completed your own essay, answer these five questions:

1. What was most difficult about this assignment?
2. What was easiest?
3. What did you learn about comparison/contrast by completing this assignment?
4. What do you think are the strengths of your comparison/contrast paragraph? What are its weaknesses?
5. What did you learn from this assignment about your own writing process—about preparing to write, about writing the first draft, about revising, and about editing?

DIVIDING AND CLASSIFYING

Three things are necessary for becoming a good
writer: a good head, a thick skin, and a soft heart.

—AUSTIN J. APP

Dividing and classifying play important roles in our daily lives. Think of how we all organize our environment:

Our coursework is separated into different binders and notebooks.
The names in our address book are divided up alphabetically.
Our shirts, socks, and sweaters all get their own dresser drawers.
Our garden supplies and household tools have separate locations in the garage.

In fact, division and classification come so naturally to us that we sometimes aren't even aware we are using them. Imagine going to a grocery store that doesn't group its merchandise logically: Dairy products wouldn't be together; salad dressings might be randomly scattered throughout the store; some breakfast foods could be in the deli section—and who knows where the rest might be? The result would be total chaos, and finding what you were looking for would be frustrating and time-consuming.

Dividing and classifying are actually mirror images of each other. **Dividing** is sorting into smaller categories, and **classifying** is grouping into larger categories. Division moves from one category to many, while classifying moves in the opposite direction, from many categories to one. For example, the general category of food can be divided or sorted into soups, salads, dairy products, beef, chicken, and so on. In like manner, soups, salads, dairy products, beef, and chicken can be grouped into the single category of food. To classify, you need to find the common trait that all the items share.

Here, from *Entrepreneur* magazine, is a paragraph that is based on division and classification. Written by Debra Phillips, the essay "Tween Beat" puts the youngest consumers into three categories to discuss their buying power. Notice how division and classification work together in this paragraph.

In his widely hailed research on child-age consumers, author and Texas A&M University marketing professor James McNeal points out that there's not one but three different children's markets. First and foremost, there's the market created by kids' direct spending. Second, there's the market stemming from kids' influence over their family's purchases. Finally, there's the market of the future—that is, courting kids to eventually become loyal adult consumers. With so much at stake, it's easy to see why so many eyes are on the tween-age kids of the baby boomers. They are the present; they are also the future.

Before continuing in this chapter, take a moment to write your own division/classification paragraph. Save your work because you will use it later in this chapter.

 WRITE YOUR OWN DIVISION/CLASSIFICATION PARAGRAPH

We all have lots of friends, and we naturally divide them into categories, whether we realize it or not. What categories do your friends fall into? Write a paragraph that introduces your categories and then explains why specific friends fit into each category.

HOW TO WRITE A DIVISION/CLASSIFICATION PARAGRAPH

To write a division/classification paragraph, keep in mind that the same items can be divided and classified many different ways. No two kitchens are exactly alike, and your friends probably don't organize their closets the same way you do. Methods of organizing schoolwork also vary from person to person. Similarly, in writing, you can divide and classify a topic differently, but following the guidelines listed here will help you create an effective division/classification paragraph.

1. *Decide on your overall purpose for writing, and state it in your topic sentence.* Dividing and classifying are not very interesting in themselves unless you are trying to make a point. In other words, division and classification should be the means of communicating a coherent message. This message is the heart of your topic sentence.

   In Debra Phillips's paragraph, for example, Phillips is using division and classification to show that the younger generation affects the economy more than most people realize. She does this by using James McNeal's division of child consumers into three categories—direct spending, influences on family buying, and future consumers.

2. *Divide your topic into categories (division); explain each category with details and examples (classification).* Since division and classification are so closely related, you will often use both of them in a single

paragraph. In fact, each one actually helps explain the other. When you choose examples, remember that they must share a common trait. You should not, for instance, classify cars on the basis of safety features and use air bags, antilock brakes, and leather seats as your examples because leather seats have nothing to do with safety.

In her paragraph, Debra Phillips uses a combination of division and classification. She establishes three categories for her topic (division) and then explains how children fit into these categories (classification). All the examples share a common trait—they all refer to types of buying markets.

3. ***Organize your categories so that they help you communicate your message clearly.*** Being logical is really the only requirement for organizing a division/classification paragraph. You want to move smoothly from one category to another with transitions that help your readers understand your reasoning.

The paragraph on child consumers is organized according to the degree of influence children have on the buying market. Phillips's first category is a small market of children who purchase directly. This market is certainly not as large as the group of children who influence their parents' purchases. Finally, in the future, when these children are grown, they will have enormous buying power of their own. So Phillips's categories move from small to large and from present to future.

DISCOVERING HOW DIVISION AND CLASSIFICATION WORK

Two additional examples will help you understand more clearly the choices you have to make when you write division/classification paragraphs. The first, by Sarah Hodgson, divides dogs' personalities into five categories and explains each. As you read it, see if you can find all five categories.

Some people may think that only humans have a real personality. Anyone who has ever had a dog knows better. Dogs, like us, have their own personalities. Some are extremely funny. I call this rowdy bunch *The Comedians*. They can be frustrating as heck, constantly dancing on the edge of good behavior. But in your most serious or sad moments, they'll make you laugh. Then we have *The Eager Beavers*, the dogs many of us dream of. They'll do anything that warrants approval. Sounds fantastic, but they'll be bad, too, if that gets attention, so even the Eager Beavers can find themselves on the "B" list if their owners aren't careful. There are also *The Sweet Peas* of the planet, quiet souls who prefer the sidelines over the spotlight. Taking the sweet thing a step too far are those dogs who are *Truly Timid*. Almost anything will freak them out. Poor creatures, they require a lot of understanding. And then there is *The Boss*. This fellow thinks a little too highly of himself. He needs lots of training to tame his egotism. Take a look at where your dog fits in, because like us, they all learn differently!

1. This paragraph doesn't simply classify the personalities of dogs for its own sake. It has a broader message. What is Hodgson's general purpose in this paragraph?

   _____

   _____

2. Does this paragraph use both division and classification?

   _____

   When does Hodgson move from one to many (division)? From many to one (classification)?

   Division: _____

   Classification: _____

3. Different methods of organization work well with different topics. How is this paragraph organized?

   _____

   The next example divides and classifies the various abilities of the human brain. It is from an essay titled "Smart Genes?" by Michael Lemonick. What is the author's purpose in this paragraph?

   When everything is going right, these different systems work together seamlessly. If you're taking a bicycle ride, for example, the memory of how to operate the bike comes from one set of neurons [nerve cells]; the memory of how to get from here to the other side of town comes from another; the nervous feeling you have left over from taking a bad spill last time comes from still another. Yet you are never aware that your mental experience has been assembled, bit by bit, like some invisible edifice [structure] inside your brain.

1. What is Lemonick's general message in this paragraph?

   _____

2. When does this paragraph move from one to many (division)? From many to one (classification)?

   Division: _____

   Classification: _____

   _____

3. How does Lemonick organize his paragraph?

   _____

REVISING AND EDITING A STUDENT PARAGRAPH

Here is a division/classification paragraph written by LaKesha Montgomery. Her paragraph focuses on the different types of interior decorators she has come across in her experience. Can you figure out when she is using division and when she is using classification?

> [1]I learned that interior decorators really fall into three different categories. [2]I also found out that they work hard after decorating my new apartment. [3]First is an interior decorator who specializes in residences. [4]This person has to work closely with people and try to get into there lifestyles. [5]So that he or she can help the customer make decisions. [6]The next type of interior decorator sells estate furniture. [7]He or she works in an upscale store called a gallery. [8]His or her main responsibility is to acquire all kinds of merchandise from estate sales and than sell it to those people who our interested in these more valuable pieces. [9]I certainly wasn't in this category. [10]I don't even know how I learned about this type of interior decorator. [11]Some interior decorators specialize in office décor. [12]They enjoy working with exotic schemes. [13]And making peoples stark office space come alive.

This paragraph is LaKesha's first draft, which now needs to be revised and edited. First, apply the Revising Checklist below to the content of LaKesha's draft. When you are satisfied that her ideas are fully developed and well organized, use the Editing Checklist on page 127 to correct her grammar and mechanics errors. Answer the questions after each checklist. Then write your suggested changes directly on LaKesha's draft.

REVISING CHECKLIST ✔

TOPIC SENTENCE
✔ Does the topic sentence convey the paragraph's controlling idea?
✔ Does the topic sentence appear as the first or last sentence of the paragraph?

DEVELOPMENT
✔ Does the paragraph contain *specific* details that support the topic sentence?
✔ Does the paragraph include *enough* details to explain the topic sentence fully?

UNITY
✔ Do all the sentences in the paragraph support the topic sentence?

ORGANIZATION
✔ Is the paragraph organized logically?

COHERENCE
✔ Do the sentences move smoothly and logically from one to the next?

Topic Sentence

1. What general message is LaKesha trying to communicate in this paragraph?

   _____

   _____

2. Put brackets around LaKesha's topic sentence. Does it capture her main point?

   _____

3. Expand LaKesha's topic sentence.

   _____

   _____

Development

1. Do the details in the paragraph describe all three types of interior decorators?

   _____

2. Where do you need more information?

   _____

3. Add a closing sentence to LaKesha's paragraph.

   _____

   _____

Unity

1. Read each of LaKesha's sentences with her topic sentence (revised, if necessary) in mind.
2. Cross out the two sentences that are not directly related to LaKesha's topic sentence.

Organization

1. Read LaKesha's paragraph again to see if all the sentences are arranged logically.
2. List the main categories LaKesha explains in this paragraph.

   _____

   _____

   _____

3. Move the one category that seems to be out of order.

4. Identify LaKesha's method of organization.

Coherence

1. Circle three transitions, repetitions, synonyms, or pronouns LaKesha uses.

2. Explain how one of these makes LaKesha's paragraph easier to read.

For a list of transitions, see page 38.

For a list of pronouns, see page 276.

Now rewrite LaKesha's paragraph with your revisions.

EDITING CHECKLIST ✔

SENTENCES

✔ Does each sentence have a main subject and verb?

✔ Do all subjects and verbs agree?

✔ Do all pronouns agree with their nouns?

✔ Are modifiers as close as possible to the words they modify?

PUNCTUATION AND MECHANICS

✔ Are sentences punctuated correctly?

✔ Are words capitalized properly?

WORD CHOICE AND SPELLING

✔ Are words used correctly?

✔ Are words spelled correctly?

Sentences

Subjects and Verbs

1. Underline the subjects once and verbs twice in your revision of LaKesha's paragraph. Remember that sentences can have more than one subject-verb set.

2. Does each of the sentences have at least one subject and verb that can stand alone?

For help with subjects and verbs, see Chapter 30.

---

3. Did you find and correct LaKesha's two fragments? If not, find and correct them now.

For help with fragments, see Chapter 31.

Subject-Verb Agreement

For help with subject-verb agreement, see Chapter 34.

1. Read aloud the subjects and verbs you underlined in your revision of LaKesha's paragraph.
2. Correct any subjects and verbs that do not agree.

Pronoun Agreement

For help with pronoun agreement, see Chapter 38.

1. Find any pronouns in your revision of LaKesha's paragraph that do not agree with their nouns.
2. Correct any pronouns that do not agree with their nouns.

Modifier Errors

For help with modifier errors, see Chapter 41.

1. Find any modifiers in your revision of LaKesha's paragraph that are not as close as possible to the words they modify.
2. Did you find and correct LaKesha's one modifier error? If not, find and correct it now.

Punctuation and Mechanics

Punctuation

For help with punctuation, see Chapters 42–45.

1. Read your revision of LaKesha's paragraph for any errors in punctuation.
2. Find the two fragments you revised, and make sure they are punctuated correctly.
3. Did you find and correct the apostrophe error in LaKesha's paragraph? If not, find and correct it now.

Mechanics

For help with capitalization, see Chapter 46.

1. Read your revision of LaKesha's paragraph for any errors in capitalization.
2. Be sure to check LaKesha's capitalization in the fragments you revised.

Word Choice and Spelling

Word Choice

For help with confused words, see Chapter 52.

1. Find any words used incorrectly in your revision of LaKesha's paragraph.
2. Did you find and correct her three confused words? If not, find and correct them now.

Spelling

For help with spelling, see Chapter 53.

1. Use spell-check and a dictionary to check the spelling in your revision of LaKesha's paragraph.
2. Correct any misspelled words.

Now rewrite LaKesha's paragraph again with your editing corrections.

REVISING AND EDITING YOUR OWN PARAGRAPH

Returning to the division/classification paragraph you wrote earlier in this chapter, revise and edit your own writing. The checklists above will help you apply what you have learned to your own paragraph.

PRACTISING DIVISION AND CLASSIFICATION

Reading Suggestions

In Chapter 26, you will find two essays that follow the guidelines you have studied in this chapter. "Rapport: How to Ignite It" by Camille Lavington divides and classifies personality types by communication styles, and "Categories of Time Use" by Edwin Bliss divides and classifies tasks to help people make better use of their time. You might want to read these selections before writing another division/classification assignment. As you read, notice how the writers use these rhetorical modes to make their points.

Writing Workshop

> **Guidelines for Writing a Division/Classification Paragraph**
>
> 1. Decide on your overall purpose for writing, and state it in your topic sentence.
> 2. Divide your topic into categories (division); explain each category with details and examples (classification).
> 3. Organize your categories so that they help you communicate your message clearly.

1. Place yourself in the picture on the previous page, and tell someone who isn't looking at the picture about the different types of products you see as you move through the outdoor market. In other words, use division and classification to describe the market.

2. Think of the many occasions in your life that require different types of clothes. For example, you would never wear to a funeral what you wear to the beach. Group the routine events in your life, and explain how various clothes in your wardrobe are appropriate for specific types of events.

3. Think of the various jobs you will be qualified for when you graduate. Classify these jobs into a few categories, and explain your interest in each category.

4. Create your own division/classification assignment (with the help of your instructor), and write a response to it.

Revising Workshop

Small-Group Activity (5–10 minutes per writer)   Working in groups of three or four, each person should read his or her division/classification to the other members of the group. Those listening should record their reactions on a copy of the Peer Evaluation Form in Appendix 2F. After your group goes through this process, give your evaluation forms to the appropriate writers so that each writer has two or three peer comment sheets for revising.

Paired Activity (5 minutes per writer)   Using the completed Peer Evaluation Forms, work in pairs to decide what you should revise in your paragraphs. If time allows, rewrite some of your sentences and have your partner check them.

Individual Activity   Rewrite your paragraph, using the revising feedback you received from other students.

Editing Workshop

Paired Activity (5–10 minutes per writer)   Exchange papers with a classmate, and use the Editing Peer Evaluation Form in Appendix 1 to identify as many grammar, punctuation, mechanics, and spelling errors as you can. If time allows, correct some of your errors and have your partner check them. Record your grammar, punctuation, and mechanics errors in the Error Log (Appendix 6) and your spelling errors in the Spelling Log (Appendix 7).

Individual Activity   Rewrite your paragraph again, using the editing feedback you received from other students.

Reflecting on Your Writing

When you have completed your own essay, answer these five questions:

1. What was most difficult about this assignment?

2. What was easiest?

3. What did you learn about division and classification by completing this assignment?

4. What do you think are the strengths of your division/classification paragraph? What are its weaknesses?

5. What did you learn from this assignment about your own writing process—about preparing to write, about writing the first draft, about revising, and about editing?

CHAPTER 12

DEFINING

Words are the tools with which we work. . . .
Everything depends on our understanding of them.

—FELIX FRANKFURTER

Part of our daily communication process is asking people for clarification and definitions.

"What do you mean by that?"
"Can you clarify 'unfair'?"
"Can you explain what you mean by 'hyper'?"
"Can someone tell me what HTML is?"

Definitions keep the world running efficiently. Whenever we communicate—in spoken or written form—we use words we all understand. If we did not work from a set of shared definitions, we would not be able to communicate at all. We use definitions to explain concrete things (crayfish, DVD, laser beam), to identify places and events (Bay of Fundy, the Capilano Bridge, provincial elections), and to discuss complex ideas (democracy, ambition, happiness).

Definition is the process of explaining a word, an object, or an idea in such a way that the audience knows as precisely as possible what you mean. A good definition of a word, for example, focuses on the special qualities of the word that set it apart from similar words. In the following paragraph, Mary Pipher defines the concept of family. She uses humorous, realistic examples to explain the responsibilities and rewards of being part of a family. See if you can pick out the main points of her definition.

> Families are the people for whom it matters if you have a cold, are feuding with your mate, or are training a new puppy. Family members use magnets to fasten the newspaper clippings about your bowling team on the refrigerator door. They save your drawings and homemade pottery. They like to hear stories about when you were young. They'll help you can tomatoes or change the oil in your car. They're the people who will come visit you in the hospital, will talk to you when you call with "a dark night of the soul," and will loan you money to pay the rent if you lose your job. Whether or not they are biologically related to each other, the people who do these things are family.

Before continuing in this chapter, take a moment to write a definition of your own. Save your work because you will use it later in this chapter.

  WRITE YOUR OWN DEFINITION

Everyone has a personal definition of the word *student*. What is your definition of this word? Explain it in a paragraph.

HOW TO WRITE A DEFINITION PARAGRAPH

Definitions vary in length from short summaries (such as dictionary entries) to longer, extended pieces (such as essays and whole books written on complex concepts like *courage*). In addition, definitions can be objective or factual (as in a textbook) or subjective (combined with personal opinion). Pipher's definition of *family* is very subjective. Whether short or long, objective or subjective, a good definition meets certain basic requirements. The following guidelines will help you write an effective definition paragraph.

1. ***State your purpose in your topic sentence.*** Sometimes a definition is used by itself (as in a classified ad for a job opening). More often, definitions are used in other types of writing, such as process analysis, comparison/contrast, and division/classification. In any case, the topic sentence in a definition paragraph should state your purpose as clearly as possible.

   In Mary Pipher's paragraph, Pipher lays out her purpose right away in her topic sentence: "Families are the people for whom it matters if you have a cold, are feuding with your mate, or are training a new puppy." She explains this definition in the rest of her paragraph.

2. ***Decide how you want to define your term or idea.*** Definitions are the building blocks of communication. Therefore, you want to be sure your audience understands how you're using certain words and key terms. Consider your audience, and define the term in a way that your readers will understand. The three possibilities are by synonym, by category, or by negation.

   By synonym: The simplest way to define a word or term is to provide a synonym or word that has a similar meaning. This synonym should be easier to understand than the word being defined. For example, "A *democracy* is a *free society*."

   By category: Defining by category is a two-step process. First, you put the word you are defining into a specific class or category: "A *democracy* is a form of government." Then you need to state how the word is different from other words in that category: "A *democracy* is a form of government based on individual freedom that is developed *by* the people and *for* the people."

By negation: When you define a word by negation, you say what the word is *not* before stating what it is. For example, "A *democracy* is not a socialist form of government. Rather it is based on freedom and independence."

In her paragraph, Pipher uses the second method to define her term. First, she puts the term *family* in the category of *people.* Then she explains how members of a family are different from other people. Your family cares "if you have a cold, are feuding with your mate, or are training a new puppy."

3. ***Use examples to expand on your definition.*** These examples should show your word in action. Concrete examples are an option for accomplishing this task.

In Pipher's paragraph, the author uses examples to expand on her definition of the word *family.* Every example is concrete, appealing to one of the five senses, and action-oriented.

> Family members use magnets to fasten the newspaper clippings about your bowling team on the refrigerator door.
>
> They save your drawings and homemade pottery.
>
> They like to hear stories about when you were young.
>
> They'll help you can tomatoes or change the oil in your car.
>
> They're the people who will come visit you in the hospital, will talk to you when you call with "a dark night of the soul," and will loan you money to pay the rent if you lose your job.

By the end of the paragraph, you have a very clear sense of what *family* means to Mary Pipher.

4. ***Organize your examples to communicate your definition as clearly as possible.*** Your examples should progress in some logical order—from most serious to least serious, from least important to most important, chronologically, or spatially. What's important is that they move in some recognizable way from one to the next.

In her paragraph, Pipher arranges her examples from least crucial (putting your bowling score on the refrigerator) to most crucial (loaning you money when you lose your job). Pipher's method of organization is subtle but important to the flow of the paragraph.

DISCOVERING HOW DEFINITION WORKS

Two more examples will help you understand more clearly how good definition paragraphs work. The first, taken from an essay by Margaret Atwood entitled "It Came from Beneath the Dust Jacket," defines what a *signature* is. What is the main point of her definition?

> A signature is deeply personal. Your handwriting used to be called your "hand," and there's such an intense connection between the hand and the brain/mind that the former stands symbolically for the latter. Anyone seeing those red ochre handprints in the Cro-Magnon cave paintings can feel what

they must have meant: I was here. This is me. My mark. Even now, our signature—our unique scrawl—represents us, on letters and legal documents and credit cards alike. Every signature is different, and thus to forge a signature so that the forgery is undetectable remains very difficult.

1.   What is this paragraph defining?

_____

2.   Does this author rely on a synonym, a category, or a negation to start off her paragraph? Explain your answer.

_____

_____

3.   What examples does Atwood use to develop her definition? List some here.

_____

_____

4.   How does Atwood organize her examples: from one extreme to another, chronologically, or spatially?

_____

_____

Explain your answer.

_____

_____

The next example defines the word *khaki*. It is from an essay titled "Up Through the Ranks" by David Feld. What is Feld's approach to this definition?

The word khaki is Urdu, a dialect of Hindustani spoken in Afghanistan. It means dust-colored. From dark tannish green to light taupe verging on cream, there is as much variance in khaki as there are shades of the earth. In fact, one of the trousers' great attractions is that they almost beg to be dirty. Virtually any type of dirt can be simply brushed off, but khakis, because of their colorations, often don't even look soiled, when, in fact, they are quite filthy.

1.   What is this paragraph defining?

_____

2. Does this author rely on a synonym, a category, or a negation at the beginning of this paragraph? Explain your answer.

_____

_____

3. What examples does Feld use to develop his definition? List some here.

_____

_____

_____

4. How does Feld organize his examples: from one extreme to another, chronologically, or spatially?

_____

Explain your answer.

_____

_____

REVISING AND EDITING A STUDENT PARAGRAPH

Here is a definition paragraph written by Inez Morales. Her paragraph defines *success*. After you read her definition, see if you can restate her definition in your own words.

¹To me, success is having an education, a decent job, and a happy, healthy family. ²In order to be successful in life people must first get a degree. ³This education will prepare them for whatever situation in life that may come up. ⁴I believe that having professional jobs like doctors, lawyers, and teachers help show a level of success. ⁵When people work in professional jobs, they has the ability to build bigger homes, and buy better cars. ⁶They are able to travel to different parts of the world with their families. ⁷Many of my friends whose parents have professional jobs don't enjoy traveling. ⁸They also don't have large families. ⁹The last element of success are having a happy and healthy family. ¹⁰Without an education, people will not be qualified for well-paying jobs. ¹¹I believe this is the formula for making it if people have all three of these in their lives, then they have success.

This paragraph is Inez's first draft, which now needs to be revised and edited. First, apply the Revising Checklist below to the content of Inez's draft. When you are satisfied that her ideas are fully developed and well organized, use the Editing Checklist on page 139 to correct her grammar and mechanics errors. Answer the questions after each checklist. Then write your suggested changes directly on Inez's draft.

REVISING CHECKLIST ✔

TOPIC SENTENCE
✔ Does the topic sentence convey the paragraph's controlling idea?
✔ Does the topic sentence appear as the first or last sentence of the paragraph?

DEVELOPMENT
✔ Does the paragraph contain *specific* details that support the topic sentence?
✔ Does the paragraph include *enough* details to explain the topic sentence fully?

UNITY
✔ Do all the sentences in the paragraph support the topic sentence?

ORGANIZATION
✔ Is the paragraph organized logically?

COHERENCE
✔ Do the sentences move smoothly and logically from one to the next?

Topic Sentence

1. What is Inez defining?

_____

2. Put brackets around Inez's topic sentence. Does it explain what she is defining?

_____

3. Make sure the topic sentence introduces all the ideas in Inez's paragraph.

Development

1. Do the details in the paragraph define success?

_____

2. Does Inez rely on synonyms, categories, or negation to develop her definition?

_____

3. Where do you need more information?

_____

4. Add at least one other detail to Inez's paragraph.

Unity

1. Read each of Inez's sentences with her topic sentence (revised, if necessary) in mind.
2. Cross out the two sentences not directly related to Inez's topic sentence.

Organization

1. Read Inez's paragraph again to see if all the sentences are arranged logically.
2. List some of the examples in Inez's paragraph in the order they appear.

_____

_____

_____

_____

_____

3. Move the one example that seems to be out of order.
4. Identify Inez's method of organization.

_____

Coherence

For a list of transitions, see page 38.

1. Circle three transitions Inez uses.
2. Add another transition to Inez's paragraph.

Now rewrite Inez's paragraph with your revisions.

EDITING CHECKLIST ✔

SENTENCES

✔ Does each sentence have a main subject and verb?

✔ Do all subjects and verbs agree?

✔ Do all pronouns agree with their nouns?

✔ Are modifiers as close as possible to the words they modify?

PUNCTUATION AND MECHANICS

✔ Are sentences punctuated correctly?

✔ Are words capitalized properly?

WORD CHOICE AND SPELLING

✔ Are words used correctly?

✔ Are words spelled correctly?

Sentences

Subjects and Verbs

1. Underline the subjects once and verbs twice in your revision of Inez's paragraph. Remember that sentences can have more than one subject-verb set.

2. Does each of the sentences have at least one subject and verb that can stand alone?

For help with subjects and verbs, see Chapter 30.

3. Did you find and correct Inez's run-on sentence? If not, find and correct it now.

For help with run-ons, see Chapter 32.

Subject-Verb Agreement

1. Read aloud the subjects and verbs you underlined in your revision of Inez's paragraph.

2. Did you find and correct the three subjects and verbs that don't agree? If not, find and correct them now.

For help with subject-verb agreement, see Chapter 34.

Pronoun Agreement

1. Find any pronouns in your revision of Inez's paragraph that do not agree with their nouns.

2. Correct any pronouns that do not agree with their nouns.

For help with pronoun agreement, see Chapter 38.

Modifier Errors

1. Find any modifiers in your revision of Inez's paragraph that are not as close as possible to the words they modify.

For help with modifier errors, see Chapter 41.

2. Rewrite sentences if necessary so that the modifiers are as close as possible to the words they modify.

Punctuation and Mechanics

Punctuation

For help with punctuation, see Chapters 42–45.

1. Read your revision of Inez's paragraph for any errors in punctuation.
2. Find the run-on sentence you revised, and make sure it is punctuated correctly.
3. Did you find and correct the two comma errors in Inez's paragraph? If not, find and correct them now.

Mechanics

For help with capitalization, see Chapter 46.

1. Read your revision of Inez's paragraph for any errors in capitalization.
2. Be sure to check Inez's capitalization in the run-on sentence you revised.

Word Choice and Spelling

Word Choice

For help with confused words, see Chapter 52.

1. Find any words used incorrectly in your revision of Inez's paragraph.
2. Correct any errors you find.

Spelling

For help with spelling, see Chapter 53.

1. Use spell-check and a dictionary to check the spelling in your revision of Inez's paragraph.
2. Correct any misspelled words.

Now rewrite Inez's paragraph again with your editing corrections.

 REVISING AND EDITING YOUR OWN PARAGRAPH

Returning to the definition paragraph you wrote earlier in this chapter, revise and edit your own writing. The checklists above will help you apply what you have learned to your own paragraph.

PRACTISING DEFINITION

Reading Suggestions

In Chapter 27, you will find two essays that follow the guidelines you have studied in this chapter. "Gentrification" by Robert Fulford shows how the creation of the word *gentrification* and its definition have changed the way people think about urban renewal. Alanna Mitchell in "Bullied by the Click of a Mouse" defines a new type of bullying: cyber bullying. You might want to read these selections before writing another definition. As you read, notice how the writers make their points though well-chosen examples and details.

Writing Workshop

Guidelines for Writing a Definition Paragraph

1. State your purpose in your topic sentence.
2. Decide how you want to define your term or idea.
3. Use examples to expand on your definition.
4. Organize your examples to communicate your definition as clearly as possible.

1. Define *parenthood* using the image shown above.
2. Define *relaxation* or *stress*, depending on your mood today.
3. Define one of the following abstract terms: *knowledge, fear, love, inferiority, wonder, pride, self-control, discipline, anger, freedom, violence, assertiveness, fellowship, friendship, courtesy, kindness.*
4. Create your own definition assignment (with the help of your instructor), and write a response to it.

Revising Workshop

Small-Group Activity (5–10 minutes per writer)   Working in groups of three or four, each person should read his or her definition to the other members of the group. Those listening should record their reactions on a copy of the Peer Evaluation Form in Appendix 2G. After your group goes through this process, give your evaluation forms to the appropriate writers so that each writer has two or three peer comment sheets for revising.

Paired Activity (5 minutes per writer)   Using the completed Peer Evaluation Forms, work in pairs to decide what you should revise in your paragraphs. If time allows, rewrite some of your sentences and have your partner check them.

Individual Activity   Rewrite your paragraph using the revising feedback you received from other students.

Editing Workshop

Paired Activity (5–10 minutes per writer)   Exchange papers with a classmate, and using the Editing Peer Evaluation Form in Appendix 1, identify as many grammar, punctuation, mechanics, and spelling errors as you can. If time allows, correct some of your errors and have your partner check them. Record your grammar, punctuation, and mechanics errors in the Error Log (Appendix 6) and your spelling errors in the Spelling Log (Appendix 7).

Individual Activity   Rewrite your paragraph again using the editing feedback you received from other students.

Reflecting on Your Writing

When you have completed your own essay, answer these five questions:

1. What was most difficult about this assignment?
2. What was easiest?
3. What did you learn about definition by completing this assignment?
4. What do you think are the strengths of your definition paragraph? What are its weaknesses?
5. What did you learn from this assignment about your own writing process—about preparing to write, about writing the first draft, about revising, and about editing?

ANALYZING CAUSES AND EFFECTS

How do I know what I think until I see what I say?

—E. M. FORSTER

We all analyze causes and effects without even realizing it. Consider the following thoughts that might have crossed your mind:

Why you find someone attractive

The reasons you thought a movie was good

The effects of cutting your English class

Your reaction to a political debate

The consequences of going out with your friends instead of studying for an exam

Wanting to know why something happens is a natural interest that surfaces early in life—"Why can't I play outside today?" Not only do we want to know *why*, but we also want to know *what* will happen as a result of our actions. In like manner, your courses often want you to analyze causes and effects. For example, an essay exam in a psychology course might ask, "Why are some people superstitious?" Or a history question might be "What were the positive effects of the formation of the Bloc Québécois?"

When we work with **causes and effects,** we are searching for connections and reasons. To understand a **cause,** we look to the past for reasons why something is the way it is. To discover an **effect,** we look to the future to figure out what the possible results of a particular action might be. In other words, we break an action or situation into parts and look at how these different parts relate to each other so that we can better understand the world around us.

In a book titled *Immigrant Kids*, Russell Freedman analyzes why the children of immigrants reject their parents' language and customs. He then discusses the results of this rejection. Can you see the difference between the causes and effects in this paragraph?

The children became Americanized much faster than their parents. Often this caused painful conflicts in immigrant families. A gap appeared between the children and their parents. The parents spoke English with heavy accents, if they spoke it at all. They clung to Old World customs and beliefs. The kids spoke English all day with their friends. They thought in American terms. More than anything else, they wanted to be accepted as equals in their adopted land. In their anxiety to become fully "American," some immigrant children rejected their Old World heritage and the traditional values of their parents. They felt embarrassed or even ashamed by their parents' immigrant ways.

Before continuing in this chapter, take a moment to analyze an event in your own life. Save your work because you will use it later in this chapter.

 WRITE YOUR OWN CAUSE/EFFECT ANALYSIS

Why did you choose the college or university you are attending today? Explain in a paragraph the events that led up to your decision and the results you expect from attending this school.

HOW TO WRITE A CAUSE/EFFECT PARAGRAPH

Writing about causes and effects requires careful critical thinking. To do this well, you need to discover connections between two or more events or ideas and explain the connection. Although this is a complex form of writing, good cause/effect paragraphs follow a few simple guidelines.

1. *Write a topic sentence that makes a clear statement about what you are going to analyze.* This should always be the first step in a cause/effect essay. You need to decide what you are analyzing and whether you are going to focus on causes (activities leading up to the event), effects (the results of an event), or both. These decisions will give focus and coherence to the rest of your paragraph.

   In Russell Freedman's paragraph, Freedman writes a very clear topic sentence: "The children became Americanized much faster than their parents." His topic sentence suggests that he will be discussing both the causes and effects of this observation.

2. *Choose facts and details to support your topic sentence.* These facts and details are the causes and effects that fully explain your topic sentence. To generate this material, try to anticipate your readers' questions and then answer them in your paragraph.

   In Freedman's paragraph, the author cites two *results* of Americanization at the beginning of the paragraph:

   often caused painful conflicts

   gap appeared between children and parents

Then he discusses seven *causes* of this situation—two from the parents' side of the conflict:

> spoke English with heavy accents
> clung to Old World customs

and five from the children's side:

> spoke English all day long
> thought in American terms
> wanted to be accepted as equals
> rejected Old World customs
> were embarrassed by their parents' immigrant ways

3. *Make sure you include the real causes and effects of your topic.* Just as you wouldn't stop reading halfway through a good murder mystery, you shouldn't stop too early in your analysis of causes and effects. For example, a student might fail a biology exam because she was sick. However, if you dig a little deeper, you may find that she missed several lectures, didn't study very much, and is exhausted holding down two jobs. Similarly, failing the exam probably has many effects: She may quit one job, promise herself to attend class regularly, and study harder for the next test. In other words, the actual causes and effects may not be the most obvious ones. This digging for the basic causes and effects will help you avoid confusing causes and effects with coincidences.

    In the sample paragraph, Freedman keeps digging for the "real" reasons for the conflict and tension in immigrant families. He first lists ways children try to become more American and finally realizes that they are basically embarrassed by their heritage.

4. *Organize your material so that it communicates your message as clearly as possible.* You should present your details in a logical order— perhaps chronologically or from one extreme to another. Chronological order follows a time sequence; from one extreme to another could involve any two extremes.

    Freedman organizes his paragraph from least serious to most serious according to the two different groups he is discussing. He first takes up the parents' point of view (from accent to customs) and then deals with the children's side (from their speaking English all day to their feelings of embarrassment and shame).

DISCOVERING HOW CAUSE-AND-EFFECT ANALYSIS WORKS

Two additional sample paragraphs will help you understand more clearly how good cause-and-effect reasoning works. The first, by Drew Appleby, examines the causes and effects of specific behaviours in the classroom. See if you can separate the causes from the effects in this paragraph.

Sometimes the behaviour of students and that of faculty becomes circular, with each contributing to the undesirable response of the other. For example, students yawn, gaze around the room, and otherwise look bored. The instructor reads this behaviour as students not caring and concludes, "If they're not interested, why should I try to be interesting? I'll just do it and get it over with." So, there's nothing but lecture, endless instructor talk, and more students get bored and yawn and gaze around.

1. What is Appleby analyzing in this paragraph?

   _____

2. Does Appleby's topic sentence capture this focus? Explain your answer.

   _____

   _____

3. What causes and effects does Appleby cite? How does each relate to the topic sentence?

Causes	**Relation to Topic Sentence**
_____	_____
_____	_____
Effects	
_____	_____
_____	_____
_____	_____

4. Do you feel that Appleby gets to the real source of student-faculty classroom behaviour? Explain your answer.

   _____

   _____

5. How does Appleby organize the details in his paragraph: chronologically or one extreme to another?

   _____

In this next example, Gisday Wa and Delgam Uukw write about how the concept of circular time affects their Gitksan and Wetśuwetén bands, located in central British Columbia. Do the authors deal with both causes and effects in this paragraph?

> In daily life, this circular vision of time gives to the Gitksan and Wetśuwetén a shared sense of identity and history. It contributes to their ethics and to the recurrent obligations they have to the natural world, and it explains experiences within that world. Their notion of a cyclic world destiny differs fundamentally from Western notions of history as a progressive unfolding of causally linked events and achievements. In their circular conception of cause and effect, the seasonal pulsations of nature, the lives of ancestors long dead, and the world-shaping transformations of the mythic era of creation have a continuous, powerful influence upon the present. *Events of the "past" are not simply history but are something that directly affects the present and future.* This places a heavy ethical responsibility for "right action" on the Gitksan and Wetśuwetén, in much the same way that Buddhists and Hindus view the effects of one's actions as reverberating far beyond the boundaries of a single life or generation.

1. What are Wa and Uukw analyzing in this paragraph?

   _____

   Does Wa and Uukw's topic sentence capture this focus? Explain your answer.

   _____

   _____

2. List one cause and one effect that Wa and Uukw cite? How does each relate to the topic sentence?

Cause	Relation to Topic Sentence
_____	_____
Effect	
_____	_____

3. Do you feel that Wa and Uukw get to the real causes and effects connected with the concept of circular time? Explain your answer.

   _____

   _____

   _____

4. How do Wa and Uukw organize the details in this paragraph?

_____

_____

REVISING AND EDITING A STUDENT PARAGRAPH

Here is a cause/effect paragraph written by a student named Matthew Machias. His paragraph analyzes the causes and effects of his experience attending a court proceeding. Do you think Matthew gets to the real causes and effects of the situation in this paragraph?

[1]A class trip to a court proceeding showed me how difficult the job of a jury can be. [2]We had finished listening to both sides present evidence, examine witnesses, and summarize their arguments. [3]We had looked at photographs of the terrible automobile accident, shots of the wreckage, close-ups of the defendant's best friend, and even photos of him being taken away. [4]We heard that Grant (the defendant) had been driving while intoxicated on the local highway at 2 a.m. after a party. [5]His blood alcohol level was .11. [6]Well over the legal limit. [7]Grant had been convicted of drunk driving on previous occasions during 1998–99. [8]Grant didn't know that his actions would lead to his best friend's death. [9]Grant had completed a special program for drunk drivers in mid-May. [10]I've heard those programs don't work well. [11]I don't know why those programs keep running. [12]Grant was driving over 130 kph while drunk, even though his licence had been suspended. [13]When Grant's friend got in the car with him that night, was Grant's friend partly to blame for his own death. [14]What a tough question this is? [15]Even though the twenty-two-year-old defendant looked like a nice person, he was guilty. [16]Grant and his friend knew what they were doing when he drove to the party that night. [17]He knew what he was doing when he took that first drink. [18]Grant's friend trusted him. [19]That was the last decision he was ever able to make. [20]After the jury filed back into the jury box. [21]The foreman read the verdict of second-degree murder. [22]I knew that the judgment was the right one, even though I still felt sorry for the defendant.

This paragraph is Matthew's first draft, which now needs to be revised and edited. First, apply the Revising Checklist below to the content of Matthew's draft. When you are satisfied that his ideas are fully developed and well organized, use the Editing Checklist on pages 150–151 to correct his grammar and mechanics errors. Answer the questions after each checklist. Then write your suggested changes directly on Matthew's draft.

REVISING CHECKLIST ✔

TOPIC SENTENCE

✔ Does the topic sentence convey the paragraph's controlling idea?

✔ Does the topic sentence appear as the first or last sentence of the paragraph?

DEVELOPMENT

✔ Does the paragraph contain *specific* details that support the topic sentence?

✔ Does the paragraph include *enough* details to explain the topic sentence fully?

UNITY

✔ Do all the sentences in the paragraph support the topic sentence?

ORGANIZATION

✔ Is the paragraph organized logically?

COHERENCE

✔ Do the sentences move smoothly and logically from one to the next?

Topic Sentence

1. What is Matthew analyzing in his paragraph?

   _____

2. Put brackets around Matthew's topic sentence. Does it capture the paragraph's focus?

   _____

3. Make sure the topic sentence introduces all the ideas in Matthew's paragraph.

Development

1. Do the details in the paragraph refer to specific causes and effects?

   _____

2. Where does Matthew deal with causes? Where does he deal with effects?

Causes	Effects
_____	_____
_____	_____
_____	_____
_____	_____
_____	_____

Unity

1. Read each of Matthew's sentences with his topic sentence (revised, if necessary) in mind.
2. Cross out the two sentences not directly related to Matthew's topic sentence.

Organization

1. Read Matthew's paragraph again to see if all the sentences are arranged logically.
2. Identify Matthew's method of organization.

   _____

3. Move the one example that seems to be out of order.

Coherence

For a list of pronouns, see page 276.

1. Circle three pronouns Matthew uses.
2. Change three references to Grant to pronouns.

   Now rewrite Matthew's paragraph with your revisions.

EDITING CHECKLIST ✔

SENTENCES
- ✔ Does each sentence have a main subject and verb?
- ✔ Do all subjects and verbs agree?
- ✔ Do all pronouns agree with their nouns?
- ✔ Are modifiers as close as possible to the words they modify?

PUNCTUATION AND MECHANICS
- ✔ Are sentences punctuated correctly?
- ✔ Are words capitalized properly?

WORD CHOICE AND SPELLING
- ✔ Are words used correctly?
- ✔ Are words spelled correctly?

Sentences

Subject and Verbs

1. Underline the subjects once and verbs twice in your revision of Matthew's paragraph. Remember that sentences can have more than one subject-verb set.
2. Does each of the sentences have at least one subject and verb that can stand alone?

For help with subjects and verbs, see Chapter 30.

3. Did you find and correct Matthew's two fragments? If not, find and correct them now.

For help with fragments, see Chapter 31.

Subject-Verb Agreement

1. Read aloud the subjects and verbs you underlined in your revision of Matthew's paragraph.
2. Correct any subjects and verbs that do not agree.

For help with subject-verb agreement, see Chapter 34.

Pronoun Agreement

1. Find any pronouns in your revision of Matthew's paragraph that do not agree with their nouns.
2. Did you find and correct the four pronoun agreement errors in Matthew's paragraph? If not, find and correct them now.

For help with pronoun agreement, see Chapter 38.

Modifler Errors

1. Find any modifiers in your revision of Matthew's paragraph that are not as close as possible to the words they modify.
2. Rewrite sentences if necessary so that the modifiers are as close as possible to the words they modify.

For help with modifier errors, see Chapter 41.

Punctuation and Mechanics

Punctuation

For help with punctuation, see Chapters 42–45.

1. Read your revision of Matthew's paragraph for any errors in punctuation.

2. Find the two fragments you revised, and make sure they are punctuated correctly.

3. Did you find and correct two errors in end punctuation in Matthew's paragraph? If not, find and correct them now.

Mechanics

For help with capitalization, see Chapter 46.

1. Read your revision of Matthew's paragraph for any errors in capitalization.

2. Be sure to check Matthew's capitalization in the fragments you revised.

Word Choice and Spelling

Word Choice

For help with confused words, see Chapter 52.

1. Find any words used incorrectly in your revision of Matthew's paragraph.

2. Correct any errors you find.

Spelling

For help with spelling, see Chapter 53.

1. Use spell-check and a dictionary to check the spelling in your revision of Matthew' paragraph.

2. Correct any misspelled words.

Now rewrite Matthew's paragraph again with your editing corrections.

REVISING AND EDITING YOUR OWN PARAGRAPH

Returning to the cause/effect paragraph you wrote earlier in this chapter, revise and edit your own writing. The checklists above will help you apply what you have learned to your own paragraph.

PRACTISING CAUSE-AND-EFFECT ANALYSIS

Reading Suggestions

In Chapter 28, you will find two essays that follow the guidelines you have studied in this chapter. In "Shedding the Weight of My Dad's Obsession," Linda Lee Andujar analyzes a lifelong problem with her father, and in "The Secret Heroes of Vimy," Pierre Berton analyzes the role Canada played in World War II. You might want to read these selections before writing another cause/effect analysis. As you read, notice how the writers make their points through well-thought-out, detailed reasoning.

Writing Workshop

Guidelines for Writing a Cause/Effect Paragraph

1. Write a topic sentence that makes a clear statement about what you are going to analyze.
2. Choose facts and details to support your topic sentence.
3. Make sure you include the real causes and effects of your topic.
4. Organize your material so that it communicates your message as clearly as possible.

1. Write an explanation of how the area in the picture above became such a wasteland. Analyze what happened before this picture was taken. Why did it happen? Or focus on what might happen in this area in the future.

2. Write a paragraph about an important event that changed your attitude toward an authority figure in your life (a parent, a religious leader, a teacher, a club sponsor, a supervisor or boss). What brought about the change? What were the results of the change?

3. Choose a major problem you see in society today, and analyze its causes and effects. Can you propose a solution to this problem?

4. Create your own cause/effect assignment (with the help of your instructor), and write a response to it.

Revising Workshop

Small-Group Activity (5–10 minutes per writer)   Working in groups of three or four, each person should read his or her cause/effect analysis to the other members of the group. Those listening should record their reactions on a copy of the Peer Evaluation Form in Appendix 2H. After your group goes through this process, give your evaluation forms to the appropriate writers so that each writer has two or three peer comment sheets for revising.

Paired Activity (5 minutes per writer) Using the completed Peer Evaluation Forms, work in pairs to decide what you should revise in your paragraphs. If time allows, rewrite some of your sentences and have your partner check them.

Individual Activity Rewrite your paragraph using the revising feedback you received from other students.

Editing Workshop

Paired Activity (5–10 minutes per writer) Exchange papers with a classmate, and using the Editing Peer Evaluation Form in Appendix 1, identify as many grammar, punctuation, mechanics, and spelling errors as you can. If time allows, correct some of your errors and have your partner check them. Record your grammar, punctuation, and mechanics errors in the Error Log (Appendix 6) and your spelling errors in the Spelling Log (Appendix 7).

Individual Activity Rewrite your paragraph again using the editing feedback you received from other students.

Reflecting on Your Writing

When you have completed your own essay, answer these five questions:

1. What was most difficult about this assignment?
2. What was easiest?
3. What did you learn about analyzing causes and effects by completing this assignment?
4. What do you think are the strengths of your cause/effect paragraph? What are its weaknesses?
5. What did you learn from this assignment about your own writing process—about preparing to write, about writing the first draft, about revising, and about editing?

ARGUING

Remember, no one is obligated to take your word for anything.

—M. L. STEIN

When was the last time you tried to talk someone into doing something? Was it when you wanted

> your wife to go to a movie you were excited to see,
>
> your parents to let you use the car,
>
> your sister to lend you money,
>
> a professor to give you a little more time to submit a paper, or
>
> the garage mechanic to fix your car without charging you more than the car was worth?

So much of what we say or do is an attempt to convince someone to do something. If you dress up for a job interview, you are trying to persuade the employer that you should be hired. If you argue with a friend about which movie to see, you are trying to persuade your friend to agree with you. And think of all the television, magazine, and billboard ads that are trying to talk you into buying a certain product. Life is filled with opportunities to argue with others and persuade them of your point of view.

The purpose of **arguing** is to persuade your readers to take some action or to think or feel a certain way. Clearly, then, arguing and persuading work closely together. Because we live in a society that allows us to voice our opinions freely, learning how to express our thoughts in a polite and reasonable way is one goal we should all strive for. The ability to argue well is a powerful tool.

In the following paragraph, David Suzuki argues for Canadians to make a commitment to the Kyoto Protocol and to find ways to become more energy efficient. Does he persuade you?

> It's interesting that within weeks of Canada agreeing to the terms of the Kyoto Protocol, temperatures soared and the country became gripped in what climatologists describe as the worst national drought in history.... Meanwhile, the federal government has been stalling and our emissions na-

tionally have soared. To meet our Kyoto commitments, Canada must find ways to encourage energy efficiency and renewable energy, and discourage waste and polluting fossil fuels. Right now, that isn't happening, and we can see the results hanging in the air in major Canadian cities. Southern Ontario has been especially hard hit with record smog. Last year, according to the Ontario Medical Association, about 1,900 premature deaths associated with air pollution occurred in Ontario, along with 47 million minor illness days.

Before continuing in this chapter, take a moment to write your own argument paragraph. Save your work because you will use it later in this chapter.

 WRITE YOUR OWN ARGUMENT

Choose a controversial issue on your campus, and write a paragraph that presents your opinion about it. When writing your paragraph, be sure to back up your opinion with reasons.

HOW TO WRITE AN ARGUMENT PARAGRAPH

When you are writing an argument, you must present evidence that convinces your readers to agree with you on a particular topic. This isn't always as easy as it sounds. All too often your reader will have a different opinion. Your evidence, therefore, must be accurate and logical. In fact, evidence is the most important ingredient in an argument. Without supporting evidence, your paragraph will be nothing more than a statement of your opinion. Convincing evidence, however, helps your readers understand and perhaps agree with your views. The following guidelines will help you organize and develop a good argument/persuasion paragraph.

1. *State your opinion on the issue in the topic sentence.* This sentence should state a position on an issue that can be argued and does not have a clear answer. It sets up your point of view and prepares your readers for the evidence you plan to give them.

    David Suzuki starts his paragraph with a sentence that the reader might be persuaded to believe: "It's interesting that within weeks of Canada agreeing to the terms of the Kyoto Protocol, temperatures soared and the country became gripped in what climatologists describe as the worst national drought in history." Suzuki's first sentence sets up the rest of his paragraph, in which he will present material that supports his position on this issue.

2. *Find out as much as you can about your audience before you write.* Knowing your audience's background and feelings toward your topic will help you choose supporting details and examples. If you are trying to convince people in two different age groups not to smoke, you might tell teenagers that cigarettes make their breath rancid, their teeth

yellow, and their clothes smell bad. On the other hand, you might persuade parents and other adults to stop smoking with some long-term statistics on lung and heart disease in smokers.

Suzuki addresses the audience as "we," including himself in the reference. He connects directly with his audience when he states, "[W]e can see the results hanging in the air in major Canadian cities." This shows that Suzuki knows that he and his readers are facing these environmental issues together. The knowledge that Suzuki has of his audience will help him make choices as he develops his argument.

3. ***Choose appropriate evidence that supports your topic sentence.*** Evidence usually takes the form of (a) facts, (b) statistics, (c) statements from authorities, or (d) examples and personal stories. You can use one of these types of evidence or a combination of them in any argument paragraph. Opinions—your own or other people's—are not evidence.

   In Suzuki's paragraph, the author cites evidence that falls into several categories:

Evidence	Type
… climatologists describe as the worst national drought in history	Statement from authority
… we can see the results hanging in the air in major Canadian cities.	An example
… according to the Ontario Medical Association	Statement from authority
… 1,900 premature deaths	Statistic
… 47 million minor illness days	Statistic

4. ***Organize your evidence so that it supports your argument as effectively as possible.*** The organization of your material in an argument paragraph depends to a great extent on the opinions of your readers. Your paragraph should be arranged from general to particular, from particular to general, or from one extreme to another. When you know that your readers already agree with you, you should arrange your paragraph from a general statement to particular examples or from most to least important. This way, your audience will move through your argument with you from beginning to end, and you will be building on their loyalty and enthusiasm. When you are dealing with readers who probably disagree with you, you should work from details and examples to a single general statement or from least to most important. With this method of organization, you can lead your readers through your reasoning step by step as you use your examples to pull them into your way of thinking.

   In his paragraph, Suzuki starts with a general statement and then organizes his information to be more specific. His information goes from a statement about soaring temperatures causing a drought, to the

Canadian government ignoring energy efficiency, to being able to see smog above major cities, to the smog being responsible for 1,900 premature deaths and 47 million minor illness days. He is trying to persuade his readers that they can't ignore the fact that their lifestyles affect the environment and their health.

DISCOVERING HOW ARGUMENT WORKS

Two additional sample paragraphs will help you understand more clearly how good arguments work. The first, by Marie Winn, argues that TV watching is an addiction. See if you can identify her evidence.

> Not unlike drugs or alcohol, the television experience allows the participant to blot out the real world and enter into a pleasurable and passive mental state. The worries and anxieties of reality are as effectively deferred by becoming absorbed in a television program as by going on a "trip" induced by drugs or alcohol. And just as alcoholics are only vaguely aware of their addiction, feeling that they control their drinking more than they really do ("I can cut it out any time I want—I just like to have three or four drinks before dinner"), people similarly overestimate their control over television watching. Even as they put off other activities to spend hour after hour watching television, they feel they could easily resume living in a different, less passive style. But somehow or other, while the television set is present in their homes, the click doesn't sound. With television pleasures available, those other experiences seem less attractive, more difficult somehow.

1. What is Winn's topic sentence?

   _____

   _____

   Does it state her opinion about a certain issue?

   _____

   Is it debatable? (Does it have more than one side?)

   _____

2. Whom do you think Winn is addressing in this paragraph? How did you come to this conclusion?

   _____

3. What evidence does the author use to support her topic sentence? How would you classify her major pieces of evidence (facts, statistics, statements from authorities, or examples/personal stories)?

Evidence	Type
_____	_____
_____	_____
_____	_____
_____	_____
_____	_____

4. How does Winn organize her paragraph: general to particular, particular to general, or one extreme to another?

_____

_____

The next paragraph is a statement from a commission report on the quality of education in schools. Its information has often been used as evidence that we need to reform our educational system. What type of evidence does the report furnish? Do you find it convincing?

We must emphasize that the variety of student aspirations, abilities, and preparation requires that appropriate content be available to satisfy diverse needs. Attention must be directed to both the nature of the content available and to the needs of particular learners. The most gifted students, for example, may need a curriculum enriched and accelerated beyond even the needs of other students of high ability. Similarly, educationally disadvantaged students may require special curriculum materials, smaller classes, or individual tutoring to help them master the material presented. Nevertheless, there remains a common expectation: We must demand the best effort and performance from all students, whether they are gifted or less able, affluent or disadvantaged, whether destined for college, the farm, or industry.

1. What is the paragraph's topic sentence?

_____

_____

_____

Does it state the authors' opinion about a certain issue?

_____

Is it debatable? (Does it have more than one side?)

_____

2. Whom do you think the authors are addressing in this paragraph? How did you come to this conclusion?

_____

_____

_____

3. The authors offer three statements to support their topic sentence. What are these statements? How would you classify each statement (fact, statistic, statement from an authority, or example/personal story)?

Evidence	Type
_____	_____
_____	_____
_____	_____

4. How do the authors organize the evidence in this paragraph?

_____

_____

REVISING AND EDITING A STUDENT PARAGRAPH

Here is a paragraph written by Anthony Barone arguing against home schooling for children. Notice how this student writer organizes and presents his evidence on this subject.

[1]Being educated at home is not in the best interest of children. [2]I do not think it should be allowed unless a child is sick or lives to far from school to go home every day. [3]Most parents say the world is too dangerous for their children who teach they're kids at home. [4]Parents also need to consider that children do not learn to work together by staying home, they need to be around other children to learn how to argue, how to solve problems, and how to develop a strong value system. [5]But if one child is unsafe. [6]All children are unsafe that I know. [7]The community should get together and make the area safe for these children. [8]Children can learn more then academic subjects

in school they can also learn about life. [9]Parents should volunteer at there child's school. [10]And pass their knowledge on to other children too.

This paragraph is Anthony's first draft, which now needs to be revised and edited. First, apply the Revising Checklist below to the content of Anthony's draft. When you are satisfied that his ideas are fully developed and well organized, use the Editing Checklist on page 163 to correct his grammar and mechanics errors. Answer the questions after each checklist. Then write your suggested changes directly on Anthony's draft.

REVISING CHECKLIST ✔

TOPIC SENTENCE
✔ Does the topic sentence convey the paragraph's controlling idea?

✔ Does the topic sentence appear as the first or last sentence of the paragraph?

DEVELOPMENT
✔ Does the paragraph contain *specific* details that support the topic sentence?

✔ Does the paragraph include *enough* details to explain the topic sentence fully?

UNITY
✔ Do all the sentences in the paragraph support the topic sentence?

ORGANIZATION
✔ Is the paragraph organized logically?

COHERENCE
✔ Do the sentences move smoothly and logically from one to the next?

Topic Sentence

1. What is the subject of Anthony's paragraph?

_____

2. What is his opinion on this subject?

_____

3. Put brackets around Anthony's topic sentence. Does it communicate the subject and his opinion on it?

_____

4. Make sure the topic sentence introduces all the ideas in Anthony's paragraph.

Development

1. What types of support does Anthony supply for his topic sentence?

Evidence	Type
_____	_____
_____	_____
_____	_____

2. Where do you need more information?

_____

_____

Unity

1. Read each of Anthony's sentences with his topic sentence (revised, if necessary) in mind.

2. Drop or rewrite any of his sentences not directly related to his topic sentence.

Organization

1. Read Anthony's paragraph again to see if all sentences are arranged logically.

2. Identify Anthony's method of organization.

_____

3. Move the one example that seems to be out of order.

Coherence

For a list of transitions, see page 38.

1. Circle three transitions, repetitions, synonyms, or pronouns Anthony uses.

For a list of pronouns, see page 276.

2. Change at least one of these in Anthony's paragraph, and explain how your change makes the paragraph easier to read.

Now rewrite Anthony's paragraph with your revisions.

EDITING CHECKLIST ✔

SENTENCES

✔ Does each sentence have a main subject and verb?

✔ Do all subjects and verbs agree?

✔ Do all pronouns agree with their nouns?

✔ Are modifiers as close as possible to the words they modify?

PUNCTUATION AND MECHANICS

✔ Are sentences punctuated correctly?

✔ Are words capitalized properly?

WORD CHOICE AND SPELLING

✔ Are words used correctly?

✔ Are words spelled correctly?

Sentences

Subjects and Verbs

1. Underline the subjects once and verbs twice in your revision of Anthony's paragraph. Remember that sentences can have more than one subject-verb set.

2. Does each of Anthony's sentences have at least one subject and verb that can stand alone?

For help with subjects and verbs, see Chapter 30.

3. Did you find and correct Anthony's two fragments? If not, find and correct them now.

For help with fragments, see Chapter 31.

4. Did you find and correct Anthony's two run-on sentences? If not, find and correct them now.

For help with run-ons, see Chapter 32.

Subject-Verb Agreement

1. Read aloud the subjects and verbs you underlined in your revision of Anthony's paragraph.

For help with subject-verb agreement, see Chapter 34.

2. Correct any subjects and verbs that do not agree.

Pronoun Agreement

1. Find any pronouns in your revision of Anthony's paragraph that do not agree with their nouns.

For help with pronoun agreement, see Chapter 38.

2. Correct any pronouns that do not agree with their nouns.

Modifier Errors

For help with modifier errors, see Chapter 41.

1. Find any modifiers in your revision of Anthony's paragraph that are not as close as possible to the words they modify.
2. Did you find and correct Anthony's two modifier errors? If not, find and correct them now.

Punctuation and Mechanics
Punctuation

For help with punctuation, see Chapters 42–45.

1. Read your revision of Anthony's paragraph for any errors in punctuation.
2. Find the two run-on sentences and two fragments that you revised, and make sure they are punctuated correctly.

Mechanics

For help with capitalization, see Chapter 46.

1. Read your revision of Anthony's paragraph for any errors in capitalization.
2. Be sure to check Anthony's capitalization in the fragments and run-on sentences you revised.

Word Choice and Spelling
Word Choice

For help with confused words, see Chapter 52.

1. Find any words used incorrectly in your revision of Anthony's paragraph.
2. Did you find and correct the four words Anthony uses incorrectly? If not, find and correct them now.

Spelling

For help with spelling, see Chapter 53.

1. Use spell-check and a dictionary to check the spelling in your revision of Anthony's paragraph.
2. Correct any misspelled words.

Now rewrite Anthony's paragraph again with your editing corrections.

REVISING AND EDITING YOUR OWN PARAGRAPH

Returning to the argument paragraph you wrote earlier in this chapter, revise and edit your own writing. The above checklists will help you apply what you have learned to your own paragraph.

PRACTISING ARGUMENT
Reading Suggestions

In Chapter 29, you will find three essays that follow the guidelines you have studied in this chapter. The first, "Open the Gates Wide" by Rudyard

Griffiths, discusses the effects of immigration on the Canadian identity. The other two essays are about the pros and cons of smoking bans: "Smoking Bans May Be Just the Ticket" by Roy MacGregor and "Butt Out? No Chance. I'd Rather Break the Law" by Rosie DiManno. These two essays offer opposing viewpoints.

You might want to read these selections before writing another argument paragraph. As you read, notice how the writers make their points through clear, well-chosen evidence.

Writing Workshop

Guidelines for Writing an Argument Paragraph

1. State your opinion on the issue in the topic sentence.
2. Find out as much as you can about your audience before you write.
3. Choose appropriate evidence that supports your topic sentence.
4. Organize your evidence so that it supports your argument as effectively as possible.

1. Explain how the subject of this photo is trying to persuade people to buy cigarettes. How does it appeal to its viewers? What line of reasoning does it follow? Write a paragraph about what the photo would say if it could talk directly to you.

2. We all have strong opinions on controversial issues. A newspaper or newscast might remind you of some of these subjects. Choose a current controversial issue, and, presenting your evidence in an essay, try to convince your classmates that your opinion is right.

3. Persuade the leader of an organization that your position on an important topic affecting the organization is the best choice. To find a topic, think of your own work experience, or talk to someone who has work experience. Organize your evidence as effectively as possible.

4. Create your own argument/persuasion assignment (with the help of your instructor), and write a response to it.

Revising Workshop

Small-Group Activity (5–10 minutes per writer)   Working in groups of three or four, each person should read his or her argument to the other members of the group. Those listening should record their reactions on a copy of the Peer Evaluation Form in Appendix 2I. After your group goes through this process, give your evaluation forms to the appropriate writers so that each writer has two or three peer comment sheets for revising.

Paired Activity (5 minutes per writer)   Using the completed Peer Evaluation Forms, work in pairs to decide what you should revise in your paragraphs. If time allows, rewrite some of your sentences and have your partner check them.

Individual Activity   Rewrite your paragraph using the revising feedback you received from other students.

Editing Workshop

Paired Activity (5–10 minutes per writer)   Exchange papers with a classmate, and using the Editing Peer Evaluation Form in Appendix 1, identify as many grammar, punctuation, mechanics, and spelling errors as you can. If time allows, correct some of your errors and have your partner check them. Record your grammar, punctuation, and mechanics errors in the Error Log (Appendix 6) and your spelling errors in the Spelling Log (Appendix 7).

Individual Activity   Rewrite your paragraph again using the editing feedback you received from other students.

Reflecting on Your Writing

When you have completed your own essay, answer these five questions:

1. What was most difficult about this assignment?
2. What was easiest?
3. What did you learn about argument by completing this assignment?
4. What do you think are the strengths of your argument paragraph? What are its weaknesses?
5. What did you learn from this assignment about your own writing process—about preparing to write, about writing the first draft, about revising, and about editing?

ESSAYS: PARAGRAPHS IN CONTEXT

Everyone agrees that a writer's sense of purpose usefully directs choices
about what to say and where and how to say it.

—C. H. KNOBLAUCH

Part III explains what an essay is. It tells you not only how to identify an
essay but also how to write one—step by step. It provides both a professional model and a student model for you to work with. Then it helps you
apply specific revising and editing guidelines to a student essay and to your
own writing.

15

RECOGNIZING AN ESSAY

In content, essays are "nonfiction." That is, they are about real-life subjects rather than made-up ones. Most essays focus on one specific subject, a single purpose, and a particular audience (for example, telling postsecondary students how to get a good job). For an essay to be successful, its method of development must suit its purpose and appeal to its target audience. A successful essay gets the reaction from the readers that its author hopes for, whether this response is to appreciate a special scene, identify with someone's grief, or leap to action on a controversial issue.

Although essays may differ a great deal in design, organization, and content, they share certain features that distinguish them from other types of writing. At the simplest level, the way an essay looks on the page tells its audience, "Here's an essay!" First, an essay usually has a title that names its general subject. Longer, more complex essays may also have subtitles. When writers move from one topic to another, they start a new paragraph by indenting a few spaces. In addition, most essays contain a thesis statement (a controlling idea for the entire essay) in the introduction. Several body paragraphs explain and support that thesis, and a conclusion draws the essay to a close.

The following essay, by Scott Russell Sanders, is from a book titled *Hunting for Hope*.

FIDELITY

by Scott Russell Sanders

1   A cause needn't be grand, it needn't impress a crowd, to be worthy of our commitment. I knew a man, a lifelong Quaker, who visited prisoners in our county jail, week in and week out, for decades. He would write letters for them, carry messages for them, fetch them clothing or books. But mainly he just offered himself, a very tall and spare and gentle man, with a full shock of white hair in his later years and a rumbling voice that never wasted a word. He didn't ask whether the prisoners were innocent or guilty of the charges that had landed them in jail. All that mattered was that they were in trouble. He didn't preach to them, didn't pick and choose between the likable and the nasty, didn't look for any return on his time. Nor did he

call attention to his kindness; I had known him for several years before I found out about his visits to the jail. Why did he go spend time with outcasts, every week without fail, when he could have been golfing or shopping or watching TV? "I go," he told me once, "in case everyone else has given up on them. I never give up."

Never giving up is a trait we honor in athletes, in soldiers, in climbers   2
marooned by avalanches, in survivors of shipwreck, in patients recovering from severe injuries. If you struggle bravely against overwhelming odds, you're liable to wind up on the evening news. A fireman rescues three children from a burning house, then goes back inside a fourth time to rescue the dog. A childless washerwoman in the deep South, who never dreamed of going to college herself, lives modestly and saves her pennies and in old age donates everything she's saved, over a hundred thousand dollars, for university scholarships. A pilot flies his flimsy plane through a blizzard, searching for a pickup truck in which a woman is trapped; gliding and banking through a whirl of white, he catches signals from her cellular phone, ever so faint; the snow blinds him, the wind tosses him around, his fuel runs low, but he circles and circles, homing in on that faint signal; then just before dark he spies the truck, radios the position to a helicopter crew, and the woman is saved. What kept him searching? "I hadn't found her yet," he tells the camera. "I don't quit so long as I have gas."

Striking examples of perseverance catch our eye, and rightly so. But in   3
less flashy, less newsworthy forms, fidelity to a mission or a person or an occupation shows up in countless lives all around us, all the time. It shows up in parents who will not quit loving their son no matter how much trouble he causes, in parents who will not quit loving their daughter even after she dyes her hair purple and tattoos her belly and runs off with a rock band. It shows up in couples who choose to mend their marriages instead of filing for divorce. It shows up in farmers who stick to their land through droughts and hailstorms and floods. It shows up in community organizers who struggle year after year for justice, in advocates for the homeless and the elderly, in volunteers at the hospital or library or women's shelter or soup kitchen. It shows up in the unsung people everywhere who do their jobs well, not because a supervisor is watching or because they are paid gobs of money but because they know their work matters.

When Jesse was in sixth grade, early in the school year, his teacher was   4
diagnosed as having breast cancer. She gathered the children and told them frankly about the disease, about the surgery and therapy she would be undergoing, and about her hopes for recovery. Jesse came home deeply impressed that she had trusted them with her news. Before going to the hospital, she laid out lesson plans for the teacher who would be replacing her. Although she could have stayed home for the rest of the year on medical leave while the substitute handled her class, as soon as she healed from the mastectomy, she began going in to school one afternoon a week, then two, then a full day, then two days and three, to read with the children

and talk with them and see how they were getting on. When a parent worried aloud that she might be risking her health for the sake of the children, the teacher scoffed, "Oh, heavens no! They're my best medicine." Besides, these children would only be in sixth grade once, and she meant to help them all she could while she had the chance. The therapy must have worked, because seven years later she's going strong. When Ruth and I see her around town, she always asks about Jesse. Is he still so funny, so bright, so excited about learning? Yes he is, we tell her, and she beams.

5   I have a friend who builds houses Monday through Friday for people who can pay him and then builds other houses on Saturday, with Habitat for Humanity, for people who can't pay him. I have another friend who bought land that had been stripped of topsoil by bad farming, and who is slowly turning those battered acres into a wildlife sanctuary by halting erosion and spreading manure and planting trees. A neighbor of ours who comes from an immigrant family makes herself available night and day to international students and their families, unriddling for them the puzzles of living in this new place. Other neighbors coach soccer teams, visit the sick, give rides to the housebound, go door to door raising funds for charity, tutor dropouts, teach adults to read; and they do these things not just for a month or a season but for years.

6   There's a man in our town who has been fighting the U.S. Forest Service for two decades, trying to persuade them to quit clear-cutting, quit selling timber at a loss, quit breaking their own rules in the Hoosier National Forest. All the while, those who make money from tearing up the woods call for more cutting, more road-building, more board feet. This man makes no money from carrying on his crusade, but he makes plenty of enemies, many of whom own chain saws and guns. He won't back down, though, because he loves the forest and loves the creatures that depend on the forest. Hearing him talk, you realize that he sees himself as one of those creatures, like any warbler or fox.

7   I could multiply these examples a hundredfold without ever leaving my county. Most likely you could do the same in yours. Any community worth living in must have a web of people faithful to good work and to one another, or that community would fall apart.

Before continuing, take a moment to record some of your own thoughts and observations. Save your work because you will use it later in Part III.

 **WRITE YOUR OWN ESSAY**

Think of someone you admire. Why do you look up to this person? What has he or she done that you admire? Write an essay explaining your feelings, observations, and thoughts about this special person.

How to Read an Essay

To learn how essays actually function, you should look at them from two different perspectives—from both reading and writing. In each case, you are studying an essay from a different angle so you can clearly understand how essays work. As you progress through these next two chapters, you will see that reading and writing are companion activities that help people create meaning. When you read an essay, you work with the writer to understand his or her message; in other words, you convert words and sentences into ideas and thoughts. When you write an essay, your job is to put your own thoughts into language that communicates your message to your reader(s). In either case, you are in a partnership with the text to create meaning from the words on the page.

Every time you read an essay in this book, you will also be preparing to write your own essay. For this reason, you should pay careful attention to both the content (subject matter) and the form (language, sentence structure, organization, and development of ideas) of each essay you read. In fact, the more aware you are of each author's techniques and strategies, the more rapidly your own writing process will mature and improve.

The questions after each essay in Part IV teach you a specific way of approaching your reading that can help you both understand what you read and discover the relationship of the writer's ideas to one another and to your own thoughts. These questions can also help clarify for you the connection between the writer's topic, his or her means of expression, and your own composing process. In other words, the questions are designed to help you understand and generate ideas, discover various choices the writers make in composing their essays, and then realize the freedom you have to make related choices in your own writing. Such an approach to the process of reading takes some of the mystery out of reading and writing and makes them manageable tasks at which anyone can succeed.

A good way to approach your reading is to discover for yourself exactly how an essay works. You will then understand more clearly the choices you can make as a writer. To accomplish this goal, choose an essay from Part IV of this book, and answer the questions that follow. Once you grapple with these questions, you will learn for yourself the various features at work in a good essay and be able to apply this new knowledge to your own writing.

The essay of your choice: _____

Author: _____

Page: _____

Answer each question in as much detail as you can.

1. What is the subject of this essay?

   _____

   _____

2. What is its thesis statement?

   _____

   _____

3. Does the thesis state the author's position on the subject?

   _____

4. How does the writer capture the reader's attention in the introduction?

   _____

   Is this strategy effective for this subject? Why or why not?

   _____

5. How many body paragraphs does the author include in this essay?

   _____

   List the topic sentence of each body paragraph:

   _____

   _____

   _____

   _____

   _____

_____

_____

_____

_____

_____

6. Does the author use enough specific details to communicate his or
    her message?

    _____

7. Do the sentences in each paragraph support the topic sentence?

    _____

8. Is the essay organized logically?

    _____

    _____

9. Do the sentences and paragraphs move smoothly and logically from
    one to the next?

    _____

    _____

10. What strategy does the author use to conclude the essay?

    _____

    _____

    Is this strategy effective? Explain your answer.

    _____

11. How does the title relate to the author's thesis statement?

    _____

    Is this an effective title? Explain your answer.

    _____

    _____

12. Did you find the essay interesting?

_____

_____

◆ *P r a c t i c e   1*   What type of reading (novels, magazines, short stories, essays, comic books, etc.) do you like most?

_____

◆ *P r a c t i c e   2*   What do you like most about reading?

_____

_____

◆ *P r a c t i c e   3*   What do you like least about reading?

_____

_____

◆ *P r a c t i c e   4*   What did you learn about reading in this chapter that can help you with your writing?

_____

_____

How to Write an Essay

As you learned in the previous chapter, writing is a companion activity to reading. In fact, you can learn a great deal about how to write by reading. When you read an essay, you can see how the writer thinks and puts words together to create meaning. Then, when you write, you are putting your own thoughts into words so that you can communicate a specific message to your reader(s). In both cases, you must work together with the words to create meaning.

Writing an essay is very similar to writing a paragraph, although we call some elements of an essay by different names than we use for similar elements in a paragraph. The following chart demonstrates the correspondences:

Paragraph	Essay
Topic sentence	Introduction with thesis statement
Examples, details, support	Body paragraphs
Concluding sentence	Concluding paragraph

Keeping these similarities in mind, you will learn in this chapter how to construct a good essay. Laying out some clear guidelines is the best place to start.

1. **Choose a subject.** You might be choosing a subject from infinite possibilities or selecting a topic from a set of writing assignments. Whatever the case, make sure you decide on a topic that you can handle comfortably within the word length required. That means you might choose a subject, like pets, and then narrow the subject further to fulfill the assignment:

    General subject: pets

      More specific: dogs

        More specific: golden retrievers

          More specific: training your golden retriever

This limited subject would be perfect for a short essay.

In the essay in Chapter 15, Scott Russell Sanders might have started with a general topic like "good deeds," limited it to the idea that good deeds don't have to be "grand," and finally settled on the message that a cause doesn't have to be "grand" to be worthwhile.

2. **Write a thesis statement about your subject.** Just as a topic sentence is the controlling idea of a paragraph, a thesis statement provides the controlling idea for an essay. It guides the writing of your entire essay. Like a high-powered telescope pointed at a distant star, your thesis statement focuses on a single aspect of your subject.

Your essay's thesis statement is also a contract between you and your readers. The thesis statement tells your readers what the main idea of your essay will be and what the body paragraphs will be about. If you don't deliver what your thesis statement promises, your readers will be confused and disappointed.

To write a thesis statement, begin by stating your position on your topic. This sentence moves you from the broad subject of your essay to your own perspective or feeling about the topic.

Topic:	Training your golden retriever
Thesis statement:	Training your golden retriever is important for your dog's safety and for your enjoyment of each other.

In this case, the writer states a position (training is important) and gives reasons for this position (safety and enjoyment).

When you feel you have a good working thesis statement, turn it into a question as an exercise to guide you through your draft. Then the rest of your essay should answer this question.

Thesis question:	In what ways is training your golden retriever important for your dog's safety and for your enjoyment of each other?

Usually, the thesis statement is the final sentence in the introduction. This placement gives the reader a road map for reading the rest of your essay.

Sanders's controlling idea or thesis appears at the beginning of his first paragraph:

> A cause needn't be grand, it needn't impress a crowd, to be worthy of our commitment.

Sanders's body paragraphs after this statement explain this thesis. His entire essay is about the benefits of performing selfless acts and being true to a cause or mission to help others in some way.

3. **Construct an introduction that leads up to your thesis statement.** The introduction to an essay is your chance to make a great first impression. Just like a firm handshake and a warm smile in a job interview, an essay's introduction should capture your readers' interest, set the tone for your essay, and state your specific purpose. Introductions often take on a funnel shape: they typically begin with general information and then narrow the focus to your position on a particular issue. Regardless of your approach, your introduction should "hook" your readers by grabbing their attention.

Some effective ways of catching your audience's attention and giving necessary background information are (1) to furnish a quotation; (2) to tell a story that relates to your topic; (3) to provide a revealing fact, statistic, or definition; (4) to offer an interesting comparison; or (5) to ask an intriguing question. Always make sure your introduction gives your readers all the information they need in order to follow your train of thought.

Sanders's introduction is a single paragraph. It starts out with his thesis statement, which is followed by a story about a man who visited prisoners and did specific chores for them for several years. The paragraph ends with a question and answer. This introduction uses a brief story, a question, and a quotation to draw its readers into the essay.

4. ***Develop as many supporting paragraphs or body paragraphs as necessary to explain your thesis statement.*** Following the introductory paragraph, an essay includes several body paragraphs that support and explain the essay's thesis. Each body paragraph deals with a topic that is directly related to your thesis statement.

At least one supporting paragraph should cover each topic in your essay. Supporting paragraphs, also called "body" paragraphs, usually include a topic sentence, which is a general statement about the paragraph's content, plus examples or details that support the topic sentence. See the chapters in Part II for methods of developing and organizing these paragraphs.

Indenting and starting a new paragraph gives your readers important information. It tells them you are moving to a new idea that will be developed in its own paragraph.

Sanders's essay contains five body paragraphs, each making a separate point that is directly related to the essay's thesis:

Paragraph	Point
2	We value never giving up.
3	"Fidelity" shows up in all kinds of people.
4	A teacher is diagnosed with breast cancer.
5	Neighbours help the needy.
6	People choose causes that they feel strongly about.

Like the foundation of a solid building, these paragraphs provide support for the position Sanders takes in his thesis statement. The stronger the supporting paragraphs are, the stronger the essay.

5. ***Write a concluding paragraph.*** The concluding paragraph is the final paragraph of an essay. In its most basic form, it should summarize the main points of your essay and remind readers of your thesis statement. It should also reflect the introduction.

The best conclusions go beyond these basic requirements and then conclude the essay with one of these creative strategies: They will (1) ask a question that provokes new ideas, (2) predict the future, (3) offer a solution to a problem, or (4) call the reader to action. Each of these options sends a specific message and creates a slightly different effect at the end of an essay. The most important responsibility of the last paragraph, however, is to bring the essay to a close.

Sanders's conclusion summarizes his main point—

I could multiply these examples a hundredfold without ever leaving my county;

extends his observations to other areas—

Most likely you could do the same in yours;

and ends by echoing his thesis and highlighting his main points—

Any community worth living in must have a web of people faithful to good work and to one another, or that community would fall apart.

Overall, his conclusion summarizes and calls his readers to action.

6. *Give your essay a catchy title.* Now that you have written a draft, you should think of a title for your essay. Much like wearing your best clothes to a job interview, your title is what your readers see first. Titles are phrases, usually no more than a few words, placed at the beginning of your essay that suggest or sum up the subject, purpose, or focus of your essay. The title chosen for this book, *Mosaics*, reflects a specific view of the writing process—a collection of brightly coloured individual pieces that fit together to form a complete whole. Whereas this title vividly conveys the textbook's purpose, the title for this chapter is a more straightforward label: "How to Write an Essay." These are just two of many approaches to creating a title.

Besides forecasting an essay's purpose, a good title catches an audience's attention. For instance, Sanders's title, "Fidelity," gets his readers' attention because they are bound to be curious about this author's use of this single word. That's exactly what a title should do—make your readers want to read your essay.

7. *Revise and edit your essay.* Revising and editing an essay are very similar to revising and editing a paragraph. A few more simple guidelines are necessary, but the process is the same. You should first apply the revising guidelines to your writing until you are satisfied with the content. Then go through the editing guidelines one by one and correct any grammar and mechanics errors in your final draft.

Sanders probably went through similar revising and editing strategies several times before his essay was published. Most professional writers consider revising and editing essential parts of the entire writing process.

◆ *P r a c t i c e 1* What type of writing (essays, short stories, poems, lists, memos, journals, letters, etc.) do you enjoy most?

Practice 2   What do you like best about writing?

_____

_____

Practice 3   What do you like least about writing?

_____

_____

Practice 4   What did you learn about writing in this chapter that can help you with your reading?

_____

_____

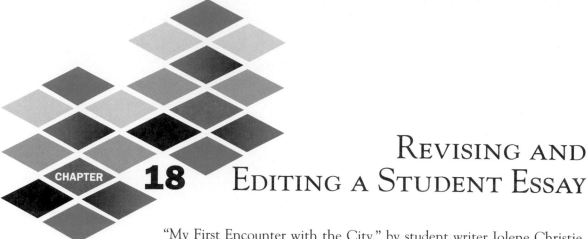

REVISING AND EDITING A STUDENT ESSAY

"My First Encounter with the City," by student writer Jolene Christie, follows the guidelines presented in Chapter 17 for writing a successful essay.

My First Encounter with the City

1   My mother is a single mother, and she lived in a small town her whole life. She had me at a very young age. I never knew my father, and she never mentioned anything about him. On numerous occasions I would ask about him, and around the age of 15, my mother decided that it might be best if I knew who my father was. I'll never forget that day.

2   I went out to do some research on my newfound father. I asked about him and tried to find out what kind of person he was. I didn't find a lot of information, but at the time it was enough for a 15-year-old. Just after my 18th birthday, I thought that I was mentally ready to take another step forward. I managed to find his phone number. It took me about six months to work up the courage to call him. I was afraid that he wouldn't believe that I am his daughter and would reject me, but I was pleasantly surprised. Now, two months later, I am excited about our first encounter, especially in the city!

3   My thoughts are interrupted as I notice that the bus is pulling into the station. People are everywhere! Some are strolling down the sidewalks gazing through store windows; others are speed-walking with their cell phones glued to their ears. I look out the window and take a deep breath. There is wall-to-wall traffic, with people honking their horns and slamming on their brakes. I can feel the terror filling up inside of me. I grab my backpack and suitcase, adjust my load, and step off the bus. Just as I step down, someone bowls me over to catch another bus. I pick up my bags from the filthy ground, readjust, and sigh. I feel as if my legs are rooted to the cement, and if I try to move them, they will turn to Jell-O.

4   I see a man walking toward me. He has a mound of long, greasy grey hair that resembles a used bird's nest. He also has a long, scraggly beard and mustache. He has beady little eyes which I can feel penetrating and paralyzing me. His clothes are ragged, ripped, and falling off of him. My heart sinks as I realize this man could be my father, Samuel Bride. I cannot align my emotions and expectations with the man who is staring directly into my eyes.

5   As I scan the station trying to find the courage to approach him, my eyes spot a man wearing a suit and tie. He is holding a sign with my name

written in black and a bouquet of white and yellow roses. I hesitantly walk over to him with an uncomfortable smile. I give him an awkward hug, and he returns the gesture. After a moment of silence, he asks me how my trip was, and I can't help but look back at the bedraggled man. I suddenly feel sorry for him, ashamed that I had desperately wanted someone else as my father. I look up at my successful and charming father and, in my anxious emotional state, can only respond with a smile.

I will never forget my first encounter with this city. I glance once more   6
at my father as we walk out of the station. I suddenly feel as if this city, this place where my father lives, has always been a part of me. I am ready to venture out toward a new life.

This is Jolene's first draft, which now needs to be revised and edited. First, apply the Revising Checklist below to the content of Jolene's draft. When you are satisfied that her ideas are fully developed and well organized, use the Editing Checklist on pages 184–185 to correct her grammar and mechanics errors. Answer the questions after each checklist. Then write your suggested changes directly on Jolene's draft.

REVISING CHECKLIST ✔

THESIS STATEMENT
✔ Does the thesis statement contain the essay's controlling idea and an opinion about that idea?

✔ Does the thesis appear as the last sentence of the introduction?

BASIC ELEMENTS
✔ Does the title draw in the reader?

✔ Does the introduction capture the reader's attention and build up to the thesis statement effectively?

✔ Does each body paragraph deal with a single topic?

✔ Does the conclusion bring the essay to a close in an interesting way?

DEVELOPMENT
✔ Do the body paragraphs adequately support the thesis statement?

✔ Does each body paragraph have a focused topic sentence?

✔ Does each body paragraph contain *specific* details that support the topic sentence?

✔ Does each body paragraph include *enough* details to explain the topic sentence fully?

UNITY
✔ Do the essay's topic sentences relate directly to the thesis statement?

✔ Do the details in each body paragraph support its topic sentence?

ORGANIZATION
- ✔ Is the essay organized logically?
- ✔ Is each body paragraph organized logically?

COHERENCE
- ✔ Are transitions used effectively so that paragraphs move smoothly and logically from one to the next?
- ✔ Do the sentences move smoothly and logically from one to the next?

Thesis Statement

1. What is Jolene's main idea in this essay?

   _____

2. Put brackets around the last sentence in Jolene's introduction. Does it introduce her main idea?

   _____

3. Rewrite Jolene's thesis statement if necessary so that it states her main point and introduces her topics.

   _____

   _____

Basic Elements

1. Give Jolene's essay an alternative title.

   _____

2. Rewrite Jolene's introduction so that it captures the reader's attention and builds up to the thesis statement at the end of the paragraph.

   _____

   _____

   _____

3. Does each of Jolene's body paragraphs deal with only one topic?

   _____

4. Rewrite Jolene's conclusion using at least one suggestion from Chapter 17, #5, pages 177–178.

_____

_____

_____

_____

Development

1. Write out Jolene's thesis statement (revised, if necessary), and list her four topic sentences below it.

Thesis statement: _____

Topic 1: _____

_____

Topic 2: _____

_____

Topic 3: _____

_____

Topic 4: _____

_____

2. Do Jolene's topics adequately support her thesis statement?

_____

3. Does each body paragraph have a focused topic sentence?

_____

4. Are Jolene's examples specific?

_____

Add another, more specific detail to one of the examples in her essay.

5. Does she offer enough examples to make her point?

_____

Add at least one new example to strengthen Jolene's essay.

Unity

1. Read each of Jolene's topic sentences with her thesis statement (revised, if necessary) in mind. Do they go together?

   _____

2. Revise them if necessary so they are directly related.
3. Read each of Jolene's paragraphs with its topic sentence in mind.
4. Drop or rewrite any sentences not directly related to the paragraph's topic sentence.

Organization

1. Review your list of Jolene's topics in item 1 under "Development," and decide if her body paragraphs are organized logically.
2. What is her method of organization?

   _____

3. Look closely at Jolene's body paragraphs to see if all her sentences are arranged logically within paragraphs.
4. Move any sentences that are out of order.

Coherence

For a list of transitions, see page 38.

1. Circle five transitions Jolene uses.
2. Explain how two of these make Jolene's essay easier to read.

   _____

   _____

Now rewrite Jolene's essay with your revisions.

EDITING CHECKLIST ✔

SENTENCES

✔ Does each sentence have a main subject and verb?

✔ Do all subjects and verbs agree?

✔ Do all pronouns agree with their nouns?

✔ Are modifiers as close as possible to the words they modify?

PUNCTUATION AND MECHANICS

✔ Are sentences punctuated correctly?

✔ Are words capitalized properly?

> WORD CHOICE AND SPELLING
> ✔ Are words used correctly?
> ✔ Are words spelled correctly?

Sentences

Subjects and Verbs

1. In paragraph 1 of your revision, underline Jolene's subjects once and verbs twice. Remember that sentences can have more than one subject-verb set.

2. Does each sentence have at least one subject and verb that can stand alone?

For help with subjects and verbs, see Chapter 30.

---

3. Correct any fragments you find.
4. Correct any run-on sentences you find.

For help with fragments, see Chapter 31.

For help with run-ons, see Chapter 32.

Subject-Verb Agreement

1. Read aloud the subjects and verbs you underlined in Jolene's first paragraph.
2. Correct any subjects and verbs that do not agree.
3. Now read aloud all the subjects and verbs in the rest of her revised paragraphs.
4. Correct any subjects and verbs that do not agree.

For help with subject-verb agreement, see Chapter 34.

Pronoun Agreement

1. Find any pronouns in your revision of Jolene's essay that do not agree with their nouns.
2. Correct any pronouns that do not agree with their nouns.

For help with pronoun agreement, see Chapter 38.

Modifier Errors

1. Find any modifiers in your revision of Jolene's essay that are not as close as possible to the words they modify.
2. Rewrite sentences if necessary so that modifiers are as close as possible to the words they modify.

For help with modifier errors, see Chapter 41.

Punctuation and Mechanics

Punctuation

1. Read your revision of Jolene's essay for any errors in punctuation.
2. Make sure any fragments and run-on sentences you revised are punctuated correctly.

For help with punctuation, see Chapters 42–45.

Mechanics

For help with capitalization, see Chapter 46.

1. Read your revision of Jolene's essay for any errors in capitalization.
2. Be sure to check her capitalization in any fragments or run-on sentences you revised.

Word Choice and Spelling

Word Choice

For help with confused words, see Chapter 52.

1. Find any words used incorrectly in your revision of Jolene's essay.
2. Correct any errors you find.

Spelling

For help with spelling, see Chapter 53.

1. Use spell-check and a dictionary to check the spelling in your revision of Jolene's essay.
2. Correct any misspelled words.

Now rewrite Jolene's essay again with your editing corrections.

REVISING AND EDITING YOUR OWN ESSAY

Returning to the essay you wrote at the end of Chapter 15, revise and edit your own writing. The checklists here will help you apply what you have learned to your own writing.

REVISING CHECKLIST ✔

THESIS STATEMENT

☐ Does the thesis statement contain the essay's controlling idea and appear as the last sentence of the introduction?

BASIC ELEMENTS

☐ Does the title draw in the reader?

☐ Does the introduction capture the reader's attention and build up to the thesis statement effectively?

☐ Does each body paragraph deal with a single topic?

☐ Does the conclusion bring the essay to a close in an interesting way?

DEVELOPMENT

☐ Do the body paragraphs adequately support the thesis statement?

☐ Does each body paragraph have a focused topic sentence?

☐ Does each body paragraph contain *specific* details that support the topic sentence?

☐ Does each body paragraph include *enough* details to explain the topic sentence fully?

UNITY

☐ Do the essay's topic sentences relate directly to the thesis statement?

☐ Do the details in each body paragraph support its topic sentence?

ORGANIZATION

☐ Is the essay organized logically?

☐ Is each body paragraph organized logically?

> **COHERENCE**
> ☐ Are transitions used effectively so that paragraphs move smoothly and logically from one to the next?
> ☐ Do the sentences move smoothly and logically from one to the next?

Thesis Statement

1. What is the main idea you are trying to convey in your essay?

   _____

2. Put brackets around the last sentence in your introduction. Does it convey your main idea?

   _____

3. Rewrite your thesis statement if necessary so that it states your main point and introduces your topics.

   _____

Basic Elements

1. Give your essay a title if it doesn't have one.

   _____

2. Does your introduction capture your reader's attention and build up to your thesis statement at the end of the paragraph?

   _____

3. Does each of your body paragraphs deal with only one topic?

   _____

4. Does your conclusion follow some of the suggestions offered in Part I?

   _____

Development

1. Write out your thesis statement (revised, if necessary) and your topic sentences.

   Thesis statement: _____

Topic sentences: _____

_____

_____

_____

2. Do your topics adequately support your thesis statement?

_____

3. Does each body paragraph have a focused topic sentence?

_____

4. Are your examples specific?

_____

   Add another more specific detail to an example in your essay.

5. Do you give enough examples to make your point?

_____

   Add at least one new example to your essay.

Unity

1. Read each of your topic sentences with your thesis statement in mind. Do they go together?
2. Revise them if necessary so that they are directly related.
3. Drop or rewrite any sentences in your body paragraphs not directly related to their topic sentence.

Organization

1. Read your essay again to see if all the paragraphs are arranged logically.
2. Review the list of your topics in item 1 under "Development." Then identify your method of organization.

_____

3. Is the order you chose for your paragraphs the most effective approach to your topic?

_____

4. Move any paragraphs that are out of order.

5. Look closely at your body paragraphs to see if all the sentences are arranged logically within paragraphs.

6. Move any sentences that are out of order.

Coherence

For a list of transitions, see page 38.

1. Circle five transitions you use.

2. Explain how two of these make your essay easier to read.

_____

_____

Now rewrite your essay with your revisions.

EDITING CHECKLIST ✔

SENTENCES

☐ Does each sentence have a main subject and verb?

☐ Do all subjects and verbs agree?

☐ Do all pronouns agree with their nouns?

☐ Are modifiers as close as possible to the words they modify?

PUNCTUATION AND MECHANICS

☐ Are sentences punctuated correctly?

☐ Are words capitalized properly?

WORD CHOICE AND SPELLING

☐ Are words used correctly?

☐ Are words spelled correctly?

Sentences

Subjects and Verbs

For help with subjects and verbs, see Chapter 30.

1. In a paragraph of your choice, underline the subjects once and verbs twice. Remember that sentences can have more than one subject-verb set.

2. Does each of your sentences have at least one subject and verb that can stand alone?

_____

For help with fragments, see Chapter 31.

3. Correct any fragments you have written.

4. Correct any run-on sentences you have written.

For help with run-ons, see Chapter 32.

Subject-Verb Agreement

1. Read aloud the subjects and verbs you underlined in the paragraph of your choice.
2. Correct any subjects and verbs that do not agree.
3. Now read aloud the subjects and verbs in the rest of your revised essay.
4. Correct any subjects and verbs that do not agree.

For help with subject-verb agreement, see Chapter 34.

Pronoun Agreement

1. Find any pronouns in your revised essay that do not agree with their nouns.
2. Correct any pronouns that do not agree with their nouns.

For help with pronoun agreement, see Chapter 38.

Modifier Errors

1. Find any modifiers in your revised essay that are not as close as possible to the words they modify.
2. Rewrite sentences if necessary so that your modifiers are as close as possible to the words they modify.

For help with modifier errors, see Chapter 41.

Punctuation and Mechanics

Punctuation

1. Read your revised essay for any errors in punctuation.
2. Make sure any fragments and run-on sentences you revised are punctuated correctly.

For help with punctuation, see Chapters 42–45.

Mechanics

1. Read your revised essay for any errors in capitalization.
2. Be sure to check your capitalization in any fragments or run-on sentences you revised.

For help with capitalization, see Chapter 46.

Word Choice and Spelling

Word Choice

1. Find any words used incorrectly in your revised essay.
2. Correct any errors you find.

For help with confused words, see Chapter 52.

Spelling

1. Use spell-check and a dictionary to check your spelling.
2. Correct any misspelled words.

For help with spelling, see Chapter 53.

Now rewrite your essay again with your editing corrections.

20 WRITING WORKSHOP

Guidelines for Writing an Essay

1. Choose a subject.
2. Write a thesis statement about your subject.
3. Construct an introduction that leads up to your thesis statement.
4. Develop as many supporting paragraphs or body paragraphs as necessary to explain your thesis statement.
5. Write a concluding paragraph.
6. Give your essay a catchy title.
7. Revise and edit your essay.

1. Find someone who does community service or volunteer work as in the photo above. What type of service does this person do? Why is the person attracted to this type of work? Who does he or she help?

What does this activity do for the community? What does it do for you?

2. You have been asked by the editor of your campus newspaper to relate your weirdest experience. Write an essay about this experience, including what you learned from it.

3. Analyze a relationship you have with another person by explaining its causes and effects.

4. Come up with your own essay assignment (with the help of your instructor), and write a response to it.

Revising Workshop

Small-Group Activity (5–10 minutes per writer)   Working in groups of three or four, each person should read his or her essay to the other members of the group. Those listening should record their reactions on a copy of the Peer Evaluation Form in Appendix 3. After your group goes through this process, give your evaluation forms to the appropriate writers so that each writer has two or three peer comment sheets for revising.

Paired Activity (5 minutes per writer)   Using the completed Peer Evaluation Forms, work in pairs to decide what you should revise in your essay. If time allows, rewrite some of your sentences and have your partner look at them.

Individual Activity   Rewrite your paper, using the revising feedback you received from other students.

Editing Workshop

Paired Activity (5–10 minutes per writer)   Exchange papers with a classmate, and use the Editing Peer Evaluation Form in Appendix 1 to identify as many grammar, punctuation, mechanics, and spelling errors as you can. If time allows, correct some of your errors and have your partner look at them. Record your grammar, punctuation, and mechanics errors in the Error Log (Appendix 6) and your spelling errors in the Spelling Log (Appendix 7).

Individual Activity   Rewrite your paper again, using the editing feedback you received from other students.

Reflecting on Your Writing

When you have completed your own essay, answer these five questions:

1. What was most difficult about this assignment?

2. What was easiest?

3. What did you learn about writing essays by completing this assignment?

4. What do you think are the strengths of your essay? What are its weaknesses?

5. What did you learn from this assignment about your own writing process—about preparing to write, about writing the first draft, about revising, and about editing?

IV

From Reading to Writing

There is no way to write unless you read and read a lot.

—Walter J. Ong

Part IV is a collection of essays that demonstrate the rhetorical modes you are studying in this book. Each chapter focuses on a different rhetorical strategy and includes two essays that show the strategy at work with other strategies. After each essay are questions that check your understanding of the selection.

21 # DESCRIBING

In the following selections, the writers provide detailed and accurate descriptions that enable readers to see for themselves the actions and events the authors experienced. In the excerpt titled "Magpies," from *The Joy Luck Club* by Amy Tan, a young girl observes the sights, sounds, smells, textures, and tastes that she encounters when she arrives at her new home. The second selection, an essay called "The Films Stink More than the Greasy Audience," by Russell Smith, describes the unpleasantness of movie-going.

Amy Tan

MAGPIES

Focusing Your Attention

1. Think of a place you are very familiar with: your room, your home, your school, your place of employment, a garden, a restaurant. Then make a list of the sights, sounds, textures, smells, and tastes that come into your mind as you think of that place.

2. In the excerpt you are about to read, a young girl recounts the many sights, sounds, smells, textures, and tastes that she encountered when she first arrived at her new home. Think of an occasion when you entered a place for the first time. What sights, sounds, textures, smells, and tastes made the strongest impressions on you?

Expanding Your Vocabulary

The following words are important to your understanding of this essay.

British Concession: areas that the Chinese allowed the British to occupy (paragraph 1)

concubines: women who were part of a man's household and were expected to fulfill his needs (paragraph 14)

mourning bands: representing grief over a person's death (paragraph 17)

1   I knew from the beginning our new home would not be an ordinary house. My mother had told me we would live in the household of Wu Tsing, who was a very rich merchant. She said this man owned many carpet fac-

tories and lived in a mansion located in the British Concession of Tientsin, the best section of the city where Chinese people could live. We lived not too far from Paima Di, Racehorse Street, where only Westerners could live. And we were also close to little shops that sold only one kind of thing: only tea, or only fabric, or only soap.

The house, she said, was foreign-built; Wu Tsing liked foreign things 2 because foreigners had made him rich. And I concluded that was why my mother had to wear foreign-style clothes, in the manner of newly rich Chinese people who liked to display their wealth on the outside. And even though I knew all this before I arrived, I was still amazed at what I saw.

The front of the house had a Chinese stone gate, rounded at the top, 3 with big black lacquer doors and a threshold you had to step over. Within the gates I saw the courtyard, and I was surprised. There were no willows or sweet-smelling cassia trees, no garden pavilions, no benches sitting by a pond, no tubs of fish. Instead, there were long rows of bushes on both sides of a wide brick walkway, and to each side of those bushes was a big lawn area with fountains. And as we walked down the walkway and got closer to the house, I saw this house had been built in the Western style. It was three stories high, of mortar and stone, with long metal balconies on each floor and chimneys at every corner.

When we arrived, a young servant woman ran out and greeted my 4 mother with cries of joy. She had a high scratchy voice: "Oh Taitai, you've already arrived! How can this be?" This was Yan Chang, my mother's personal maid, and she knew how to fuss over my mother just the right amount. She had called my mother Taitai, the simple honorable title of Wife, as if my mother were the first wife, the only wife.

Yan Chang called loudly to other servants to take our luggage, called 5 another servant to bring tea and draw a hot bath. And then she hastily explained that Second Wife had told everyone not to expect us for another week at least. "What a shame! No one to greet you! Second Wife, the others, gone to Peking to visit her relatives. Your daughter, so pretty, your same look. She's so shy, eh? First Wife, her daughters . . . gone on a pilgrimage to another Buddhist temple. . . . Last week, a cousin's uncle, just a little crazy, came to visit, turned out not to be a cousin, not an uncle, who knows who he was. . . ."

As soon as we walked into that big house, I became lost with too many 6 things to see: a curved staircase that wound up and up, a ceiling with faces in every corner, then hallways twisting and turning into one room then another. To my right was a large room, larger than I had ever seen, and it was filled with stiff teakwood furniture: sofas and tables and chairs. And at the other end of this long, long room, I could see doors leading into more rooms, more furniture, then more doors. To my left was a darker room, another sitting room, this one filled with foreign furniture: dark green leather sofas, paintings with hunting dogs, armchairs, and mahogany desks. And as I glanced in these rooms, I would see different people, and Yan Chang would explain: "This young lady, she is Second Wife's servant. That one, she is nobody, just the daughter of cook's helper. This man takes care of the garden."

7   And then we were walking up the staircase. We came to the top of the stairs, and I found myself in another large sitting room. We walked to the left, down a hall, past one room, and then stepped into another. "This is your mother's room," Yan Chang told me proudly. "This is where you will sleep."

8   And the first thing I saw, the only thing I could see at first, was a magnificent bed. It was heavy and light at the same time: soft rose silk and heavy, dark, shiny wood carved all around with dragons. Four posts held up a silk canopy, and at each post dangled large silk ties holding back curtains. The bed sat on four squat lion's paws, as if the weight of it had crushed the lion underneath. Yan Chang showed me how to use a small step stool to climb onto the bed. And when I tumbled onto the silk coverings, I laughed to discover a soft mattress that was ten times the thickness of my bed in Ningpo.

9   Sitting in this bed, I admired everything as if I were a princess. This room had a glass door that led to a balcony. In front of the window door was a round table of the same wood as the bed. It too sat on carved lion's legs and was surrounded by four chairs. A servant had already put tea and sweet cakes on the table and was now lighting the houlu, a small stove for burning coal.

10   It was not that my uncle's house in Ningpo had been poor. He was actually quite well-to-do. But this house in Tientsin was amazing. And I thought to myself, My uncle was wrong. There was no shame in my mother's marrying Wu Tsing.

11   While thinking this, I was startled by a sudden clang! clang! clang! followed by music. On the wall opposite the bed was a big wooden clock with a forest and bears carved into it. The door on the clock had burst open, and a tiny room full of people was coming out. There was a bearded man in a pointed cap seated at a table. He was bending his head over and over again to drink soup, but his beard would dip in the bowl first and stop him. A girl in a white scarf and blue dress was standing next to the table, and she was bending over and over again to give the man more of this soup. And next to the man and girl was another girl with a skirt and short jacket. She was swinging her arm back and forth, playing violin music. She always played the same dark song. I can still hear it in my head after these many years—ni-ah! nah! nah! nah! nah-ni-nah!

12   This was a wonderful clock to see, but after I heard it that first hour, then the next, and then always, this clock became an extravagant nuisance. I could not sleep for many nights. And later, I found I had an ability: To not listen to something meaningless calling to me.

13   I was so happy those first few nights, in this amusing house, sleeping in the big soft bed with my mother. I would lie in this comfortable bed, thinking about my uncle's house in Ningpo, realizing how unhappy I had been, feeling sorry for my little brother. But most of my thoughts flew to all the new things to see and do in this house.

14   I watched hot water pouring out of pipes not just in the kitchen but also into washbasins and bathtubs on all three floors of the house. I saw cham-

ber pots that flushed clean without servants having to empty them. I saw rooms as fancy as my mother's. Yan Chang explained which ones belonged to First Wife and the other concubines, who were called Second Wife and Third Wife. And some rooms belonged to no one. "They are for guests," said Yan Chang.

On the third floor were rooms for only the men servants, said Yan 15 Chang, and one of the rooms even had a door to a cabinet that was really a secret hiding place from sea pirates.

Thinking back, I find it hard to remember everything that was in that 16 house; too many good things all seem the same after a while. I tired of anything that was not a novelty. "Oh, this," I said when Yan Chang brought me the same sweet meats as the day before. "I've tasted this already."

My mother seemed to regain her pleasant nature. She put her old 17 clothes back on, long Chinese gowns and skirts now with white mourning bands sewn at the bottoms. During the day, she pointed to strange and funny things, naming them for me: bidet, Brownie camera, salad fork, napkin. In the evening, when there was nothing to do, we talked about the servants: who was clever, who was diligent, who was loyal. We gossiped as we cooked small eggs and sweet potatoes on top of the houlu just to enjoy their smell. And at night, my mother would again tell me stories as I lay in her arms falling asleep.

If I look upon my whole life, I cannot think of another time when I felt 18 more comfortable: when I had no worries, fears, or desires, when my life seemed as soft and lovely as lying inside a cocoon of rose silk.

Thinking Critically About Content

1. List two details from this essay for each of the five senses: seeing, hearing, touching, smelling, and tasting. How do these details *show* rather than tell the readers the narrator's impressions of her new house?

2. In one or more complete sentences, state the main character's point of view.

3. What does the narrator mean when she says, "If I look upon my whole life, I cannot think of another time when I felt more comfortable: when I had no worries, fears, or desires, when my life seemed as soft and lovely as lying inside a cocoon of rose silk" (paragraph 18)? Why do you think she is so comfortable in these surroundings?

Thinking Critically About Purpose and Audience

4. What dominant impression does the writer create in this description? How does this impression change throughout the essay?

5. Do you think readers who have never been to China can appreciate and enjoy this essay? Explain your answer.

6. What specific observations are most interesting to you? Why? In what ways do these observations help you imagine the entire scene?

Thinking Critically About Paragraphs

7. If a paragraph is unified, all of its sentences are related to one central idea. Based on this explanation, is paragraph 12 unified? Explain your answer.

8. Look closely at paragraph 17, and explain how it is organized. (Refer to pages 20–25 for information on organization.)

9. Choose one body paragraph, and decide if it has enough details. What is the most interesting detail in the paragraph?

10. Write a paragraph describing the inner feelings of the main character when she finally settles into her new home.

Russell Smith

THE FILMS STINK MORE THAN THE GREASY AUDIENCE

Focusing Your Attention

1. Do you enjoy going to the movies? What part do you like the best? Do you enjoy the entire experience or just the actual movie?

2. Have you ever considered that going to the movies might be an unpleasant experience? The essay you are about to read compares movie-goers to farm animals. The author wonders why movie-going has become our primary entertainment. Do you agree at all with this rant or do you think that the author would be better off staying at home?

Expanding Your Vocabulary

The following words are important to your understanding of this essay.

> **dilated:** widened, expanded (paragraph 2)
>
> **viscous:** sticky, doesn't flow (paragraph 2)
>
> **angst:** anxious, apprehensive (paragraph 3)
>
> **amplified:** increased, exaggerated (made louder) (paragraph 5)

1 It's time someone came out and said that not only are movies terrible, but that the whole experience of going to movies is highly unpleasant. How is it possible that this sensory stressfest has become the most popular entertainment of the contemporary age?

2 How can people possibly enjoy the lining up, the waiting with coats on for tickets, then the shuffling with the heated herd toward a crowded, windowless room? And when you get to that butter-scented trough, with its seats piled high with coats and scarves, the representatives of humanity who surround you are anxious: They are focused on their feed. This focus is quite dramatic. Their eyes are glazed and dilated, their shoulders are hunched over their cartons, they are stuffing themselves with viscous oil

products with orange cheeze whip on fried nachos, with yellow "topping," with gallon jugs of liquid sugar. They have the concentration of chess players, of athletes before contests, of the starving. Do you like this, the greedy scrabbling in greasy boxes, the whole herd determinedly chomping and chewing and slurping . . . don't you feel even a little bit as if you're in the pig barn, at exactly the moment the big trough full of ground intestines slops over for all to rush towards and snuffle in?

They will settle down, after 15 or 20 intense minutes. Once they have had their fill of trans fats, they wipe the chemical film from their faces and they start talking to each other. This is where my angst goes up a whole notch on the hystero-meter. Because I have been trying to distract myself from the nauseating smells and the comical cacophony of crunching by watching the slides on the screen. These slides test your knowledge of Hollywood stars. They are there to remind you of death, of your inevitable subsumption into the great terrifying artistic void that is movieland. They are there to remind you that you do actually know all the stars' names, even without wanting to: As soon as you see the blurry visage and the clue "went postal" you murmur, automatically, Kevin Costner, and then you are amazed at yourself. How do you know every Hollywood star's name? It has happened by osmosis; you are so immersed in it every day, like a nacho chip in a tub of yellow goop, that it has seeped into your pores.

Anyway. The slides are at least better than hearing your neighbours begin to talk. The sociological lessons learned from overhearing conversations in cinemas are even more depressing. One learns that most people like to communicate by announcing what food they like to eat and what food they don't like to eat. This is an interactive discussion: Each participant takes a turn. You may change the subject slightly in the second or third rounds—you may, for example, announce how tired you are today as compared to how tired you were yesterday or on Saturday, and then everyone may follow suit with similar admissions. This apparently amuses and interests most people, for it can go on for some time.

You will think that there is a merciful God when the lights finally dim, because the movie is about to start and save you from the insane boredom of your surroundings. But you will be very, very sadly mistaken. Because this is the beginning of the ads. These are ads you must watch. When you are watching television, you can change the channel during ads, you can get up and have a sherry. But here you are trapped, and the ads are amplified. Everyone sits docilely munching and slurping and watching extremely loud ads on a big screen for a half-hour. And they pay to do so. They pay to have various cheery jingles and swooshing automobiles blared at them for a half-hour. No one seems remotely uncomfortable or bored.

Who can make it this far into the movie-watching experience without being so agitated, so depressed, so foul-tempered that even the greatest masterpiece would not provide anything, at this point, remotely resembling pleasure? At this point I have wanted to leave for half an hour, and that desire to leave will simply continue for the length of the film.

7   I don't even need to go into how disappointing that great payoff invariably is. You've heard me on this before: It doesn't help that 90 per cent of
films shown here and discussed here are made by the great schmaltz factories, the megastudios of southern California. So that the great treat of this
experience, the feature presentation that is the point of all this suffering, is
going to contain a lot of very emotional music which lets you know when to
feel sad or happy or scared, and a lot of huge close-ups of the sad faces of
famous actors, and very probably a final scene with a sun-dappled forest
with a deer emerging to remind our characters of their natural wonder. . . .
(I'm thinking here of the film *Kinsey*, which I was persuaded to see because
otherwise intelligent critics, their minds numbed by exposure to schmaltz of
even more preposterous gooeyness, had proclaimed it brilliant, and which
turned out to be, of course, another Hollywood weeper made according to
the strictest rules of narrative convention.)

8   Honestly, why, why, why do we pay to have ads broadcast at us at insane
volume? Why do we pay to have productive hours of our lives removed and
replaced with the sameness, the predictability, the boredom of the grave?
Explain it to me.

Thinking Critically About Content

1. What is the narrator's mood in this article? Do the sounds, sights, and
   smells in the theatre affect his mood?

2. Find at least one detail for each of the five senses. Does Russell Smith
   draw on one sense more than another?

3. What does the author mean when he describes Hollywood studios as
   "schmaltz factories"?

Thinking Critically About Purpose and Audience

4. What dominant impression does Smith create in this essay?

5. Who do you think Smith's primary audience is?

6. In your opinion, does Smith intend to change his readers' minds or is
   he just letting off steam?

Thinking Critically About Paragraphs

7. Smith uses alliteration in several places (groups of words all starting
   with the same letter). What effect does this usage have on the reader?

8. The paragraphs in this essay follow a particular order. What is that
   order, and why is it used?

9. What is the topic sentence in paragraph 4? Do all the sentences in
   that paragraph relate to the topic sentence? Explain your answer.

10. Write a paragraph about an event that you did not enjoy. Make sure
    you use vivid descriptions about the parts of the event that bothered
    you. Feel free to rant!

Writing Topics: Describing

Before you begin to write, you might want to review the writing process in Part I.

1. In the first selection, Amy Tan draws on impressions from all the senses to show how her main character observes her new home. Think of a place that is very important to you, a place that is a part of your life now or that was part of your life in the past. Write a description of that place, drawing on as many of the senses as possible—seeing, hearing, touching, smelling, and tasting—so that your readers can experience this place the way you did.

2. How healthy are you? Write a description of the foods that you eat and the exercise that you get in a normal week. In what ways are you taking good care of yourself so that you have a chance for a long, healthy life?

3. What do you think are the most important features of a good description? Why are they important? What effect do they have on you?

NARRATING

In the following essays, the authors tell stories that are realistic and make a point. In "How Do I Look," Joan Clark writes about the effect of focusing on her own appearance. In "I Was a Teenage Hijabi Hockey Player," Sheema Khan, in reaction to implied stereotyping by co-workers, writes about her love of both playing and watching hockey.

Joan Clark

HOW DO I LOOK?

Focusing Your Attention

1. Do you consider that it is important for a woman (or a man, for that matter) to look her best? How much time do you spend grooming?

2. In the short story you are about to read, the title "How Do I Look" refers to the question the writer routinely asks her husband when they are about to go out. Have you ever asked this question? Would you expect or want an honest answer to this question if you asked it?

Expanding Your Vocabulary
The following words are important to your understanding of this essay.

nourished: well-fed in appearance (paragraph 3)

ambivalent: of two minds (paragraph 4)

rampantly: in an unrestrained or uncontrolled manner (paragraph 5)

verboten: German for *forbidden* (paragraph 6)

prostrations: lying face down, associated with worship (paragraph 7)

feckless: careless and irresponsible (paragraph 8)

discourse: discussion (paragraph 13)

pragmatic: practical, dealing with facts (paragraph 13)

When I was seventeen I began smearing cherry jelly bean on my lips in 1
lieu of the lipstick my father had forbidden me to wear because, he said, he did not want me looking like a hussy. I had come across the word "hussy" in my reading and knew it to be a woman with loose morals, a scarlet lady, a

trollop. I did not know why my father got it into his head that my wearing lipstick was immoral; my mother and older sister wore lipstick and their morals were far from slack. I did know that the notion came from my father's Cape Breton Presbyterianism and from a wish to protect me from overweening vanity. As my mother put it, he did not want to turn my head.

2   There was little danger of that. My parents rarely commented on my appearance except to caution me to stand up straight. Occasionally my mother would pass on a received compliment. The one I remember most clearly came from Mrs. Roper, the chinless, dumpy woman who worked in the stationery store that in our town passed as a bookstore. Mrs. Roper told my mother that I was better looking than I used to be.

3   Backhanded though this compliment was, I was grateful for it and did not stop to wonder what I used to look like before Mrs. Roper's comment. I did not dwell on the thought that my mother had not passed on a compliment so much as a sober observation of fact. Mrs. Roper's comment gave me hope. Tall and skinny—at five foot eight I weighed one hundred pounds—like many teenaged girls I nourished the secret hope that one day I could be beautiful.

4   This did happen once, on my high school graduation night. On that occasion my grandfather looked at the strapless dress of layered net my sister had sewn for me and called me a princess. Later the same night my sister's friend, Charlotte, said I looked beautiful. I put these words inside the fortune teller's ball where I stored my erratic and ambivalent stirrings for romance.

5   My father could not protect me from physical vanity. As soon as I set foot on the university campus I became rampantly vain. The presence, at last, of all those real men (older and, I thought, more experienced) set me to brushing my hair one hundred strokes a night, camouflaging pimples with beige acne cream, arranging my banlon sweater so that my breasts looked just so. All this fussing was time consuming, some of the sessions lasting up to half an hour. I was trying to achieve a look I hoped my father would approve of— a soft, natural beauty, nothing tartish or cheap. This was the Breck look of the shampoo ads, which aimed for an understated, virginal beauty.

6   Given the fact that I had little money, it would have been simpler to have abandoned lipstick, powder and blonde hair rinse and go on dates just as I was. Such a thought never occurred to me. This was, after all, the mating game, a game I enthusiastically embraced. I relished the complications of attaining beauty. And I believed that my looks could be improved by way of self-attention. Wasn't it logical that all those hours spent in front of the mirror would result in the enhancement of my appearance? These attentions were undertaken even if my date was a stroll alongside a brook or a ramble through an orchard. On those occasions I went for the casual, country look—the scarf or sweater contrived to look thrown on, ditto the artfully tousled hair. Fortunately I had "big" hair that lent itself to looking windblown. The women at my college continued this casual look throughout the winter; no matter how fierce the wind, wearing hats was verboten, coats were left unbuttoned, and even in the bitter cold our legs were bare (and blue). Not for us those ugly beige nylons.

There were of course lapses in these prostrations to vanity, if only   7
because I needed time to catch my breath and renew my resolve. These
plateaus of doubt usually came to me in the basement of the library where,
every morning by nine o'clock, I would be huddled against the radiator in
the theology reading room, beneath a small window through which I
watched the intermittent passage of feet—an occupation consistent with
reading Plato's *Allegory of the Cave*. I remember these interludes of reading
and study as hours of bliss: the smell of drying wool and dry books, the gulp-
ing of hot water pipes, the luminous rectangle of light falling on my page.

Though I was not interested in reading the theology books on the shelves   8
and was unacquainted with anyone who did, in the solitude of that room I
would sometimes imagine myself as the wife of a theologue or, even better,
a missionary. There I stood in an ill-fitting dress, my hair cropped short, my
face scrubbed and beaming as I strove to be of service to others and to God.
At other times I would imagine myself as a pure-hearted nun who had
given herself over to a life of contemplation and prayer. These imaginings
fed my appetite for melodrama. They were the Presbyterian version of
sackcloth and ashes, a reminder that my attentions to vanity, not to mention
men, were misguided and shallow. If I continued this folly, not only would
my grades suffer but, as my father feared, I would become a fallen woman
or—and this was far worse to my way of thinking—a dim-witted blonde.
Should I not reform before it was too late? Perhaps I ought to stop wearing
lipstick and powder altogether. Perhaps I ought to model myself after those
dowdy girls in residence who did not give their appearance a second
thought—girls who had so little vanity or self-preservation that they did not
often wash their hair. But these false aspirations and feckless doubts van-
ished the moment I was called to the telephone and asked for a date.

I continued to follow the slavish rituals of surface grooming until I mar-   9
ried and took myself out of the mating game. It came as a relief to slough
them off to make room for my new preoccupations. Except for a pass with
lipstick and comb, I was unwilling to give time to looking any better than I
did. In any case, within a few years of marrying I had children to look after;
there was no time for self-ministrations. Even a daytime bath was out of the
question. I barely had time to wash my hair, let alone use a blonde rinse.
Once I fell into writing, which I did after the birth of my eldest son, I was
unwilling to give leftover time to anything that did not feed the Word.

Which is not to suggest that my nods to vanity entirely disappeared.   10
When the doorbell rang I tied a kerchief over my unwashed hair, hooked my
bra and made a swipe with the lipstick. When I put on nylons, earrings and
dress before going out for the occasional evening, I would say to my husband, "How do I look?" My husband obligingly would tell me that I looked
fine or lovely or ravishing, whatever it took to get us out of the house on time.

After my children left home I had time—if I wanted to use it—to improve   11
my appearance. Now my efforts to improve were attempts to look not better
but younger, or at least not to look my age. I was not unhappy with my age,
but I began noticing that if I disclosed it I was treated differently, too often as

a matron or as somebody's mother. I was addressed as ma'am. I did not take kindly to this, not wanting to mother anyone except my children. I did not like the assumptions made about aging, especially the one articulated by writers and seized upon by critics that by age sixty a writer's best working years were over. It was not until I was confronted with ageism that I thought of attention to physical vanity as a strategy for survival.

12   By now, of course, I had met dozens of people who carried physical vanity further than I had ever been prepared to go: the glam who wouldn't dash to the superette without a forty-minute fine-tuning job; the woman who waited until after her lover fell asleep before removing eyelashes and wig; the man with gold medallions who had a chest-plate implant beneath his unbuttoned shirt. I had seen countless magazine makeovers and marvelled at the sacrifices that women especially were prepared to make at the altar of beauty: tooth filing and straightening, chin and eye tucks, silicone breasts and liposuctions, diet and exercise regimes intended to achieve twigginess. All of this made my father's old-fashioned attempts not to turn my head quaint and even touching, almost—though not entirely—beside the point.

13   The hole in my father's discourse is obvious. Contrary to leading to my downfall, physical vanity has probably done me more good than harm. My early efforts to improve my looks may not have been commendable but they were strategically sound. If I had known that at seventeen, I would have defied my father, bought a tube of Cherry Ripe and eaten the jelly beans. To a point, physical vanity is not only a pragmatic response to the realities with which we live and work, but is an incentive to take better care of our health. I suspect that being vain helps us live longer.

14   Nevertheless, when I apply lip liner and pluck chin hair, there is someone with me in the mirror, standing slightly behind me. She is wearing a baggy shirt to cover the bulge. Her grey hair is cropped short. She wears no eyeshadow or mascara. Her gaze is as clear and guileless as a nun's. She is waiting, though not with impatience. She knows that I am travelling steadily toward a room where the only objects on top of the dresser are a bar of soap, a toothbrush and a comb.

Thinking Critically About Content

1. Joan Clark opens her essay with a reference to comments by her father. Read the rest of the essay and note how many times she comes back to her father's opinion. Why do you think it matters to her?

2. In paragraph 9, the writer talks about the "slavish rituals of surface grooming" that she stops when she marries. Why does she use the word "surface" here? Explain your answer.

3. What is a "received compliment" and why does the author use that example to explain her mother to her readers?

Thinking Critically About Purpose and Audience

4. What do you think Clark's purpose is in this essay? Explain your answer.

5. What type of audience do you think would most understand and appreciate this recollection?

6. Paragraph 12 brings the reader into the present. What details in this paragraph underline the fact that the author is talking about the present?

Thinking Critically About Paragraphs

7. Paragraph 13 seems to be the real conclusion to the essay, referring back to the opening. Has the point the author makes in this paragraph been sufficiently signalled in the rest of the essay? Does it matter? Explain your answer.

8. What specific details does Clark use in paragraph 9? What do these details add to the paragraph?

9. What is the effect of the final paragraph in the essay?

10. Write a paragraph about the effect of comments that your parents made to you when you were younger, and describe how they have affected the way you perceive yourself now.

Sheema Khan

I WAS A TEENAGE HIJABI HOCKEY PLAYER

Focusing Your Attention

1. Do you have a sport that is totally in your blood and that you love to play as well as watch? What is that sport?

2. This narrative is about what it is like for a young Muslim woman to play hockey and have to convince others that she loves the rough and aggressive game. What is it about your sport that you love? Are you typical of the type of athlete that plays that sport? Does it matter, as long as you love to play?

Expanding Your Vocabulary

The following words are important to your understanding of this essay.

incredulously: disbelievingly (paragraph 1)

hijabis: women who wear the Muslim headscarf, or hajib (paragraph 1)

phenomenal: outstanding, extraordinary (paragraph 2)

zenith: the high point (paragraph 2)

hapless: unfortunate, without luck (paragraph 5)

teetotalling: abstaining from alcohol (paragraph 8)

wistfully: sad, yearning, thoughtful (paragraph 9)

prescribed: to establish rules (paragraph 10)

1   "When I used to play hockey," I began telling my co-workers over lunch. All of a sudden, eyes looked up in disbelief. "You played hockey?" asked a friend incredulously. "Yes," I replied with a smile, thinking, "Doesn't every Canadian play hockey at some point in their life?" And then it hit me. Muslim women, especially *hijabis*, aren't expected to be interested in sports, let alone play. Perhaps a calming sport like croquet. But hockey?

2   Come on! I grew up cheering the Montreal Canadiens. My allegiance to the Habs was minted during their phenomenal upset Stanley Cup win in 1971 that featured a law student/goalie named Ken Dryden (I still have his rookie card). My love of the game reached its zenith during that magical September of 1972. I still remember cheering passionately with the rest of my school when Paul Henderson scored in Game 8.

3   During the '70s, I, like many Montrealers, became spoiled by the Canadiens dynasty. Every May, my friends and I would line up on Ste-Catherine Street to see the "annual" Stanley Cup parade. One year, we lingered near City Hall, and were rewarded with meeting Bob Gainey, Yvan Cournoyer and Ken Dryden. My seven-year-old brother refused to wash his hand for days.

4   I grew up playing street hockey, driveway hockey and table hockey.

5   I was both Danny Gallivan and Yvan Cournoyer, describing the play-by-play of an electrifying rush leading to a goal with seconds left to play. At the time, there was no organized hockey for girls—only ringette. Later in high school, I found a recreational league and laced up every week. In one game, I had a breakaway from the blue line. I was Guy Lafleur, ready to swoop in on the hapless goalie. As I lunged toward the puck, I tripped over the pick of my figure skates, falling flat on my face. Goodbye, figure skates.

6   Once I bought my prized hockey skates, I had to learn to skate all over again (I kept falling over the front edges of my pick-less hockey skates). At McGill, I didn't have the talent to make the varsity women's team. So I played intramural hockey, joining a women's engineering team called the Tachyons (named after a subatomic particle by the lone physicist on the team). Some didn't know how to skate. But that never mattered. We just enjoyed the thrill of hockey. I still remember one pre-game warm-up when I was knocked out cold after colliding head-on with a player from the other team. We had both been skating at full speed in opposite directions, passing a puck the length of the rink to our respective teammates—heads down. You get the picture. Good thing we were playing the med-school team that night.

7   After moving to Boston for graduate school, I inquired about intramural hockey. There was a league for men, but none for women.

8   Why not start one? And so, a teetotalling Muslim Canuck introduced women's intramural hockey at Harvard. I was one of the few who could lift the puck off the ice. My friends from California and Florida seemed to have the most fun, even though few knew how to skate. It was the sheer thrill of playing hockey that brought out the smiles.

9   Now middle-aged, three pregnancies later, I look back wistfully at my hockey-playing days. I am not yet a hockey parent. If I do go down that

road, I will look to the example of Daniele Sauvageau—the legendary coach of the Canadian women's Olympic hockey team that won gold in 2002—for maintaining grace and poise under pressure.

I have found other Muslim women who share a passion for hockey, 10 including one friend who recently played for a varsity team in Alberta. On the ice, there was no problem (hockey equipment lends itself to maintaining modesty in attire, as opposed to, say, swimming). It was off the ice where negotiations were made in good faith. Teammates understood when she excused herself from beer excursions and the "girls' night out." They went out of their way to help her find a place to pray on road trips. But perhaps the most awkward issue she faced—and one that many observant Muslim women still face—was the casual nudity of the locker room. Modesty is prescribed in Islam, not merely between men and women, but between members of the same gender as well. Locker rooms, showers, open-concept washrooms—all pose challenges to Muslims. Those of us who play sports often dash in and out of dressing rooms, usually with our eyes glued to the floor.

It is now May, and our household sorely misses the National Hockey 11 League playoffs. Having completed a season of pond hockey, my kids and I are ready to play a few weeks of street hockey. The only difference from my childhood days is that now I imagine myself as Hayley Wickenheiser, scoring with only seconds left to play.

Thinking Critically About Content

1. What do Sheema Khan's co-workers assume about her athletic abilities?

2. Why does the author put quotation marks around the word "annual" in the third paragraph?

3. Khan now imagines herself as Hayley Wickenheiser when she plays road hockey. What change does this represent since the time she was a child?

Thinking Critically About Purpose and Audience

4. Why do you think Khan wrote this essay?

5. Who is Khan's primary audience?

6. The essay is full of examples of hockey games she has played. What is the effect of this use of examples?

7. The author is attempting to teach us about her part of the Canadian mosaic by showing how it operates within that most Canadian of activities, hockey. Do you feel that you learned something? Describe what you learned.

Thinking Critically About Paragraphs

8. In paragraph 10, which is longer than most of the other paragraphs, Khan writes more generally about Muslim women who

play hockey. Why is this paragraph placed toward the end of the essay? What is the effect?

9. Why does Khan focus on her current hockey games with her children in the final paragraph? Is this an effective conclusion?

10. Write a paragraph about a specific game you played at school. Use the first person and give specific, concrete details.

Writing Topics: Narrating

Before you begin to write, you might want to review the writing process in Part I.

1. Think about a time you participated in a team—either at a sporting event or for a school project. What did you learn about the way different people handle teamwork? Write a narrative on teamwork using your own experiences on the team.

2. Look at an old picture of yourself and imagine what you might have been thinking back then. Write a paragraph in the voice of the person you were then, using the present tense.

3. What do you think are the most important features of a good story? Why are they important? What effect do they have on you?

ILLUSTRATING

The two essays in this chapter show how authors use examples in essays. The first essay, "It's Not You, It's Me ... and You're Weird" by Leah McLaren, uses examples to catalogue types of attitude. In the second essay, "Goin' Down the Road," Jonathon Gatehouse uses statistics and personal stories to illustrate why people are leaving a small town in Newfoundland.

Leah McLaren

"IT'S NOT ME, IT'S YOU ... AND YOU'RE WEIRD"

Focusing Your Attention

1. Have you ever felt responsible for other people's actions? Has there been a time in your life when you realized some people are just different and there's nothing you can do about it? Have you ever felt as though things were awkward but the person you were with thought nothing of it?

2. The essay you are about to read illustrates how the "It's not you, it's me" attitude can affect one's life. Has it affected you in any way?

Expanding Your Vocabulary

The following words and names are important to your understanding of this essay.

David Miller: mayor of the city of Toronto (paragraph 2)

Dalton McGuinty: premier of Ontario (paragraph 2)

Michael Bloomberg: mayor of the city of New York (paragraph 2)

John Kerry: Democratic candidate who ran against George W. Bush and lost in the 2004 U.S. presidential election (paragraph 2)

lobotomize: surgical interruption of nerve tracts to and from the frontal lobe of the brain; often results in cognitive and personality changes (paragraph 3)

plight: predicament, situation from which escape is difficult (paragraph 3)

demented: affected with madness or insanity (paragraph 5)

subjectivity: judgment based on individual personal impressions, feelings, and opinions rather than external facts (paragraph 5)

eccentric: a person with an unusual or odd personality (paragraph 9)

pretense: pretending with intention to deceive (paragraph 10)

banal: obvious and dull (paragraph 10)

unpretentiously: understated; exhibiting restrained good taste (paragraph 10)

Hal Hartley: independent filmmaker whose deadpan "comedies" (e.g., *The Unbelievable Truth*) have become favourites with critics (paragraph 10)

1   "It's not you, it's me ..." is a phrase that everyone will utter—and have uttered back at them—at least once in his or her life. So mused the funny and insightful columnist Ben Rayner in the Toronto Star last Sunday. He's right, of course, but it got me to wondering. What about all the times in life when the opposite is true? When it's definitely *not* me, it's you.

2   Specifically, I was thinking of the guy who keeps leaving messages on my answering service at work imploring me, in the most heartbreakingly polite manner, to help him get out of the mental institution to which his parents recently had him committed. They're after his money, he says, and he wants me to let Mayor David Miller, Premier Dalton McGuinty, Michael Bloomberg and John Kerry know before it's too late.

3   He makes wry jokes about being lobotomized and always leaves a return phone number and the name of his doctor. He thinks I might already have heard about his plight because, in his mind, he's famous in the outside world. I've never called him back because I can't think of what to say, except that I hope he's okay, which, in light of what he's going through, seems pretty goddamn pathetic. The bottom line is, what can I do? It's not me, it's him.

4   He is a rather extreme example of what I [have] come to call the it's-not-me-it's-you type. Don't get me wrong, I'm not saying all such people are delusional. In some ways, they are saner than the rest of us. Allow me to explain.

5   The it's-not-me-it's-you people never make any effort to conceal their moods from the outside world. Like the rest of us, they exist entirely within the bounds of their own demented subjectivity, but, unlike the rest of us, they never bother to pretend otherwise. If they are annoyed, they grunt; if they are happy, they laugh and if they are feeling untalkative, you can't get a word out of them with a bottle of Scotch and a crowbar.

6   The it's-not-me-it's-you guy is the sort of person you are introduced to at a party and have a four-minute conversation with that leaves you feeling utterly confounded. For days afterward, you are left wondering: "What did I say to offend that man so badly that he walked over to the cheese board in the middle of our conversation?" Only later will it occur to you that he probably just wanted some cheese. Remember: It's not you, it's him.

7   While it's-not-me-it's-you people are difficult to get to know, once you befriend them, they can be the most fun people in the world to hang out

with. Once you recognize their strangeness for what it is—an inborn trait that has absolutely no reflection on your character whatsoever—you can relax and bask in the warm glow of their weirdness.

Take my friend Chris. The first time I met him, he took me to dinner at a Peruvian restaurant where we ate deep-fried potato wedges drowned in Cheese Whiz. It was unclear whether it was a date. I don't remember much about our conversation except that it was strangely disjointed. The oddness of the evening was aided by the incessant blaring of South American soap operas from the television in the corner. 8

I went home feeling as though I'd said something terribly wrong. But the next time I saw Chris, he seemed glad to see me and remarked on what a nice time he'd had. I realized that I had also had a nice time, and that the weirdness I'd felt was simply the way you feel around an eccentric person with whom you are not yet well acquainted. 9

There is no pretense toward normalcy with the it's-not-me-it's-you person. No plastering over holes in the conversation with banal small talk. No avoiding the issue, yet at the same time, no direct confrontation. Nothing is particularly obvious and nothing is particularly hidden. Time spent with them is just naturally, unpretentiously bizarre. The conversation is off-kilter, the silences awkward and plentiful. It's actually kind of fun, in a Hal Hartley movie kind of a way. 10

In our most pure and unselfconscious moments, all of us become this kind of person. When we are babies, for instance. Or when we are on the brink of death. Or if we are just very sleepy. These are the times when mood and identity are the least influenced by other people's behaviour. Whether we are at our best or our worst at these moments is incidental—the important thing is that we are being exactly who we are. Which is, uh, pretty strange. 11

The it's-not-me-it's-you person knows and follows the golden rule of all social situations: that above all, no one is thinking about you. Everyone else is thinking about themselves, just like you. 12

Not that the strangely abrupt ending of this column is you. No, I'm pretty sure this time it's me. 13

Thinking Critically About Content

1. What examples from this essay illustrate most clearly the "It's not me, it's you" attitude?

2. How are "It's not you, it's me" people saner than the rest of us? Do you agree with the author? Explain your answer.

3. Does the essay change the way you view the world? Would you rather be "It's not me, it's you" or "It's not you, it's me"? How did the essay affect your answer?

Thinking Critically About Purpose and Audience

4. Why did Leah McLaren write this article?

5. What type of audience would most understand and appreciate this essay?

6. Do you think the essay is successful? What would you change? Explain your answer.

Thinking Critically About Paragraphs

7. Examine paragraph 5. Is there an effective concluding sentence that reflects the topic sentence? Would you write something different? What would you write?

8. How does McLaren organize details in paragraph 10? Would you change anything? Explain your answer.

9. Which paragraph is the most illustrative? Why?

10. Write a paragraph describing an awkward "It's not you, it's me" situation that you once found yourself in.

Jonathon Gatehouse

GOIN' DOWN THE ROAD

Focusing Your Attention

1. Are you from a town that most people leave in order to find work? Are you from a town people move to in order to find work? How does this affect you?

2. The essay you are about to read illustrates the problems that the residents of Newfoundland face when trying to find employment in their own communities. Would you leave the place where you were born and raised in order to find work? Explain your answer.

Expanding Your Vocabulary

The following words are important to your understanding of this essay.

abide: put up with something or somebody unpleasant (paragraph 1)

expats: short form for *expatriates*; people who have left their home country to live and work in another country (paragraph 1)

perilous: fraught with danger (paragraph 3)

conceivably: within the realm of possibility (paragraph 3)

sentinel: lookout, a person employed to watch for something to happen (paragraph 3)

acronyms: abbreviations coined from the initial letter of each successive word in a term or phrase (e.g., RCMP) (paragraph 6)

sheath: protective covering (paragraph 11)

out-migration: emigration; migration from a place, especially from one's native country in order to settle in another (paragraph 12)

1   On a slate-coloured morning, the ladies down at Noseworthy's Grocery in Green Island Brook are ticking off the list of heartbreak and resignation.

"Denny went yesterday. Don Macey, Junior Macey, Ramsey and Ricky went last Thursday. Wilfred Hughes left on Monday. And there's three more truck-loads heading for Alberta after the weekend." Nobody's keeping a strict count anymore, but best estimates are 70 or 80 of the village's 200 remaining residents will be gone by the end of June, to look for work once the last of the lobster pots are pulled from the water. Some will come back in late fall, but each year more and more families decide they can't abide the months of separation. There's no one to buy your house, so you just lock it up, maybe put some boards on the windows as extra protection against the storms that whip across the Strait of Belle Isle. And join the thousands of other Newfoundland expats scattered across the country, with keys and memories stashed away in safe places.

A little distance along the gravel road, Wallace Hughes is sitting at his   2 kitchen table wondering if that's how his story will end too. "One winter is all it takes. Why come back home when you can go out there and work and have money?" He's spent the morning tying up loose ends, chopping wood, setting up a swing set in the front yard for his daughter. In a couple of days, he's joining the exodus, bound for Edmonton and a job labouring with a landscape crew. The ruddy-faced 47-year-old has never been away from home before, but there isn't much choice. Last summer, after years of strug-gle, he was forced to sell the takeout stand and arcade he had run for more than two decades. It's the same situation as his neighbour, who used to operate the town's only gas station. You just have to look across the harbour to the empty wharf and shuttered cod plant to see why. "Everyone fished. No one ever went away," Hughes says as he stares out the window. "It was that little bit of extra money in the summer that kept you going."

In the dozens of tiny communities that skirt the shore of the Northern   3 Peninsula—as if the original settlers, having survived the perilous cross-ing of the Atlantic, were content to cling to the New World's edges—it's a familiar tale. Nearly 20 per cent of the population has left over the last decade. The 20,000 who remain [are] now conceivably outnumbered by the moose that overrun the vast inland bush and stand sentinel every cou-ple of kilometres along the roadways. Over the past five years, Newfound-land's economy—fuelled by the Hibernia oil project off the Avalon Peninsula—has grown faster than that of any other province. But the boom towns are 12 hours away by car from the island's northern tip, where unemployment hovers around 24 per cent.

In Big Brook, the end has already come, with the last three families opt-   4 ing this past February for government relocation to be closer to schools, medical help and shopping. In other villages such as Grandois on the peninsula's eastern coast (pronounced "grand-eyes"—as with many spots on the former French Shore, not even vaguely like the language you learned in school), the ghost-town future is in sight.

It was home to approximately 100 when, right after Canada Day, 1992,   5 Fisheries Minister John Crosbie announced the closure—first "temporary," now quasi-permanent—of the cod fishery. Now, most of the homes have been abandoned, boats and nets left to rot on the landings. Cannibalized cars ("machines" in local parlance) sit rusting in the parking spaces next to the dormant processing plant. There are only four school-age children among the 14 remaining families. All 11 of Leo and Ida McGrath's kids have moved. "There used to be a time when you had to go just outside the harbour and drop your nets and they would be filled. The hills here were covered with drying fish," says the 67-year-old Leo, born and raised in Grandois, long before light and power, or even the road, arrived. "Now, it's not legal to go and get yourself one for the table."

6   It's not like governments, first the federal Conservatives, then the Liberals, didn't try to help. There have been a dizzying array of acronyms since some 40,000 people in the four Atlantic provinces and Quebec—30,000 of them in Newfoundland and Labrador—saw their livelihood drastically diminish or altogether disappear. Billions have been spent on emergency assistance and "transition" programs such as NCARP, AGAP, CFAR, and the granddaddy of them all, TAGS. But the people of the Northern Peninsula have little to show for it, despite steady representation at the cabinet table—Crosbie, then Brian Tobin, now Gerry Byrne, parliamentary secretary to the minister of health.

7   "It was the make-work syndrome," says Greg Mercer, a former provincial assistant deputy minister for intergovernmental affairs and once Tobin's chief fixer for the riding. "They were moving rocks from one side of the road to the other. It was something done to keep communities alive, but it's nothing that anybody would stand up and say they were proud of." People retrained for jobs that mostly didn't exist—at least not where they lived. Others just grimly concentrated on getting enough work to qualify for Employment Insurance. Hard choices delayed by hopes that the fishery would someday bounce back. "It's a real eye-opener, not just for rural Newfoundland but rural Canada," says Mercer. "The level of continuing support these people need versus the handouts we were giving them."

8   Along the wharves in Port au Choix, where the rich cod stocks and massive processing plant once provided residents with some of the highest per capita incomes in the country, there is more anger than gratitude. "The mainlanders talk about the money they sends down here," Dwight Spence says as he sprawls in the captain's chair of his 55-foot boat, the Cape Ashley. "But my God, look what we've been giving—trees, water, minerals, fish, oil—everything we got. Now, we're educating our young people and giving them one-way tickets out. Who benefits?"

9   A fisherman for 38 years, Spence made a solid living, employed several crew and never filed for EI during his first quarter-century in business. Now, as he watches the dock workers off-load the 40,000 pounds of shrimp in his hold, he's unsure if he will be able to make it to the end of the season to apply for his cheques. Three days of back-breaking work, 100 km out and back with a full catch, and he probably won't break even.

10   Too many communities now fight for a share of the ever-shrinking pie. Quotas for crab, turbot, shrimp and halibut are spread thinly over Atlantic Canada, and the seasons are shorter than ever. The world market is flooded, prices are a fraction of what they used to be, fuel and insurance

costs have skyrocketed. Who's to blame? Spence isn't the type to sheath his sharp tongue. Politicians set the quotas, make the trade-offs, pay people to sit at home, keep hope alive where it should have died. "We've been mismanaged," he says. "Sold out. We've been traded for every other commodity in the world. And we're left here poor as piss."

Twelve per cent of Port au Choix's population has left since 1996. The local 11 fish plant, which once operated almost year-round and employed 450, is now open for a few weeks each summer and has work for only 150. And like the whole peninsula, the town is greying at an alarming rate. The remaining workers are in their 40s or 50s, and their children leave when they graduate (the nearest high school is now nine kilometres away). Vachon Noel, 28, Port au Choix's mayor, is an exception. He can count on one hand the members of his high-school graduating class who remain. Friends—two retrained as millwrights, the other as a carpenter—will soon leave because they can't find work. "You just can't make a sensible income," he says. "There are so many opportunities abroad, why would you stay home?"

There are bright spots on the peninsula. St. Anthony is constructing a 12 new $10-million cold storage facility that should see business at its locally owned fish plant expand—a major turnaround less than two years after Mayor Ern Simms staged a mock funeral for the town to protest the loss of a crab licence. Rocky Harbour, in the heart of Gros Morne National Park, already attracts 150,000 visitors a year, and is building for more. The Dark Tickle Company in St. Lunaire-Griquet, which makes gourmet jams and other products, is exporting around the world. But the economy still rises and falls with the tide of the fishery. And despite the out-migration of close to 15,000 people over the last decade, the government buzzword "sustainability" seems a long way off.

Judy Tucker and Edna Hedderson used to earn a decent living boning 13 and filleting cod. When the fishery shut down, they lost their jobs, as did their husbands. Both women received assistance money and retraining. Judy ended up clearing walking trails on a program that lasted just long enough to give her the 14 qualifying weeks for EI. Edna found a part-time spot as a home-care assistant, earning barely enough to cover the cost of gas. In 2000, they landed positions as Vikings at Norstead, a recreation of a Norse village the local tourist authority opened across the road from the L'Anse aux Meadows national historic site. Judy now spends her summers in a smoky longhouse, chatting with tourists and cooking over an open-pit fire. Edna makes pottery in an outdoor kiln. Their new jobs don't pay as much as the fish plant in St. Anthony did, but it's a living—and a second income that their families sorely need to survive. "You can get by on a little here," says Edna. "We own our own homes. We get a lot of food from the sea. And moose and wild game from the bush. We make our own bread." Judy giggles. "We live like the Norsemen—off the land."

There aren't many left in their communities—just 30 people in L'Anse 14 aux Meadows where Judy lives, and only 18, mostly elderly households, in Edna's home of Hay Cove, the next village over. The spot where the first European settlers arrived 1,000 years ago is slowly emptying out. The tourists come in increasing numbers each summer to learn about Canada's ancient past. Someday soon they might need a recreated village to show how Newfoundlanders used to live, too.

Thinking Critically About Content

1. What is the main concern for people in Newfoundland? Why has 20 per cent of the population left?

2. How does closing a fishery affect the people of Newfoundland? What are some examples of ways people have tried to cope with the closings?

3. Why would people stay? Would you stay? Where would you go? What if you had family to worry about, too? Explain your answer.

Thinking Critically About Purpose and Audience

4. What is Jonathon Gatehouse's purpose in writing this essay?

5. Who is the primary audience?

6. What examples convince you that there is a problem in Newfoundland?

Thinking Critically About Paragraphs

7. Examine paragraph 1. Does the topic sentence reflect the concluding sentence? Do the support sentences support the topic? Explain your answer.

8. Which paragraph do you think is the most illustrative of the population leaving Newfoundland? Explain your answer.

9. Examine paragraph 4. What would you add or delete in order to make it a better structured illustrative paragraph? Explain your answer.

10. Write a paragraph illustrating what a historian might say about your town when looking back from the future.

Writing Topics: Illustrating

Before you begin to write, you might want to review the writing process in Part I.

1. Different attitudes make relationships interesting. Use examples to illustrate different attitudes among your friends.

2. What are some attractions that keep people in your hometown? Use examples to illustrate why you would want to stay, even if there was little employment.

3. What do you think writers should consider first when choosing examples to support a topic sentence? Why are these criteria most important when working with examples?

ANALYZING A PROCESS

CHAPTER **24**

The following essays explain different events or processes; in other words, they tell you how to do something or how something happened the way it did. The first, "A Financial Primer for New Graduates with Loans" by James Daw, offers practical suggestions for getting and staying out of debt. It demonstrates how to do something. "How We Kept the Farm" by Eugene Warwaruk explains the lengths a family went to to keep their farm from creditors. It demonstrates the how-something-happened process analysis.

James Daw

A FINANCIAL PRIMER FOR NEW GRADUATES WITH LOANS

Focusing Your Attention

1. Think of a time when you had to explain to someone how to do something. Was the task difficult or easy? Did the person understand and follow your directions?

2. In the process analysis essay you are about to read, the writer tells us how to manage money and control debt. Do you manage your money efficiently? Have you ever been in debt? Do you know how to avoid debt?

Expanding Your Vocabulary

The following words are important to your understanding of this essay.

inclination: an attitude of mind, especially one that favours one alternative over others (paragraph 8)

consolidate: unite into one (paragraph 16)

1   A second-year law student expects to have about $78,000 in loans when she graduates, and she wonders how to plan for her future.

2   Debt repayment will be her primary focus for several years. A home, car, family, investments and retirement planning can come later. But these goals will be easier to achieve if she handles her debts well, and quickly.

3   She will have about $30,000 in government student loans, a professional line of credit of $43,000 and an interest-free family loan of $5,000.

4   Students typically have up to 10 years to repay their government loans, and five years to repay a bank credit line. Special concessions are available in special cases. Some professional schools may offer bursaries, interest relief, promissory notes or other assistance for those in difficult financial straits. All of these options should be explored where necessary.

5   But this particular law student—let's call her Sarah—expects to make $67,000 as an articling student with a major firm, and more if she is hired after being called to the bar.

6   So she should be able to handle the minimum annual payments of about $14,000 at today's low interest rates, plus make extra payments that will reduce her total interest costs. (See www.canlearn.ca for a student loan calculator and other information.)

7   The trick for graduates is to live like a student as long as they can after graduation in order to put themselves on a sound financial footing.

8   "You live like a student for so long, the first inclination when you get out is to start living," says Murray Baker of Vancouver, the author of The Debt-Free Graduate, How To Survive College Or University Without Going Broke (Money Smarts: $16.95). "But if you graduate with a lot of student debt, you may have to delay that a little bit longer."

9   Graduates who rush out to buy a car and new furniture on credit will hem themselves in, warns Baker. If they hate their new job, or the employer hates them, they may owe more than the possessions are worth to sell.

10   Certain additional expenses cannot be avoided. For example, a job with a major law firm will likely require fancier clothes than law school. But used clothing stores that sell on consignment, Value Village stores located near well-to-do neighbourhoods and warehouse outlets can help keep down costs.

11   Other strategies include living close to your job to save on transportation costs, sharing accommodation, car pooling or joining and renting occasionally from one of a growing number of auto co-operatives.

12   Some tips on paying debt are offered by Baker and by Bradley Roulston of MAP Inc. in Mississauga, a certified financial planner, chartered life underwriter and contributor to Educating Youth, A Tool Kit For Secondary Students available at www.cfp-ca.org.

13   Always make the minimum loan payments or you could endanger your future access to credit. This could prevent you from making major purchases, acquiring a cellphone or setting up a business or independent practice.

14   Approach family about putting up security to hold down interest costs, and talk to the lender about other ways to reduce costs, such as debt consolidation.

15   Use extra cash to pay the loan with the highest interest rate first. Pay credit cards before credit line loans, and government student loans last. Pay student debts before worrying about retirement savings.

16   Do not consolidate the government student loan with other debt. Your repayment schedule will be less flexible, and you will lose the non-refundable tax credit on interest. In Ontario, the tax credit provides a refund of about 21.3 per cent of the interest cost.

Once a graduate enters the workforce, the ability to earn income 17
becomes his or her most important asset. It's that asset that gives banks the
confidence to lend such large sums without security. One of the greatest
risks to losing that asset will be disability. So the graduate should take
steps to protect against a temporary loss of income through the purchase
of disability insurance.

Roulston recommends graduates see a certified financial planner soon 18
after starting a new job to plan for retiring debts, and setting priorities for
meeting future goals and managing the risks of adult life.

Most planners will offer a free consultation, which gives both the plan- 19
ner and the client time to assess their compatibility.

A fee-only planner might charge as little as $250 to $500 to provide a grad- 20
uate with a written plan, while a planner who relies on sales commissions for
income may do a plan for free in the hope of obtaining business later.

You can find a list of CFPs working in your area and their method of 21
compensation at www.cfp-ca.org, the Web site of their professional over-
sight body, the Financial Planners Standards Council.

Thinking Critically About Content

1. Why should you still live like a student after you graduate? What are
   some ways you can keep down costs?

2. Why should you always make the minimum loan payments? How
   could your future be affected?

3. Why should you not consolidate your government loans with other
   debts?

Thinking Critically About Purpose and Audience

4. What is James Daw's purpose in writing this article?

5. Who do you think Daw's audience is? Did he write the article in a
   way that it can reach his target audience?

6. Which guidelines are most likely to help you now and in the future?
   Explain your answer.

Thinking Critically About Paragraphs

7. Often when describing a process, the writer gets lost in telling the
   reader the steps of the process and forgets about proper paragraph
   structure. Do you see any evidence of this in Daw's article? What
   would you do to improve the paragraph structure in Daw's article?
   Explain your answer.

8. Choose several steps and put them into one paragraph. Add a topic
   and concluding sentence. Do you feel this new paragraph helps the
   process or hinders it? Explain your answer.

9. Is the order of guidelines well organized? Would you change anything? Explain your answer.

10. Write a paragraph to explain the process you go through to save (or
    not save) money.

Eugene Warwaruk

HOW WE KEPT THE FARM

Focusing Your Attention

1. What lengths would you go to to save your family home/business/ farm …?

2. The following essay shows what four brothers did to save the family farm. Have you ever done jobs that you didn't like in order to reach a goal?

Expanding Your Vocabulary

The following words are important to your understanding of this essay.

reservoir: a large or extra supply of something (paragraph 4)

confidants: people to whom private matters are confided (paragraph 9)

metaphor: a figure of speech in which an expression is used to refer to something that it does not literally denote in order to suggest a similarity (paragraph 11)

1   It was always a fight. It seemed every night a different creditor would call, and Dad would do his best to explain why he couldn't pay the bill. Crowded around the table, we ate supper silently, listening as he pleaded for more time. Then he would sink into his chair and try to muster the appetite to eat his cold food. I felt sick with despair, jumping when he snapped at Mom for having supper late again. Everyone knew that with seven kids to look after, it was a miracle anyone ate before 9 p.m.

2   The bank lent Dad tons of money to raise cattle through the 1970s on our farm near Erickson, Man. Feeding cattle was like playing the stock market. What was lost on one bunch was made up on the next. Then the market nose-dived—while Dad bought a big bunch of calves at $1.35 per pound. Selling at 72 cents per pound, we lost $110,000. That was 1981.

3   Every spring through the '80s, Dad somehow convinced the bank to give us another chance. By the time we got the money, the planting season was so late that the crop froze, so we would harvest the following spring, pushing that year back. And so the cycle continued.

4   Farmers need a deep reservoir of hope. Dad was no different. He looked forward to every harvest with a renewed sense of optimism. "Looks like a bumper crop this year," he'd say. "You'll see, this year's going to be different."

5   My older brothers, Chris and Lawrence, and I had questions and doubts. Do I even want to farm? How can we buy fuel, or groceries? If you'd handled it this way, we wouldn't be in this mess. Everyone pointed fingers. Sometimes I wondered if I could last much longer in all the negativity.

6   Mom also had a deep reservoir of hope, but it was for her family and her marriage. The farm crisis took a terrible toll on two people already suf-

fering from loneliness and lack of communication. Mom and Dad finally separated in 1989.

My youngest brother Eric, fiercely independent, went off to university   7
with his Governor General's Medal for academic excellence. Chris and Lawrence chose to stay, accepting that if they left, there would be no farm to come back to. As a middle child, I felt like I was the glue, keeping everyone together. I was painfully aware that if any of us got discouraged enough to quit, it would all be over.

In '93, it was all over. Almost. Buried under a mountainous debt, we   8
faced an impossible decision. Too proud to give up and move on, we leased our land from our lender, hoping to save up enough money to buy it back. We were allowed one five-year term to do it, with one three-year extension.

In the midst of all this, Lawrence, Chris and I made ends meet somehow.   9
We worked together market gardening, picking small spruce trees and growing gourmet potatoes. That led to a concession trailer. We served burgers, fries and ice cream all over southern Manitoba in '97 and '98. Driving from festival to festival, we laughed and argued, schemed and reminisced. We were brothers, partners, confidants and best friends.

But by the fall of '98, with Eric finishing a film degree and me enrolled in a   10
journalism course, we were all slowly drifting away, along with the dwindling hope of saving that farm. We, "the boys," needed a new project—and against all advice, decided to open a café in Winnipeg. Lawrence and Chris moved into the one-bedroom apartment Eric and I shared. The four of us worked feverishly for five months. Eric pulled out his Latin dictionary to find a name.

Lux Solé Café opened in March, 1999. Meaning "Light from the Sun"   11
(we had to add the accent on Sole so people would pronounce it properly), it was a perfect metaphor to connect our rural roots with the homemade food we served. A friendly neighbourhood took us under its wing and our reputation spread throughout the city. Everyone asked how four farm boys landed in a funky café. "It's a long story," I would grin.

But the farm was running out of time. The deadline to buy it back was   12
December, 2000. Our only asset was our restaurant. Lux Solé was like a colt gingerly taking its first steps. Our family depended on it the way we had depended on the farm. Would that farm ruin us one more time?

I made the call. I showed our banker, Rob, how four brothers poured   13
their lives into this 50-seat café—as they had poured their lives into a farm. If we could mortgage the restaurant, I told him, we could buy our farm back.

As November, 2000, loomed, Chris and I happened to be in the tiny   14
office in Lux Solé's basement when Rob called. All I remember saying is, "Great, I'll be down to sign everything" as evenly as I could. Looking at Chris, I saw my tears reflected in his eyes. We called upstairs to tell everyone it was a go. Then we called Dad at home on the farm.

I helped Chris and Lawrence open a second location, Lux Solé Down-   15
town, in March, 2001. And Dad, now 63, harvested a bumper hay crop last fall.

Originally published in Maclean's *in 2002. Eugene Warwaruk and his brothers still operate Lux Solé, with future franchise plans, while maintaining the family farm.*

Thinking Critically About Content

1. Did each brother want to be a farmer? Why did the brothers want to save the farm?

2. How did finances affect the family? Was a "reservoir of hope" enough in the end?

3. How was the café a perfect metaphor?

Thinking Critically About Purpose and Audience

4. What do you think is the purpose of this essay?

5. Who would be the most interested in this essay?

6. Is the opening description of the dad trying to pay the bills an effective way of getting the reader's attention? Explain your answer.

Thinking Critically About Paragraphs

7. How do paragraphs 8–11 demonstrate how something happened? Which of these four paragraphs best describes this process? Explain your answer.

8. Look closely at paragraph 12. Is it properly structured? What parts are effective? What parts are ineffective? Explain your answer.

9. Does each paragraph have an effective topic sentence? Which ones would you change? Why?

10. Imagine your ultimate dream in life. What would you do to attain that dream? Answer in paragraph format.

Writing Topics: Analyzing a Process

Before you begin to write, you might want to review the writing process in Part I.

1. In the first essay, James Daw discusses different ways a graduate can pay down debt. Does living like a student as long as you can after graduation seem like a reasonable solution to student debt? What steps do you hope to take in order to pay down debt after graduation?

2. Think of something in life that you want as much as the brothers in Warwaruk's essay wanted to keep their farm. Then explain your plan for achieving this goal or accomplishing this mission you have set for yourself.

3. Which type of process analysis do you find more interesting— how-to essays or background explanations? Explain your answer.

COMPARING AND CONTRASTING

The following essays show how comparison and contrast work in a complete essay. The first, "London in My Life" by David Suzuki, is from Suzuki's book *Time to Change*. The second, "From Wretched Ugliness to Glamour Doll-dom" by Zebedee Nungak, discusses the perceived beauty of Inuit women from 150 years ago to the present day.

David Suzuki

LONDON IN MY LIFE

Focusing Your Attention

1. Have you ever been back to a place that you used to live in years ago and noticed how much it had changed? Were the changes for the better? Were you sorry to see some of the changes?

2. In the essay you are about to read, the writer compares and contrasts various characteristics of London, Ontario, in the fifties with the modern-day city. What do you think are some of the differences? What are the similarities?

Expanding Your Vocabulary

The following words are important to your understanding of this essay.

sustained: supported or maintained (paragraph 1)

sanctity: sacredness, holiness (paragraph 2)

sequestered: removed, set apart (paragraph 3)

assimilation: the process whereby a minority group adopts the customs of the prevailing culture (paragraph 3)

sterile: lacking imagination or vitality (paragraph 11)

estranged: cut off from, alienated (paragraph 11)

bittersweet: producing a mix of pain and pleasure (paragraph 17)

Having passed the half century mark in age, I have reluctantly and with 1
astonishment become a member of the elders in society. As I reflect on the changes that have happened during the brief span of my family's and my

own life here, it becomes clear that the enormous changes in that time cannot be sustained. All across the planet, people in towns and cities undergoing explosive growth in population and economic development have reason to pay attention to the experience of their elders.

2   My grandparents were driven out of Japan by poverty at the beginning of this century and came to Canada to seek their fortune. They had no intention of staying in what they considered a primitive and backward country. All they wanted was some of its wealth to take back home. My grandparents were aliens in an unfamiliar landscape with which they had no historical or cultural link, let alone a sense of reverence for its sanctity. Instead, Canada to them represented an opportunity, the land was a commodity full of resources to exploit. My grandparents became a part of a massive assault on the "New World" initiated by Columbus's arrival and causing vast ecological and human catastrophe.

3   Following the Second World War, my family moved to Ontario, the industrial heartland of Canada and the most populous province in the country. First in Leamington, then London, I grew up in a land named after the homelands of the European settlers. There were few reminders that this area had long been occupied by people with proud histories, people who had been mistakenly labelled "Indians" by the newcomers. But lumped together as red Indians were dozens of nations, including Algonquins, Mohawks, Cree, and Ojibway. Today, most aboriginal people of Canada are invisible, sequestered on reserves or extinguished through forced assimilation.

4   In London, we lived on the northwest edge of town next to the railway tracks along whose banks I would pick asparagus in the spring and hunt for insects in summer. One year I worked on a vegetable farm only a kilometre or so down the railway line. A few blocks east of our house was the Thames River, which was full of catfish, carp, bass, and sunfish, which I would catch for my family to eat. The first softshell turtle I ever saw was in the Thames. In the spring, striped bass, pickerel, and pike would jam the river on their way to spawning grounds.

5   Bicycling west on Oxford Street, I would quickly run out of pavement and hit the gravel road. In about 20 minutes, I'd be at my grandparents' four-hectare farm at the end of Proudfoot Lane. But first I'd always stop at the large swamp beside the road to look for frogs, snakes, and damselflies. Many times I returned home with boots full of mud and bottles with frog eggs and dragonfly larvae. The woods surrounding the swamp always beckoned with the promise of a glimpse of a fox, skunk, raccoon, or owl.

6   My grandparents' farm was a child's paradise. Besides large vegetable and berry patches to be raided, there were several hundred chickens to be fed, eggs to be gathered, and fences mended. At the end of the fields, a creek ran year-round. That was where I dipped for darters, discovered freshwater clams, and hunted snails. In the fields, pheasants tooted like trains, groundhogs sunbathed in front of their burrows, and hawks skimmed above the ground in search of rodents.

In the 35 years since my boyhood, the Thames River has been saturated   7
with industrial effluent and agricultural runoff accumulating along its
length. The river was too convenient for dumping garbage and chemical
wastes. Now there are few clams, crayfish, or minnows to be seen. Lon-
doners today recoil at any suggestion of eating fish from the Thames or
asparagus from the tracks.

When I arrived in London in 1950, its population was just over 90,000.   8
Five years later, we were proud when the city passed 100,000. By 1960, it
had almost doubled to over 185,000 and reached a quarter of a million 10
years after that. Today, London boasts 300,000 people. This spectacular rate
of growth was accompanied by a booming economy and a sense of civic
pride. But at what cost?

The road to my grandparents' farm is now a wide highway, with the city   9
extending all the way to the village of Byron. My grandparents' farm is
occupied by a cluster of high-rise apartments, while the creek has been
tamed to run through culverts. My beloved swamp is covered by an
immense shopping mall and parking lot, while the woods beside it have
given way to a huge housing complex. Along the Thames River and all
around the city, once-productive agricultural land has been converted to
housing subdivisions.

Within my lifetime, the ecological devastation has been massive. But   10
when my grandparents immigrated to North America, the real holocaust
had already occurred. Only 200 years ago, Ontario was covered by a
dense, ancient forest, the plains of the midwest reverberated under the
hooves of 60 million bison, while the skies were darkened for days on end
when billions of passenger pigeons passed by. By the beginning of this century, they were all gone, yet we have learned little from that unprecedented
ecological annihilation and continue our destructive rampage so that we
can see the destruction going on before our eyes.

In the topsy-turvy world of economics, farmland, swamps, woods,   11
rivers, and ponds adjacent to expanding cities acquire value that makes it
inevitable for them to be developed. So the animals and plants that belong
there disappear, leaving our children to grow up in an increasingly sterile
human-created environment. And with diminished opportunities to experience nature, our future generations become all the more estranged from
the real systems that support their lives.

My hometown of London is a microcosm of what has been happening   12
around the planet, but particularly in the New World and especially since
the Second World War. Seen from a plane above Canada today, the country is crisscrossed by geometric straight lines of highways and rectangles of
clear-cuts and agricultural fields. Everywhere the imprint of human beings
has been stamped on the land in mathematical precision that pays no
attention to geographic and biological realities. We act as if our political
subdivisions of the land are meaningful and fail to observe the realities of
"bioregions," ecosystems and watersheds to which living things have
evolved and fit.

13   Our alienation from the land is so great that we have no sense that it is sacred or that our ability to exploit it is a great privilege accompanied by responsibility. Impelled by our faith in our technological prowess and scientific knowledge, we assault the planet as if it is limitless and endlessly self-renewing. Like an exotic species introduced to a new environment, we feel no natural restraints, only the deadly belief that all of nature is there for us to use as a resource in any way we wish.

14   This story was repeated in different parts of the world. Driven by a profound disconnection from the land, newcomers sought to tame it and its human and nonhuman occupants. The combination of technological power and the Western attitude of rightful dominion over nature was unstoppable. That has been the legacy passed on to the present time.

15   Seen from another perspective, beginning with respect for the unique flora and fauna of the continent and extending to the indigenous people whose cultures were so exquisitely evolved to live in rich harmony with the land, technological optimism and economic greed of the invaders become a policy that is shortsighted and arrogant.

16   It can be argued that one of the great tragedies that led to the current crisis in wilderness destruction was the attempt by colonizing peoples to re-create their familiar European surroundings in alien lands. In Canada and Australia, forests, grassy plains, and swamps were forced to resemble bits of home. And the introductions of species such as sparrows, foxes, and rabbits were ecological catastrophes.

17   Each visit to my childhood roots becomes a bittersweet mix of memories that remind me of the price we have paid for the way we now live.

Thinking Critically About Content

1. What do you think David Suzuki means when he says of his grandparents, "the land was a commodity full of resources to exploit"?

2. The word *holocaust* has been the target of much discussion and debate (see Dictionary.com). Suzuki uses it in paragraph 10 to describe ecological devastation. Is this a fair use of the word? Explain why or why not.

3. Have you seen in your own lifetime the kind of changes Suzuki refers to? Do you agree or disagree with Suzuki that these changes are devastating?

Thinking Critically About Purpose and Audience

4. Why do you think Suzuki wrote this essay?

5. Who would be most interested in this essay?

6. Who would be likely to disagree with the essay? Explain your answer.

7. Suzuki uses the city of London, Ontario, to make his case. However, the last few paragraphs broaden out to the rest of the world. What is the effect of this technique?

Thinking Critically About Paragraphs

8. If a paragraph is unified, all of its sentences refer to the idea expressed in the topic sentence. In paragraph 6, four sentences follow the topic sentence. How do these four sentences relate to the paragraph's topic sentence?

9. Suzuki uses a narrative style throughout the essay. Is this a good style for an essay that depends on comparison and contrast to make its point?

10. Write a paragraph about a visit to your own grandparents' home, comparing it to your own home.

Zebedee Nungak

FROM WRETCHED UGLINESS TO GLAMOUR DOLL-DOM

Focusing Your Attention

1. How do we determine who is beautiful and who isn't? Does the Barbie doll represent a realistic ideal of beauty in a multicultural country like Canada?

2. In the essay you are about to read, the author questions both historical and current ideals of beauty. Why do we find certain looks beautiful? Does society play a part in how we feel?

Expanding Your Vocabulary

The following words are important to your understanding of this essay.

unadorned: without decoration or makeup (paragraph 2)

reflective: thoughtful (paragraph 3)

irresistible: having an overpowering appeal (paragraph 7)

The recently announced creation and marketing of an Inuk Barbie doll has triggered some questions within me. It has also reminded me of the vivid, plain, uncomplimentary descriptions of Inuit women by a series of Qallunaat (white) explorers who first encountered Inuit in their natural "uncivilized" state. 1

From the raw, unadorned impressions of Inuit women as wretchedly unattractive to the glamour of mass market doll-ery is a great leap by any measure. 2

First, though, the questions: Will the doll's name still be Barbie? And, if so, who determined that Barbie is a typical name for an Inuk woman? Will its body proportions merely follow the standard tall, slender, leggy Barbie of the Qallunaat ideal of beauty? Or will Inuk Barbie be reflective of bodily reality, and therefore be more chunky? Will there be an Inuk Ken doll to fol- 3 low? Why will Inuk Barbie be available only in Canada? Isn't Eskimo beauty good enough for export outside Canada?

4   Now, consider what some Qallunaat explorers in the Arctic had to say about Inuit women: British explorer Sir John Ross, visiting an Eskimo encampment on Boothia Peninsula, Jan. 10, 1830, wrote: "The females were certainly not beautiful but they were at least not inferior to their husbands, and were not less well behaved ... one girl of thirteen was even considered to have a pretty face."

5   American explorer E.K. Kane, in High Arctic Greenland in 1853–55, came up with a uniquely contradictory description of one particular Eskimo woman: "Six Esquimaux, three of them women,—that ugly beauty, Nessark's wife, at the head of them,—had come off to the boats for shelter from the gale."

6   American polar explorer Robert Peary had this to say about Inuit women in 1909: "The accomplishments of the Eskimo woman are of the useful rather than the ornamental kind.... As the Eskimos are not highly romantic, a woman's skill in dressing skins and in making clothes largely determines the quality of husband she is likely to get. The Eskimo men have not a very critical eye for feminine beauty, but they are strong in appreciation of domestic accomplishments."

7   Earlier, in 1894, Peary described a woman who was the subject of duels of strength among some Inuit men: "Ahtooksungwah ... had a form like a walrus. Her glistening face was considerably broader than it was long, she stood about four feet six inches high, and weighed about three hundred pounds, her figure resembling a number of stuffed pillows fastened together. To my mind, her curves were a trifle heavy, but she evidently realized the Eskimo ideal of beauty, and being a widow besides, she was irresistible. Many were her suitors."

8   So here we have a teenaged girl noted for possessing the unusual novelty of a pretty face, a woman specifically described as being an "ugly beauty", and an irresistible Eskimo beauty ... who had the form of a walrus, with a figure resembling a number of stuffed pillows fastened together! None of this is anywhere near talking about future Barbie dolls!

9   Peary and most of the Qallunaat who made first contact with Inuit went out of their way to take note of the perceived lack of physical beauty among Inuit women. Contrary to this impression, though, some Inuit women were desirable enough to conceive children with. Peary himself fathered children by an Inuk woman, and he certainly was not the only one. In Canada, about 40 to 45 per cent of Inuit can trace some Qallunaat ancestry, which is plentiful testimony that not all Inuit women were repulsive in appearance.

10   Beauty, it is said, is in the eye of the beholder. And ugliness, where observed, must definitely be relative. Why do we now have so many Qallunaat ningauk's (sons and brothers-in-law), who have taken Eskimo wives? Has there been a beauty evolution among our women in the 400-plus years since Qallunaat have been around?

11   Or, Qallunaat standards have shifted and corrected themselves to a reality more accurate than the times when ugliness of Eskimo women was grossly misdefined to be the rule and not the exception.

On the other hand, not an ugly Qallunaat woman appeared in the 12 Arctic for ages! Arnaapik, or fair woman, was a common nickname for many of them. It has taken a longer while for Qallunaat women to be "wife-able" by Eskimo men, but there are now many more than a handful of them, all lovingly called ukuak (daughter-in-law)!

The transformation of Inuit women from savage ugliness to Barbie doll- 13 dom should be tracked in documentary detail. This work would be a perfect opportunity for collaboration by Eskimologists (those who study Inuit ways), and Qallunologists (those who study Qallunaat ways).

They will likely discover that reality resides somewhere between all 14 Eskimo women being ugly and all Qallunaat women being beautiful.

Thinking Critically About Content

1. In which paragraph can you find the controlling idea or thesis of this essay?

2. Are you surprised by the comments in the quotations the author uses from 150 years ago? Explain your answer.

3. In paragraph 12, Zebedee Nungak writes that it took a long time for white women to be considered "wife-able" in the Arctic. What do you think he means?

Thinking Critically About Purpose and Audience

4. Why do you think Nungak wrote this essay?

5. Who do you think is the primary audience for this essay? Does the tone Nungak uses relate to the probable audience? How?

6. Nungak asks many rhetorical questions in his writing (questions with no answers). For example, he asks, "Has there been a beauty evolution among our women in the 400-plus years since Qallunaat have been around?" Why do you think he uses this technique? Was is the effect?

7. What is the tone of paragraph 13? Do you think such a person as a Qallunologist exists? If not, why has Nungak invented the word to use here?

Thinking Critically About Paragraphs

8. Underline all the transitional words or phrases in the essay. Do these words and phrases help move the reader from one paragraph to another? Explain your answer. (Refer to page 38 for information on transitions.)

9. Nungak's tone is often ironic. Find examples and explain how the irony works.

10. *Eskimo*, *Inuit*, and *Inuk* are all used by the author to describe his people. Does the essay make the different meanings of these terms clear to you? Do an online search and write a paragraph comparing and contrasting these terms.

Writing Topics: Comparing and Contrasting

Before you begin to write, you might want to review the writing process in Part I.

1. In the first essay, David Suzuki talks about the differences he sees between London, Ontario, of the 1950s and the city today. Compare and contrast your own town or city today with how it was when you were a child.

2. What process do you have to go through to come up with an interesting comparison or contrast? How is it different from the process you go through for other rhetorical modes?

3. Compare your high school experiences with your college or university experiences. Begin by listing similarities and differences.

DIVIDING AND CLASSIFYING

The essays that follow show both division and classification at work. The first, "Rapport: How to Ignite It" by Camille Lavington, divides and classifies types of people. In the second, "Categories of Time Use," Edwin Bliss breaks common tasks into five categories.

Camille Lavington
RAPPORT: HOW TO IGNITE IT

Focusing Your Attention

1. Do you get along easily with others? Do you like different types of people?

2. The essay you are about to read classifies the different personality traits in people. What are your dominant personality traits? What impression do you usually make on people? How do you know you make this particular impression?

Expanding Your Vocabulary

The following words are important to your understanding of this essay.

rapport: chemistry between people (title)

reticent: reserved, shy (paragraph 2)

Henry Kissinger: U.S. secretary of state during the Nixon administration (paragraph 2)

persona: image, public identity (paragraph 2)

affinity: liking, attraction (paragraph 4)

endowed: gifted (paragraph 4)

remedied: fixed, corrected (paragraph 6)

hyperactive: energetic (paragraph 9)

intrusive: pushy (paragraph 9)

paradoxically: surprisingly, contrary to what was expected (paragraph 9)

reservoir: supply (paragraph 9)

eliciting: bringing forth, drawing out (paragraph 13)

osmosis: effortless learning, absorption (paragraph 17)

ESP: intuition, insight (paragraph 17)

cosmic: coming from the universe (paragraph 17)

charismatic: charming (paragraph 17)

nonconformity: difference from the norm (paragraph 17)

prudent: cautious (paragraph 21)

affluent: wealthy (paragraph 22)

frivolities: matters of little importance (paragraph 23)

cerebral: intellectual (paragraph 24)

stick-in-the-mud: an old-fashioned or unprogressive person (paragraph 24)

empathetic: kindly, sensitive to the feelings of others (paragraph 25)

modified: adapted, changed (paragraph 25)

got strokes: was praised or rewarded (paragraph 25)

spontaneous: impulsive (paragraph 26)

all is not hearts and flowers: the situation is not entirely positive (paragraph 26)

psychoanalyze: try to explain the thoughts and emotions of others (paragraph 26)

benchmarks: criteria, milestones, points of reference (paragraph 29)

1   It happens in a flash, based entirely on surface cues, but people use first impressions to make sometimes irreversible judgments.

2   So don't be reticent about the talent you've been given. It's your obligation to share it with the world, and your personality is the driving force behind your talent. As Henry Kissinger once said, history is fueled not by impersonal forces, but by personalities. If yours is out of sync, it may need some work. That doesn't mean adopting a phony persona; it simply means adjusting your communicating style in order to relate better to others.

3   Understanding your own personality makes it easier to spot someone with whom you'd like to connect. There are simple signs that signal personality types, and you can recognize them—even in strangers.

4   We are all a combination of many personality traits, but most people have a stronger affinity for one. Or you may be one of those rarely gifted individuals who are *evenly* endowed in *every* style.

5   **Introverts** are deep thinkers who prefer time alone to read, or stare at their computer screens, or gaze into outer space. They strive for, and appreciate, excellence. Ironically, introverts often have meaningful friendships. These are their positive qualities. But, as with all personality types, there are negative aspects: Introverts have a tendency to be suspicious and wor-

ried. Introverts can also be intellectual snobs who are unaccepting of others and perfectionists to a fault. They may be self-centered and have friends who are jealous of them.

Much of introversion is caused by shyness and lack of experience. Of all the personality traits, I think that introversion is the one characteristic that most needs to be remedied. Why? Introversion borders on selfishness. By hanging back during interactions with others, introverts are protecting themselves. A conversation is like a canoe that requires the exertion of both participants to keep moving forward; an introvert isn't engaging his paddle. It's everyone's job to contribute to relationships and to make others comfortable.   6

Extroverts aren't perfect, but society tends to reward their behavior. They have many good qualities, including their friendliness and magnetism. Energetic and sparkling, they inspire others. They like people, variety, and action. Extroverts like to chat a lot. They get their energy from other people.   7

You won't see an extrovert going to the movies alone, eating dinner alone, taking a vacation alone. Extroverts are born leaders. It should come as no surprise that most CEOs and politicians are extroverts.   8

Still, extroverts can be hyperactive and intrusive. They need to be the center of attention at all times, and have a habit of boasting. They're looking for a vote of confidence from the outside, even if they have to solicit it. Paradoxically, this is sometimes because they don't tap into their own reservoir of strength and thus haven't learned their own value.   9

The easiest way to achieve rapport with others is to remember that time together is either a learning or an entertaining experience. With this attitude, you'll always be eager to draw people into any dialogue by inviting them to add a comment or an opinion—rather than draining other people's energy by dominating or shortchanging the conversation.   10

Lock two extroverts in a room, and each will complain that the other is a poor conversationalist. (An extrovert thinks a good conversationalist is someone who is interested in what *he* has to say.)   11

Sensers are just-the-facts people, and they get that way by using their objective senses, rather than their intuition, to gather information. A senser relies on his eyes and ears for clues. Practical and bottom-line oriented, sensers are doers who want action and want it now. They are competitive and highly organized, and they set high standards for themselves.   12

Sensers are master manipulators who have a talent for eliciting the response they want from people; many actors, comedians, and salespeople are sensers for just that reason. Sensers prefer to wear comfortable clothing, but peer pressure means so much to them that they will give in to the current vogue and wear what people they admire are wearing.   13

On the negative side, sensers can be self-involved, arrogant, and status-seeking. They tend to act first and think later. Also, they can be domineering and lacking in trust.   14

Sometimes you will be thrown off by a senser's easygoing manner because of his sense of humor, but don't waste his time. Get to the point   15 quickly; remember that he's action-oriented and looking for short-term personal gain. If you have no previous knowledge about his temperament, take a look around for clues. A senser decorates his walls and bookshelves with personal trophies and memorabilia that remind him of his conquests.

16   You will lose points if you ever try to upstage a senser. This type, of all of the others, wants to be the center of interest, as indicated by all of the personal trophies on his walls.

17   **Intuitors** make up a scant 10% of the population. So you're dealing with a rare bird. Albert Einstein is the classic intuitor—a genius who didn't speak until he was six years old. Intuitors gather information through a sort of osmosis, absorbing ESP signals and cosmic energy. Creative, imaginative, and original, they are driven by inspiration and a powerful intellect. Intuitors see the big picture in spite of a tenuous grasp of the details. Intuitors can be quite charismatic, although they tend to be unaware of their effect on people. They are also magnets to each other—finding their counterparts in the arts, sciences, wherever. Their nonconformity makes them dress in unusual combinations. In fact, they'll wear anything.

18   On the other hand, intuitors can drive others to madness. At times they're unrealistic and impractical. They're allergic to focusing on details. Fantasy-bound, they can be long on vision and short on action.

19   To approach an intuitor, spark her curiosity. When picking the brain of an intuitor, ask her to problem-solve without following any rules. You want to hear her unedited ideas.

20   If you're trying to impress an intuitor, don't waste time. You'll lose her attention if you give her a lot of background. Instead, respect her right-brain ability to jump to the heart of the matter in a flash.

21   **Thinkers** are the mainstay of society. They make life better because of their strong work ethic and high standards. Deliberate, prudent, and objective thinkers dwell in the world of rationality and analysis. Thinkers like to sleep on it. Many are effective communicators, possibly because they consider carefully before they speak. They make good jurors, who wait until closing arguments are concluded before weighing the evidence carefully. Their checkbooks are balanced.

22   Thinkers tend to like tailored, conservative clothing. If they're affluent, they have a tie that shows they met the rigid qualifications for entry to a top-ranked school. Teaching is a profession often favored by thinkers.

23   Thinkers can get trapped in their love of analysis, becoming overcautious and indecisive. They can be frustrating in a relationship by being too rigid, impersonal, and unemotional. Some of them walk around with monster superiority complexes, trying at every turn to prove they're smarter than others. Some don't care how they look, because they're trying to send a message: *I have too big a brain to concern myself with frivolities like appearance.* But they're not out to hurt anyone; they forget their own feelings as well as the feelings of others. Thinkers often forget to stop and smell the roses.

24   These cerebral types can sound like sticks-in-the-mud, but don't take them lightly. Some of the finest minds in the world fall into this category. Put this trait together with extroversion and you've got one remarkable leader.

Feelers operate from the heart and the gut. They're warm and always 25 observing interactions among people and interpreting them: *Why didn't she invite me to that meeting? Was that look he gave me a sign of disapproval?* Feelers read between the lines. They are nurturing and empathetic. Their need for an emotional response can have an odd side effect: Whatever childhood behavior got attention from their parents is the one they'll pursue in a modified form as adults—so a feeler child who got strokes for bringing home straight A's will turn into a feeler adult who works overtime at the office.

Feelers are not trendsetters; they are more comfortable in the main- 26 stream, following traditional values. They like colorful clothes that reflect their emotions. They are loyal, spontaneous, and persuasive. But all is not hearts and flowers. Feelers overreact and get defensive if things don't go their way. Their need to psychoanalyze everyone gets them into trouble as they over-personalize every interaction, stirring up conflict. Some are guilt-ridden, ruled by thoughts of what they've done wrong.

Judges aren't any more judgmental than the rest of us. Any personality 27 type can be judgmental.

If you are a judge, you like to think you have some control over life. 28 Judges are structured and organized; they want to finish things and move along. They set standards for themselves and for others and follow them. Judges are surprised every time someone fails to live up to his or her agreement, as if that were unusual. Judges set goals and meet them—thriving on the resulting sense of closure.

Dealing with a judge is simple: Make a commitment, and live up to it. 29 Set goals, and use benchmarks to measure your performance by objective standards. Fail to meet a judge's expectations of you, and you'll travel a rocky road.

Perceivers are always receptive to more information or stimulation 30 before acting. They take each day as it comes and don't kick themselves for letting chores slide into tomorrow. Perceivers generally grew up in either an unstructured environment or a very structured one against which they rebel as adults. These people can be very kind to others because they're kind to themselves. They don't become angry because you're late or take offense if you ask them a personal question. They see life as a process. A lot of artistic people fall into this category.

Pressure tactics just don't work with perceivers, but perceivers are so easy 31 to be around that they are certainly worth rewarding with a little patience.

Once you've discovered what makes the other person tick—which traits 32 are getting in the way of good communication between the two of you—then you have to decide what to do with that information.

Thinking Critically About Content

1. What are the eight different personality types that Lavington outlines in her essay?

2. Are these personality traits evenly distributed in you, or is one dominant? Explain your answer.

3. Do you agree with Lavington when she says, "Don't be reticent about the talent you've been given. It's your obligation to share it with the world" (paragraph 2)?

Thinking Critically About Purpose and Audience

4. What do you think Lavington's purpose is in this essay?

5. Who do you think is her primary audience?

6. When did you last make an important judgment based on a first impression of someone? Was your impression fairly accurate?

Thinking Critically About Paragraphs

7. Explain how the topic sentence works in paragraph 7. Does it supply the controlling idea for the entire paragraph? Are the other sentences in this paragraph related to the topic sentence?

8. Why do you think Lavington discusses these personality types in this particular order? What is her rationale for moving from one type to the next?

9. How does Lavington start her essay? Is it effective?

10. Write an alternative conclusion to Lavington's essay.

Edwin Bliss

CATEGORIES OF TIME USE

Focusing Your Attention

1. Do you use your time wisely? Where could you improve your time management skills?

2. In the essay you are about to read, the author lays out five categories of tasks for organizing our daily lives. These categories will help you realize that each chore and activity in your life has a different status. Do you find that you get to all the tasks that you need to complete in a particular day? Or do you procrastinate beyond your deadlines? Explain your answer.

Expanding Your Vocabulary

The following words and name are important to your understanding of this essay.

escalated: increased rapidly (footnote to paragraph 2)

simultaneously: at the same time (paragraph 3)

precedence: priority (paragraph 3)

preliminary: initial, beginning (paragraph 6)

clamor: shout (paragraph 8)

marginally: only slightly (paragraph 10)

diversionary: distracting (paragraph 10)

subjective: differing from person to person (paragraph 13)

Ernest Hemingway: 1899–1961, an American writer (paragraph 14)

theological: related to religion (paragraph 14)

scrutiny: inspection, examination (paragraph 14)

in vain: without success (paragraph 15)

allocating: assigning (paragraph 15)

Tasks can be broken down into five categories: 1

1. Important and Urgent
2. Important but Not Urgent
3. Urgent but Not Important
4. Busy Work
5. Wasted Time

1. Important and Urgent

These are the tasks that *must* be done immediately or in the near future.   2
Examples: Your boss demands a certain report by 10 A.M. tomorrow. Or your
engine blows a gasket. Or the labor pains are three minutes apart. Or it's
April 15, and you haven't finished your income tax form.*

Now, unless these situations all develop simultaneously (God forbid!),   3
you can cope with them. Because of their urgency and their importance,
they take precedence over everything else, and procrastination is out of the
question. It is not here that we find our time management problems.

2. Important but Not Urgent

Attention to this category is what divides effective individuals from inef-   4
fective ones.

Most of the really important things in our lives are not urgent. They can   5
be done now or later. In many cases they can be postponed forever, and in
too many cases they are. These are the things we "never get around to."

Examples: that special course you want to take to upgrade your profes-   6
sional skills; that new project you would like to suggest to your boss after
you find time to do the preliminary fact-finding; that article you've been
meaning to write; that diet you've intended to begin; that annual medical
checkup you've planned to get for the past three years; that visit to a lawyer
to have your will drawn; that retirement program you've been planning to
establish.

All of these tasks have one thing in common: Despite their importance,   7
affecting as they do your health, your wealth, and your family's welfare, they

---

*This is an example of a task that began in Category 2 and escalated to Category 1 now that
you have reached the deadline.

will be postponed indefinitely unless you yourself initiate action. If your activities are keyed to other people's priorities or to system-imposed deadlines that make things "urgent," you will never get around to your own priorities.

3. Urgent but Not Important

8   In this category are those things that clamor for immediate action but that we would assign a low priority if we examined them objectively.

9   For example, someone asks you to chair a fund drive or to give a speech or to attend a meeting. You might consider each of these low priority, but someone is standing in front of you waiting for an answer and you accept because you cannot think of a graceful way to decline. Then, because these tasks have built-in time limits, they get done, while Category 2 items get moved to the back burner.

4. Busy Work

10   There are many tasks that are marginally worth doing but are neither urgent nor important. We often do them ahead of more important things because they are *diversionary*—they provide a feeling of activity and accomplishment while giving us an excuse to put off tackling those Category 2 tasks that have a far greater benefit.

11   One aerospace executive, for example, told me of going to his office the previous Saturday morning to do some work he had been postponing. He decided first to organize the materials on his desk. Having done so, he decided that while he was at it he might as well straighten up the desk drawers. He spent the rest of the morning reorganizing drawers and files.

12   "I left the office feeling vaguely disappointed that I hadn't accomplished what I went in for," he said, "but I consoled myself with the thought that I had been very busy doing some worthwhile things. I realize now that I was playing games with myself—working on low-priority tasks to give myself an excuse for further delay on the far more essential task I originally had assigned myself."

5. Wasted Time

13   The definition of wasted time is subjective, of course.

14   Ernest Hemingway is quoted as having defined "immoral" as "anything you feel bad after." I don't know whether that definition will stand up to theological scrutiny, but I do think it can be applied to wasted time. Television viewing, for example, can be time well spent if we come away feeling that we have been enlightened or entertained. But if afterward we feel that the time would have been better spent mowing the lawn or playing tennis or reading a good book, then we can chalk up that time as wasted.*

15   People who scramble madly to get control of their time often look in vain for things in this category upon which to blame their inefficiency. I am con-

---

*By any sane person's standards, about 95 percent of all television viewing must be put in this category, which is something to think about the next time you reach for that remote control.

vinced, however, that with most people this is not where the problem lies. It lies rather with allocating too much time to things in Categories 3 and 4 rather than to those in Category 2.

Thinking Critically About Content

1. Explain Bliss's five categories of time use.

2. Based on Bliss's explanation, do you complete Category 2 tasks in a timely manner? Explain your answer.

3. List the tasks you perform in a typical day, and classify each in terms of Bliss's categories. Do his categories cover all of your tasks? Would you add any other categories to his essay? Explain your answer.

Thinking Critically About Purpose and Audience

4. Why do you think Bliss wrote this essay?

5. Who would be most interested in this essay?

6. Does this essay make you feel more or less stressed than you already do about time management? Explain your answer.

Thinking Critically About Paragraphs

7. What examples does Bliss use to explain Category 5? Add two more examples to this list.

8. Underline five transitions in the final three paragraphs. Then explain how they make the discussion of Category 5 smooth and coherent. (Refer to page 38 for more information on transitions.)

9. Choose one paragraph, and decide whether or not it has enough details. Explain your answer.

10. Write an alternative introduction to Bliss's essay.

Writing Topics: Dividing and Classifying

Before you begin to write, you might want to review the writing process in Part I.

1. In the first essay, Camille Lavington divides and classifies the personality types she sees in the human race. Using her essay as a reference, explain what category you fit into and why you fit there.

2. Using Edwin Bliss's categories, divide a typical week of your homework into categories. Then explain each category.

3. How do division and classification work together? Refer to one of the reading assignments in Chapter 26 to respond to this question.

27

DEFINING

Here are two essays that show how definition works in the context of a full essay. "Gentrification" by Robert Fulford shows how a word can influence opinion and action. The second essay, "Bullied by the Click of a Mouse" by Alanna Mitchell, defines electronic bullying, or cyber bullying.

◆◆◆━━━━◆━━━━◆◆◆

Robert Fulford

GENTRIFICATION

Focusing Your Attention

1. Do you think a word with a particular meaning can influence the way you think? Does the idea sometimes come before the word?

2. The essay you are about to read discusses the phenomenon of wealthy people buying into run-down neighbourhoods, and questions whether this phenomenon is as bad as the term that describes it implies. What has happened to the downtown area of your city?

Expanding Your Vocabulary

The following words are important to your understanding of this essay.

> **metaphorical:** a figure of speech where one thing represents another symbolically (paragraph 2)
>
> **communiqué:** official announcement (paragraph 2)
>
> **intractable:** difficult to manage or manipulate (paragraph 3)
>
> **decrepit:** weak, worn out with age (paragraph 5)
>
> **consolidated:** joined in one system (paragraph 9)
>
> **demonize:** to represent as evil (paragraph 11)

1   In urban politics, "gentrification" has for many years been a curse, a one-word bundle of anger and resentment. In 1999 a candidate for mayor of San Francisco solemnly pledged that if elected he would make "war on any and all gentrification." In 2000 a Toronto weekly paper, eye, discussed "Toronto's silent war over gentrification."

Those wars were of course purely metaphorical. On Monday in Mon-   2
treal, members of an organization called the Anti-Gentrification Committee, springing from God knows what political swamp, made the metaphor
dangerously literal by committing war-like acts. They terrified residents of
the Hochelaga-Maisonneuve district by leaving six suspicious-looking
packages at condominium construction sites and sales offices. The police
bomb squad found the packages harmless, but a communiqué from the
Anti-Gentrification Committee threatened more vicious action in future.

Whoever they are, the Montreal radicals express an extreme version of   3
a widely held opinion. Urban activists and scholars on several continents
have convinced themselves that there's something fundamentally wrong
and selfish about improving a neighbourhood. That seems to me precisely
the reverse of the truth. In fact, the gentrification movement has helped
solve, through the spontaneous decisions of millions of citizens, what once
seemed a grave and intractable problem.

Forty years ago, the same sort of people who are now averse to gentri-   4
fication were worrying that "white flight" was destroying the inner cities.
Across the U.S., white middle-class families were moving to the suburbs
because downtown neighbourhoods were increasingly populated by
blacks. By leaving, the middle classes shrank the tax base of the cities,
eroding schools and other services. Everyone claimed that downtowns
were dying, even where race was not a major factor.

But the 1960s and 1970s brought a big change for the better—or so it   5
seemed. Middle-class families began taking over cheap, decrepit housing
and improving it. Districts that were called "slums" only a few years earlier sprang back to life. In the early stages this was called "neighbourhood
revitalization."

In 1964, however, it acquired a new and sinister name and ceased to be   6
an obviously benign process. Ruth Glass, a British sociologist, invented the
word "gentrification" as a reaction against the transformation of London
neighbourhoods. She decided that the new movement was eliminating
cheap rental housing and driving out the poor.

Glass took the extremely conservative view that districts should remain   7
the way they were when she first glimpsed them. She didn't know or care
that at some level all neighbourhoods are in transition all the time. She
believed that time should be stopped in its path.

As a package for her misgivings, "gentrification" was a clever choice. It   8
had a sophisticated sound, as well as ironic echoes of the rural gentry
depicted in the novels of Jane Austen. It carried overtones of snobbery and
class superiority—even if many gentrifiers had been among the urban poor
only a generation or a decade earlier. Glass also imported into town planning another word, "invaded," which is what the middle classes supposedly
did to the districts of the poor. She used another term, still uglier: "colonising."

By 1973 Glass was treating the improvement of every London slum as a   9
tragedy: "There is very little left of the poorer enclaves of Hampstead and

Chelsea: In these boroughs, the upper-middle-class takeover was consolidated some time ago. The invasion has since spread to Islington, Paddington, North Kensington."

10   As a term of abuse, "gentrification" proved such a huge success that it went into some dictionaries with Glass's own social interpretation attached; Merriam-Webster says it's "the process of renewal and rebuilding accompanying the influx of middle-class or affluent people into deteriorating areas that often displaces earlier, usually poorer residents." Recently in *The New York Times*, A.O. Scott depicted gentrification (he was discussing a former slum in Brooklyn) as a transformation that's "full of aspiration and oppression, progress and callousness."

11   Seldom has a single word done so much to distort perception. In a sense it resembles "elitist." Both words demonize creative impulses that are common to much of humanity by depicting ambition and the search for personal betterment as a form of evil.

12   Much of the world now agrees with Glass that gentrification cheats the poor, though the evidence has never been strong. Recent economic studies in Boston and New York have suggested that the opposite is the case. They claim that gentrification can benefit the poor by increasing the tax base, bringing middle-class energy to the job of improving the schools, and introducing economic variety. Many older residents, they discovered, are not pushed out. What disappears instead is the "monoculture of poverty." It's replaced by the kind of economic mix that's essential to social health. Reuben Greenberg, the police chief of Charleston, S.C., claims that "Urban problems are caused not by poverty, but by the concentration of poverty."

13   No one will claim, though, that benefits can be shown in each case of gentrification. Every renovated district has its own qualities and its own economic results. But certainly no serious research supports the belief that gentrification consistently hurts the poor. This widespread foolishness demonstrates how thinking can be imprisoned by language, even by just one well-chosen word.

Thinking Critically About Content

1. What does Robert Fulford mean when he describes the word *gentrification* as "a one-word bundle of anger and resentment"?

2. What is the writer's attitude to Ruth Glass, the sociologist who invented the word *gentrification*? What words or phrases indicate his attitude?

3. What previous phenomenon does Fulford compare to gentrification? Why does he make the comparison?

Thinking Critically About Purpose and Audience

4. Why do you think Fulford wrote this essay?

5. Who do you think is his primary audience?

6. Would the argument presented in this essay be persuasive to the organization mentioned in paragraph 2? What details would Fulford need to add to reach that audience?

Thinking Critically About Paragraphs

7. In paragraph 8, Fulford returns to the idea of the "bundle" referred to in the opening paragraph, giving us his version of the connotations (non-literal meanings) of the word. What is his tone in this paragraph?

8. The central paragraphs of this essay are presented in a particular order. What is that order and why is it used?

9. Fulford says in paragraph 2 that the wars were strictly metaphorical. He uses several metaphors in this essay. What are they and how are they used?

10. Write a paragraph defining either *elitist* or *invaded* from Fulford's point of view.

Alanna Mitchell

BULLIED BY THE CLICK OF A MOUSE

Focusing Your Attention

1. Do you use instant messaging? Do you have a cellphone that contains a digital camera? How do you feel about the power of others to send your personal information or image to thousands of people?

2. In the essay you are about to read, the author defines the latest form of bullying. How would you define bullying? Does sending unflattering photos of someone over the internet sound like a form of bullying to you?

Expanding Your Vocabulary

The following words are important to your understanding of this essay.

scorn: contempt, disdain (paragraph 1)

rampant: out of control (paragraph 2)

bafflegab: gobbledygook, nonsense (paragraph 14)

empathy: identifying with another's feelings (paragraph 14)

debilitating: draining strength or energy (paragraph 14)

covert: sheltered, secretive (paragraph 21)

In one case, it was a Japanese teen photographed in his school change room by a camera phone. In a U.S. case, it was an ex-girlfriend's head shot pasted electronically onto a pornographic picture. In a third, it was a full-figured Canadian boy acting out Star Wars moves in a homemade video. In each case, the hurtful image was beamed around the digital universe, the better to heap scorn upon the victim. 1

It's called cyber bullying. Already common in North America, it is about to become rampant, driven by the army of Internet-connected camera cell- 2 phones that preteens and teenagers received as gifts over the recent holiday season, experts warn.

3   "I hate to say it, but this issue is going to get worse before it gets better," Bill Belsey said from his home in Alberta. Mr. Belsey is one of the world's foremost experts on the phenomenon and the creator of the website www.cyberbullying.ca.

4   Cyber bullying—also known as digital bullying or Internet bullying—is harassment that takes place using an electronic medium. That can be through e-mails, instant messaging, chat rooms on the Internet, small text messages, on-line voting booths, and even websites set up especially to mock and humiliate.

5   Girls usually get bullied about their appearance, and boys about their sexual orientation.

6   The phenomenon has grown over the past three or four years throughout North America as teenagers and preteens become ever more closely attached to the Internet. Until now, this has often meant that a student—to be bullied digitally—needed to be sitting at a computer connected to high-speed or a telephone line. This is what is changing, and quickly.

7   Now, teens and preteens in North America are following the lead of their cellphone-toting counterparts in the United Kingdom, other parts of Europe and Japan by becoming huge consumers of cellphones that hook wirelessly to the Internet. These often have picture and instant text-messaging features, some of the points that make them such popular gifts.

8   Instant messaging, for example, is expanding at a faster rate now than e-mail grew at the same stage of its evolution, Mr. Belsey said. An Environics Research Group survey taken in 2002, before the holiday surge of Internet-connected mobile phones, showed that nearly 60 per cent of Canadian students used chat rooms and instant messaging even then, he said.

9   The trend means that cyber bullying is poised to become far more widespread, faster and even harder for adults to monitor, said Glenn Stutzky, a professor at the school of social work at Michigan State University and one of the key researchers in cyber bullying.

10   "It's like kids 11 to 17 have created a cyber community, an interactive world largely unknown to adults and unsupervised," Prof. Stutzky said.

11   He and Mr. Belsey say that cyber bullying is worse than the regular schoolyard kind because it knows no bounds of time, space or geography. A bullied child used to be able to go home to escape. Now, bullying can happen when a child is in his or her own bedroom with a cellphone.

12   Because this is such a new issue, many adults are not aware of it. It also tends to be under the radar for police, even when the bullying includes threats. The Calgary police have issued a warning on the phenomenon, explaining that written death threats are a different beast from schoolyard taunts. Mr. Belsey said the Calgary force is one of the first in North America to peg cyber bullying as a major problem.

13   Part of the concern is that cyber bullying is often even more cruel than the in-person kind.

That's because the cyber bullies can often hide their true identities with 14
digital bafflegab and dodge reprisals, Prof. Stutzky said. Being anonymous and far away, they are also immune to the tears of the bullied and
removed from feeling empathy for them, he said. The result is painful and
sometimes debilitating.

"Bullying, when it comes into our lives, comes in a way that takes over 15
our lives," Prof. Stutzky said. "It's like domestic violence. You know it's only a
matter of time before it comes again. It hurts because your life is no longer
your own; someone else is in control."

The most famous Canadian example is G.,* who became known 16
around the world as the "Star Wars Kid" last year after some schoolmates
got their hands on a video he had made of himself wielding a golf ball
retriever as a light sabre and providing his own sound effects.

The 15-year-old's homemade video ended up digitized and placed on a 17
file-sharing network and has been downloaded by millions of interested
spectators around the world. Clones of the pudgy would-be combatant
have been digitally inserted into versions of Benny Hill, The Matrix, Mortal
Kombat, The Hulk and The Lord of the Rings.

G. was so wounded by the unflattering attention that he has been under 18
psychiatric care and finished last year's school session at a child psychia-
try ward. His parents have launched a lawsuit.

Technology has advanced so quickly since then that G.'s ordeal is no 19
longer so cumbersome to implement, nor so rare.

Take the case that Mr. Belsey heard this summer of a Japanese boy, hot 20
and sweaty after his gym class, who was getting dressed in what he
thought was the privacy of the school's change room.

One of his classmates, moved to ridicule by the boy's large size, took a 21
covert picture of him with a cellphone camera. Within seconds, the picture
was flying to the cellphones of the sweaty boy's schoolmates through
instant messaging. By the time the boy was dressed and back in class, he
was the laughingstock of the school.

A 16-year-old Japanese girl told Mr. Belsey of the nightmare that hap- 22
pened after she broke up with her boyfriend. The boy knew all her contact
numbers, including e-mail, cellphone and street address, and posted them
on sex-oriented websites all over Japan. People were driving by her home
and instant-messaging her.

Paul Denison, principal of Nicholson Catholic College, a high school in 23
Belleville, Ont., said he has seen so many victims of cyber bullying in his
office and that of his school counsellors that he has launched a campaign
at the school to make parents and students aware that it is happening and
is not acceptable. Mr. Belsey recently did a series of seminars at the school
in aid of that.

"We don't have a lot of good ways of intervening," Mr. Denison said. 24
"Right now, the phase we're in is awareness."

*G.'s full name has been removed to protect his identity.

25   To Mr. Belsey, North American adults have a chance to tackle the problem before it becomes as entrenched as it is in other countries, and before the technology here catches up to advances in Japan and Britain which he says are three or four generations ahead.

26   "We have a window of opportunity to get ahead of this," he said.

27   Mr. Belsey has some tips on how to do this. He said parents and educators need to learn the technology so they can figure out what's going on and start to talk about it. They also need to set up guidelines for appropriate use of the technology.

28   Children need to refuse to respond to cyber bullying taunts, be careful not to give out personal information such as passwords and to tell adults if harassment goes on. And schools should focus on explaining to students and parents that cyber bullying is just as serious as any other kind and make sure they know who to talk to in school administration if it does happen.

Thinking Critically About Content

1. Alanna Mitchell develops her definition of cyber bullying with real-life examples. Which of the examples communicates most clearly to you what cyber bullying is? Explain your answer.

2. The author does not offer a definition of cyber bullying until paragraph 4. Why do you think she does not put the definition in the first paragraph?

3. Is the author guilty of cyber bullying herself, considering she uses real names (removed here) in at least one case in the essay?

Thinking Critically About Purpose and Audience

4. Why do you think Mitchell wrote this essay, particularly at the time she did?

5. Who do you think is Mitchell's audience for this essay? Explain your answer.

6. Does this essay make you feel sympathy for the people involved? Does the sympathy depend on your having experienced some form of bullying yourself?

7. Mitchell starts her essay with several examples. What do you think her purpose is in starting this way?

Thinking Critically About Paragraphs

8. Paragraph 5 is just one sentence long with no explanations or examples. Why do you think the author chose to write the paragraph in this way? Do her examples in the rest of the essay back up what she says in this paragraph?

9. The author quotes a number of experts in this essay. What is the effect of expert opinion?

10. Write a paragraph defining *schoolyard bully* using examples from your own experience.

Writing Topics: Defining

Before you begin to write, you might want to review the writing process in Part I.

1. In the first essay, Robert Fulford defines *gentrification*. Write your own definition of *suburbia* or of another aspect of city life, such as downtown or ethnic neigbourhoods (Little Italy, Chinatown).

2. Using Alanna Mitchell's method of development through examples, define *blogging*.

3. Now that you have studied different approaches to the process of definition, what makes a definition effective or useful for you? Apply what you have studied about definition to your answer.

CHAPTER **28**

ANALYZING CAUSES AND EFFECTS

The two essays in this chapter show cause and effect at work. The first essay, "Shedding the Weight of My Dad's Obsession," deals with the lifelong burden of an insensitive father. In the second essay, "The Secret Heroes of Vimy," Pierre Berton explains how leadership and training helped the Canadian Army win the Battle of Vimy Ridge.

Linda Lee Andujar

SHEDDING THE WEIGHT OF MY DAD'S OBSESSION

Focusing Your Attention

1. Do you have a personal problem that plagues you consistently? What is this problem?

2. The essay you are about to read explains how the author finally shed an emotional burden she carried since her childhood. How do you deal with emotional problems? Where did you learn your "survival skills"? What do you do to find security and safety when you are upset about something?

Expanding Your Vocabulary

The following words are important to your understanding of this essay.

Bluebird: entry-level organization for future Girl Scouts (paragraph 1)

clambered: climbed awkwardly (paragraph 4)

timber (Canadian spelling: timbre): distinctive character or quality (paragraph 5)

authoritarian regimens: strict regulations (paragraph 5)

incarceration: imprisonment (paragraph 7)

skirmish: battle (paragraph 8)

amphetamines: stimulants that lessen appetite (paragraph 9)

diuretics: drugs that increase the production of urine (paragraph 9)

metabolism: bodily process that changes food into energy (paragraph 11)

Instead of selling the Camp Fire candy, I ate it. Eight boxes of it. Each   1
Bluebird in our fourth-grade troop was assigned 12 boxes of chocolate
candy to sell for a dollar a box. I sold four boxes to my family and then ran
out of ideas for selling the rest.

As the days passed and the stack of candy remained in a corner of my   2
room, the temptation to eat it overwhelmed my conscience. Two months
after we'd been given the goodies, the troop leader announced that the
drive was over and we were to bring in our sales money, along with any
unsold candy, to the next Tuesday meeting. I rushed home in a panic and
counted $4 in my sales money envelope and 12 boxes of candy gone.

I thought of the piggy bank filled with silver dollars that my father kept   3
on a shelf in his closet. It was a collection that he added to but never spent.
I tried to push this financial resource out of my mind, but Tuesday was
approaching, and I still had no money.

By Monday afternoon I had no choice. I tiptoed into my parents' bed-   4
room, pulled the vanity chair from Mother's dressing table, and carried it to
the walk-in closet. There was the piggy bank smiling down at me from the
high shelf. After stacking boxes on the chair, I reached up and laid hands
on the bank. When I had counted out eight silver dollars, I returned the pig
to its place and clambered down. For days I felt bad about my theft, but
what I felt even guiltier about was eating all those treats.

Throughout my childhood, my parents weighed me every day, and   5
Daddy posted the numbers on my bedroom door. He never called me fat,
but I came to learn every synonym. He discussed every health aspect of
obesity endlessly. The daily tone and timber of our household was affected
by Dad's increasingly authoritarian regimens.

I remember one Friday night, months after the candy caper. I heard the   6
garage door rumble shut, and I knew that Daddy was home. He came in
the back door, kissed Mother, and asked what my weight was for the day.
Mother admitted that I was still a pound over the goal he had set. "Get a pil-
low and a book, Linda," he said.

He firmly ushered me to the bathroom, then shut and locked the door   7
behind me. As the door was closing, I caught a glimpse of Mother and my
sister looking on as though they were witnessing an execution. For the next
two days, the only time I was allowed out was for meals. It was late Sunday
evening when I was finally released from my cell, supposedly taught a
lesson by my incarceration.

The bathroom episode was one skirmish in a long war that had begun   8
when, unlike my older sister, I failed to shed the "baby fat" many children
are born with. Although I was cheerful, affectionate, and good-natured,
none of these qualities interested my father. He had one slender child—he
meant to have two. It was simply a matter of my self-discipline.

My slightly chubby figure had become a target for my physician father's   9
frustration as he struggled to establish his medical practice. Dad told me

constantly that if I was a pound overweight, I would be teased at school and nobody would like me. I stayed away from the other kids, fearing harsh words that never came. When I was 16, Daddy came up with the ultimate punishment: any day that I weighed more than 118 pounds (the weight my father had deemed ideal for my 5-foot, 4-inch frame) I'd have to pay him. In an attempt to shield me from this latest tactic, my exhausted, loving mother secretly took me to an internist friend of the family who prescribed what he described as "diet pills"—amphetamines and diuretics. Although the pills caused unpleasant side effects like light-headedness, taking them landed me a slim figure and, two years later, an engineer husband.

10   I quit the hated amphetamines at 27 and accepted my divorce as a result of my weight gain. I became a single, working mother devoted to raising my son and daughter. Over time, I realized that people liked my smile and my laugh and, contrary to my father's predictions, didn't shun me because of my size.

11   Many years ago, at my annual physical, I mentioned to my doctor that I couldn't eat the same quantity of food that normal people eat without getting bigger. He kindly reassured me that people do indeed have different metabolisms, some more efficient than others. This discussion ultimately helped me to accept my size and shed the emotional burden carried over from my childhood.

12   My sister and her husband have a daughter who was pudgy as a child. They asked me what they should do about her weight "problem." My reply, "Don't make it an issue. Let her find her own weight level." To their great credit, they did.

Thinking Critically About Content

1. What is Andujar analyzing in this essay?

2. The author is very honest and open about the causes and effects of her weight problem. What is the most fundamental cause and the ultimate effect?

3. What does Andujar seem upset about when she says, "Although I was cheerful, affectionate, and good-natured, none of these qualities interested my father" (paragraph 8)?

Thinking Critically About Purpose and Audience

4. What do you think Andujar's purpose is in this essay?

5. Who do you think is her primary audience?

6. Explain the essay's title.

Thinking Critically About Paragraphs

7. Andujar opens her essay with the story about the Camp Fire candy. Do you think this is an effective beginning? Explain your answer.

8. Paragraph 5 gives us a hint of what the real problem is in Andujar's life. How does the writer organize her details in that paragraph?

9. What is the topic sentence of paragraph 9? Do all the sentences in that paragraph support this topic sentence? Explain your answer.

10. Write a paragraph about the role of a particular relative in your life. Are you very emotionally attached to this person? How did you become so close?

Pierre Berton

THE SECRET HEROES OF VIMY

Focusing Your Attention

1. Think of a time when you acted or did something without carefully analyzing the situation. What were the results?

2. In the essay you are about to read, Major-General Byng uses training methods and techniques that were looked down upon by the British Army. Major-General Byng's seemingly radical ideas led to the Canadian Army capturing Vimy Ridge in World War II. Have you ever found your way out of a situation using tactics that your friends thought would never work?

Expanding Your Vocabulary

The following words are important to your understanding of this essay.

> **Vimy Ridge:** located almost 12 kilometres northeast of Arras, France, and occupied by the Germans in 1914 (paragraph 1)
>
> **impregnable:** able to withstand attack, impossible to take by storm (paragraph 1)
>
> **thwarted:** defeated, disappointingly unsuccessful (paragraph 3)
>
> **South African Light Horse:** a regiment of soldiers in South Africa, dating back to the Boer War (paragraph 5)
>
> **Boer War:** a war fought in South Africa, 1899–1902 (paragraph 5)
>
> **Somme:** the main Allied attack on the Western Front in 1916 during World War I (paragraph 6)
>
> **cronies:** friends, pals, buddies (paragraph 6)
>
> **colonial:** refers to a colony, which is an organized settlement in a foreign land (paragraph 18)

On Easter Monday, 1917, the four divisions that made up Canada's military contribution to the First World War attacked and captured Vimy Ridge, the supposedly impregnable German stronghold in northern France. 1

The French had thrown 20 divisions against the ridge in three massive attacks that failed at a cost of 150,000 casualties. The British followed suit 2 with no better success. The Canadian Corps, fighting together for the first time, did the job in less than eight hours.

3   This was the first major Allied victory in the Great War—a bright spot in an otherwise disappointing battle of Arras. How did the Canadians succeed when much larger forces had been thwarted?

4   First, they were a band of brothers. The Canadians were fighting under the command of the British who kept breaking up the Corps, moving units about like chess pieces, but the Canadian high command resisted, insisting the four divisions be brought together.

5   They were fortunate, too, in that the British officer chosen to lead them was a veteran of the South African Light Horse whose personality had been tempered in the freewheeling atmosphere of the Boer War a decade earlier. Under Major-General Julian Byng, the social gap that separated enlisted men in the British Army from their officers did not exist. In the Canadian Corps, the lowliest infantry soldier was treated as an adult so that each one knew his job. If an officer was struck down, his men could replace him.

6   One of Byng's first moves was to send Canada's Arthur Currie, then commander of the First Division, to the bloody battlefield of the Somme, to analyze why that campaign had failed. The result was a return to tactics that had been abandoned during the long static war. Currie had each platoon organized into a self-contained fighting unit—a tightly knit group of cronies, all interchangeable in the event of casualties.

7   Lieutenant-Colonel Andrew McNaughton, as counter-battery officer, was instructed to pinpoint all the German guns on Vimy Ridge and dispose of them before the attack. This was considered tactical nonsense by old-time British gunners. And when Harold Hemming, a young McGill graduate, made a major breakthrough in "flash spotting," an experimental method of locating a gun's position by triangulating its muzzle flashes, the British scoffed. "You take all the fun out of war," he was told.

8   But McNaughton not only adopted Hemming's technique, he sought the help of an impressive trio of scientists considered dangerous radicals by the British Army. All had become experts in the new science of sound ranging— a method of identifying enemy artillery positions by recording sound waves.

9   Because of these modern techniques, every German gun on the ridge was knocked out before the assault, save for those the enemy had purposely kept silent until the final hour.

10   Another key to the Vimy victory was Lieutenant-Colonel Raymond Brutinel, a French-born businessman who had made his fortune in the West and, when the war broke out, been instrumental in establishing the Canadian Machine Gun Corps. As well as commanding the force, he was an innovator who had developed a radical theory based on using "indirect" fire (a theory pooh-poohed by the British and French high commands, to whom the weapon was just a fancy rifle).

11   "Indirect fire" meant that, instead of firing directly at the enemy, the machine gun could be used to fire over the heads of assaulting troops,

harassing road crossings, thwarting carrying parties, and sweeping the front to prevent the Germans from repairing wire.

Brutinel was given his lead by Currie. In almost every trench raid, 12 machine-gun fire was used to intensify the box barrage that held the Germans in a cage of exploding steel. After Vimy, indirect fire, scorned so long by the brass hats, was adopted by all Allied armies.

The thoroughness and scope of the intensive training that preceded the 13 attack was entirely new to the British Army. Miles of white and coloured tapes were used to mark out full-scale replicas of the German trench system. By April, every infantry soldier from bottle washer to general officer knew the kind of ground he would have to cover—every fold, every pimple, every depression, every shell hole. Enemy trenches were outlined with tape, while strongholds, pillboxes, even barbed-wire entanglements were marked and labelled.

Entire divisions were put through manoeuvres. Because the troops 14 would have to advance behind a "creeping barrage"—a curtain of exploding steel—that advance had to be choreographed to the second; men's lives depended on it. Officers on horseback carried flags to represent the advancing screen of shrapnel. Over and over again, the troops practised the "Vimy Glide," walking at the rate of 100 yards every three minutes while instructors checked their watches.

At the First Army's headquarters, a Plasticine model of the Vimy sector 15 showed the German trench system in detail, with all the topographical features. Byng himself often turned up to explain and to guide. "Make sure every man knows his task," he would say to the sergeants and brigadiers who rubbed shoulders as they examined the model. "Explain it to him again and again. Encourage him to ask questions."

In no previous British-led offensive had so little been left to chance. The 16 knowledge that nothing had been overlooked seeped down to the newest private soldier and contributed to the high morale of the Canadian Corps.

That high morale produced a victory that helped to turn the tide in the 17 war. The stunning success led to promotions—Byng took command of the entire British Third Army, and was succeeded by Currie, the first Canadian to lead the Canadian Corps.

But it also gave Canada what it needed most: a mythology to help in its 18 transformation from a colonial backwater to a confident and increasingly independent nation.

Thinking Critically About Content

1. What is Pierre Berton analyzing in this essay?

2. Explain two causes and two effects of planning for Vimy Ridge.

3. Berton highlights the British resistance to Byng's methods. What effect did this resistance have on Byng? On the troops? On the outcome? What effect does Berton's highlighting the British resistance have on the reader?

Thinking Critically About Purpose and Audience

4. Why do you think Berton wrote this essay?

5. Who do you think the audience is? Explain your answer.

6. What effect does this essay have on the sense of Canadian identity? British identity?

Thinking Critically About Paragraphs

7. What effect do the statistics in paragraph 2 have on the reader? Is this an effective placement for the paragraph? Explain your answer.

8. Analyze the causes and effects outlined in paragraph 6. What were the results? How were these results accomplished?

9. Examine the information in paragraphs 13–16. Are the causes that "produced a victory that helped to turn the tide in the war" clearly outlined? Explain your answer.

10. What situation have you been in where training, or lack of training, affected you and the results you produced? Write your answer in paragraph form.

Writing Topics: Analyzing Causes and Effects

Before you begin to write, you might want to review the writing process in Part I.

1. Linda Andujar's father felt that her weight problem was simply a matter of self-discipline. What role does self-discipline play in most of our daily lives? Explain your answer.

2. In "The Secret Heroes of Vimy," Pierre Berton describes the effect of the training that the Canadian Corps received for the Battle of Vimy Ridge. Try to remember your first day on a job. How did training affect your future performance?

3. How would looking closely at causes and effects help you live a better life? How would the process of discovering causes and effects help you think through your decisions and problems more logically? Explain your answer.

ARGUING

29

The three essays in this chapter let you see argument at work. The first essay, "Open the Gates Wide" by Rudyard Griffiths, draws clear relationships between immigration and the Canadian identity.

The next two essays present two different points of view on smoking legislation. The first of these, written by Roy MacGregor, argues that smoking bans are positive and even help smokers quit smoking. The second, written by Rosie DiManno, argues that smoking bans should not exist and that there is no proof that second-hand smoke is harmful.

OPEN THE GATES WIDE

Focusing Your Attention

1. What do you feel is an integral part of the Canadian identity? Try to list as many items as possible.

2. Have you immigrated to Canada? Do you know someone who has immigrated to Canada? What is there about Canada that would make you want to live here?

Expanding Your Vocabulary

The following words are important to your understanding of this essay.

> **contentious:** involving or likely to cause controversy (paragraph 1)
>
> **mantra:** spiritual or sacred syllables or sounds that contain in their essence divine cosmic power (paragraph 2)
>
> **advocacy:** active support, especially the act of pleading or arguing for something (paragraph 5)

1

Immigration: its effect on our collective identity is one of the most compelling and often contentious issues facing Canada today. But so much of our thinking about the subject is framed by debate about its impact on the economy. As someone who spends his working life dealing with Canadian history—but who likes to look to the future as well—I'd like to make another point about the subject of new people coming to our shores: far from diluting Canada's identity, as some critics like to suggest, immigrants offer our best hope for future of strengthening it.

2   The problem, before we even get to my thesis, is the degree to which all discussion about immigration seems to revolve around economic considerations. Consider the preliminary findings of the 2001 census, which showed that new immigrants were mostly responsible for the four-per-cent growth in the population of Canada since 1996. From Jean Chrétien on down, government officials recited the mantra that increased immigration is key to future economic development. This argument encourages us to see immigration primarily as an economic good. But when you start to talk about cultural consequences of immigration, politicians invariably discuss official multiculturalism, a 30-year-old policy that is increasingly unpopular with Canadians for its promotion of a hyphenated national identity.

3   Canadian attitudes towards immigration mirror and then diverge from the government line. A recent Léger Marketing survey indicates that three-quarters of Canadians think immigrants make an economic contribution to the country. But the same poll finds that half of Canadians feel we accept too many immigrants. Forty per cent think Canada is too open to political refugees. Alongside polite support for immigration, many of us wouldn't mind a less competitive job market, or living in communities where people look like "us," eat the same foods and speak the same language. The Léger poll suggests that our commitment to immigration is skin-deep—self-interest and economic preservation still trump social tolerance.

4   Those figures imply that anti-immigrant sentiment still runs high. One way to change that is to make the point that the closer you look, the more you realize that immigrants, despite their disparate cultural interests, strengthen our common values in very deliberate and specific ways. In fact, we should double immigration rates not for economic reasons, but to ensure the preservation of a common set of Canadian values and way of life.

5   In five years of exhaustive polling by my organization—the Dominion Institute, a history advocacy organization—the data has consistently shown that immigrants know more about Canada and Canadian history than natural-born citizens. That applies not only to knowledge of Canada's civic institutions and the way government functions, but also to such issues as Confederation and the patriation of the constitution. Some argue that this is mere trivia—the product of newcomers having to write a basic citizenship exam. But this kind of knowledge represents cultural capital that makes our society work: it allows us as citizens to talk intelligently together about the public good.

6   Immigrants bring unique experience of what it means to be Canadian. For most immigrants, coming to Canada is the result of a rational choice. It may sometimes be an ambiguous one, where memories of a lost homeland mix with the problems of integrating into a new society, but it's still a conscious decision. Because they're the emotional product of both their homeland and adopted country, they constantly question what it means to be Canadian.

By contrast, those of us born here often take Canada for granted. We 7 assume that the country as we have known it in our lifetimes will continue: our contribution to that process is to vote and, perhaps, renew our passport every five years.

A healthy dose of self-examination is good for everyone. In the next 8 decade, many of the traditional hallmarks of the Canadian identity—things like universal health care, an independent military, and border controls between our country and the United States—could be either abolished or radically reworked by the forces of continental integration. As these institutions diminish or disappear, we'll have to rebuild our collective identity around a set of commonly held values that define what it means to be Canadian. While it's hard to predict the composition of those new values, the self-examination that immigrants bring will be essential to figuring out who we are as a nation—and what we hope to accomplish together.

Thinking Critically About Content

1. What is Rudyard Griffiths's main argument about immigration?
2. Paragraphs 3 and 4 offer a rebuttal to Griffiths's argument. What is the rebuttal? Does he effectively bring the "con" information back to the "pro" side?
3. What sort of support does Griffiths use for his argument? Is it organized in an effective way?

Thinking Critically About Purpose and Audience

4. What do you think Griffiths's purpose is in writing this essay?
5. Who do you think would be more persuaded by this essay, someone Canadian-born or a Canadian immigrant? Were you persuaded?
6. An essential part of persuasion is to pull your reader into your argument. Has Griffiths done this effectively? What are some other effective or ineffective aspects of his argument? Explain your answer.

Thinking Critically About Paragraphs

7. Analyze the opening paragraph. Does Griffiths begin his argument essay with an effective introductory paragraph? What is his thesis? Is it located in an effective position?
8. Analyze paragraph 6. Does it have an effective topic and concluding sentence? Are the support sentences organized in an effective order? Does his argument come across clearly? Would you change anything? Explain your answer.
9. Analyze the final paragraph. Is it an effective concluding paragraph? Does it wrap up his argument? Are you persuaded to believe his point? What would you do differently in the conclusion? Explain your answer.
10. Choose a side of the immigration argument and write a paragraph arguing your position.

ARGUING A POSITION

Focusing Your Attention

1. If you were asked to take a strong position on a topic of great importance to you and society, what are some of the topics you would consider?

2. In the two essays you will be reading, one writer tries to persuade readers that smoking bans have a positive influence on helping smokers to quit, while the other argues that smoking should not be banned and that smokers have no effect on non-smokers. Although you haven't read either essay, which one do you think you will agree with?

Roy MacGregor

SMOKING BANS MAY BE JUST THE TICKET—ESPECIALLY FOR THOSE WHO STILL LIGHT UP

Expanding Your Vocabulary

The following words are important to your understanding of this essay.

zealot: a fervent and even militant proponent of something (paragraph 1)

abhor: find repugnant or hateful (paragraph 3)

1   I'm not exactly sure when I became a zealot.

2   But a week ago, while checking into a hotel near the St. Lawrence River, my nose began twitching the second the key opened the door to my room for the night.

3   I immediately went over to the window, held the drapes in hand and ran that same twitching nose over them—not to wipe, but to check for that stale, telltale smell that so many of us have come to abhor.

4   Next step was to sweep the room. Not for hidden microphones to catch me talking in my sleep or small cameras to catch me in my boxers, but for the one sure sign that I'd been had: an *ashtray*.

5   There were two, each with a box of matches supplied.

6   Two minutes later I was back at the front desk, begging for a "No Smoking" room. None being available, I briefly thought of heading for another hotel before, finally, coming to my senses. I slept fine. I am alive today.

7   It is astonishing how much has changed in the very different worlds of smoking and non-smoking. Non-smoking seats in airplanes were once but a couple of rows near the back, rarely filled. There was no such thing as

smoke-free hotel rooms, no bars where you could see from one side of the room to the other.

This column once would never have been salvaged without an editor taking a deep sigh and lighting up before firing up the copydesk chainsaw. 8

The fact that smoking is no longer allowed in planes and, increasingly, not in bars, restaurants and public places is a bit of a hot-button issue among those who still use the car lighter for something other than plugging in a cellphone. 9

Editorials have been written against the tyranny of the now majority— approximately one in five adult men and women smokes—and railing against the "bullying" tactics of the non-smoking public. 10

The tobacco manufacturers even have a current radio campaign to get people to surf onto their website, www.mychoice.ca, which claims it is "committed to restoring common sense, balance and civility to the way Canada's adult smokers are treated by their federal, provincial and municipal politicians." 11

The idea, obviously, is to give a voice to the millions of Canadians who smoke but who do not have a say against higher tobacco taxes and the possibility of "province-wide bans" on smoking in public places, perhaps even in private vehicles. 12

The manufacturers may indeed have a point about civility. A list of "Words of Wisdom" skipping through this week's e-mail includes: "Isn't having a smoking section in a restaurant like having a peeing section in a swimming pool?" The presumption of all this talk, of course, is that any no-smoking regulations are entirely for the benefit of those who do not smoke. 13

And yet, a fascinating study released only yesterday by Statistics Canada suggests that bans on smoking—in the home or workplace, preferably in both—are having a beneficial impact on those smokers who would like to quit. 14

The study, "Smoking: One Step Forward, One Step Back," by Margot Shields, found that those who smoke fewer cigarettes a day, even if they wish to smoke more, found it much easier to quit. Daily smokers who spent chunks of their days in smoke-free environments—at home, work, or both—smoked less. 15

"This is a good news story," says Shields. 16

Paul McDonald agrees. The professor of Health Studies at the University of Waterloo has been going over the results of a detailed study of 2,000 smokers in Canada, the United States, the United Kingdom and Australia. Even to his surprise, the survey found that around 90 per cent of those studied "regretted" that they had ever taken up smoking in the first place. 17

Starting up was the easy part. Quitting was another question entirely. 18

And what the Statscan study appears to indicate, says McDonald, is that smoking bans might be just what these particular smokers need. 19

"The presumption has always been," he says, "that when people advocate a smoking ban, it's to help protect non-smokers. 20

20   "In fact, it turns out that there may be even more benefits to smokers than to non-smokers." There has been, he says, a "gross misunderstanding" about quitting in that it has been presumed that quitting is determined by the individual—choosing to quit for health or money reasons, or through sheer personal willpower—when one of the strongest factors is the environment and the people surrounding the smoker.

21   A smoke-free workplace alone, says McDonald, appears to push the success rate for those trying to quit up as much as 20 per cent. And given the effect smoking has on health-care costs, says McDonald, "this helps everybody, not just one group." No-smoking rules, he would say, are much more than just sops to those who can't stand the smell of stale cigarette smoke in a hotel room.

22   "The message here is good news," says McDonald. "These sorts of things do work."

Rosie DiManno

BUTT OUT? NO CHANCE. I'D RATHER BREAK THE LAW

Expanding Your Vocabulary

The following words and name are important to your understanding of this essay.

> **social engineering:** controlling and shaping people's attitudes and behaviour through legislation or techniques of behaviourist psychology (paragraph 9)
>
> **Mel Lastman:** mayor of Toronto, 1998–2003 (paragraph 20)
>
> **lotus-eaters:** refers to the men in Homer's *Odyssey* who ate lotus fruit and became dreamy and lethargic (paragraph 20)

1   Watching Larry King Live the other night, I was taken aback—as was the host—when a studio guest casually lit a cigarette whilst chatting. King interrupted his interview to remark that he couldn't remember the last time he'd seen someone smoking on TV. But, as a polite host, he didn't ask his guest to butt out. Of course, this particular guest was Tony Sirico, who plays Paulie Walnuts on The Sopranos, a role to which he brings the informed experience of a man who actually spent some five years in the hoosegow before becoming an actor specializing in Wiseguy roles.

2   I love Paulie Walnuts. And now I love Tony Sirico too.

3   It's not often that we come across mavericks anymore, individualists who don't give a fig for rules of convention and decorum, nor anti-smoking laws for that matter. In North America, roughly speaking, about one in four adults still smokes. But you won't see TV characters lighting up, unless the intention is to convey a figure of poor morals, a disagreeable sort, a criminal or a creep.

I know a lot of non-smoking creeps. Actually, if we're going to generalize   4
and stigmatize, most of the creeps I know don't smoke. Further, the creepiest
of all are those who don't smoke and won't let others smoke. And, while I
don't know him personally, I'd characterize Joe Mihevc, chairman of Toronto's
board of health, as a capital-C creep after hearing him fulminate about Zero
Tolerance for smokers, as if they were drug dealers or wife beaters.

The health board is the architect of Toronto's new municipal bylaw   5
which will prohibit smoking in all Toronto restaurants. As of Friday, smoking will be 100 per cent banned in restaurants, with both owners and
patrons subject to fines ranging from $205 to $5,000. What next? Shall we
wear little yellow triangles on our chests?

One hopes smokers and proprietors will ignore the bylaw, just as they   6
did back in 1997, when the city was forced to back down after mass non-
compliance. Once more into the breach! Onward nicotine soldiers!

There are 72 smoking bylaw officers lurking out there, sharpening their   7
pencils, preparing to take names and kick butts. But there are far more of us
than there are them—24 per cent of the population, according to just
released statistics; 35 per cent of men and 30 per cent of women aged 20–24,
the largest smoking group. Despite all the draconian efforts of government
and anti-smoking zealots, sales and production of cigarettes by tobacco
manufacturers actually went up in the first three months of this year—10.1
billion cigarettes sold, a 5 per cent increase over the same period last year.
Supply meeting demand. Therein lies the strongest evidence that all those
restrictions and tactics—forbidding tobacco companies from sponsoring
sports and entertainment, the ghoulish packaging on cigarette packs,
gazillions of dollars spent on public education—have accomplished squat.

The niconazis—and I remind you again that Adolf Hitler was the first and   8
most ga-ga anti-smoking legislator—don't care to be reminded of their astonishing failures. Nor do they wish to be reminded that the largest study ever
undertaken on second-hand smoke—involving seven European countries
over 10 years—could find no statistical link between passive smoke and lung
cancer. This study was co-ordinated by the World Health Organization which,
dismayed by the results, tried to bury the information before finally forced to
publish the study in 1998. WHO's International Agency for Research on Cancer
reluctantly acknowledged that the 16–17 per cent relative risk of contracting
lung cancer from exposure to a smoking spouse or a smoking environment at
work was "statistically non-significant" and could just as easily be attributed
to random chance. Further, the study found "no relationship between childhood exposure to second-hand smoke at home and lung cancer."

But this isn't really about health, is it? It's about social engineering and   9
discrimination against smokers because non-smokers don't like us, don't
like the smell, can't even stand the optics of cigarette smoke.

I'll admit that it bothers me to see young people smoking outside school   10
or at the mall. There's no doubt smoking is harmful to the smoker, that it
leads to lung cancer and respiratory illness. My solution, if I had a smoking
adolescent in my home, would be to force that kid to chain-smoke a couple

of packs of unfiltered Players, one fag after another, until he or she turned green and was retching. Guaranteed, this experience will render the neophyte smoker strongly disinclined towards firing up a dart again. If you can keep teens from smoking, it's unlikely they'll take up the habit later on.

11   But I'm not a teenager. I'm an adult. Actually, I'm an adult who goes for long stretches without smoking, without even thinking about smoking. The niconazis would have you believe no such creature exists. As per usual, they lie. Just as most people who use recreational drugs aren't junkies, will never become junkies, most smokers are not hopeless addicts and they will not die of lung cancer.

12   So, if I've just finished a restaurant meal and want to have a cigarette, in my smoking section of the establishment, among other like-minded adults, what's it to the rest of you? Because you don't like it? Huh. You must be confusing me with someone who gives a damn.

13   In any event, the new bylaw is wildly unfair and discriminatory. Proprietors will have to designate their establishment as either a restaurant or a bar, with smoking permitted in the latter—at least until 2004, when bars, bingo parlours, even private clubs and Legion halls will ostensibly become smoke-free. (As if.) Bars must not allow anyone younger than 19 on to the premises. The argument is that children in restaurants should not be subjected to smoke—and damn the scientific evidence about non-existent harm.

14   The fact is, most restaurants also operate as bars, with the clientele often changing between lunch and dinner. But now they must declare themselves as one or the other. By allowing minors—essentially, by catering to the family trade—you are, ipso facto, a restaurant, exclusively. No smoking. Yet there are no similar restrictions on serving alcohol.

15   Mihevc claims he has received only a handful of protests. I don't believe him. This is the man who wants to create a world where a beer and a smoke in front of a TV screen over the bar will be ancient history, wiped out by enforced "social change." Perhaps Mihevc should remember what happened to Peter Tabuns, his equally dogmatic health chair predecessor, who was subsequently crushed at the polls.

16   It was a pleasant surprise, four years ago, when Toronto smokers refused to be cowed by anti-smoking legislation. Who'd have thought we had such nerve in us? I think of this every time I visit places like Vancouver, where smoking is not allowed anywhere and people huddle outside bars to pound a quick cig. Miserable sheep. What a bunch of pussies.

17   The law will be a hardship for restaurateurs because they are most vulnerable to heavy-handed punishment.

18   But the rest of us should keep in mind that smoking bylaw officers do not have the legal authority to demand that patrons produce identification.

19   No ID, no ticket.

20   If reformed smoker Mayor Mel Lastman and his cohorts on city council want to turn all smokers into scofflaws, they will create a monster. Such schemes work only with a compliant population. But we are not so obsequious. We are not, shudder, Vancouver lotus-eaters.

I don't pretend this is a noble cause. Perhaps it's even ignoble. That's 21
what I like about it.

Don't want to kiss my ashtray mouth? Then kiss my butt. 22

Thinking Critically About Content

1. What statistics are referenced in each essay? How do they serve each argument?

2. What is the main argument for each essay?

3. Why do you think each author cites authorities and examples? Which essay uses authorities and examples to back up its claims more effectively?

Thinking Critically About Purpose and Audience

4. What type of audience would be interested in these essays? Explain your answer.

5. What tone do the authors use? How does the tone affect the reader? How does the tone affect the argument?

6. Which essay do you agree with? Did you agree with that position before you read the argument? Did any part of either essay make you change your mind? Explain your answer.

Thinking Critically About Paragraphs

7. Each author uses a narrative to capture the audience's attention. Which opening do you think is more effective? Explain your answer.

8. Compare the conclusions. Do they both reflect the main topic of each argument?

9. Which paragraph is most convincing in each essay? What makes it so convincing?

10. Write a paragraph arguing for or against your views on smoking bans.

Writing Topics: Arguing and Persuading

Before you begin to write, you might want to review the writing process in Part I.

1. "Open the Gates Wide" argues for the importance of immigration in Canada. According to Rudyard Griffiths, immigrants know more about Canadian politics and history than natural-born citizens do. How will knowing about Canada and its background aid Canadians in arguing for universal health care, an independent military, border control, and other traditional hallmarks of the Canadian identity?

2. The two essays on banning smoking cite opposite views. Which side of the argument do you agree with? Attempt to convince a peer who is on the other side. Gather as much evidence as you can before you begin to write.

3. How can being able to develop good arguments and persuade people of your point of view help you in real life? How might this ability give you the edge over other people in the job market?

The Handbook

This part of *Mosaics* provides you with a complete handbook for editing your writing. You can use it as a reference tool as you write or as a source of instruction and practice in areas of your writing that need work.

This handbook consists of an introduction and eight units:

The chapters in each unit start with a self-test to help you identify your strengths and weaknesses in that area. The answers to these tests are in Appendix 8. Then the chapters teach specific sentence skills and provide exercises so you can practise what you have learned. Each chapter also asks you to write your own sentences and then work with another student to edit each other's writing. At the end of each unit, two review tests are provided that ask you to apply to sentences and paragraphs all that you have practised in the unit.

The Editing Symbols on the inside back cover will give you marks for highlighting errors in your papers. In addition, the Error Log (Appendix 6) and Spelling Log (Appendix 7) will help you tailor the instruction to your own needs and keep track of your progress.

INTRODUCTION: PARTS OF SPEECH, PHRASES, AND CLAUSES

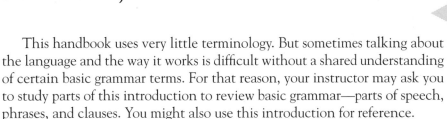

This handbook uses very little terminology. But sometimes talking about the language and the way it works is difficult without a shared understanding of certain basic grammar terms. For that reason, your instructor may ask you to study parts of this introduction to review basic grammar—parts of speech, phrases, and clauses. You might also use this introduction for reference.

This section has three parts:

Parts of Speech
Phrases
Clauses

PARTS OF SPEECH

Test Yourself

In the following paragraph, label two examples of each of the parts of speech listed here:

verbs (v)	adverbs (adv)
nouns (n)	prepositions (prep)
pronouns (pro)	conjunctions (conj)
adjectives (adj)	interjections (int)

The personality trait that I like best about myself is my healthy sense of humour. No matter how bad a situation is, I can usually find something funny to say to cheer everyone up. When Toby's ancient car was stolen, I told him it was a piece of junk anyway, and I felt sorry for the foolish person who stole it. Man, we laughed so hard, imagining the car thief broken down on the side of the road somewhere in town. Oh, there are some things that I don't even try to joke about, like death and diseases. A person would have to be extremely insensitive to joke about those situations.

(Answers are in Appendix 8.)

Every sentence is made up of a variety of words that play different roles. Each word, like each part of a coordinated outfit, serves a distinct function. These functions fall into eight categories:

1. Verbs
2. Nouns
3. Pronouns
4. Adjectives
5. Adverbs
6. Prepositions
7. Conjunctions
8. Interjections

Some words, such as *is*, can function in only one way—in this case, as a verb. Other words, however, can serve as different parts of speech depending on how they are used in a sentence. For example, look at the different ways the word *burn* can be used:

Verb:	The farmers **burn** the fields after every harvest.
	(*Burn* is a verb here, telling what the farmers do.)
Noun:	Yolanda's **burn** healed well.
	(*Burn* functions as a noun here, telling what healed.)
Adjective:	My mom found two **burn** marks on the sofa.
	(*Burn* is an adjective here, modifying the noun *marks*.)

Verbs

The **verb** is the most important word in a sentence because every other word depends on it in some way. Verbs tell what's going on in the sentence.

There are three types of verbs: action, linking, and helping. An **action verb** tells what someone or something is doing. A **linking verb** tells what someone or something is, feels, or looks like. Sometimes an action or linking verb has **helping verbs**—words that add information, such as when an action is taking place. A **complete verb** consists of an action or linking verb and all the helping verbs.

Action:	We **started** the fire too close to the tent.
Action:	Mark **voted** in the election.
Linking:	We **felt** really smart.
Linking:	It **was** the most embarrassing moment in my life.
Helping:	She **will be** arriving tomorrow.
Helping:	I **have** been so tired lately.

Complete Verb: She **will be arriving** tomorrow.

Complete Verb: I **have been** so tired lately.

REVIEWING VERBS

Define each of the following types of verbs, and give an example of each.

Action: _____

_____

Linking: _____

_____

*Helping:*_____

_____

What is a complete verb? Give an example with your definition.

_____

_____

◆ *P r a c t i c e 1* **Identifying** In each of the following sentences, under-line the complete verbs. Some sentences have more than one verb.

1. We left on our fishing expedition when we got off work.

2. My brother has felt guilty since he took my money.

3. People sometimes think more than they act.

4. The first sign of trouble came almost immediately.

5. Next weekend we will be going Christmas shopping at the mall.

◆ *P r a c t i c e 2* **Completing** Fill in each blank in the following paragraph with a verb.

Last weekend we (1) _____ to go shopping at a nearby outlet mall. Before we got out of the city limits, Maryl (2) _____ that she was really thirsty and Kurt (3) _____ hungry. So we stopped at the first convenience store we saw. While Kurt and Maryl were inside the store, I

(4) _____ steam coming from under the hood of my car.
After checking it out, I (5) _____ water leaking from the
radiator, so we cancelled the trip and went home.

◆ *P r a c t i c e   3*   **Writing Your Own**   Write a sentence of your own for
each of the following verbs.

1. had been going _____

2. chuckled _____

3. appeared _____

4. did become _____

5. whispers _____

Nouns

People often think of **nouns** as "naming words" because they identify—
or name—people (*friend, Brian, dad, officer*), places (*town, lake, Kamloops*),
or things (*tree, boat, table, belt*). Nouns also name ideas (*freedom, democracy*), qualities (*honesty, courage*), emotions (*fear, anxiety*), and actions
(*competition, negotiations*). A **common noun** names something general
(*actor, mountain, pop, restaurant*). A **proper noun** names something specific
(*Kiefer Sutherland, Whistler Mountain, Pepsi, Burger King*).

Hint: To test whether a word is a noun, try putting *a*, *an*, or *the* in front
of it:

Nouns: a friend, an apple, the love
NOT Nouns: a silly, an around, the sing

This test does not work with proper nouns:

NOT   a Ken, the Halifax

REVIEWING NOUNS

What is a noun?

_____

_____

> **What is the difference between a common noun and a proper noun? Give an example of each.**
>
> Common noun: _____
>
> _____
>
> Proper noun: _____
>
> _____

◆ *P r a c t i c e   4*   **Identifying**   Underline all the nouns in the following sentences.

1. Students in college have many responsibilities.
2. Before my friend ran in the marathon, she trained for months.
3. Last fall, my husband and I bought our first house.
4. David nodded his head while I presented my ideas.
5. Ontario is known for its many lakes and excellent universities.

◆ *P r a c t i c e   5*   **Completing**   Fill in each blank in the following paragraph with a noun that will make each sentence complete.

My best (1) _____ is my brother Ben. He is 18, about six feet tall with curly brown hair. He is really a neat (2) _____. I have to say that he is unusual and does his own thing. For example, he likes to wear (3) _____ during the wintertime. When he goes out, people usually point and stare. Ben just shakes his (4) _____ and keeps on walking. But Ben's best qualities are his (5) _____ and his (6) _____ to help people.

Pronouns

Pronouns can do anything nouns can do. In fact, **pronouns** can take the place of nouns. Without pronouns, you would find yourself repeating nouns and producing boring sentences. Compare the following sentences, for example:

Maxine picked up **Maxine's** cellphone and called **Maxine's** friend Sam to say **Maxine** was on **Maxine's** way.

Maxine picked up **her** cellphone and called **her** friend Sam to say **she** was on **her** way.

There are many different types of pronouns, but you only need to focus on the following four types for now.

Most Common Pronouns

Personal (refer to people or things)

Singular:	*First Person:*	*I, me, my, mine*
	Second Person:	*you, your, yours*
	Third Person:	*he, she, it, him, her, hers, his, its*
Plural:	*First Person:*	*we, us, our, ours*
	Second Person:	*you, your, yours*
	Third Person:	*they, them, their, theirs*

Demonstrative (point out someone or something)

Singular:	*this, that*
Plural:	*these, those*

Relative (introduce a dependent clause)

who, whom, whose, which, that

Indefinite (refer to someone or something general, not specific)

Singular:	*another, anybody, anyone, anything, each, either, everybody, everyone, everything, little, much, neither, nobody, none, no one, nothing, one, other, somebody, someone, something*
Plural:	*both, few, many, others, several*
Either Singular or Plural:	*all, any, more, most, some*

Hint: When any of these words are used with nouns, they are pronouns used as adjectives.

Adjective:	She can have **some cookies.**
Pronoun:	She can have **some.**

Adjective:	I want **that car.**
Pronoun:	I want **that.**

REVIEWING PRONOUNS

What is a pronoun?

_____

Define the four most common types of pronouns, and give two examples of each.

Personal: _____

Demonstrative: _____

Relative: _____

Indefinite: _____

◆ *P r a c t i c e 6* **Identifying** Underline all the pronouns in the following sentences. Don't underline pronouns that are really adjectives.

1. Some of the vegetables were shipped from Ontario.
2. I don't believe he could have committed such crimes.
3. Whoever took the last piece of pie should confess!
4. If we help each other, we can finish by Sunday.
5. This is the last time I spend any of my money calling a psychic hotline.

◆ *P r a c t i c e 7* **Completing** In the following paragraph, replace the nouns in parentheses with pronouns.

     Have you ever received an anonymous card or letter? I did. In fact, I received several cards. To this day I still don't know who sent (1) _____ (the cards). I remember when I got the first card. (2) _____ (The card) was written in a scratchy handwriting and signed "Your Secret Admirer." Of course, I asked my friends Amy and Beth whether (3) _____ (Amy and Beth) knew who had sent it. Though (4) _____ (Amy and Beth) denied it, I think Amy was more involved than (5) _____ (Amy) admits.

Adjectives

Adjectives modify—or describe—nouns or pronouns. Adjectives generally make sentences clear and vivid.

Without Adjectives: We had our rods, a cooler, and some sandwiches for the trip.

With Adjectives: We had our **trusty fly** rods, a **white plastic** cooler, and **several tuna** sandwiches for the trip.

REVIEWING ADJECTIVES

What is an adjective?

_____

Give three examples of adjectives.

_____   _____   _____

◀ *P r a c t i c e 8*   **Identifying** Underline all the adjectives in the following sentences.

1. Her long red hair bounced as she walked down the sunlit street.
2. Carl's successful career results from his hard work and pure determination.
3. Ali's poor old car needs two new tires and a complete under-the-hood check.
4. If you want to go on the camping trip, turn in the registration slip.
5. My little brother lost the remote control for our big-screen TV.

◀ *P r a c t i c e 9*   **Completing** Fill in each blank in the following paragraph with an adjective.

We went to a (1) _____ play at the Little Theatre on campus. It was a (2) _____ comedy written by a (3) _____ student at our school. The lead actor was a (4) _____ guy who kept everyone laughing with his (5) _____ faces and clever lines.

Adverbs

Adverbs modify—or describe—adjectives, verbs, and other adverbs. They do *not* modify nouns. Adverbs also answer the following questions:

How?	carefully, fast, quickly, slowly
When?	yesterday, lately, early, now
Where?	outside, here, there, deeply
How often?	usually, seldom, regularly, promptly
To what extent?	very, almost, too, hardly

Hint: Notice that adverbs often end in *-ly*. That might help you recognize them.

REVIEWING ADVERBS

What is an adverb?

_____

What are the five questions that adverbs answer?

_____ _____ _____ _____ _____

Give one example of an adverb that answers each question.

_____ _____ _____ _____ _____

◆ *P r a c t i c e 1 0* **Identifying** Underline all the adverbs in the following sentences.

1. My curious cat sat very quietly for a few seconds before she quickly pounced on the fly.

2. Steve was quite upset after badly missing the shot.

3. We will never do business with the Simpsons again.

4. Often Mr. Ringold asks, "Are you working hard or hardly working?"

5. I don't necessarily think we need to go there tomorrow.

◆ *P r a c t i c e 11*   **Completing** Fill in each blank in the following paragraph with an adverb.

(1) _____ I decided to find a new job, a (2) _____ easy task, or so I thought. I began by (3) _____ going through the phone book and listing each business that I thought would be hiring (4) _____. After calling ten businesses that said they weren't hiring, I (5) _____ realized this job hunt would be more difficult than I first thought.

Prepositions

Prepositions indicate relationships among the ideas in a sentence. Something is *up, down, next to, behind, around, near,* or *under* something else. A preposition is always followed by a noun or a pronoun called the **object of the preposition.** Together, they form a **prepositional phrase.**

Preposition	+	Object	=	Prepositional Phrase
of	+	the supplies	=	of the supplies
for	+	the lake	=	for the lake

Here is a list of some common prepositions.

Common Prepositions

about	beside	into	since
above	between	like	through
across	beyond	near	throughout
after	by	next to	to
against	despite	of	toward
among	down	off	under
around	during	on	until
as	except	on top of	up
at	for	out	upon
before	from	out of	up to
behind	in	outside	with
below	in front of	over	within
beneath	inside	past	without

Hint: *To* + a verb (as in *to go, to come, to feel*) is not a prepositional phrase. It is a verb phrase, which we will deal with later in this unit.

REVIEWING PREPOSITIONS

What is a preposition?

_____

Give two examples of prepositions:

_____   _____

What is a prepositional phrase?

_____

Give two examples of prepositional phrases:

_____   _____

Practice 12 **Identifying** Underline all the prepositions in the following sentences.

1. James said the concert by the college jazz band would take place during the last week of May.
2. Carl was with us when we talked after the party.
3. Before the movie, we talked among ourselves in a downtown park.
4. Sharon was lying on the couch watching *Jeopardy* on TV when I walked into the room.
5. Colin looked under his bed and inside his closet, but he never found his math book.

Practice 13 **Completing** Fill in each blank in the following paragraph with a preposition.

One day as I waited (1) _____ the bus, a tall man sat down (2) _____ me on the bench and began talking (3) _____ the weather. I agreed that it certainly had been hot (4) _____ the city. As we were talking, a police officer came around the corner and began walking (5) _____ the sidewalk toward us. For some strange reason, the man quickly stood up and walked away.

Conjunctions

Conjunctions connect groups of words. Without conjunctions, most of our writing would be choppy and boring. The two types of conjunctions are easy to remember because their names state their purpose: *Coordinating conjunctions* link equal ideas, and *subordinating conjunctions* make one idea subordinate to—or dependent on—another.

Coordinating conjunctions connect parts of a sentence that are of equal importance or weight. These parts can be **independent clauses,** a group of words with a subject and verb that can stand alone as a sentence (see page 286). There are only seven coordinating conjunctions.

Coordinating Conjunctions

---

and, but, or, nor, for, so, yet

Coordinating: I wanted to explore the caves, **and** Greg wanted to go up in a hot air balloon.

Coordinating: Our adventure turned into a nightmare, **but** we learned an important lesson.

Subordinating conjunctions join two ideas by making one dependent on the other. The idea introduced by the subordinating conjunction becomes a **dependent clause,** a group of words with a subject and a verb that cannot stand alone as a sentence (see page 287). The other part of the sentence is an independent clause.

Dependent Clause
Subordinating: I don't know **when** I will return.

Dependent Clause
Subordinating: **If we save enough money**, we can go to the Calgary Stampede.

Here are some common subordinating conjunctions.

Common Subordinating Conjunctions

after	because	since	until
although	before	so	when
as	even if	so that	whenever
as if	even though	than	where
as long as	how	that	wherever
as soon as	if	though	whether
as though	in order that	unless	while

REVIEWING CONJUNCTIONS

What is a coordinating conjunction?

_____

_____

Name the seven coordinating conjunctions.

_____ _____ _____ _____ _____ _____ _____

What is a subordinating conjunction?

_____

_____

Write a sentence using a subordinating conjunction.

_____

◀ *Practice 14* **Identifying** Underline all the conjunctions in the following sentences.

1. I hate going grocery shopping, though I love to cook.
2. Whether or not you're ready for it, becoming a parent will change your life.
3. You can't rent a car unless you have a credit card.
4. Nicole would make a great attorney, and she would get paid to argue.
5. I thought this class was easy until we took the midterm.

◀ *Practice 15* **Completing** Fill in each blank in the following paragraph with a conjunction.

　　(1) _____ I work two jobs and go to school, I have little spare time. Whenever possible, I try very hard to find time for myself. (2) _____ I have so many things to do, I sit down and write out everything in the order it has to be done. I try to make a schedule, (3) _____ I have a tendency to get side-tracked. For example, (4) _____ I have homework, it has to be my first priority. But (5) _____ work and school are finished, I make sure I save time for my friends.

Interjections

Interjections are words that express strong emotion, surprise, or disappointment. An interjection is usually followed by an exclamation point or a comma.

Interjection: **Help!** The boat is drifting away.

Interjection: **Wow,** what an unbelievable game!

Other common interjections include *aha, awesome, great, hallelujah, neat, oh, oops, ouch, well, whoa, yeah,* and *yippee.*

REVIEWING INTERJECTIONS

What is an interjection?

_____

_____

Write a sentence using an interjection.

_____

Practice 16   **Identifying** Underline all the interjections in the following sentences.

1. Yeah! We got the best seats in the house!
2. Man, my legs are tired after running ten kilometres.
3. Oh, I almost forgot that I have a dentist appointment.
4. That was the best grade I've ever received in math. Hallelujah!
5. Ouch! I stubbed my toe.

Practice 17   **Completing** Fill in each blank in the following paragraph with an interjection.

(1) _____, was I tired last night! I woke up yesterday morning at the crack of dawn, climbed into the shower, and slipped on the bar of soap before I could even get my eyes completely open. (2) _____! Then I got into my car and, (3) _____, it wouldn't start. After calling a friend to give

me a ride to work, I got to my desk to find an emergency project that needed to be completed before the end of my shift. (4) _____, I worked on it all day, though I had to stay late to finish it. (5) _____! I am so glad that day is over!

PHRASES

Test Yourself

Underline the phrases in the following sentences.

- After the concert, we decided to get some food.
- To get a good grade on the test, I know I have to study harder.
- Ben lives in the brick house at the end of the block behind the park.
- I am going to get a job this year.
- Do you want to see a movie with us?

(Answers are in Appendix 8.)

A **phrase** is a group of words that function together as a unit. Phrases cannot stand alone, however, because they are missing either a subject, a verb, or both.

Phrases:	the black mountain bike, a happy person
Phrases:	turned up the music, cruised the mall, opened my present
Phrases:	after school, in the back room, by myself, on the green grass
Phrases:	telling us the answer, to be fooled

Notice that all these groups of words are missing either a subject, a verb, or both.

REVIEWING PHRASES

What is a phrase?

_____

_____

Give two examples of phrases.

_____   _____

◆ *P r a c t i c e   1 8*   **Identifying**   Underline eight phrases in the following sentences.

1.   Looking out the window, I watched the countryside from the train.

2.   I like to do adventurous things like skydiving and rock climbing.
3.   My favourite vacation was our trip to the Bahamas three years ago.
4.   Customers should have completed their deposit slips.
5.   Save energy by turning off the lights after everyone has left the room.

◆ *P r a c t i c e   1 9*   **Completing**   Fill in each blank in the following paragraph with a phrase.

Sang went (1) _____ early because he had worked overtime yesterday afternoon. But since his roommate was cleaning the apartment, (2) _____, and (3) _____, Sang knew he would not be able to sleep. Tony, Sang's roommate, wanted everything clean because his parents (4) _____. His last chore was to get a can of air freshener (5) _____ and spray it around the apartment.

CLAUSES

Test Yourself

Underline the clauses in the following sentences.

•   Mallory will get what she wants out of life because she is assertive.
•   Since you don't have time to go to dinner, I'll bring you some food.
•   If Rachel is going to leave first, she needs a map.
•   We finished painting, and then we celebrated.
•   I enjoyed the book the most when Harry Potter got the sorcerer's stone.

(Answers are in Appendix 8.)

Like phrases, **clauses** are groups of words. But unlike phrases, a clause always contains a subject and a verb. There are two types of clauses: *independent* and *dependent*.

An **independent clause** contains a subject and a verb and can stand alone and make sense by itself. Every complete sentence must have at least one independent clause.

Independent Clause: We planned our vacation very carefully.

Now look at the following group of words. It is a clause because it contains a subject and a verb. But it is a **dependent clause** because it is introduced by a word that makes it dependent, *since*.

Dependent Clause: **Since** we planned our vacation very carefully.

This clause cannot stand alone. It must be connected to an independent clause to make sense. Here is one way to complete the dependent clause and form a complete sentence.

Dependent   Independent

<u>**Since** we planned our vacation very carefully</u>, <u>we had a great time</u>.

Hint: Subordinating conjunctions (such as *since, although, because, while*) and relative pronouns (*who, whom, whose, which, that*) make clauses dependent. (For more information on subordinating conjunctions, see page 282, and on relative pronouns, see page 276.)

REVIEWING CLAUSES

For a group of words to be a clause, it must have a _____

and a _____ .

What is an independent clause?

_____

_____

What is a dependent clause?

_____

_____

Name the two kinds of words that can begin a dependent clause.

_____   _____

Name five subordinating conjunctions.

_____ _____ _____ _____ _____

Name the five relative pronouns.

_____ _____ _____ _____ _____

◆ *P r a c t i c e   2 0*   **Identifying** Each of the following sentences is made up of two clauses. Circle the coordinating or subordinating conjunctions and relative pronouns. Then label each clause either independent (Ind) or dependent (Dep).

1. When Veronica got up, she made her bed and brushed her teeth.
2. The truck swerved toward his car, and Jason veered to the side of the road.
3. Unless you are planning to major in science, you don't need to take chemistry.
4. I am familiar with the person who won the contest.
5. Until he makes the team, Chan will continue to practise his swing.

◆ *P r a c t i c e   2 1*   **Completing** Add an independent or dependent clause that will complete each sentence and make sense.

Matt is an artist (1) who _____. (2) He
_____. He buys supplies with half of his earnings,
(3) and _____. His most recent drawing won a
prize, (4) which _____. He says he will never sell it
(5) because _____.

REVIEW

You might want to reread your answers to the questions in all the review boxes before you do the following exercises.

◆ *Review   P r a c t i c e   1*   **Identifying** Use the following abbreviations to label the underlined words in these sentences.

v	Verb	adv	Adverb
n	Noun	prep	Preposition
pro	Pronoun	conj	Conjunction
adj	Adjective	int	Interjection
ph	Phrase	cl	Clause

1. <u>Hey</u>, remember to meet with <u>your</u> <u>counselor</u> <u>before</u> choosing your <u>classes</u>.

2. Stacy <u>works</u> as a <u>telephone</u> salesperson and <u>has</u> to meet a <u>daily</u> quota.

3. An <u>education</u> enables people to obtain knowledge, <u>confidence</u>, <u>and</u> marketable skills.

4. There is <u>nothing</u> better than a <u>warm</u> fire on a <u>cold</u> day.

5. If you <u>maintain</u> a B+ average, you will <u>likely</u> qualify <u>for</u> grants <u>or</u> scholarships.

◆ *Review P r a c t i c e 2* **Completing** Fill in each blank in the following paragraph with an appropriate word, phrase, or clause, as indicated.

    I saved money for six months to buy a new (1) _____ (noun) for my (2) _____ (adjective) car. I found a store where I could (3) _____ (verb) this product, (4) _____ (conjunction) I waited an extra week for it to go on sale. The store was located (5) _____ (preposition) town, but it was worth the drive. (6) _____ (interjection)! I had wanted this thing for a long time! On my next day off work, I (7) _____ (adverb) drove to the store and made the purchase. I talked to the salesperson for about an hour, and (8) _____ (pronoun) assured me I was making a wise purchase. But when (9) _____ (clause), the item I had saved so long for did not work properly, and I completely lost my temper. I picked the thing up and angrily threw it (10) _____ (phrase).

◆ *Review P r a c t i c e 3* **Writing Your Own** Write your own paragraph about your favourite pet. What did you name it? What kind of animal was it?

◆ *Review P r a c t i c e 4* **Editing Your Writing** Exchange paragraphs from Review Practice 3 with a classmate, and do the following:

1. Circle any words that are used incorrectly.
2. Underline any phrases that do not read smoothly.
3. Put an X in the margin where you find a dependent clause that is not connected to an independent clause.

Then return the paragraph to its writer, and use the information in the Introduction to edit your own paragraph. Record your errors on the Error Log in Appendix 6.

CHAPTER 30

SUBJECTS AND VERBS

✔ CHECKLIST for Identifying Subjects and Verbs

> ✔ Does each of your sentences contain a subject?
> ✔ Does each of your sentences contain a verb?

Test Yourself

Circle the subjects and underline the verbs in each sentence.

- We really liked the movie.
- Melissa and Brian left early.
- She is in class.
- Clean your room.
- The Masons have never remodeled their kitchen.
- She checked the oil and put air in the tires.

(Answers are in Appendix 8.)

A sentence has a message to communicate, but for communication to take place, it must have a subject and a verb. The subject is the topic of the sentence or what the sentence is about. The verb is the sentence's motor. It moves the message forward to its destination. Without these two parts, the sentence is not complete.

SUBJECTS

To be complete, every sentence must have a subject. The **subject** tells who or what the sentence is about.

> **Subject**
> ↓
> **She** never liked movies at all.
> Mystery **novels** appeal to everyone.

Compound Subjects

When two or more separate words tell what the sentence is about, the sentence has a **compound subject.**

Compound Subject: **Hamburgers** and **hotdogs** are my favourite foods.

Compound Subject: **Margaret** and **I** watch movies every night.

Hint: Note that *and* is not part of the compound subject.

Unstated Subjects

Sometimes a subject does not actually appear in a sentence but is understood. This occurs in commands and requests. The understood subject is always *you*, meaning either someone specific or anyone in general.

Command: Call your boss in the morning.

Unstated Subject: **(You)** call your boss in the morning.

Request: Pass me the salt, please.

Unstated Subject: **(You)** pass me the salt, please.

Subjects and Prepositional Phrases

The subject of a sentence cannot be part of a prepositional phrase. A **prepositional phrase** is a group of words that begins with a **preposition,** a word like *in, on, under, after,* or *from.* Here are some examples of prepositional phrases:

in the hall	**next to** me	**on** the stairs	**before** dinner
under your pillow	**with** Brad	**behind** the car	**instead of** you
after lunch	**into** the cave	**around** the block	**across** the street
from the mayor's office	**during** the day	**for** the child	**at** home

(See page 280 for a more complete list of prepositions.)

If you are looking for the subject of a sentence, first cross out all the prepositional phrases. Then figure out what the sentence is about.

~~After dinner~~, my friend and I went home.

^s
The classified ads ~~in the local newspaper~~ were misleading.

^s
One ~~of our cows~~ got ~~into a neighbouring pasture~~ last night.

REVIEWING SUBJECTS

What is a subject?

_____

What is a compound subject?

_____

_____

What is an unstated subject?

_____

How can you find the subject of a sentence?

_____

_____

◆ *P r a c t i c e   **1**   **Identifying** Cross out the prepositional phrases in each of the following sentences, and then underline the subjects.

1. The boxers stood in their corners.
2. One of the artists is showing his paintings at the Mira Godard Gallery in Toronto.
3. Manuel and Jack are both good guitar players.
4. After the first of the year, I will begin preparing my taxes.
5. Start working on your term paper immediately.

◆ *P r a c t i c e   **2**   **Completing** Fill in each blank in the following sentences with a subject without using a person's name.

1. _____ slept fitfully last night.
2. _____ strutted across the stage to a cheering crowd.
3. Sitting high above the pool, _____ thought about life.

4. Sometimes _____ comes out all wrong.

5. _____ are always backing out at the last moment.

VERBS

To be complete, a sentence must have a verb as well as a subject. A **verb** tells what the subject is doing or what is happening.

Verb
↓

She   never **liked** movies at all.
Mystery novels   **appeal** to everyone.

Action Verbs

An **action verb** tells what a subject is doing. Some examples of action verbs are *run, skate, discuss, hurt, allow, forget, pretend, hope, laugh, increase, listen,* and *hurry*.

Action Verb: The players **raced** down the court.

Action Verb: The bus **stopped** at the bus stop.

Linking Verbs

A **linking verb** connects the subject to other words in the sentence that say something about it. Linking verbs are also called **state-of-being verbs** because they do not show action. Rather, they say that something "is" a particular way. The most common linking verb is *be* (*am, are, is, was, were*).

Linking Verb: The cats **are** in the other room.

Linking Verb: He **was** very happy to see her.

Other common linking verbs are *become, feel, look, appear,* and *seem*.

Linking: She **became** a lawyer.

Linking: Mom **feels** sick.

Linking: His beard **looks** rough and scratchy.

Linking: Ashley and Jack **appear** very worried.

Linking: My brother **seems** happy with his choice of career.

Some words, like *smell* and *taste,* can be either action verbs or linking verbs.

Action: I **smell** a skunk.

Linking: This rose **smells** so fragrant.

Action: I **tasted** the stew.

Linking: It **tasted** very good.

Compound Verbs

Just as a verb can have more than one subject, some subjects can have more than one verb. These are called **compound verbs.**

Compound Verb: She **watches** and **feeds** his dog on the weekends.

Compound Verb: I **visit** my grandparents and **play** cards with them.

Hint: A sentence can have both a compound subject and a compound verb.

s   s   v   v

Gus and **Burt ran** from the car and **dove** into the water.

Helping Verbs

Often the **main verb** (the action verb or linking verb) in a sentence needs help to convey its meaning. **Helping verbs** add information, such as when an action took place. The **complete verb** consists of a main verb and all its helping verbs.

Complete Verb: The horses **are** galloping to the finish line.

Complete Verb: Angelica **did** feel angry.

Complete Verb: They **might** come with us.

Complete Verb: Maybe we **should have** gone to the library.

Complete Verb: My favourite teacher **used to give** a quiz every week.

Complete Verb: Duane **will** not **be** graduating this year.

Hint: Note that *not* isn't part of the helping verb. Similarly, *never, always, only, just,* and *still* are never part of the verb.

Complete Verb: I **have** never **been** so **insulted** in my life.

The most common helping verbs are

be, am, is, are, was, were
have, has, had
do, did

Other common helping verbs are

may, might
can, could
will, would
should, used to, ought to

REVIEWING VERBS

What is a verb?

_____

What is the difference between action and linking verbs?

_____

_____

Give an example of a compound verb. _____

Give an example of a helping verb. _____

What is the difference between a subject and a verb?

_____

_____

◆ *P r a c t i c e   3*   **Identifying** Underline the complete verbs in each of the following sentences.

1. The workers became tired early.
2. *Flare* has been recognized as a very popular magazine.
3. One young woman with too many problems left school early.
4. If she succeeds, she feels happy and fulfilled.
5. Don't encourage her.

◆ *P r a c t i c e   4*   **Completing** Fill in each blank in the following sentences with a verb. Avoid using *is*, *are*, *was*, and *were* except as helping verbs.

1. Dmitri _____ extremely lucky.
2. The field workers _____ tired.
3. My manager _____ crossword puzzles every day.
4. Both the instructors and the deans _____ patiently for the meeting to begin.
5. Computers _____ our daily lives.

CHAPTER REVIEW

You might want to reread your answers to the questions in all the review boxes before you do the following exercises.

◆ ***Review P r a c t i c e 1* Identifying** Underline the subjects once and the verbs twice in each of the following sentences. Cross out the prepositional phrases first.

1. The competitors eyed one another warily and looked ready for the game.
2. Sculptors work from a variety of raw material.
3. David was quite a good piano player.
4. After April 15th, she will begin her campaign for office.
5. Every year, her parents put money into her college fund.

◆ ***Review P r a c t i c e 2* Completing** Fill in the missing subject(s) or verb(s) in each of the following sentences.

1. _____ got the best seats in the house.
2. Usually _____ just waited and hoped for someone else to volunteer.
3. Mark and Mabel _____ to stay at the fancy hotel.
4. Every day _____ leaves the house to go to work in the grocery store.
5. Carrying the grand piano _____ a difficult task.

◆ ***Review P r a c t i c e 3* Writing Your Own** Write a paragraph explaining what you would do if you won the lottery.

◆ ***Review P r a c t i c e 4* Editing Through Collaboration** Exchange paragraphs from Review Practice 3 with another student, and do the following:

1. Circle the subjects.
2. Underline the verbs.

Then return the paragraph to its writer, and edit any sentences in your own paragraph that do not have both a subject and a verb. Record your errors on the Error Log in Appendix 6.

FRAGMENTS

✅ CHECKLIST for Identifying and Correcting Fragments

✔ Does each sentence have a subject?
✔ Does each sentence have a verb?

Test Yourself

Put an X by the sentences that are fragments.

- _____ We were hoping that the test would be easy.
- _____ Which he did not see at first.
- _____ She wanted to become a musician.
- _____ Running to catch the plane, with her suitcase flying.
- _____ Since the newspaper had reported it.

(Answers are in Appendix 8.)

One of the most common errors in college or university writing is the fragment. A fragment is a piece of a sentence that is punctuated as a complete sentence but does not express a complete thought. Once you learn how to identify fragments, you can avoid them in your writing.

ABOUT FRAGMENTS

A complete sentence must have both a subject and a verb. If one or both are missing or if the subject and verb are introduced by a dependent word, you have only part of a sentence, a **fragment.** Even if it begins with a capital letter and ends with a period, it cannot stand alone and must be corrected in your writing. The five most common types of fragments are explained in this chapter.

Type 1: Afterthought Fragments
He works out at the gym. **And runs several kilometres a week.**

Type 2: *-ing* Fragments

Finding no food in the refrigerator. Betty went to the store.

Type 3: *to* Fragments

The company sponsored a national training program. **To increase its sales by 20 per cent.**

Type 4: Dependent-Clause Fragments

Since he bought a Chevy Blazer. His insurance has gone up.

Type 5: Relative-Clause Fragments

I climbed Mt. Everest. **Which is the tallest mountain in the world.**

Once you have identified a fragment, you have two options for correcting it. You can connect the fragment to the sentence before or after it, or you can make the fragment into an independent clause.

Ways to Correct Fragments

Correction 1:   *Connect the fragment to the sentence before or after it.*

Correction 2:   *Make the fragment into an independent clause:*

   (a) add the missing subject and/or verb, or

   (b) drop the subordinating word before the fragment.

We will discuss these corrections for each type of fragment.

REVIEWING FRAGMENTS

What is a sentence fragment?

_____

_____

What are the five types of fragments?

_____   _____

_____   _____

_____

What are the two ways to correct a fragment?

1. _____

2. _____

IDENTIFYING AND CORRECTING FRAGMENTS

The rest of this chapter discusses the five types of fragments and the corrections for each type.

Type 1: Afterthought Fragments

Afterthought fragments occur when you add an idea to a sentence but don't punctuate it correctly.

Fragment: He works out at the gym. **And runs several kilometres a week.**

The phrase *And runs several kilometres a week* is punctuated and capitalized as a complete sentence. Because this group of words lacks a subject, however, it is a fragment.

Correction 1:   *Connect the fragment to the sentence before or after it.*

Example: He works out at the gym **and** runs several kilometres a week.

Correction 2:   *Make the fragment into an independent clause.*

Example: He works out at the gym. **He** runs several kilometres a week.

The first correction connects the fragment to the sentence before it or after it. The second correction makes the fragment an independent clause with its own subject and verb.

REVIEWING AFTERTHOUGHT FRAGMENTS

What is an afterthought fragment?

_____

Give an example of an afterthought fragment.

_____

What are the two ways to correct an afterthought fragment?

1. _____

2. _____

_____

◆ *P r a c t i c e   **1 A**   **Identifying** Underline the afterthought fragments in each of the following sentences.

1. The competition was tough. We were all afraid to play them. Including me.
2. With his face against the window. He could see his keys lying on the end table.
3. She stayed up late last night. Now she's sleeping. In class.
4. Spring is my favourite time of year. With all the flowers in bloom. And lovers holding hands.
5. Aikio was very nervous. Before her job interview. I hope she calms down.

◆ *P r a c t i c e   **1 B**   **Correcting** Correct the fragments in Practice 1A by rewriting each sentence.

◆ *P r a c t i c e   **2**   **Completing** Correct the following afterthought fragments using both correction 1 and correction 2. Rewrite any corrected sentences that you think could be smoother.

1. She found a beautiful vase at the yard sale. Also some antique chairs.

   _____

2. Benny studied really hard. Lisa, too.

   _____

3. My mom makes the best brownies. Sometimes with walnuts and frosting.

   _____

4. They married December 6. In Las Vegas.

   _____

5. The mysterious woman stood in the doorway. And stared at him.

   _____

Type 2: *-ing* Fragments

Words that end in *-ing* are forms of verbs but cannot be the main verbs in their sentences. For an *-ing* word to function as a verb, it must have a helping verb with it (see page 294).

Fragment: **Finding no food in the refrigerator.** Shoshana went to the store.

Finding is not a verb in this sentence because it has no helping verb. Also, this group of words is a fragment because it has no subject.

Correction 1:   *Connect the fragment to the sentence before or after it.*

Example: **Finding no food in the refrigerator,** Shoshana went to the store.

Correction 2:   *Make the fragment into an independent clause.*

Example: **She found no food in the refrigerator.** Shoshana went to the store.

Hint: When you connect an *-ing* fragment to a sentence, insert a comma between the two sentence parts. You should insert the comma whether the *-ing* part comes at the beginning or the end of the sentence.

Dennis went to the store, **finding no food in the refrigerator.**
Finding no food in the refrigerator, Dennis went to the store.

REVIEWING *-ing* FRAGMENTS

How can you tell if an -ing word is part of a fragment or is a main verb?

_____

_____

Give an example of an -ing fragment.

_____

What are the two ways to correct an -ing fragment?

1. _____

2. _____

_____

What kind of punctuation should you use when you join an -ing fragment to another sentence?

_____

◆ **P r a c t i c e   3 A   Identifying** Underline the *-ing* fragments in each of the following sentences.

1. Driving like a maniac. She made the trip in 10 hours.
2. Yvonne joined a health club. Thinking that would motivate her to exercise.
3. Threatening the east coast. The hurricane grew in force.
4. Drew cleaned his house thoroughly. Vacuuming, dusting, and washing windows.
5. He's at the student union. Hanging out.

◆ **P r a c t i c e   3 B   Correcting** Correct the fragments in Practice 3A by rewriting each sentence.

◆ **P r a c t i c e   4   Completing** Correct each of the following *-ing* fragments using both methods. Remember to insert a comma when using correction 1.

1. We'll either walk or drive. Depending on the weather.

   _____

2. You can find him at home every night. Playing his electric guitar.

   _____

3. The car lurched and stopped suddenly. Spilling the pop onto the seat.

   _____

4. Loving every minute on stage. She is a talented performer.

   _____

5. Mrs. Weeks volunteers at the hospital. Delivering flowers and cards to patients.

   _____

Type 3: *to* Fragments

When *to* is added to a verb (*to see, to hop, to skip, to jump*), the combination cannot be a main verb in its sentence. As a result, this group of words is often involved in a fragment.

Fragment: The company sponsored a national training program. **To increase its sales by 20 per cent.**

Since *to* + a verb cannot function as the main verb of its sentence, *to increase its sales by 20 per cent* is a fragment as it is punctuated here.

Correction 1:   *Connect the fragment to the sentence before or after it.*

Example: The company sponsored a national training pro-gram **to increase its sales by 20 per cent.**

Correction 2:   *Make the fragment into an independent clause.*

Example: The company sponsored a national training program. **It decided to increase its sales by 20 per cent.**

Hint: A *to* fragment can also occur at the beginning of a sentence. In this case, insert a comma between the two sentence parts when correcting the fragment.

To increase its sales by 20 per cent, the company sponsored a national training program.

REVIEWING *to* FRAGMENTS

What does a to fragment consist of?

_____

Give an example of a to fragment.

_____

What are the two ways to correct a to fragment?

1. _____

2. _____

_____

◆ *P r a c t i c e* **5 A**   **Identifying** Underline the *to* fragments in each of the following sentences.

1. We want to stay home tonight. To see the Juno awards.
2. To get an A in English. That's Cheryl's goal.
3. Would you please call Jerry? To remind him to bring his cooler.

4. The environmental group Greenpeace will be there. To protest whaling.

5. I have only one New Year's resolution. To stop smoking.

◆ *P r a c t i c e*   **5 B**   **Correcting**   Correct the fragments in Practice 5A by rewriting each sentence.

◆ *P r a c t i c e*   **6**   **Completing**   Correct the following *to* fragments using both correction 1 and correction 2. Try putting the fragment at the beginning of the sentence instead of always at the end. Remember to insert a comma when you add the *to* fragment to the beginning of a sentence.

1. To improve her strength and flexibility. She has started a new exercise program.

   _____

2. He works full time and takes classes at night. To get his degree in accounting.

   _____

3. Megan and Bethany are saving their money. To go to Florida for spring vacation.

   _____

4. To warn approaching ships. The captain sounded the foghorn.

   _____

5. He bought two packages of coffee. To be sure he didn't run out.

   _____

Type 4: Dependent-Clause Fragments

A group of words that begins with a **subordinating conjunction** (see the following list) is called a **dependent clause** and cannot stand alone. Even though it has a subject and a verb, it is a fragment because it depends on an independent clause to complete its meaning. An **independent clause** is a group of words with a subject and a verb that can stand alone. (See pages 286–287 for help with clauses.)

Here is a list of some commonly used subordinating conjunctions that create dependent clauses.

Subordinating Conjunctions

after	*because*	*since*	*until*
although	*before*	*so*	*when*
as	*even if*	*so that*	*whenever*
as if	*even though*	*than*	*where*
as long as	*how*	*that*	*wherever*
as soon as	*if*	*though*	*whether*
as though	*in order that*	*unless*	*while*

Fragment: <u>Since</u> he bought a Chevy Blazer. His insurance has gone up.

This sentence has a subject and a verb, but it is introduced by a subordinating conjunction, *since*. As a result, this sentence is a dependent clause and cannot stand alone.

Correction 1:   *Connect the fragment to the sentence before or after it.*

Example: **Since he bought a Chevy Blazer,** his insurance has gone up.

Correction 2:   *Make the fragment into an independent clause.*

Example: ~~Since~~ **He** bought a Chevy Blazer. His insurance has gone up.

Hint: If the dependent clause comes first, put a comma between the two parts of the sentence. If the dependent clause comes second, the comma is not necessary.

Since he bought a Chevy Blazer, his insurance has gone up.
His insurance has gone up **since he bought a Chevy Blazer.**

REVIEWING DEPENDENT-CLAUSE FRAGMENTS

What is a dependent-clause fragment?

_____

What types of words make a clause dependent?

_____   _____

What is an independent clause?

_____

Give an example of a dependent-clause fragment.

_____

What are the two ways to correct a dependent-clause fragment?

1. _____

2. _____

   _____

◆ *P r a c t i c e   7 A*   **Identifying** Underline the dependent-clause fragments in each of the following sentences.

1. Let's wait under this awning. Until it stops raining.
2. We rented the apartment on Lee Street. So that I can walk to campus.
3. Ana took two Aspirin. Because she has a headache.
4. If you are interested. I can show you how to install the new software.
5. Wait one minute, please. While I get my coat.

◆ *P r a c t i c e   7 B*   **Correcting** Correct the fragments in Practice 7A by rewriting each sentence.

◆ *P r a c t i c e   8*   **Completing** Correct the following dependent-clause fragments using both correction 1 and correction 2. When you use correction 1, remember to add a comma if the dependent clause comes first.

1. Although Jeff doesn't have any money. He manages to go to every Raptors game.

   _____

2. As long as you're up. Would you please get me a drink?

   _____

3. I don't watch much TV. Unless Oprah is on.

   _____

4. You can save a lot of money. If you clip coupons.

    _____

5. The cheque book is on the kitchen counter. Where I left it.

    _____

Type 5: Relative-Clause Fragments

A **relative clause** is a dependent clause that begins with a relative pronoun: *who, whom, whose, which,* or *that.* When a relative clause is punctuated as a sentence, the result is a fragment.

Fragment: I climbed Mt. Everest. **Which is the tallest mountain in the world.**

Which is the tallest mountain in the world is a clause fragment that begins with the relative pronoun *which.* This word automatically makes the words that follow it a dependent clause, so they cannot stand alone as a sentence.

Correction 1:   *Connect the fragment to the sentence before or after it.*

Example: I climbed Mt. Everest, **which** is the tallest mountain in the world.

Correction 2:   *Make the fragment into an independent clause.*

Example: I climbed Mt. Everest. **It** is the tallest mountain in the world.

REVIEWING RELATIVE-CLAUSE FRAGMENTS

How is a relative-clause fragment different from a dependent-clause fragment?

_____

_____

Give an example of a relative-clause fragment.

_____

What are the two ways to correct a relative-clause fragment?

1. _____

2. _____

◆ *P r a c t i c e   9 A* **Identifying** Underline the relative-clause fragments in the following sentences.

1. For psychology, I have Professor Shannon. Whose wife also teaches psychology.
2. She takes courses online. Which allows her to also work full time.
3. Ronya is going to stay with her sister. Who lives in Regina.
4. He's thinking of getting a laptop computer. That he can take on trips.
5. Traffic was bumper to bumper. Which always makes me impatient.

◆ *P r a c t i c e   9 B* **Correcting** Correct the fragments in Practice 9A by rewriting each sentence.

◆ *P r a c t i c e   1 0* **Completing** Correct the following relative-clause fragments using both correction 1 and correction 2.

1. The shark circled the boat. Which made me very nervous.

   _____

2. She's dating Kevin. Whom I dated last year.

   _____

3. The movie stars Tom Hanks. Who has already won two Oscars.

   _____

4. He read every short story. That was published in 2004.

   _____

5. He watched the professor. Whose glasses kept slipping down her nose.

   _____

CHAPTER REVIEW

You might want to reread your answers to the questions in all the review boxes before you do the following exercises.

◆ *R e v i e w   P r a c t i c e   1* **Identifying** Underline the fragments in the following paragraph.

The worst day of my life was last week. My sister promised to help me move into my new apartment. And didn't show up. Which I couldn't believe at first. When I called her to make arrangements, I should have known I was in trouble. Because she didn't sound like she was listening to me on the phone. This was my first clue. Anyway, I was counting on her. A big mistake. I kept expecting her to arrive all night. But she never came. I found out afterwards. That she forgot. This was what it was like growing up with her too. She remembered what she wanted to remember. And not any more. Which got her this far in life. But how much more can her family and friends forgive and forget?

◆ *Review   Practice   2*   **Correcting** Correct all the fragments you underlined in Review Practice 1 by rewriting the paragraph.

◆ *Review   Practice   3*   **Writing Your Own** Write a paragraph about your favourite restaurant. Where is this restaurant? What does it specialize in? Why do you like it? What is your favourite meal?

◆ *Review   Practice   4*   **Editing Through Collaboration** Exchange paragraphs from Review Practice 3 with another student, and do the following:

1. Put brackets around any fragments that you find.
2. Identify the types of fragments that you find.

Then return the paragraph to its writer, and use the information in this chapter to correct any fragments in your own paragraph. Record your errors on the Error Log in Appendix 6.

CHAPTER 32

FUSED SENTENCES AND COMMA SPLICES

✅ CHECKLIST for Identifying and Correcting Fused Sentences and Comma Splices

> ✔ Are any sentences run together without punctuation?
> ✔ Are any sentences incorrectly joined with only a comma?

Test Yourself

Mark any incorrect sentences here with a slash between the independent clauses that are not joined properly.

- Jennifer was elected Academic President, I voted for her.
- The beach is a great getaway we're fortunate it's only 45 minutes away.
- He wanted to participate, but he wasn't sure of the rules.
- Casey is hard to get to know she hides her thoughts and feelings well.
- I hope I get into Dr. Jones's class, I hear he's the best teacher to get.

(Answers are in Appendix 8.)

When we cram two separate statements into single sentences without correct punctuation, we create what are called *fused sentences* and *comma splices*. These run-on sentences generally distort our message and cause problems for our readers. In this chapter, you will learn how to identify and avoid these errors in your writing.

IDENTIFYING FUSED SENTENCES AND COMMA SPLICES

Whereas a fragment is a piece of a sentence, **fused sentences** and **comma splices** are made up of two sentences written as one. In both cases, the first sentence runs into the next without the proper punctuation between the two.

Fused Sentence:	The car slowly rolled to a stop we hopped out.
Comma Splice:	The car slowly rolled to a stop, we hopped out.

Both of these sentences incorrectly join two independent clauses. The difference between them is one comma.

A **fused sentence** is two sentences "fused" or jammed together without any punctuation. Look at these examples:

Fused Sentence:	Kinya's favourite event is the pole vault he always scores very high in it.

This example consists of two independent clauses with no punctuation between them:

1. Kinya's favourite event is the pole vault.
2. He always scores very high in it.

Fused Sentence:	My brother loves to cook he doesn't like others to cook for him.

This example also consists of two independent clauses with no punctuation between them:

1. My brother loves to cook.
2. He doesn't like others to cook for him.

Like a fused sentence, a **comma splice** incorrectly joins two independent clauses. However, a comma splice puts a comma between the two independent clauses. The only difference between a fused sentence and a comma splice is the comma. Look at the following examples:

Comma Splice:	Kinya's favourite event is the pole vault, he always scores very high in it.
Comma Splice:	My brother loves to cook, he doesn't like others to cook for him.

Both of these sentences consist of two independent clauses. But a comma is not the proper punctuation to separate these two clauses.

REVIEWING FUSED SENTENCES AND COMMA SPLICES

What are the two types of run-on sentences?

_____   _____

What is the difference between them?

_____

_____

◆ *P r a c t i c e   1*   **Identifying** Put a slash between the independent clauses that are not joined correctly.

1. Cedric goes out on a date every Saturday night he usually spends less than $20.
2. Margaret Atwood wrote the novels *The Handmaid's Tale* and *Oryx and Crake* she won the Governor General's Award for fiction.
3. The party begins at six, but the food isn't served until seven, there's a choice between chicken and beef.
4. The carnation is my favourite flower, but I still like the rose it is also beautiful.
5. Peanut butter and chocolate is my favourite ice cream flavour, but macadamia nuts in vanilla ice cream is a close second, the peanut butter makes my taste buds tingle.

◆ *P r a c t i c e   2*   **Identifying** For each incorrect sentence in the following paragraph, put a slash between the independent clauses that are not joined properly.

The day I started my first job was the most frustrating day of my life. I arrived at the restaurant early no one showed me which door to enter so I stood outside banging on the wrong door for several minutes. One of the cooks heard me, he laughed and told the other employees. This embarrassed me from the start. I didn't know that my white shirt was wrong either, it had two pockets instead of one. Sherri, my manager, pointed this out. She said the personnel director should have told me about the dress code I said he had told me nothing but wear a white shirt. Anyway, the most frustrating part of the day was watching videos about setting a table, serving, and performing other duties. It was boring I had worked two years at the country club and knew what to do. I wanted to get out on the floor. The day was too long, I knew things had to get better!

CORRECTING FUSED SENTENCES AND COMMA SPLICES

You have four different options for correcting your run-on sentences.

1. Separate the two sentences with a period, and capitalize the next word.
2. Separate the two sentences with a comma, and add a coordinating conjunction (*and, but, for, nor, or, so,* or *yet*).

3. Change one of the sentences into a dependent clause with a subordinating conjunction (such as *if, because, since, after,* or *when*) or a relative pronoun (*who, whom, whose, which,* or *that*).

4. Separate the two sentences with a semicolon.

Correction 1: Use a Period

Separate the two sentences with a period, and capitalize the next word.

> Kinya's favourite event is the pole vault**. He** always scores very high in it.
>
> My brother loves to cook**. He** doesn't like others to cook for him.

◆ *Practice* **3** **Correcting** Correct all the sentences in Practice 1 using correction 1.

◆ *Practice* **4** **Correcting** Correct the paragraph in Practice 2 using correction 1.

Correction 2: Use a Coordinating Conjunction

Separate the two sentences with a comma, and add a coordinating conjunction (*and, but, for, nor, or, so,* or *yet*).

> Kinya's favourite event is the pole vault**, so** he always scores very high in it.
>
> My brother loves to cook**, but** he doesn't like others to cook for him.

◆ *Practice* **5** **Correcting** Correct all the sentences in Practice 1 using correction 2.

◆ *Practice* **6** **Correcting** Correct the paragraph in Practice 2 using correction 2.

Correction 3: Create a Dependent Clause

Change one of the sentences into a dependent clause with a subordinating conjunction (such as *if, because, since, after,* or *when*) or a relative pronoun (*who, whom, whose, which,* or *that*).

> Kinya's favourite event is the pole vault **because** he always scores very high in it.
>
> **Even though** my brother loves to cook, he doesn't like others to cook for him.

For a list of subordinating conjunctions, see page 305.

Hint: If you put the dependent clause at the beginning of the sentence, add a comma between the two sentence parts.

Because he always scores very high in it, Kinya's favourite event is the pole vault.

◆ *P r a c t i c e* **7**   **Correcting** Correct all the sentences in Practice 1 using correction 3.

◆ *P r a c t i c e* **8**   **Correcting** Correct the paragraph in Practice 2 using correction 3.

Correction 4: Use a Semicolon

Separate the two sentences with a semicolon.

Kinya's favourite event is the pole vault**;** he always scores very high in it.

My brother loves to cook**;** he doesn't like others to cook for him.

You can also use a **transition,** a word or an expression that indicates how the two parts of the sentence are related, with a semicolon. A transition often makes the sentence smoother. It is preceded by a semicolon and followed by a comma.

Kinya's favourite event is the pole vault**; as a result,** he always scores very high in it.

My brother loves to cook**; however,** he doesn't like others to cook for him.

Here are some transitions commonly used with semicolons.

Transitions Used with a Semicolon Before and a Comma After

also	*for instance*	*in fact*	*of course*
consequently	*furthermore*	*instead*	*otherwise*
finally	*however*	*meanwhile*	*similarly*
for example	*in contrast*	*nevertheless*	*therefore*

◆ *P r a c t i c e* **9**   **Correcting** Correct all the sentences in Practice 1 using correction 4.

◆ *P r a c t i c e* **1 0**   **Correcting** Correct the paragraph in Practice 2 using correction 4.

REVIEWING METHODS OF CORRECTING FUSED SENTENCES
AND COMMA SPLICES

What are the four ways to correct a fused sentence or comma splice?

1. _____

2. _____

3. _____

4. _____

Why is correcting fused sentences and comma splices important?

_____

CHAPTER REVIEW

You might want to reread your answers to the questions in all the review boxes before you do the following exercises.

◆ *Review Practice 1* **Identifying** Label each of the following sentences as fused (F), comma splice (CS), or correct (C).

1. _____ The small girls fidgeted in their colourful outfits they waited for their cue to go on stage.

2. _____ A hubcap came off the car as the car continued down the street.

3. _____ Alanna grabbed for the pen that worked she didn't want to forget his phone number.

4. _____ Stanley waited, but Tia never showed up, her car must have gotten stuck.

5. _____ Now that winter is approaching, the ski slopes will get very crowded.

◆ *Review Practice 2* **Completing** Correct the fused sentences and comma splices in Review Practice 1.

◆ *Review Practice 3* **Writing Your Own** Write a paragraph about a first in your life (for example, your first date, your first pizza, your first job).

♦ *Review   P r a c t i c e   4*   **Editing Through Collaboration** Exchange paragraphs from Review Practice 3 with another student, and do the following:

1. Put brackets around any sentences that have more than one independent clause.
2. Circle the words that connect these clauses.

Then return the paragraph to its writer, and use the information in this chapter to correct any run-on sentences in your own paragraph. Record your errors on the Error Log in Appendix 6.

UNIT TESTS

Here are some exercises that test your understanding of all the material in this unit: Subjects and Verbs, Fragments, and Fused Sentences and Comma Splices.

Unit Test I

A. Underline the subjects once and the verbs twice in the following sentences. Cross out the prepositional phrases first. Then put the fragments in brackets ([ ]), and put a slash (/) between the run-on sentences.

1. She has transferred to university. After she went to our local community college.
2. I called the business office and inquired about my account balance the credit clerk told me that the company owed me money.
3. She bought a used Toyota. That she can drive between home and school.
4. Musicians and entertainers make great money after their "big break."
5. Before you make your plane reservations. Check the Internet prices.
6. Yesterday Val won the art contest at the mall it was judged by three professionals.
7. Mom planted a little garden this year. Some lettuce, spinach, and tomatoes.
8. Bowing and smiling. The actors appeared for yet another curtain call.
9. The Board of Education conducted a poll 23 per cent of the students like gym classes, but 37 per cent dislike gym classes and the rest have no opinion.
10. Both of the children are in daycare.
11. All the kids love Mr. Kaufmann. Whose gingerbread cookies are a hit.

12. Agriculture is a very risky occupation. Since it depends on the weather.

13. Every year, her parents put money into her RESP.

14. To change your telephone message. Press SET and speak clearly.

15. If you're going to the store, we need cat food and paper towels. And something for dinner tonight.

16. You have all the ingredients here. To make a nutritious smoothie.

17. The 12 beautiful, mint green roses that I got during my wedding brunch were lovely, they lasted for two weeks after the event.

18. The first three scenes in the horror film were frightening.

19. Though Samuel signed up early, he still didn't get into summer school so many people applied.

20. On their vacation, Brent and Miranda felt and acted like royalty.

B. Correct the fragments and run-on sentences in Part A by rewriting each incorrect sentence.

Unit Test II

A. Underline the subjects once and the verbs twice in the following paragraph. Cross out the prepositional phrases first. Then put the fragments in brackets (| |), and put a slash (/) between the run-on sentences.

I went to the beach. During my summer vacation. My friends Christine and Jennifer went with me, we had such a great time. We spent one week at a hotel. Which was right on the beach. We had saved our money all spring. To be able to afford such a nice hotel room. Since we were so close. We spent nearly every moment at the beach. Christine would not play volleyball with us, she said that she was not good enough. Realizing we were just playing for fun. She soon joined our game. When our week was over. We were not ready to go home. I cannot wait for another vacation with Christine and Jennifer they are the best!

B. Correct the fragments and run-on sentences in Part A by rewriting the paragraph.

CHAPTER 33

REGULAR AND IRREGULAR VERBS

☑ CHECKLIST for Using Regular and Irregular Verbs

> ✔ Are regular verbs in their correct forms?
> ✔ Are irregular verbs in their correct forms?

Test Yourself

Underline the complete verb in each of the following sentences. Then mark an X if the form of the verb is incorrect.

- _____ We brang our new neighbour a pizza for dinner.
- _____ My brother married on February 14—Valentine's Day.
- _____ He drug the heavy suitcase down the street.
- _____ This CD costed $15.
- _____ My roommate's waterbed has sprang a leak.

(Answers are in Appendix 8.)

All verbs are either regular or irregular. *Regular verbs* form the past tense and past participle by adding *-d* or *-ed* to the present tense. If a verb does not form its past tense and past participle this way, it is called an *irregular verb*.

REGULAR VERBS

Here are the *principal parts* (*present*, *past*, and *past participle* forms) of some regular verbs. They are **regular verbs** because their past tense and past participle end in *-d* or *-ed*. The past participle is the verb form often used with helping verbs like *have*, *has*, or *had*.

Some Regular Verbs

PRESENT TENSE	PAST TENSE	PAST PARTICIPLE (USED WITH HELPING WORDS LIKE *HAVE, HAS, HAD*)
talk	talked	talked
sigh	sighed	sighed
drag	dragged	dragged
enter	entered	entered
consider	considered	considered

The different forms of a verb tell when something happened—in the *present* (I *walk*) or in the *past* (I *walked*, I *have walked*, I *had walked*).

REVIEWING REGULAR VERBS

What is a regular verb?

_____

_____

Identify three forms of a regular verb.

_____   _____   _____

◆ **P r a c t i c e   1   Identifying** Put an X to the left of the incorrect verb forms in the following chart.

Present Tense	**Past Tense**	**Past Participle**
1. _____ skip	_____ skipt	_____ skipped
2. _____ paint	_____ painted	_____ painted
3. _____ danced	_____ dance	_____ danced
4. _____ play	_____ played	_____ playen
5. _____ cook	_____ cooked	_____ cooken

◆ *Practice 2* **Completing** Write the correct forms of the following regular verbs.

	Present Tense	**Past Tense**	**Past Participle**
1. act	_____	_____	_____
2. invent	_____	_____	_____
3. follow	_____	_____	_____
4. drag	_____	_____	_____
5. create	_____	_____	_____

IRREGULAR VERBS

Irregular verbs do not form their past tense and past participle with *-d* or *-ed*. That is why they are irregular. Some follow certain patterns (*sing, sang, sung; ring, rang, rung; drink, drank, drunk; shrink, shrank, shrunk*). But the only sure way to know the forms of an irregular verb is to spend time learning them. As you write, you can check a dictionary or the following list.

Irregular Verbs

PRESENT	PAST	PAST PARTICIPLE (USED WITH HELPING WORDS LIKE *HAVE, HAS, HAD*)
am	was	been
are	were	been
be	was	been
bear	bore	borne, born
beat	beat	beaten
begin	began	begun
bend	bent	bent
bid	bid	bid
bind	bound	bound
blte	bit	bitten
blow	blew	blown
break	broke	broken
bring	brought (not *brang*)	brought (not *brung*)
build	built	built
burst	burst (not *bursted*)	burst

buy	bought	bought
choose	chose	chosen
come	came	come
cost	cost (not *costed*)	cost
cut	cut	cut
deal	dealt	dealt
do	did (not *done*)	done
draw	drew	drawn
drink	drank	drunk
drive	drove	driven
eat	ate	eaten
fall	fell	fallen
feed	fed	fed
feel	felt	felt
fight	fought	fought
find	found	found
flee	fled	fled
fly	flew	flown
forget	forgot	forgotten
forgive	forgave	forgiven
freeze	froze	frozen
get	got	got, gotten
go	went	gone
grow	grew	grown
hang[1] (a picture)	hung	hung
has	had	had
have	had	had
hide	hid	hidden
hear	heard	heard
hurt	hurt (not *hurted*)	hurt
is	was	been
know	knew	known
lay	laid	laid
lead	led	led
leave	left	left
lend	lent	lent
lie[2]	lay	lain
lose	lost	lost

meet	*met*	*met*
pay	*paid*	*paid*
prove	*proved*	*proved, proven*
put	*put*	*put*
read [rēēd]	*read* [rĕd]	*read* [rĕd]
ride	*rode*	*ridden*
ring	*rang*	*rung*
rise	*rose*	*risen*
run	*ran*	*run*
say	*said*	*said*
see	*saw* (not *seen*)	*seen*
set	*set*	*set*
shake	*shook*	*shaken*
shine[3] (a light)	*shone*	*shone*
shrink	*shrank*	*shrunk*
sing	*sang*	*sung*
sink	*sank*	*sunk*
sit	*sat*	*sat*
sleep	*slept*	*slept*
speak	*spoke*	*spoken*
spend	*spent*	*spent*
spread	*spread*	*spread*
spring	*sprang* (not *sprung*)	*sprung*
stand	*stood*	*stood*
steal	*stole*	*stolen*
stick	*stuck*	*stuck*
stink	*stank* (not *stunk*)	*stunk*
strike	*struck*	*struck, stricken*
strive	*strove*	*striven*
swear	*swore*	*sworn*
sweep	*swept*	*swept*
swell	*swelled*	*swelled, swollen*
swim	*swam*	*swum*
swing	*swung*	*swung*
take	*took*	*taken*
teach	*taught*	*taught*
tear	*tore*	*torn*
tell	*told*	*told*

think	*thought*	*thought*
throw	*threw*	*thrown*
understand	*understood*	*understood*
wake	*woke*	*woken*
wear	*wore*	*worn*
weave	*wove*	*woven*
win	*won*	*won*
wring	*wrung*	*wrung*
write	*wrote*	*written*

1. *Hang* meaning "execute by hanging" is regular: *hang, hanged, hanged.*
2. *Lie* meaning "tell a lie" is regular: *lie, lied, lied.*
3. *Shine* meaning "brighten by polishing" is regular: *shine, shined, shined.*

REVIEWING IRREGULAR VERBS

What is the difference between regular and irregular verbs?

_____

_____

What is the best way to learn how irregular verbs form their past tense and past participle?

_____

◆ **P r a c t i c e   3   Identifying** Put an X to the left of the incorrect verb forms in the following chart.

Present Tense	**Past Tense**	**Past Participle**
1. _____ bust	_____ bursted	_____ burst
2. _____ ring	_____ rung	_____ rung
3. _____ took	_____ taken	_____ taken
4. _____ sleep	_____ slept	_____ slepted
5. _____ drink	_____ drank	_____ drunk

◆ *P r a c t i c e 4* **Completing** Write the correct forms of the following
irregular verbs.

	Present Tense	Past Tense	Past Participle
1. hide	_____	_____	_____
2. sing	_____	_____	_____
3. bring	_____	_____	_____
4. write	_____	_____	_____
5. cost	_____	_____	_____

USING *LIE/LAY* AND *SIT/SET* CORRECTLY

Two pairs of verbs are often used incorrectly—*lie/lay* and *sit/set*.

Lie/Lay

	Present Tense	Past Tense	Past Participle
lie (recline or lie down)	lie	lay	(have, has, had) lain
lay (put or place down)	lay	laid	(have, has, had) laid

The verb *lay* always takes an object. You must lay something down:

Lay down *what?*
Lay down *your books.*

Sit/Set

	Present Tense	Past Tense	Past Participle
sit (get into a seated position)	sit	sat	(have, has, had) sat
set (put or place down)	set	set	(have, has, had) set

Like the verb *lay*, the verb *set* must always have an object. You must set
something down:

Set *what?*
Set *the presents* over here.

REVIEWING *Lie/Lay* AND *Sit/Set*

What do lie *and* lay **mean?**

_____

What are the principal parts of lie *and* lay?

_____

What do sit *and* set **mean?**

_____

What are the principal parts of sit *and* set?

_____

Which of these verbs always take an object?

_____

◆ *P r a c t i c e* **5** **Identifying** Choose the correct verb in the following sentences.

1. She has always (set, sat) in the front row.
2. Please (set, sit) the box of tissues on the nightstand.
3. You have (laid, lain) on the couch all morning.
4. At the concert, we (set, sat) with Howie and Carol.
5. The installers are coming to (lay, lie) the new carpeting.

◆ *P r a c t i c e* **6** **Completing** Fill in each blank in the following sentences with the correct form of *lie/lay* or *sit/set*.

1. I like to _____ next to the window on an airplane.
2. She has _____ out the clothes she will take on her trip.
3. _____ the box on the table.
4. I'm exhausted. I have to _____ down.
5. _____ the tray over here.

CHAPTER REVIEW

You might want to reread your answers to the questions in all the review boxes before you do the following exercises.

◄ *Review   Practice   1*   **Identifying**   Write out the past tense and past participle of each verb listed here, and then identify the verb as either regular or irregular.

Present Tense	Past Tense	Past Participle	Type of Verb
1. react	_____	_____	_____
2. hesitate	_____	_____	_____
3. sing	_____	_____	_____
4. treat	_____	_____	_____
5. bring	_____	_____	_____
6. suffer	_____	_____	_____
7. read	_____	_____	_____
8. stink	_____	_____	_____
9. take	_____	_____	_____
10. speak	_____	_____	_____

◄ *Review   Practice   2*   **Completing**   Fill in each blank in the following sentences with a regular or irregular verb that makes sense.

1. No one believed that he had _____ the lottery.

2. I was so tired, I _____ home.

3. Because I have a cold, I have _____ in bed all day.

4. Brian has always _____ a wonderful father to his daughter.

5. Every time the choir performs, my grandfather _____ to the concert.

◄ *Review   Practice   3*   **Writing Your Own**   Write a paragraph explaining how active or inactive you are in life. What are the reasons for the choices you have made regarding your level of daily activity?

◆ *Review   Practice   4*   **Editing Through Collaboration** Exchange paragraphs from Review Practice 3 with another student, and do the following:

1. Circle any verb forms that are not correct.
2. Suggest a correction for these incorrect forms.

Then return the paragraph to its writer, and use the information in this chapter to correct the verb forms in your own paragraph. Record your errors on the Error Log in Appendix 6.

CHAPTER 34

SUBJECT-VERB AGREEMENT

☑ CHECKLIST for Correcting Subject-Verb Agreement Problems

> ✔ Do all subjects agree with their verbs?

Test Yourself

Underline the subjects once and the complete verbs twice in the following sentences. Put an X by the sentence if its subject and verb do not agree.

- _____ Ben and Tess has become great friends.
- _____ Each of the nurses are with a patient.
- _____ Macaroni and cheese are my favourite food.
- _____ There are two trains to Moncton in the morning.
- _____ Everyone are ready to leave.

(Answers are in Appendix 8.)

Almost every day, we come across situations that require us to reach an agreement with someone. For example, you and a friend might have to agree on which movie to see, or you and your manager might have to agree on how many hours you'll work in the coming week. Whatever the issue, agreement is essential in most aspects of life—including writing. In this chapter, you will learn how to resolve conflicts in your sentences by making sure your subjects and verbs agree.

SUBJECT-VERB AGREEMENT

Subject-verb agreement simply means that singular subjects must be paired with singular verbs and plural subjects with plural verbs. Look at this example:

Singular: **He lives** in Thunder Bay.

The subject *he* is singular because it refers to only one person. The verb *lives* is singular and matches the singular subject. Here is the same sentence in plural form:

Plural: **They live** in Thunder Bay.

The subject *they* is plural, more than one person, and the verb *live* is also plural.

REVIEWING SUBJECT-VERB AGREEMENT

What is the difference between singular and plural?

_____

What kind of verb goes with a singular subject?

_____

What kind of verb goes with a plural subject?

_____

◆ **P r a c t i c e   1   Identifying** Underline the verb that agrees with its subject in each of the following sentences.

1. On her vacations, Sylvia (enjoys, enjoy) reading romance novels.
2. Jerry (has, have) a large coin collection.
3. During the day, the farmhands (works, work) in the fields.
4. Unfortunately, the paycheques (was, were) lost in the mail.
5. The twins (does, do) not look alike.

◆ **P r a c t i c e   2   Completing** Fill in each blank in the following sentences with a present-tense verb that agrees with its subject.

1. The new clothing styles _____ bad on me.
2. Bob _____ his mom to visit.
3. Every night the news _____ the latest disasters.
4. During the evening, Jake _____ for many hours.
5. The football team usually _____ its games.

WORDS SEPARATING SUBJECTS AND VERBS

With sentences that are as simple and direct as *He lives in Thunder Bay,* checking that the subject and verb agree is easy. But problems can arise when words come between the subject and the verb. Often the words between the subject and verb are prepositional phrases. If you follow the advice given in Chapter 30, you will be able to find the subject and verb: *Cross out all the prepositional phrases in a sentence. The subject and verb will be among the words that are left.* Here are some examples:

                                     s   v

Prepositional Phrases: The **map** ~~of Nahanni National Park~~ **is** ~~in a small suitcase~~.

When you cross out the prepositional phrases, you can tell that the singular subject, *map,* and the singular verb, *is,* agree.

                                    s   v

Prepositional Phrases: **Classes** ~~at my college~~ **begin** ~~in August~~.

When you cross out the prepositional phrases, you can tell that the plural subject, *classes,* and the plural verb, *begin,* agree.

REVIEWING WORDS SEPARATING SUBJECTS AND VERBS

What words often come between subjects and verbs?

_____

What is an easy way to identify the subject and verb in a sentence?

_____

◀ **P r a c t i c e   3   Identifying** Underline the subject once and the verb twice in each of the following sentences. Cross out the prepositional phrases first. Put an X to the left of any sentence in which the subject and verb do not agree.

1. _____ Her behaviour in front of adults make us all sick.

2. _____ The blooming trees in the orchard are making me sneeze.

3. _____ Unlike John, Katie gives to the poor.

4. _____ The house in the mountains were for sale for one year.

5. _____ Oscar, along with his two sisters, are studying law.

◆ *P r a c t i c e 4* **Completing** Fill in each blank in the following sentences with a present-tense verb that agrees with its subject.

1. Many students at my college _____ business administration.

2. Angie, along with the entire math class, _____ the day could start over.

3. The police, despite many obstacles, _____ many criminals every day.

4. Most teachers at all grade levels _____ the work they do.

5. The buses in town _____ many students to school.

MORE THAN ONE SUBJECT

Sometimes a subject consists of more than one person, place, thing, or idea. These subjects are called **compound** (as discussed in Chapter 30). Follow these three rules when matching a verb to a compound subject:

1. When compound subjects are joined by *and*, use a plural verb.

   Plural: The **heat** and **humidity were** hard on Simone.

   The singular words *heat* and *humidity* together make a plural subject. Therefore, the plural verb *were* is needed.

2. When the subject appears to have more than one part but the parts refer to a single unit, use a singular verb.

   Singular: **Peanut butter and jelly is** Mindy's favourite sandwich.

   Peanut butter is one item and *jelly* is one item, but Mindy does not eat one without the other, so they form a single unit. Because they are a single unit, they require a singular verb—*is*.

3. When compound subjects are joined by *or* or *nor*, make the verb agree with the subject closest to it.

   Singular: Neither **leeches** nor miserable **weather was** enough to keep her from her goal.

   The part of the compound subject closest to the verb is *weather*, which is singular. Therefore, the verb must be singular—*was*.

   Plural: Neither miserable **weather** nor **leeches were** enough to keep her from her goal.

   This time, the part of the compound subject closest to the verb is *leeches*, which is plural. Therefore, the verb must be plural—*were*.

REVIEWING SUBJECT-VERB AGREEMENT WITH MORE THAN
ONE SUBJECT

*Do you use a singular or plural verb with compound subjects joined
by* and?

_____

Why should you use a singular verb with a subject like macaroni and
cheese?

_____

If one part of a compound subject joined by or *or* nor *is singular and the
other is plural, how do you decide whether to use a singular or plural
verb?*

_____

◆ **P r a c t i c e   5   Identifying** Underline the verb that agrees with its
subject in each of the following sentences. Cross out the prepositional
phrases first.

1. The golfers and their caddies (looks, look) ready to play.
2. Ham and cheese (are, is) my favourite kind of sandwich.
3. Either the professor or his teaching assistants (grades, grade) exams.
4. The Raptors and the Leafs (is, are) both Toronto teams.
5. Checkers and chess (take, takes) a lot of concentration.

◆ **P r a c t i c e   6   Completing** Fill in each blank in the following sentences with a present-tense verb that agrees with its subject. Avoid *is* and
are. Cross out the prepositional phrases first.

1. Music and film _____ the senses with pleasure.
2. Either Ottawa or Montreal _____ our choice for a weekend
   trip.
3. Ice cream and cake _____ me happy after a stressful day.
4. Neither my cheque book nor my credit cards _____ me out of
   debt when I have no money.
5. Teachers and counselors _____ the influence they have over
   their students.

VERBS BEFORE SUBJECTS

When the subject follows its verb, the subject may be hard to find, which
makes the process of making subjects and verbs agree difficult. Subjects

come after verbs in two particular situations—when the sentence begins with *Here* or *There* and when a question begins with *Who, What, Where, When, Why,* or *How.* Here are some examples:

Verb Before Subject: Here **are** the **decorations** ~~for the party~~.

Verb Before Subject: There **is iced tea** ~~in the refrigerator~~.

In sentences that begin with *Here* or *There*, the verb always comes before the subject. Don't forget to cross out prepositional phrases to help you identify the subject. One of the words that's left will be the subject, and then you can check that the verb agrees with it.

                                    v   s
Verb Before Subject: Who **is** that **woman** ~~in red~~?

                                        v   s
Verb Before Subject: Where **are** the application **forms?**

                                      v   s   v
Verb Before Subject: What time **are you leaving** ~~for school~~?

In questions that begin with *Who, What, When, Where, Why,* and *How,* the verb comes before the subject, as in the first two examples, or is split by the subject, as in the last example.

REVIEWING VERBS BEFORE SUBJECTS

Where will you find the verb in sentences that begin with Here *or* There?

_____

Where will you find the verb in questions that begin with Who, What, Where, When, Why, *and* How?

_____

◆ *P r a c t i c e   7*   **Identifying** Underline the subject once and the verb twice in each of the following sentences. Cross out the prepositional phrases first.

1. Where is the speaker for tonight's program?
2. There are scholarships available for next year.
3. Who was the winner of the Queen's–Western game?
4. Here comes the judge with his briefcase.
5. Where is the best place to pitch my tent?

◆ *P r a c t i c e   8* **Completing** Fill in each blank in the following sentences with a verb that agrees with its subject. Cross out the prepositional phrases first.

1. What _____ that strange noise in the basement?
2. There _____ several reasons for staying in school.
3. Why _____ Michelle so quiet?
4. Here _____ the tree I planted on Mother's Day.
5. When _____ he _____ smoking?

COLLECTIVE NOUNS

Collective nouns name a group of people or things. Examples include such nouns as *army*, *audience*, *band*, *class*, *committee*, *crew*, *crowd*, *family*, *flock*, *gang*, *jury*, *majority*, *minority*, *orchestra*, *team*, and *troop*. Collective nouns can be singular or plural. They are singular when they refer to a group as a single unit. They are plural when they refer to the individual actions or feelings of the group members.

                                          s   v
Singular: The marching **band plays** at all home games.

Band refers to the entire unit or group. Therefore, it requires the singular verb *plays*.

                                          s   v
Plural: The marching **band get** their new uniforms today.

Here *band* refers to the individual members, who will each get a new uniform, so the plural verb *get* is used.

REVIEWING COLLECTIVE NOUNS

When is a collective noun singular?

_____

When is a collective noun plural?

_____

◆ *P r a c t i c e   9* **Identifying** Underline the correct verb in each of the following sentences. Cross out the prepositional phrases first.

1. The crew (is, are) talking to their loved ones on the phone.
2. The minority (is, are) still a vocal group.
3. The family (was, were) watching TV, eating, and sleeping when the fire alarm began screaming.
4. The class (feels, feel) proud of raising enough money for a field trip.
5. The carnival troupe (performs, perform) in the spring.

◆ *P r a c t i c e   1 0*   **Completing** Fill in each blank in the following sentences with a present-tense verb that agrees with its subject. Cross out the prepositional phrases first.

1. The audience always _____ their seats when the show starts.
2. The school band _____ old favourites when they perform on Saturday.
3. Our team _____ wearing their letter sweaters.
4. Our committee _____ people who take action immediately.
5. A group of tourists _____ arriving at noon.

INDEFINITE PRONOUNS

Indefinite pronouns do not refer to anyone or anything specific. Some indefinite pronouns are always singular, and some are always plural. A few can be either singular or plural, depending on the other words in the sentence. When an indefinite pronoun is the subject of a sentence, the verb must agree with the pronoun. Here is a list of indefinite pronouns.

Indefinite Pronouns

ALWAYS SINGULAR		ALWAYS PLURAL	EITHER SINGULAR OR PLURAL
another	*much*	*both*	*all*
anybody	*neither*	*few*	*any*
anyone	*nobody*	*many*	*more*
anything	*no one*	*others*	*most*
each	*nothing*	*several*	*none*
either	*one*		*some*
everybody	*other*		
everyone	*somebody*		
everything	*someone*		
little	*something*		

S   V
Singular: **No one answers** the phone when a customer calls.

S   V
Everybody simply **listens** to the ringing phone.

S   V   V
Plural: **Many get** up and **walk** away.

S   V
Others remain seated, tired, and unmotivated.

The pronouns that can be either singular or plural are singular when they refer to singular words and plural when they refer to plural words.

S   V
Singular: **Some** of Emily's time **was** spent daydreaming.

Some is singular because it refers to *time*, which is singular. The singular verb *was* agrees with the singular subject *some*.

S   V
Plural: **Some** of Emily's friends **were** late.

Some is plural because it refers to *friends*, which is plural. The plural verb *were* agrees with the plural subject *some*.

REVIEWING INDEFINITE PRONOUNS

What is an indefinite pronoun?

_____

When are all, any, more, most, *and* some *singular or plural?*

_____

_____

◆ **P r a c t i c e   1 1**   **Identifying** Underline the verb that agrees with its subject in each of the following sentences. Cross out the prepositional phrases first.

1. Of all the guests, none (was, were) dressed appropriately.
2. Someone (sneak, sneaks) into my room while I am gone.
3. Some never (seem, seems) to learn from their own mistakes.

4. In reference to the candidates, any who wish to apply for the job (need, needs) to fill out an application.

5. Somebody always (take, takes) Tabitha to lunch on Wednesdays.

◆ **Practice 12** **Completing** Fill in each blank in the following sentences with a present-tense verb that agrees with its subject. Cross out the prepositional phrases first.

1. No one _____ he's innocent of the crime.

2. Each of the oranges _____ spoiled.

3. None of the cars _____ power windows or a rear window defroster.

4. Only a few of the senior employees _____ three weeks of vacation a year.

5. Most of my supply _____ gone.

CHAPTER REVIEW

You might want to review your answers to the questions in all the review boxes before you do the following exercises.

◆ *Review Practice 1A* **Identifying** Underline the subject once and the verb twice in each of the following sentences. Cross out the prepositional phrases first. Then put an X to the left of each sentence in which the subject and verb do not agree.

1. _____ The orchestra with new instruments gets paid every Tuesday.

2. _____ Here are all the pieces to the puzzle.

3. _____ Neither the cheese nor the vegetables was fresh.

4. _____ The class down the hall is studying math.

5. _____ Anyone with questions can speak to the manager.

◆ *Review Practice 1B* **Correcting** Correct the subjects and verbs that don't agree in Review Practice 1A by rewriting the incorrect sentences.

◆ *Review Practice 2* **Completing** Fill in each blank in the following sentences with a present-tense verb that agrees with its subject.

1. Despite their ages, Angelica and Cindy _____ playing with each other at school.

2. The family with the most children _____ always seated first.

3. How _____ the levers and pulleys work?

4. Some of your apples _____ ripe.

5. Neither the curtains nor the comforter _____ the paint in the room.

◆ *Review   Practice   3*   **Writing Your Own**   Write a paragraph about an experience you have had participating on a team or observing a team. This could be in athletics, at work, in a club, at home, or at church.

◆ *Review   Practice   4*   **Editing Through Collaboration**   Exchange paragraphs from Review Practice 3 with another student, and do the following:

1. Underline the subject once in each sentence.
2. Underline the verbs twice.
3. Put an X by any verbs that do not agree with their subjects.

Then return the paragraph to its writer, and use the information in this chapter to correct any subject-verb agreement errors in your own paragraph. Record your errors on the Error Log in Appendix 6.

VERB TENSE

✅ CHECKLIST for Correcting Tense and Voice Problems

> ✔ Are verb tenses consistent?
> ✔ Are sentences written in the active voice?

Test Yourself

Label each sentence I if its verb tenses are inconsistent or P if it uses the passive voice.

- _____ When my brother won the gold medal, my father looks very proud.
- _____ All new employees are trained by a professional.
- _____ The child was saved by the firefighters.
- _____ My friend got home early, so we go to the movies.
- _____ The student was given the answers in advance.

(Answers are in Appendix 8.)

Verbs communicate the action and time of each sentence. So it is important that you use verb tense consistently. Also, you should strive to write in the active, not the passive, voice. This chapter provides help with both of these sentence skills.

CONSISTENT VERB TENSE

Verb tense refers to the time an action takes place—in the present, the past, or the future. The verb tenses in a sentence should be consistent. That is, if you start out using one tense, you should not switch tenses unless absolutely necessary. Switching tenses can be confusing. Here are some examples:

Present

NOT   When the sun **sits** high in the sky and the cloud

Present   Past

cover **is** just right, we **saw** the water glistening.

Present

CORRECT   When the sun **sits** high in the sky and the cloud

Present   Present

cover **is** just right, we **see** the water glistening.

Past

NOT   They **climbed** Mt. Robson last week when the

Present

snowfall **is** heavy.

Past

CORRECT   They **climbed** Mt. Robson last week when the

Past

snowfall **was** heavy.

Future

NOT   The astronauts **will finish** training this week, and

Present

then they **lead** the first mission to Mars.

Future

CORRECT   The astronauts **will finish** training this week, and

Future

then they **will lead** the first mission to Mars.

REVIEWING CONSISTENT VERB TENSES

Why should verb tenses be consistent?

_____

What problem do inconsistent verb tenses create?

_____

◆ *P r a c t i c e   **1 A***   **Identifying** In the following sentences, write C if the verb tense is consistent or I if it is inconsistent.

1. _____ The explorers will be leaving early in the morning and returned late at night.

2. _____ My dogs, Zak and Apollo, enjoy a day at the park and will love to play on the beach.

3. _____ Explaining the assignments to my sick roommate was hard, and it tried my patience.

4. _____ The summer movies looked interesting but will be big disappointments.

5. _____ The game was won with brute strength and is fun to watch.

◆ *P r a c t i c e   **1 B***   **Correcting** Correct the verb-tense errors in Practice 1A by rewriting the inconsistent sentences.

◆ *P r a c t i c e   **2***   **Completing** Fill in each blank in the following sentences with consistent verbs.

1. The stores _____ many sales and _____ a lot of money.

2. Most people _____ comedies and _____ tragedies.

3. Most people _____ forward to vacations because they _____ to rest.

4. Students _____ hard before they _____ final exams.

5. Sarah _____ her bike and _____ a scooter.

USING THE ACTIVE VOICE

In the **active voice,** the subject performs the action. In the **passive voice,** the subject receives the action. Compare the following two examples:

Passive Voice: The employees **were charged** with disturbing the peace **by the police.**

Active Voice: The **police charged** the employees with disturbing the peace.

The active voice adds energy to your writing. Here is another example. Notice the difference between active and passive.

Passive Voice: The water **was boiled** for the pasta **by Carmen.**

Active Voice: **Carmen boiled** the water for the pasta.

REVIEWING ACTIVE AND PASSIVE VOICE

What is the difference between the active and passive voice?

_____

_____

Why is the active voice usually better than the passive?

_____

◆ **P r a c t i c e   3 A   Identifying** Write A if the sentence is in the active voice and P if it is in the passive voice.

1. _____ The mail was opened by Sarah.

2. _____ Albert and Walter are sending flowers to their girlfriends.

3. _____ My purse was stolen by someone!

4. _____ The judge sentenced the criminals to serve five years.

5. _____ I would like to walk on the beach with you.

◆ **P r a c t i c e   3 B   Correcting** Rewrite the passive sentences in Practice 3A in the active voice.

◆ **P r a c t i c e   4   Completing** Complete the following sentences in the active voice.

1. Many styles of jeans _____.

2. A can of pop _____.

3. A bowl of beans _____.

4. A vacation _____.

5. The baseball _____.

CHAPTER REVIEW

You might want to reread your answers to the questions in all the review boxes before you do the following exercises.

◆ **Review   P r a c t i c e   1   Identifying** Label each sentence I if the verb tenses are inconsistent, P if it is in the passive voice, or C if it is correct. Then correct the inconsistent and passive sentences by rewriting them.

1. _____ All of the chocolate doughnuts have been eaten by José.

2. _____ Mr. Johnson walks five kilometres every day, but has eaten whatever he likes.

3. _____ The children were read to by Grandma Ginny.

4. _____ The lawns and gardens have always been groomed by Mr. Shultz, our gardener.

5. _____ The blue team raced down the hill, jumped the hurdles in their path, and then will cross the finish line.

◆ **Review Practice 2 Completing** Fill in the blanks with consistent active verbs.

1. Andrew always _____ the heat in summer and _____ the cold in winter.

2. The Key Club at our school _____ a bake sale and _____ all the money to charity.

3. The award-winning racehorse _____ through its routine.

4. Evan _____ to visit Tony in Red Lake, but he _____ after only two days.

5. The soup for our dinner _____ on the stove.

◆ **Review Practice 3 Writing Your Own** Write a paragraph about your favourite course. What do you like most about it? Why is it your favourite? Stay in the present tense, and use the active voice.

◆ **Review Practice 4 Editing Through Collaboration** Exchange paragraphs from Review Practice 3 with another student, and do the following:

1. Circle all verbs that are not consistent in tense.

2. Underline any verbs in the passive voice.

Then return the paragraph to its writer, and use the information in this chapter to correct any verb consistency or voice errors in your own paragraph. Record your errors on the Error Log in Appendix 6.

UNIT TESTS

Here are some exercises that test your understanding of all the material in this unit: Regular and Irregular Verbs, Subject-Verb Agreement, and Verb Tense (Consistent/Inconsistent and Active/Passive).

Unit Test I

A. Underline all the verb errors in the following sentences.

1. Yesterday he laid in the sun too long and got burned.
2. Raymond's invitation was turned down by Sally.
3. She jump on the couch and turn up the volume.
4. Mr. Wilson said he has spoke to them.
5. I work the early shift, but now I worked the late shift.
6. Amy said that you was going to bring the charcoal and grill.
7. The coach ain't going to let you skip practice.
8. Yesterday I sit my alarm clock for 7:00 a.m.
9. The runner who won last year have come in first again.
10. He don't have his driver's licence with him.
11. Last week, Justin join the Canadian Armed Forces.
12. Britta need to declare a major.
13. Some workers at the plant expects to go on strike.
14. The police and RCMP often works on cases together.
15. We have both fell behind in our reading assignments.
16. When is the fireworks starting?
17. The cheerleading squad dance wildly every time the basketball team make a shot.
18. No one really think that he will run for re-election.
19. Robin and Jack expected to arrive early, so they drive quickly to get there.
20. Jordan was asked his name by the hotel clerk.

B.   Correct the verb errors in Part A by rewriting each incorrect sentence.

Unit Test II

A. Underline the verb errors in the following paragraph.

People in small towns often has few choices when deciding how to spend their Friday and Saturday nights. Many small towns still had an old movie theatre. The movie theatre usually have only one screen. Also, the theatre rarely got movies until they are out for at least two or three weeks. In big cities, theatres like this are put out of business by newer, flashier, multi-screen theatres. However, in a small town, the old theatre was providing one of the few sources of entertainment and is full most weekends. Without the theatre, many people ain't got nothing to do except set around.

B. Correct the verb errors in Part A by rewriting the paragraph.

PRONOUN PROBLEMS

☑ CHECKLIST for Using Pronouns

> ✔ Are all subject pronouns used correctly?
> ✔ Are all object pronouns used correctly?
> ✔ Are all possessive pronouns used correctly?
> ✔ Are pronouns used in *than* or *as* comparisons in the correct form?
> ✔ Are the pronouns *this*, *that*, *these*, and *those* used correctly?

Test Yourself

Correct the pronoun errors in the following sentences.

- The toy was her's to begin with.
- Bradley told Megan and I the funniest story.
- He can run a lot faster than me.
- Those there ballet shoes are Laura's.
- Ted and me are going to the game tonight.

(Answers are in Appendix 8.)

Pronouns are words that take the place of nouns. They help us avoid repeating nouns. In this chapter, we'll discuss five types of pronoun problems: (1) using the wrong pronoun as a subject, (2) using the wrong pronoun as an object, (3) using an apostrophe with a possessive pronoun, (4) misusing pronouns in comparisons, and (5) misusing demonstrative pronouns.

PRONOUNS AS SUBJECTS

Single pronouns as subjects usually don't cause problems.

Subject Pronoun: **I** went to the movies with Jamie.

Subject Pronoun: **They** moved to St. John's.

You wouldn't say "*Me* went to the movies" or "*Them* moved to San Francisco." But an error often occurs when a sentence has a compound subject and one or more of the subjects is a pronoun.

NOT	**The Cardinals** and **us** tied for first place.
CORRECT	**The Cardinals** and **we** tied for first place.
NOT	**Him** and **me** will wait on the porch.
CORRECT	**He** and **I** will wait on the porch.

To test whether you have used the correct form of the pronoun in a compound subject, try each subject alone:

Subject Pronoun?	**The Cardinals** and **us** tied for first place.
Test:	**The Cardinals** tied for first place. **YES**
Test:	**Us** tied for first place. **NO**
Test:	**We** tied for first place. **YES**
Correction:	**The Cardinals** and **we** tied for first place.

Here is a list of subject pronouns.

Subject Pronouns

Singular	Plural
I	*we*
you	*you*
he, she, it	*they*

REVIEWING PRONOUNS AS SUBJECTS

Name two subject pronouns.

_____   _____

How can you test whether you are using the correct pronoun as the subject of a sentence?

_____

◆ *P r a c t i c e   1*   **Identifying** Underline the pronouns used as subjects in each of the following sentences.

1. Her favourite china pattern was no longer made because it was over 50 years old.

2. Paul got his feet massaged since he had worked hard all week.

3. We figured that the machinery had a crack in it.

4. They played a game of hockey just for a charitable organization.

5. "Some days are better than others for them," he said.

◆ *P r a c t i c e   2*   **Completing** Fill in each blank in the following paragraph with a subject pronoun.

Ron and Selma love to ride their bikes early in the morning. Selma bikes for pleasure, so _____ rides in the countryside. On the other hand, Ron plans to race in competitions, so _____ often bikes at the local university's track. Sometimes, however, _____ bike together in the city. _____ gives them a chance to visit each other. Personally, _____ think it's wonderful that they have an interest in common.

PRONOUNS AS OBJECTS

One of the most frequent pronoun errors is using a subject pronoun when the sentence calls for an object pronoun. The sentence may require an object after a verb, showing that someone or something receives the action of the verb. Or it may be an object of a preposition that is required (see page 280 for a list of prepositions).

NOT	She invited Bob and **I** to dinner.
CORRECT	She invited Bob and **me** to dinner.

NOT	This is between you and **I.**
CORRECT	This is between you and **me.**

Like the subject pronoun error, the object pronoun error usually occurs with compound objects. Also like the subject pronoun error, you can test whether you are using the correct pronoun by using each object separately.

Object Pronoun?	She invited **Bob and I** to dinner.
Test:	She invited **Bob** to dinner. **YES**
Test:	She invited **I** to dinner. **NO**
Test:	She invited **me** to dinner. **YES**
Correction:	She invited **Bob and me** to dinner.

Here is a list of object pronouns.

Object Pronouns

Singular	Plural
me	us
you	you
him, her, it	them

REVIEWING PRONOUNS AS OBJECTS

In what two places are pronouns used as objects?

_____   _____

How can you test whether you have used the correct pronoun as the object in a sentence?

_____

Practice 3 Identifying Underline the correct object pronoun in each of the following sentences.

1. Crystal accidentally hit (he, him) with the ping-pong ball.
2. She played the violin for (us, we).
3. The mischievous child spilled milk all over Dana and (I, me).
4. Her grandmother took (she, her) shopping for a prom dress.
5. Mary picked a bouquet of flowers for (them, they).

Practice 4 Completing Fill in each blank in the following sentences with an object pronoun.

1. Alyssa gave _____ a Valentine's Day card.
2. Beau, my dog, bit Tina on the leg, but he didn't hurt _____.
3. I bought something for _____.
4. Scoobie Doo gave _____ a tour of Canada's Wonderland.
5. My grandmother lent _____ the family pearls for the wedding.

POSSESSIVE PRONOUNS

Possessive pronouns show ownership (*my* wallet, *his* suitcase, *our* trip). (See page 276 for a list of pronouns.) An apostrophe is used with nouns to show ownership (*Tara's* car, the *clock's* hands, the *children's* toys). But an apostrophe is never used with possessive pronouns.

Possessive Pronouns

Singular	Plural
my, mine	our, ours
your, yours	you, yours
his, her, hers	their, theirs

NOT   That hairbrush is **her's.**

CORRECT   That hairbrush is **hers.**

NOT   The umbrella by the door is **your's.**

CORRECT   The umbrella by the door is **yours.**

NOT   The puppy wanted **it's** tummy scratched.

CORRECT   The puppy wanted **its** tummy scratched.

REVIEWING POSSESSIVE PRONOUNS

When do you use an apostrophe with a noun?

_____

Do possessive pronouns take apostrophes?

_____

◆ *P r a c t i c e 5* **Identifying** Underline the correct possessive pronoun in each of the following sentences.

1. Krista gave her hair and clothes a quick pat.
2. The Corvette needs its windshield fixed.
3. I believe that book on the dresser is yours.
4. Their bikes were left unattended, so they were stolen.
5. That dog should have its nails trimmed.

◆ *P r a c t i c e   6* **Completing** Fill in each blank in the following sentences with a possessive pronoun.

1. _____ vacation to Mexico was fun and exciting, but not so relaxing.

2. The games are _____.

3. The grandfather clock is broken, but _____ face is still in good condition.

4. _____ sister makes the best chocolate fudge cake.

5. The dogs performing in the circus are _____.

PRONOUNS IN COMPARISONS

Sometimes pronoun problems occur in comparisons with *than* or *as*. An object pronoun may be mistakenly used instead of a subject pronoun. To find out if you are using the right pronoun, you should finish the sentence as shown here.

NOT	She can run a mile much faster than **me**.
CORRECT	She can run a mile much faster than **I** [can run a mile].

NOT	Paula is not as good a cook as **him**.
CORRECT	Paula is not as good a cook as **he** [is].

Hint: Sometimes an object pronoun is required in a *than* or *as* comparison. But errors rarely occur in this case because the subject pronoun sounds so unnatural.

NOT	Susan likes him more than she likes **I**.
CORRECT	Susan likes him more than she likes **me**.

REVIEWING PRONOUNS IN COMPARISONS

What causes pronoun problems in comparisons?

_____

_____

How can you test whether to use a subject pronoun or an object pronoun in a than *or as comparison?*

_____

_____

◀ *P r a c t i c e* **7** **Identifying** Underline the correct pronoun in each of the following comparisons.

1. Brenda can sew better than (we, us).
2. The kittens are much friskier than (they, them).
3. Martha isn't as outspoken as (he, him).
4. She is nicer to her friends than to (I, me).
5. My husband can fix a car as well as (him, he).

◀ *P r a c t i c e* **8** **Completing** Fill in each blank in the following sentences with an appropriate pronoun for comparison.

1. Because Natalie grew up on a ranch, she is more relaxed around horses than _____.
2. She is a more accurate proofreader than _____.
3. Robert is just as smart as _____.
4. He makes you just as crazy as he makes _____.
5. Those girls ate more food than _____ .

DEMONSTRATIVE PRONOUNS

There are four demonstrative pronouns: *this, that, these,* and *those.* **Demonstrative pronouns** point to specific people or objects. Use *this* and *these* to refer to items that are near and *that* and *those* to refer to items farther away. Look at the following examples.

Demonstrative (near):	**This** tastes great.
Demonstrative (near):	**These** are delicious peaches.
Demonstrative (farther):	**That** will be decided later.
Demonstrative (farther):	**Those** are the clothes she brought with her.

Sometimes demonstrative pronouns are not used correctly.

	Incorrect	Correct
NOT	this here, that there	this, that
NOT	these here, these ones	these
NOT	them, those there, those ones	those

NOT	**Them** are the boots she wants.
CORRECT	**Those** are the boots she wants.

| **NOT** | I'd like to order **these here** pictures. |
| **CORRECT** | I'd like to order **these** pictures. |

| **NOT** | I made **those ones** by hand. |
| **CORRECT** | I made **those** by hand. |

| **NOT** | **Those there** are the ones I ordered. |
| **CORRECT** | **Those** are the ones I ordered. |

When demonstrative pronouns are used with nouns, they become adjectives.

Pronoun: **This** is his.
Adjective: **This notebook** is his.

Pronoun: **Those** are words you may regret.
Adjective: You may regret **those words.**

The problems that occur with demonstrative pronouns can also occur when these pronouns act as adjectives.

| **NOT** | Please hand me **that there** hammer. |
| **CORRECT** | Please hand me **that** hammer. |

REVIEWING DEMONSTRATIVE PRONOUNS

Name the four demonstrative pronouns.

_____   _____   _____   _____

Give two examples of errors with demonstrative pronouns.

_____

_____

◆ *P r a c t i c e* **9 A**   **Identifying** Underline the demonstrative pronoun errors in each of the following sentences.

1. These here dishes are dirty and those need to be put away.
2. Yes, these ones can be taken back to the warehouse.
3. Them classes are the hardest I have ever taken.
4. I decided those ones will do nicely for the game.
5. That there belongs to the girl waiting in line.

◆ *P r a c t i c e 9 B* **Correcting** Correct the demonstrative pronoun errors in Practice 9A by rewriting the incorrect sentences.

◆ *P r a c t i c e 1 0* **Completing** Fill in each blank in the following sentences with a logical demonstrative pronoun.

1. Later on today, _____ will be answered.

2. When seen from up close, _____ looks quite large.

3. _____ are the best seats in the house.

4. _____ should be displayed in the window.

5. Mary had never seen any of _____ before.

CHAPTER REVIEW

You might want to reread your answers to the questions in all the review boxes before you do the following exercises.

◆ *Review P r a c t i c e 1* **Identifying** Underline the pronoun errors in each of the following sentences.

1. The ring is her's.
2. Our's is the best short story out of those.
3. He is a better singer than me.
4. These here are our cars which are expected to sell.
5. The children and us went for a Sunday drive in his new convertible.

◆ *Review P r a c t i c e 2* **Completing** Correct the pronoun errors in Review Practice 1 by rewriting the incorrect sentences.

◆ *Review P r a c t i c e 3* **Writing Your Own** Write a paragraph about the town you grew up in. What is one vivid memory you have of that place?

◆ *Review P r a c t i c e 4* **Editing Through Collaboration** Exchange paragraphs from Review Practice 3 with another student, and do the following:

1. Circle all pronouns.
2. Put an X through any that are not in the correct form. Check that all the subject and object pronouns are used correctly. Also check that possessive pronouns, pronouns used in comparisons, and demonstrative pronouns are used correctly.

Then return the paragraph to its writer, and use the information in this chapter to correct the pronoun errors in your own paragraph. Record your errors on the Error Log in Appendix 6.

CHAPTER 37

PRONOUN REFERENCE AND POINT OF VIEW

✓ CHECKLIST for Correcting Problems with Pronoun Reference and Point of View

> ✔ Does every pronoun have a clear antecedent?
> ✔ Are pronouns as close as possible to the words they refer to?
> ✔ Do you maintain a single point of view?

Test Yourself

Underline the pronouns in these sentences. Then put an X over any pronouns that are confusing or unclear.

- Emily and Grace decided that she would try out for the team.
- They say you should drink eight glasses of water a day.
- I take the bus because you can save a lot of money that way.
- The reporter did not check her facts or talk to the main witness, which she regretted.
- It says to notify the dean if you are dropping a class.

(Answers are in Appendix 8.)

Any time you use a pronoun, it must clearly refer to a specific word. The word it refers to is called its **antecedent.** Two kinds of problems occur with pronoun references: The antecedent may be unclear, or the antecedent may be missing altogether. You should also be careful to stick to the same point of view in your writing. If, for example, you start out talking about "I," you should not shift to "you" in the middle of the sentence.

PRONOUN REFERENCE

Sometimes a sentence is confusing because the reader can't tell what a pronoun is referring to. The confusion may occur because the pronoun's antecedent is unclear or is completely missing.

Unclear Antecedents

In the following examples, the word each pronoun is referring to is unclear.

Unclear: On the shelf, a camera sat next to a small tape recorder. As Mr. Crutcher reached for **it,** the shelf began to tip.
(Was Mr. Crutcher reaching for the camera or the tape recorder? Only Mr. Crutcher knows for sure.)

Clear: On the shelf, a camera sat next to a small tape recorder. As Mr. Crutcher reached for **the camera,** the shelf began to tip.

Clear: On the shelf, a camera sat next to a small tape recorder. As Mr. Crutcher reached for **the tape recorder,** the shelf began to tip.

Unclear: Sarah agreed with April that **she** shouldn't get involved.
(Does *she* refer to Sarah or April? Only the writer knows.)

Clear: Sarah agreed with April that **Sarah** shouldn't get involved.

Clear: Agreeing with April, **Sarah** vowed that **she** wouldn't get involved.

How can you be sure that every pronoun you use has a clear antecedent? First, you can proofread carefully. Probably an even better test, though, is to ask a friend to read what you have written and tell you if your meaning is clear or not.

Missing Antecedents

Every pronoun should have a clear antecedent, the word it refers to. But what happens when there is no antecedent at all? The writer's message is not communicated. Two words in particular should alert you to the possibility of missing antecedents: *it* and *they*.

The following sentences have missing antecedents:

Missing Antecedent: In a recent study on teenage pregnancy, **it** says that counseling has a dramatically positive effect.
(What does *it* refer to? It has no antecedent.)

Clear: **A recent study on teenage pregnancy** says that counseling has a dramatically positive effect.

Missing Antecedent: **They** say that the early bird catches the worm.
(Who is *they*?)

Clear: **An old saying** claims that the early bird catches the worm.

REVIEWING PRONOUN REFERENCE

What is an antecedent?

_____

How can you be sure every pronoun you use has a clear antecedent?

_____

_____

What two words warn you that an antecedent may be missing?

_____   _____

♦ **P r a c t i c e   1 A**   **Identifying** Underline the pronouns in each of the following sentences. Then put an X next to any sentences with missing or unclear antecedents.

1. _____ Five hot dog vendors were on the same street, and they were each trying to outsell the others.

2. _____ The safety technician and the fire fighter gave her speech in the park.

3. _____ Barbara's birthday and Sam's anniversary are coming soon; it is the same day as Valentine's Day.

4. _____ In a recent study, it said, "Four times out of five, shoppers prefer Hallmark cards."

5. _____ They say that most students have some debts.

♦ **P r a c t i c e   1 B**   **Correcting** Correct the sentences with pronoun errors in Practice 1A by rewriting them.

♦ **P r a c t i c e   2**   **Completing** Correct the unclear or missing pronoun references in the following sentences by rewriting the sentences. Pronouns that should be corrected are underlined.

1. It says in the paper that tickets go on sale tomorrow.

   _____

2. I put the letters in my bag. Then I peeled an apple and an orange for a snack before I realized I hadn't addressed <u>them</u>.

   _____

   _____

3. Trish told Diana that <u>she</u> was going to have to move.

   _____

4. Mario told Lendel that <u>he</u> should go on a diet.

   _____

5. Both Pat and Danielle went to Humber College together. Then <u>she</u> finished her degree at the University of Western Ontario.

   _____

   _____

SHIFTING POINT OF VIEW

Point of view refers to whether a statement is made in the first person, the second person, or the third person. Each person—or point of view—requires different pronouns. The following chart lists the pronouns for each point of view.

Point of View	
First Person:	*I, we*
Second Person:	*you, you*
Third Person:	*he, she, it, they*

If you begin writing from one point of view, you should stay in that point of view. Do not shift to another point of view. For example, if you start out writing "I," you should continue with "I" and not shift to "you." Shifting point of view is a very common error in college and university writing.

Shift: If **a person** doesn't exercise regularly, **you** can lose flexibility and strength.

Correct: If **a person** doesn't exercise regularly, **he or she** can lose flexibility and strength.

Shift: I consulted a financial advisor because **you** can save money on interest payments.

Correct: I consulted a financial advisor because **I** can save money on interest payments.

REVIEWING POINT OF VIEW

What is point of view?

_____

_____

What does it mean to shift point of view?

_____

◆ **P r a c t i c e   3 A**   **Identifying** Underline the pronouns that shift in point of view in the following sentences.

1. A person should avoid eating too much fat if you don't want to become overweight.
2. I think that the new tax laws should be revised because they are so complicated that you can't understand them.
3. Doctors must go to school for many years before they can practise medicine.
4. Since students have so little free time, you should always try to manage your time efficiently.
5. You should try to save money whenever you can because we never know when we might need it.

◆ **P r a c t i c e   3 B**   **Correcting** Correct the point-of-view errors in Practice 3A by rewriting the incorrect sentences.

◆ **P r a c t i c e   4**   **Completing** Complete the following sentences with pronouns that stay in the same point of view.

1. I went shopping at the mall because I heard that _____ could get some good bargains there.
2. A driver should always pay attention to others on the road if _____ wants to avoid being in an accident.
3. The show was sold out so they checked the Internet since _____ can usually find tickets for sale there.
4. If a person wants to make friends, _____ should try to smile at others.
5. I always cook more than enough food for the picnic, for _____ never know how many people will attend.

CHAPTER REVIEW

You might want to reread your answers to the questions in all the review boxes before you do the following exercises.

◆ *Review   Practice   1*   **Identifying** Label the following sentences U if the antecedent is unclear, M if the antecedent is missing, or S if the sentence shifts point of view. Then correct the pronoun errors by rewriting the incorrect sentences.

1. _____ Alvin bought bananas, oranges, and apples at the store because you know fruit is healthy.

2. _____ They say a chef should train at home and abroad to be successful.

3. _____ You should hurry because we always need extra time.

4. _____ After my dog bit my neighbour's dog, he got sick.

5. _____ It is said that "every good dog deserves a bone."

◆ *Review   Practice   2*   **Completing** Correct the pronoun errors in the following sentences by rewriting each incorrect sentence.

1. Mary and Samantha are best friends, and she is my best friend too.

2. It is said that all people are created equal.

3. I am going to buy the most expensive dishwasher because you know that's the only way to get the best.

4. We have both chocolate and vanilla bon-bons, but it tastes better.

5. They believe that second-hand cigarette smoke can cause cancer.

◆ *Review   Practice   3*   **Writing Your Own** Using a variety of pronouns, write a paragraph about something you have learned from your friends this week.

◆ *Review   Practice   4*   **Editing Through Collaboration** Exchange paragraphs from Review Practice 3 with another student, and do the following:

1. Underline all pronouns.

2. Draw arrows to the words they modify.

3. Put an X through any pronouns that do not refer to a clear antecedent or that shift point of view.

Then return the paragraph to its writer, and use the information in this chapter to correct any pronoun-reference and point-of-view errors in your own paragraph. Record your errors on the Error Log in Appendix 6.

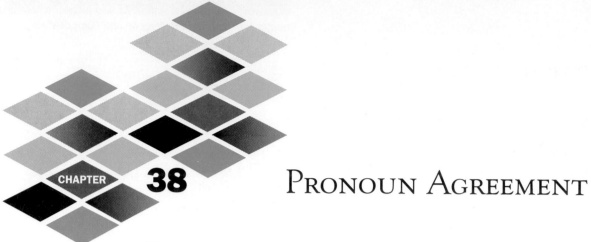

CHAPTER 38

PRONOUN AGREEMENT

☑ CHECKLIST for Correcting Pronoun Agreement Problems

✔ Do all pronouns and their antecedents agree in number (singular or plural)?

✔ Do any pronouns that refer to indefinite pronouns agree in number?

✔ Are any pronouns used in a sexist way?

Test Yourself

Underline the pronoun in each sentence, and draw an arrow to its antecedent. Put an X over any pronouns that do not agree with their antecedents.

• Harriett and Maureen walked their dogs in the park.

• Each person is responsible for their own transportation.

• Although the pieces of furniture were used, it looked new.

• Someone left their dirty dishes in the sink.

• Everyone contributed his work to the assignment.

(Answers are in Appendix 8.)

As you learned in Chapter 30, subjects and verbs must agree for clear communication. If the subject is singular, the verb must be singular; if the subject is plural, the verb must be plural. The same holds true for pronouns and the words they refer to—their *antecedents*. They must agree in number—both singular or both plural. Usually, pronoun agreement is not a problem, as these sentences show:

Singular: Jacob told **his** client to buy more stock.

Plural: Wendy and Aaron did **their** laundry yesterday.

INDEFINITE PRONOUNS

Pronoun agreement may become a problem with indefinite pronouns. Indefinite pronouns that are always singular give writers the most trouble.

NOT	**One** of the students turned in **their** paper late. (How many students were late? Only *one*, so use a singular pronoun.)
CORRECT	**One** of the students turned in **her** paper late.
CORRECT	**One** of the students turned in **his** paper late.

NOT	**Somebody** left **their** keys on the table. (How many people left keys? One person, so use a singular pronoun.)
CORRECT	**Somebody** left **her** keys on the table.
CORRECT	**Somebody** left **his** keys on the table.

Here is a list of indefinite pronouns that are always singular.

Singular Indefinite Pronouns

another	*either*	*much*	*one*
anybody	*everybody*	*neither*	*other*
anyone	*everyone*	*nobody*	*somebody*
anything	*everything*	*no one*	*someone*
each	*little*	*nothing*	*something*

Hint: A few indefinite pronouns can be either singular or plural, depending on their meaning in the sentence. These pronouns are *any*, *all*, *more*, *most*, *none*, and *some*.

Singular: **All** of the senior class had **its** picture taken.

Plural: **All** of the seniors had **their** pictures taken.

In the first sentence, *class* is considered a single body, so the singular pronoun *its* is used. In the second sentence, the *seniors* are individuals, so the plural pronoun *their* is used.

REVIEWING INDEFINITE PRONOUNS

Why should a pronoun agree with the word it refers to?

_____

Name five indefinite pronouns that are always singular.

_____ _____ _____ _____ _____

◀ *Practice 1* **Identifying** Underline the correct pronoun from the choices in parentheses, and be prepared to explain your choices.

1. Neither of the boys could give (his, their) opinion on the subject.
2. Before someone can appear on the program, (he or she, they) must audition.
3. Some of the bookstores put (its, their) books on sale for Father's Day.
4. Tom and Jack decided to hold (his, their) meetings on the first Thursday of each month.
5. Each of the dancers showed (his or her, their) dedication by practising four hours a day.

◀ *Practice 2* **Completing** Fill in each blank in the following sentences with a pronoun that agrees with its antecedent.

1. Joshua and Timothy explained _____ method for cleaning chimneys.
2. Everyone should take the time to wash _____ clothes.
3. Each of the trees has lost _____ leaves.
4. Matthew asked _____ brother to fix the car.
5. Because of the cold weather, someone will have to share _____ warm clothes.

AVOIDING SEXISM

In the first section of this chapter, you learned that you should use singular pronouns to refer to singular indefinite pronouns. For example, the indefinite pronoun *someone* requires a singular pronoun, *his* or *her*, not the plural *their*. But what if you don't know whether the person referred to is male or female? Then you have a choice: (1) You can say "he or she" or "his or her"; (2) you can make the sentence plural; or (3) you can rewrite the sentence to avoid the problem altogether. What you should not do is ignore half the population by referring to all humans as males.

NOT	If **anyone** wants to join us, then **they** can.
NOT	If **anyone** wants to join us, then **he** can.
CORRECT	If **anyone** wants to join us, then **he or she** can.
CORRECT	**People** who want to can join us.
NOT	**Everyone** paid **their** dues this month.
NOT	**Everyone** paid **his** dues this month.
CORRECT	**Everyone** paid **his or her** dues this month.
CORRECT	**All students** paid **their** dues this month.

Sexism in writing can also occur in ways other than with indefinite pronouns. We often assume that doctors, lawyers, and bank presidents are men and that nurses, schoolteachers, and secretaries are women. But that is not very accurate.

NOT	You should ask your **doctor** what **he** recommends. (Why automatically assume that the doctor is a male instead of a female?)
CORRECT	You should ask your **doctor** what **he or she** recommends.
NOT	The **policeman** gave me a warning but no ticket. (Since both men and women serve on police forces, the more correct term is *police officer* or *officer.*)
CORRECT	The **police officer** gave me a warning but no ticket.
NOT	**A nurse** cannot let **herself** become too emotionally involved in **her** work. (Why leave the men who are nurses out of this sentence?)
CORRECT	**A nurse** cannot let **him- or herself** become too emotionally involved in **his or her** work.
CORRECT	**Nurses** cannot let **themselves** become too emotionally involved in **their** work.

REVIEWING SEXISM IN WRITING

What is sexism in writing?

_____

What are two ways to get around the problem of using male pronouns to refer to both women and men?

_____   _____

Give two other examples of sexism in writing.

_____   _____

◆ *P r a c t i c e*   **3 A**   **Identifying**   Underline the sexist references in the following sentences.

1. At least one student did not memorize his test material.
2. A judge will always give her verdict at the end of the trial.
3. A navy officer can wear his white uniform to weddings.
4. A mailman knows he must deliver the mail rain or shine.
5. A passenger usually can't fit all her luggage in the overhead bin.

◆ *Practice 3B* **Correcting** Correct the sexist pronouns in Practice 3A by rewriting the incorrect sentences.

◆ *Practice 4* **Completing** Fill in each blank in the following sentences with an appropriate pronoun.

1. An athlete is always determined to overcome _____ injury.
2. The contestant who sells the most candy can choose _____ own prize.
3. An airplane pilot always has to make sure _____ remains alert and awake.
4. A teacher should always explain _____ assignments.
5. A truck driver can pull _____ truck over to sleep for a few hours.

CHAPTER REVIEW

You might want to reread your answers to the questions in all the review boxes before you do the following exercises.

◆ *Review Practice 1* **Identifying** Underline and correct the pronoun errors in the following sentences.

1. Neither of the women went to their parents' house for Thanksgiving.
2. Each of the students picked up their test from the Psychology Department office.
3. A newspaper writer can work on his assignment for months.
4. Anyone can learn how to sew if they are patient.
5. A neat gardener always sweeps up after he mows the lawn.

◆ *Review Practice 2* **Completing** Correct the following pronoun errors by rewriting the following sentences.

1. A doctor can choose his specialty from many different options.

   _____

2. Every one of the nurses has had their uniform cleaned for inspection.

   _____

3. Each of the people thought of their family as the story was being told.

   _____

4. A sales clerk is never allowed to take her vacation in December.

_____

5. Everyone should have to watch her own performance on videotape.

_____

◆ ***Review Practice 3*** **Writing Your Own** Write a paragraph explaining what you think the qualities of a good teacher are.

◆ ***Review Practice 4*** **Editing Through Collaboration** Exchange paragraphs from Review Practice 3 with another student, and do the following:

1. Underline any pronouns.
2. Circle any pronouns that do not agree with the words they refer to.

Then return the paragraph to its writer, and use the information in this chapter to correct any pronoun agreement errors in your own paragraph. Record your errors on the Error Log in Appendix 6.

UNIT TESTS

Here are some exercises that test your understanding of all the material in this unit: Pronoun Problems, Pronoun Reference and Point of View, and Pronoun Agreement.

Unit Test I

A. Underline the pronoun errors in the following sentences.

1. The pilot was ready in the private plane to take he and she on the flight.
2. Kim cooked a delicious meal for we after the meeting.
3. Anybody can create their own painting.
4. Margaret didn't want to see Vivian because she didn't want to get involved.
5. That backpack is her's.
6. Jeremy is much more enthusiastic about our vacation than me.
7. I am going to take a walk on the beach since you can always benefit from a little fresh air.
8. A steelworker must always know he could go on strike.

9.   The waiters gathered around she and sang "Happy Birthday."

10.   The cat didn't want it's food.

11.   A secretary must be able to identify her mistakes.

12.   This here is just too hard for me to do.

13.   We performed our dance routine just as well as them.

14.   At the store, an ice chest was next to a lawn chair in a window display, but it was expensive.

15.   In the summer, you and me should go swimming in the river.

16.   I will give you these ones if you will give me those ones.

17.   Something in the speakers sounded like they had broken.

18.   I always carry an umbrella with me since you can never tell when it's going to rain in Vancouver.

19.   Antonio is a much better painter than me.

20.   The officer and the inmates want peace in his or her environment.

B. Correct the pronoun errors in Part A by rewriting each incorrect sentence.

Unit Test II

A. Underline the pronoun errors in the following paragraph.

In a recent study, it shows that a student involved in some sort of music program scores more highly on their standardized tests. It is not clear what about music education leads to this improvement in your skills. They now agree that music education is a valuable asset to all students. However, many school boards have cut all or most of it's music education programs. Them cite rising costs and plummeting resources as the cause for the elimination of these here programs. Because of pressures from their communities and provincial governments, the boards feel they need to focus on teaching the basics: reading, writing, and arithmetic. Unfortunately, in the long run, dumping music education to focus on the basics will do we a great disservice. Music is not less important than them. Anyone who is concerned about music education should write to their MPP or MLA to support it.

B. Correct the pronoun errors in Part A by rewriting the paragraph.

ADJECTIVES

✅ CHECKLIST for Using Adjectives Correctly

> ✔ Are all adjectives that show comparison used correctly?
>
> ✔ Are the forms of *good* and *bad* used correctly?

Test Yourself

Underline the adjectives in the following sentences. Then put an X over the adjectives that are used incorrectly.

- The grey stingrays were very beautiful.
- We were more happier when the rain cooled the hot day.
- This is the worstest cold I've ever had.
- This textbook is more better than that one.
- She is the oldest of the two sisters.

(Answers are in Appendix 8.)

Adjectives are modifiers. They help us communicate more clearly (I have a *red* sweater; I want a *blue* one) and vividly (her voice was *soft* and *gentle*). Without adjectives, our language would be drab and boring.

USING ADJECTIVES

Adjectives are words that modify—or describe—nouns or pronouns. Adjectives often tell how something or someone looks: *dark, light, tall, short, large, small*. Most adjectives come before the words they modify, but with linking verbs (such as *is, are, look, become,* and *feel*), adjectives follow the words they modify.

Adjectives Before a Noun:	We ate the **moist, sweet** cake.
Adjectives After a Linking Verb:	The cake was **moist** and **sweet**.

REVIEWING ADJECTIVES

What are adjectives?

_____

Where can you find adjectives in a sentence?

_____

◆ **P r a c t i c e   1   Identifying** In the following sentences, underline the adjectives and circle the words they modify.

1. I could eat a large elephant for lunch.
2. My biology class is difficult but interesting.
3. The good news is that her older brother volunteers for the Boy Scouts.
4. She owns an antique store.
5. Our yard has both flowering trees and evergreen trees.

◆ **P r a c t i c e   2   Completing** Fill in each blank in the following sentences with logical adjectives.

When my (1) _____ brother Nathan was in high school, he became (2) _____ at math. The teacher wanted to teach concepts according to the textbook, but Nathan always seemed to find a (3) _____ way to solve the math problems. Though he would have the right answers, the teacher would often take off points because of the process he used. After having (4) _____ conversations with the teacher, Nathan convinced her that he was (5) _____. He got an A in the course and became a good friend of the teacher's.

COMPARING WITH ADJECTIVES

Most adjectives have three forms: a **basic** form, a **comparative** form (used to compare two items or indicate a greater degree), and a **superlative** form (used to compare three or more items or indicate the greatest degree).

For positive comparisons, adjectives form the comparative and superlative in two different ways.

1. For one-syllable adjectives and some two-syllable adjectives, use *-er* to compare two items and *-est* to compare three or more items.

Basic	Comparative (used to compare two items)	Superlative (used to compare three or more items)
tall	taller	tallest
old	older	oldest
hot	hotter	hottest

2. For some two-syllable adjectives and all longer adjectives, use *more* to compare two items and *most* to compare three or more items.

Basic	Comparative (used to compare two items)	Superlative (used to compare three or more items)
careful	more careful	most careful
relaxed	more relaxed	most relaxed
content	more content	most content

For negative comparisons, use *less* to compare two items and *least* to compare three or more items.

Basic	Comparative (used to compare two items)	Superlative (used to compare three or more items)
beautiful	less beautiful	least beautiful
familiar	less familiar	least familiar

Hint: Some adjectives are not usually compared. For example, one task cannot be "more complete" or "more impossible" than another. Here are some more examples.

complete	*favourite*	*square*
dead	*horizontal*	*supreme*
empty	*impossible*	*unanimous*
equal	*pregnant*	*unique*

REVIEWING ADJECTIVE FORMS
....

When do you use the comparative form of an adjective?

_____

When do you use the superlative form of an adjective?

_____

How do one-syllable and some two-syllable adjectives form the comparative and superlative in positive comparisons?

_____

How do some two-syllable adjectives and all longer adjectives form the comparative and superlative in positive comparisons?

_____

How do you form negative comparisons?

_____

◆ ***Practice 3* Identifying** Underline the adjectives, and note whether they are basic (B), comparative (C), or superlative (S).

1. _____ The grass is always greener on the other side.

2. _____ Your car will look good if you wash it.

3. _____ Voters today are more educated.

4. _____ The longest mile of the marathon is the last one.

5. _____ My mother often asked my older brother to help her with the cooking.

◆ ***Practice 4* Completing** Fill in each blank in the following paragraph with the correct comparative or superlative form of the adjective in parentheses.

Yesterday was the (1) _____ (rainy) day of the entire year. Consequently, my garden is looking (2) _____ (beautiful) today than it did two days ago. I have also seen the (3) _____ (slimy) earthworms on the sidewalk, wiggling faster than ever to get back into the dirt. Though I was pleased to see my flowers starting to bloom, I became even (4) _____ (excited) when I saw the tulip bulbs breaking through the ground. That means in a few weeks, my garden will be the (5) _____ (spectacular) one on the block.

COMMON ADJECTIVE ERRORS

Two types of problems occur with adjectives used in comparisons.

1. Instead of using one method for forming the comparative or superlative, both are used. That is, both *-er* and *more* or *less* are used to compare two items, or both *-est* and *most* or *least* are used to compare three or more items.

   NOT   The top shelf is **more longer** than the bottom shelf.

   CORRECT   The top shelf is **longer** than the bottom shelf.

   NOT   That is the **most silliest** hat I've ever seen.

   CORRECT   That is the **silliest** hat I've ever seen.

2. The second type of error occurs when the comparative or superlative is used with the wrong number of items. The comparative form should be used for two items and the superlative for three or more items.

   NOT   Barb's chili recipe is the hott**est** of the **two.**

   CORRECT   Barb's chili recipe is the hott**er** of the **two.**

   NOT   Ross is the young**er** of the **three** brothers.

   CORRECT   Ross is the young**est** of the **three** brothers.

REVIEWING COMMON ADJECTIVE ERRORS

Can you ever use -er + more or -est + most?

_____

When do you use the comparative form of an adjective?

_____

When do you use the superlative form of an adjective?

_____

◆ **P r a c t i c e   5 A   Identifying** Underline the adjectives in the following sentences that are used incorrectly in comparisons. Mark sentences that are correct C.

1. _____ I always thought Sasha was more better at math than I was.

2. _____ Terry is the wildest of all her friends.

3. _____ Sean is the stronger of his five cousins.

4. _____ I've owned both a cat and a dog, and the cat was the cleanest of the two.

5. _____ The most happiest day of my life was the day I got married.

◀ *Practice 5B* **Correcting** Correct the adjective errors in Practice 5A by rewriting the incorrect sentences.

◀ *Practice 6* **Completing** Choose the correct adjective forms in the following paragraph to complete the sentences.

The (1) _____ (latest/most latest) fads in cars are hard to keep up with. The (2) _____ (more common/most common) of the many options now available is a car that uses both solar energy and natural gas for power. That way, if the solar cells are empty, the natural gas keeps the car running. What would be (3) _____ (sadder/more sadder) than running out of fuel while trying to meet a deadline or get to the hospital? Natural gas is (4) _____ (more cleaner/cleaner) than the gasoline used by most cars today. Between these two sources, natural gas is the (5) _____ (easier/easiest) on the environment.

USING *GOOD* AND *BAD* CORRECTLY

The adjectives *good* and *bad* are irregular. They do not form the comparative and superlative like most other adjectives. Here are the correct forms for these two irregular adjectives:

Basic	Comparative (used to compare two items)	Superlative (used to compare three or more items)
good	better	best
bad	worse	worst

Problems occur with *good* and *bad* when writers don't know how to form their comparative and superlative forms.

NOT	more better, more worse, worser, most best, most worst, bestest, worstest
CORRECT	better, worse, best, worst

These errors appear in sentences in the following ways:

NOT   That is the **bestest** play I have ever seen.

CORRECT   That is the **best** play I have ever seen.

NOT   His health is getting **more worse** as time goes by.

CORRECT   His health is getting **worse** as time goes by.

REVIEWING *Good* AND *Bad*

What are the three forms of good?

_____   _____   _____

What are the three forms of bad?

_____   _____   _____

◆ *P r a c t i c e* **7 A** **Identifying** In the following sentences, underline the forms of *good* and *bad* used correctly, and circle the forms of *good* and *bad* used incorrectly.

1. I got a C in chemistry, but did more better in Spanish.
2. The most best drawing is a bowl of fruit.
3. Even though he practised, his soccer skills got more and more bad.
4. Going to work is better now that I am a manager.
5. I like my hair bestest when it is curly.

◆ *P r a c t i c e* **7 B** **Correcting** Correct the errors with *good* and *bad* in Practice 7A by rewriting the incorrect sentences.

◆ *P r a c t i c e* **8** **Completing** Using the correct forms of *good* or *bad*, complete the following paragraph.

Dusting is definitely the (1) _____ household chore. I can't think of anything (2) _____ than having to take everything off a shelf just to wipe a rag across it. It would be (3) _____ to buy those cans of compressed air and just spray the dust away instead of wiping the dust away. I can think of so many (4) _____ things to do with my time than dusting. But according to Dear Abby, the (5) _____ housekeepers have dust-free furniture.

CHAPTER REVIEW

You might want to reread your answers to the questions in all the review boxes before you do the following exercises.

◆ *Review   Practice   1*   **Identifying** Label the following adjectives basic (B), comparative (C), superlative (S), or not able to be compared (X).

1. _____ most lovable

2. _____ stickier

3. _____ final

4. _____ heavier

5. _____ more genuine

◆ *Review   Practice   2*   **Completing** Supply the comparative and superlative forms (both positive and negative) for each of the following adjectives.

	Basic	Comparative	Superlative
1.	tight	_____	_____
2.	crooked	_____	_____
3.	long	_____	_____
4.	smart	_____	_____
5.	greasy	_____	_____

◆ *Review   Practice   3*   **Writing Your Own** Write a paragraph describing one of the most memorable people you have ever met. What did the person look like? How did he or she talk? What did he or she wear? Where did you meet this person? Why is this person so memorable?

◆ *Review   Practice   4*   **Editing Through Collaboration** Exchange paragraphs from Review Practice 3 with another student, and do the following:

1. Underline all the adjectives.
2. Circle those that are not in the correct form.

Then return the paragraph to its writer, and use the information in this chapter to correct any adjective errors in your own paragraph. Record your errors on the Error Log in Appendix 6.

ADVERBS

 CHECKLIST for Using Adverbs

> ✔ Are all adverbs that show comparison used correctly?
>
> ✔ Are *good/well* and *bad/badly* used correctly?

Test Yourself

Underline the adverbs in the following sentences. Then put an X over the adverbs that are used incorrectly.

- We were led quickly out the back door.
- He hugged her tight when he saw her.
- Tina left early because she wasn't feeling good.
- She feels badly that she couldn't stay.
- I can't never meet on Tuesdays because I work that night.

(Answers are in Appendix 8.)

Like adjectives, adverbs help us communicate more clearly (she walked *quickly*) and more vividly (she stopped *suddenly*). They make their sentences more interesting.

USING ADVERBS

Adverbs modify verbs, adjectives, and other adverbs. They answer the questions *how? when? where? how often?* and *to what extent?* Look at the following examples.

How:	Zachary dusted the antiques **carefully.**
When:	The antique shop **always** opens on time.
Where:	The antique shop is **here.**
How often:	I shop there **regularly.**
To what extent:	The shop is **extremely** busy on Saturdays.

Some words are always adverbs, including *here, there, not, never, now, again, almost, often,* and *well.*

Other adverbs are formed by adding *-ly* to an adjective:

Adjective	**Adverb**
quiet	quietly
perfect	perfectly
strange	strangely

Hint: Not all words that end in *-ly* are adverbs. Some, such as *friendly, early, lonely, chilly,* and *lively,* are adjectives.

REVIEWING ADVERBS

What are adverbs?

_____

What five questions do adverbs answer?

_____ _____ _____ _____ _____

List four words that are always adverbs.

_____ _____ _____ _____

How do many adverbs end?

_____

◆ *P r a c t i c e 1* **Identifying** In the following sentences, underline the adverbs, and circle the words they modify.

1. The little boy cried loudly.
2. That was a very good movie.
3. Walk quickly to the car because it's raining.
4. We never miss our favourite TV show.
5. The dimly lit restaurant served horrible food.

◆ *P r a c t i c e 2* **Completing** Fill in each blank in the following sentences with an adverb that makes sense.

Tom was (1) _____ tired after spending the day at Niagara Falls. He (2) _____ changed his clothes and (3) _____ crawled into bed. But before he closed his eyes, he heard a mosquito (4) _____ buzzing around his head. Fortunately, his fatigue overpowered the buzzing, and he (5) _____ fell asleep.

COMPARING WITH ADVERBS

Like adjectives, most adverbs have three forms: a **basic** form, a **comparative** form (used to compare two items), and a **superlative** form (used to compare three or more items).

For positive comparisons, adverbs form the comparative and superlative forms in two different ways:

1. For one-syllable adverbs, use *-er* and *-est* to form the comparative and superlative.

Basic	Comparative (used to compare two items)	Superlative (used to compare three or more items)
fast	faster	fastest
near	nearer	nearest
far	farther	farthest

2. For adverbs of two or more syllables, use *more* to compare two items and *most* to compare three or more items.

Basic	Comparative (used to compare two items)	Superlative (used to compare three or more items)
beautifully	more beautifully	most beautifully
awkwardly	more awkwardly	most awkwardly
loudly	more loudly	most loudly

For negative comparisons, adverbs, like adjectives, use *less* to compare two items and *least* to compare three or more items.

Basic	Comparative (used to compare two items)	Superlative (used to compare three or more items)
often	less often	least often
frequently	less frequently	least frequently
vividly	less vividly	least vividly

Hint: Like adjectives, certain adverbs are not usually compared. Something cannot last "more eternally" or work "more uniquely." The following adverbs cannot logically be compared.

endlessly	*eternally*	*infinitely*
equally	*impossibly*	*invisibly*

REVIEWING ADVERB FORMS

When do you use the comparative form of an adverb?

_____

When do you use the superlative form of an adverb?

_____

How do one-syllable adverbs form the comparative and superlative in positive comparisons?

_____

How do adverbs of two or more syllables form the comparative and superlative in positive comparisons?

_____

How do you form negative comparisons with adverbs?

_____

◆ *P r a c t i c e 3* **Identifying** Underline the adverbs, and note whether they are basic (B), comparative (C), or superlative (S).

1. _____ Can you drive faster?

2. _____ This house is the most beautifully painted one in the neighbourhood.

3. _____ My sister speaks more kindly to me when Mom is in the room.

4. _____ The crowd yelled loudly when the referee made a bad call.

5. _____ They completed the project most efficiently.

◆ *P r a c t i c e 4* **Completing** Fill in each blank in the following paragraph with the correct comparative or superlative form of the adverb in parentheses.

Sasha gave the (1) _____ (creatively) presented oral report in the science class. Her visual aids were (2) _____ (colorfully) decorated than Paul's, and Paul is an art major. Sasha even spoke (3) _____ (clearly) than Odella, who is a speech major. But best of all, she approached the assignment (4) _____ (cleverly) than the best student in the class. She based her presentation on a popular TV game show. Everyone could identify with the information she presented, and (5) _____ (importantly), she kept our attention.

ADJECTIVE OR ADVERB?

One of the most common errors with modifiers is using an adjective when an adverb is called for. Keep in mind that adjectives modify nouns and pronouns, whereas adverbs modify verbs, adjectives, and other adverbs. Adverbs *do not* modify nouns or pronouns. Here are some examples.

NOT   She spoke too **slow.** [adjective]

CORRECT   She spoke too **slowly.** [adverb]

NOT   He was **real** happy with the decision. [adjective]

CORRECT   He was **really** happy with the decision. [adverb]

REVIEWING THE DIFFERENCE BETWEEN ADJECTIVES
AND ADVERBS

How do you know whether to use an adjective or an adverb in a sentence?

_____

_____

Give an example of an adverb in a sentence.

_____

Give an example of an adjective in a sentence.

_____

◆ *Practice* **5A** **Identifying** Underline the adverbs in the following sentences. Write C next to the sentences that are correct.

1. _____ She talked too quick for me to understand.

2. _____ Your car engine runs so quiet.

3. _____ I patiently read the same picture book five times.

4. _____ This is a nice decorated dorm room.

5. _____ The ducks began to quack loud when they saw us.

◆ *Practice* **5B** **Correcting** Correct the adverb errors in Practice 5A by rewriting the incorrect sentences.

◆ *Practice* **6** **Completing** Choose the correct adverb to complete the sentences in the following paragraph.

Last August, we drove to London to visit a couple of friends that we hadn't seen in a (1) _____ (real/really) long time. She is a doctor at a London-area hospital, and he stays (2) _____ (incredible/incredibly) busy doing his artwork and taking care of their two kids. After we arrived, they took us to Victoria Park, and we laughed (3) _____ (loudly/loud) at the kids playing. When it was time for us to go, we (4) _____ (repeated/repeatedly) promised not to wait so long before the next visit. We hugged each other (5) _____ (tightly/tight) and said goodbye.

DOUBLE NEGATIVES

Another problem that involves adverbs is the **double negative**—using two negative words in one clause. Examples of negative words include *no, not, never, none, nothing, neither, nowhere, nobody, barely,* and *hardly.* A double negative creates the opposite meaning of what is intended.

NOT   We **never** had **no** break today.

The actual meaning of these double negatives is "we did have a break today."

CORRECT   We had **no** break today.

NOT   Jim does **not** owe me **nothing.**

The actual meaning of these double negatives is "Jim does owe me something."

> **CORRECT**   Jim does **not** owe me **anything.**

Double negatives often occur with contractions.

> **NOT**   My mom doesn't **hardly** get any time to herself.

The actual meaning of these double negatives is "My mom gets a lot of time to herself."

> **CORRECT**   My mom **doesn't** get much time to herself.

Using two negatives is confusing and grammatically wrong. Be on the lookout for negative words, and use only one per clause.

REVIEWING DOUBLE NEGATIVES
....

What is a double negative?

_____

List five negative words.

_____ _____ _____ _____ _____

Why should you avoid double negatives?

_____

◆ *P r a c t i c e 7 A*   **Identifying** Mark each of the following sentences either correct (C) or incorrect (X).

1. _____ I don't think you owe me nothing.

2. _____ Michelle couldn't hardly wait to go to the Bahamas.

3. _____ Bryan can't barely fit in Tony's tennis shoes.

4. _____ The last one in is not really a rotten egg.

5. _____ Having a driver's licence doesn't say nothing about your driving skills.

◆ *P r a c t i c e 7 B*   **Correcting** Correct the double negatives in Practice 7A by rewriting the incorrect sentences.

◆ *P r a c t i c e 8* **Completing** Choose the correct negative modifiers to complete the following paragraph.

The first time I went furniture shopping, I was (1) _____ (hardly/not hardly) concerned with the quality of the furniture. I just wanted things that looked good, and I (2) _____ (didn't/didn't never) think about how long they would last. I bought a plaid couch and was excited about decorating my living room around it, so I spent even more money on curtains, pillows, and wall hangings. Soon, I had a party at my house, and that couch was (3) _____ (not never/never) so abused. One of my friends, who must weigh (4) _____ (scarcely/not scarcely) less than 300 pounds, plopped down on the couch, and it immediately broke. He apologized repeatedly, but no matter how he tried to fix it, there (5) _____ (wasn't nothing/was nothing) he could do. That's when I learned to buy things that last.

USING *GOOD/WELL* AND *BAD/BADLY* CORRECTLY

The pairs *good/well* and *bad/badly* are so frequently misused that they deserve special attention.

Good is an adjective; *well* is an adverb. Use *good* with a noun (n) or after a linking verb (lv).

                                     n

Adjective: What a **good** dog.

                                    lv

Adjective: The soup tastes **good.**

Use *well* for someone's health or after an action verb (av).

                     lv

Adverb: I am **well,** thank you. [health]

                     av

Adverb: She plays **well** with others.

Bad is an adjective; *badly* is an adverb. Use *bad* with a noun (n) or after a linking verb (lv). Always use *bad* after *feel* if you're talking about emotions.

                                n

Adjective: That looks like a **bad** cut.

                                lv
   Adjective: I feel **bad** that I lost the tickets.

Use *badly* with an adjective (adj) or after an action verb (av).

                                        adj
   Adverb: The steak is **badly** burned.

                        av
   Adverb: She drives **badly**.

REVIEWING *Good/Well* AND *Bad/Badly*

When should you use the adjective good?

_____

When should you use the adverb well?

_____

When should you use the adjective bad?

_____

When should you use the adverb badly?

_____

◆ *P r a c t i c e* **9 A**   **Identifying** Label each of the following sentences either correct (C) or incorrect (X).

   1. _____ Gwyneth said she felt good enough to travel.

   2. _____ Don't talk so bad about Mike.

   3. _____ That one bad play cost us the game.

   4. _____ I want to do good in this class so my GPA improves.

   5. _____ Tamika writes well.

◆ *P r a c t i c e* **9 B**   **Correcting** Correct the adverb errors in Practice 9A by rewriting the incorrect sentences.

◆ *P r a c t i c e* **1 0**   **Completing** Choose the correct modifiers to complete the following paragraph.

Remember when you were in third grade and wanted so (1) _____ (bad/badly) to have lots of friends? The worst feeling in the world is to be teased and shunned by peers. And third graders are very (2) _____ (good/well) at creating nicknames that stay with a person for life. Nicknames often point out something unusual about your physical features or an activity you don't play very (3) _____ (good/well). Whatever kids find to tease you about, they repeat it and repeat it until you feel (4) _____ (bad/badly) about yourself—until you never want to return to school again. That is why parents should discourage name-calling and teasing. A child's self-image will affect how (5) _____ (good/well) he or she handles all aspects of life.

CHAPTER REVIEW

You might want to reread your answers to the questions in all the review boxes before you do the following exercises.

◆ *Review Practice 1* **Identifying** Underline the correct word in each of the following sentences.

1. The committee was (real, very) tired by the end of the day.
2. Justin walked (most, more) slowly than Alec.
3. *The Simpsons* has been on TV (continued, continuously) for years.
4. We don't have (no, any) candy to offer the children.
5. The golden retriever ran more (quicklier, quickly) than the German shepherd.

◆ *Review Practice 2* **Completing** Fill in each blank in the following paragraph with an adverb that makes sense. Try not to use any adverb more than once.

Working as a telemarketer is much (1) _____ difficult than you might expect. It requires people to work (2) _____ long hours and to put up with rudeness. For instance, I've had to work for up to 13 hours without any more than a 10-minute break and a 30-minute lunch. The people that a telemarketer must call are not (3) _____ nice. Some are (4) _____ rude.

Many people hang up (5) _____ when they learn I'm a telemarketer. They could at least say, "Thank you, but I'm (6) _____ not interested." With this job, I must (7) _____ remind myself to keep a positive attitude and (8) _____ give up. I (9) _____ want to succeed at this job, but I don't know if I am (10) _____ strong enough.

♦ ***Review Practice 3* Writing Your Own** Write a paragraph explaining a favourite pastime of yours. What does the activity involve? Why do you like it? What does it do for you?

♦ ***Review Practice 4* Editing Through Collaboration** Exchange paragraphs from Review Practice 3 with another student, and do the following:

1. Underline all the adverbs.
2. Circle those that are not in the correct form.
3. Put an X above any double negatives.

Then return the paragraph to its writer, and use the information in this chapter to correct any adverb errors in your own paragraph. Record your errors on the Error Log in Appendix 6.

CHAPTER 41

MODIFIER ERRORS

✅ CHECKLIST for Identifying and Correcting Modifier Problems

> ✔ Are modifiers as close as possible to the words they modify?
> ✔ Are any sentences confusing because the words that the modifiers refer to are missing?

Test Yourself

Underline the modifier problem in each sentence.

- When we arrived at the concert, Sandy told her mother that she should call home.
- Before going to the store, the car needed gas.
- The teacher told the students their grades would be posted before she dismissed them.
- To enter the contest, the application must be submitted by Friday.
- We found the magazine and put it in a safe place that had an article about saving money.

(Answers are in Appendix 8.)

As you know, a modifier describes another word or group of words. Sometimes, however, a modifier is too far from the words it refers to (*misplaced modifier*), or the word it refers to is missing altogether (*dangling modifier*). As a result, the sentence is confusing.

MISPLACED MODIFIERS

A modifier should be placed as close as possible to the word or words it modifies, but this does not always happen. A **misplaced modifier** is too far from the word or words it refers to, making the meaning of the sentence unclear. Look at these examples.

NOT   Brad yelled at his roommate **in his underwear.**

(Who is wearing the underwear—Brad or Brad's roommate? The modifier *in his underwear* must be moved closer to the word it modifies.)

CORRECT	**In his underwear,** Brad yelled at his roommate.
CORRECT	Brad yelled at his roommate, who was **in his underwear.**
NOT	The students were told to turn in their papers **after the bell.**

(This sentence has two meanings. Were the students supposed to turn in their papers after the bell rang? Or after the bell rang, did someone tell them to turn in their papers?)

CORRECT	The teacher told the students to turn in their papers **after the bell.**
CORRECT	**After the bell,** the teacher told the students to turn in their papers.

Certain modifiers that limit meaning are often misplaced, causing problems. Look at how meaning changes by moving the limiting word *only* in the following sentences:

Only Laverne says that Shirley was at home in the evening.
(Laverne says this, but no one else does.)

Laverne **only** says that Shirley was at home in the evening.
(Laverne says this, but she doesn't really mean it.)

Laverne says that **only** Shirley was at home in the evening.
(Shirley—and no one else—was at home in the evening.)

Laverne says that Shirley was **only** at home in the evening.
(Shirley didn't leave the house in the evening.)

Laverne says that Shirley was at home **only** in the evening.
(Shirley was at home in the evening but out the rest of the day.)

Here is a list of common limiting words.

almost	*hardly*	*merely*	*only*
even just	*just*	*nearly*	*scarcely*

Reviewing Misplaced Modifiers

What is a misplaced modifier?

_____

How can you correct a misplaced modifier?

_____

◈ *Practice 1A* Identifying Underline the misplaced modifiers in the following sentences.

1. Stolen from his car, Henry saw his wallet at a pawn shop.
2. The flowers bloomed when the weather changed in the front yard.
3. Wearing her school colours, Javier went to the football game with Susan.
4. The officers quickly wanted to solve the crime.
5. I sold my old desk when I left college at a yard sale.

◈ *Practice 1B* Correcting Correct the misplaced modifiers in Practice 1A by rewriting the incorrect sentences.

◈ *Practice 2* Completing Fill in each blank in the following paragraph with a modifier that makes sense.

In the (1) _____ city of Winnipeg, Sam can see himself (2) _____ walking across the stage to receive his degree. This goal was (3) _____ but he thinks now that he will make it (4) _____. He always has doubts about himself, but he is slowly learning (5) _____.

DANGLING MODIFIERS

Modifiers are "dangling" when they have nothing to refer to in a sentence. **Dangling modifiers** (especially those starting with an *-ing* word or with *to*) often appear at the beginning of a sentence. Here is an example.

NOT   **Having lived in Montreal for 20 years,** the traffic is horrible.

A modifier usually modifies the words closest to it. So the phrase *Having lived in Montreal* modifies *traffic*. But traffic doesn't live in Montreal. In fact, there is no logical word in the sentence that the phrase modifies. It is left dangling. You can correct a dangling modifier in one of two ways—by inserting the missing word that is being referred to or by rewriting the sentence.

CORRECT   **Having lived in Montreal for 20 years, Carrie** will tell you that the traffic is horrible.

CORRECT   **Carrie has lived in Montreal for 20 years,** and she will tell you that the traffic is horrible.

NOT	**To order more food,** the coupon must be presented in person.
CORRECT	**To order more food, you** must present the coupon in person.
CORRECT	You must present the coupon in person **to order more food.**

NOT	The refrigerator was full **after buying groceries.**
CORRECT	**After buying groceries, we** had a full refrigerator.
CORRECT	The refrigerator was full **after we bought more groceries.**
CORRECT	**After buying groceries, we** filled the refrigerator with them.

REVIEWING DANGLING MODIFIERS

What is a dangling modifier?

_____

How do you correct a dangling modifier?

_____

_____

◆ *P r a c t i c e   3 A*   **Identifying** Underline the dangling modifiers in the following sentences.

1. After price-checking for hours, the stereo at Costco was the best deal.
2. To register for the dance, the money must be paid a week in advance.
3. The restaurant was very busy waiting 10 minutes for a table.
4. Sitting on the blanket, the sun shone brightly during our family picnic.
5. To meet with your counselor, an appointment must be made.

◆ *P r a c t i c e   3 B* **Correcting** Correct the dangling modifiers in Practice 3A by rewriting the incorrect sentences.

◆ *P r a c t i c e   4* **Completing** Fill in the blanks with modifiers in the following paragraph.

(1) _____, Cheryl sets out to weed her garden and trim her bushes. Her yard has really been neglected (2) _____, because she was taking classes and had two part-time jobs. Her evenings (3) _____ are her favourite times. She knows she can rest then (4) _____. She can also dream about the future during these times (5) _____.

CHAPTER REVIEW

You might want to reread your answers to the questions in all the review boxes before you do the following exercises.

◆ *Review Practice 1* **Identifying** Underline the modifier errors in the following sentences.

1. Singing and cheering, the van full of students pulled off.
2. Broken for almost two months, we finally bought a new flat-screen television.
3. My parents tried as a young child to teach me right from wrong.
4. To build endurance and muscle tone, a health plan should be followed.
5. While talking on the telephone, my alarm clock went off.

◆ *Review Practice 2* **Completing** Rewrite the sentences in Review Practice 1 so that the phrases you underlined are as close as possible to the words they modify.

◆ *Review Practice 3* **Writing Your Own** Write a paragraph about the career you hope to have after college or university and your plans to begin working in this field.

◆ *Review Practice 4* **Editing Through Collaboration** Exchange paragraphs from Review Practice 3 with another student, and do the following:

1. Underline any misplaced modifiers.
2. Put brackets around any dangling modifiers.

Then return the paragraph to its writer, and use the information in this chapter to correct any modifier problems in your own paragraph. Record your errors on the Error Log in Appendix 6.

UNIT TESTS

Here are some exercises that test your understanding of all the material in this unit: Adjectives, Adverbs, and Modifier Errors.

Unit Test I

A. Underline the modifier errors in the following sentences.

1. The Dodge Neon is the more popular car in its class.
2. Sam didn't hardly go to class this term.
3. The little boys in the class were more good at reading than the little girls.
4. Helen touched the cactus very gentle.
5. He was never more busier than after he started that big project.
6. The snake was coiled up tight.
7. Sara was nervous and sang bad at the recital.
8. Dale Earnhardt died sudden during a race in February 2001.
9. I never get nothing good on my birthday.
10. To pass this class, no more than three absences are allowed.
11. The roller coaster turned sharp, and we held on for our lives.
12. A young person shouldn't never start smoking.
13. Using bleach made my shirts more whiter.
14. Nobody did none of the work but me.
15. Seeing my grandfather in the hospital is the most worst memory I have.
16. He wanted to go so bad.
17. You can really dress good if you want to.
18. Of my two uncles, the youngest one is the most fun.
19. The car must be driven for at least 100 kilometres to know if you bought a lemon.
20. Basketball is best to play than to watch.

B. Correct the modifier errors in Part A by rewriting each incorrect sentence.

Unit Test II

A. Underline the modifier errors in the following paragraph.

Family picnics do not seem like nothing to get excited about.
However, as many Canadians long for a more simpler time, they are

becoming more popular. Spending a Saturday at the park, the grass is covered with families enjoying time away from their busy lives. Each family participating in this enjoyable activity has a more unique way of spending the afternoon. Some families like to play volleyball or other sports. Other families may simply spend the time daydreaming together while lounging on their blankets. For some families, eating good food is the better of all of these activities. The most important part of any family picnic is having fun, so planning the worse picnic is even more impossible than boiling water wrong. Family picnics are the more better way to spend a spring afternoon!

B.　Correct the modifier errors in Part A by rewriting the paragraph.

COMMAS

CHECKLIST for Using Commas

✔ Are commas used to separate items in a series?

✔ Are commas used to set off introductory material?

✔ Is there a comma before *and, but, for, nor, or, so,* and *yet* when they are followed by an independent clause?

✔ Are commas used to set off interrupting material in a sentence?

✔ Are commas used to set off direct quotations?

✔ Are commas used correctly in numbers, dates, addresses, and letters?

Test Yourself

Add commas to the following sentences.

- We went to the mall and we saw a great movie.
- When we get really tired we act really silly.
- "He's taking flying lessons" said Steven.
- The job market however is starting to look better.
- On Saturday we went hiking fishing and camping.
- He was born August 5 1987 in St. Thomas Ontario.

(Answers are in Appendix 8.)

The **comma** is the most frequently used punctuation mark, but it is also the most often misused. Commas make reading sentences easier because they separate the parts of sentences. Following the rules in this chapter will help you write clear sentences that are easy to read.

COMMAS WITH ITEMS IN A SERIES

Use commas to separate items in a series. This means that you should put a comma between all items in a series.

Series: I ordered a pizza with mushrooms, sausage, and green peppers.

Series: He washed the dishes, swept the floor, and took out the garbage.

Series: Susan plans to move out when her parents give her permission, when she has enough money, and when she learns how to cook.

Sometimes this rule applies to a series of adjectives in front of a noun, but sometimes it does not. Look at these two examples.

Adjectives with Commas: The **cool**, **sweet** plums were delicious.

Adjectives Without Commas: The **loose top** button fell off the TV.

Both of these examples are correct. So how do you know whether or not to use commas? You can use one of two tests. One test is to insert the word "and" between the adjectives. If the sentence makes sense, use a comma. Another test is to switch the order of the adjectives. If the sentence still reads clearly, use a comma between the two words.

Test 1:   The **cool and sweet** plums were delicious. **OK, so use a comma**

Test 2:   The **sweet, cool** plums were delicious. **OK, so use a comma**

Test 1:   The **loose and top** button fell off the TV. **NO comma**

Test 2:   The **top loose** button fell off the TV. **NO comma**

REVIEWING COMMAS WITH ITEMS IN A SERIES

Why use commas with items in a series?

_____

Where do these commas go?

_____

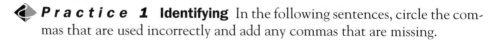 **Practice 1** **Identifying**   In the following sentences, circle the commas that are used incorrectly and add any commas that are missing.

1. I need to go to the store for bread, milk, and, eggs.

2. My favourite teams are the Leafs, the Oilers, and the Habs.

3. The best things about a college education are the social aspects, the wide variety of instruction, and the career opportunities, college offers.

4. Love, peace and goodwill are my wish for you.

5. To complete this fun exciting course successfully, you must write four papers, take two tests and give one oral report.

◆ *P r a c t i c e   2*   **Completing**   Add the missing commas to the following paragraph.

When I get to the coffee house, I'm going to find a big comfortable couch order a latte and read today's newspaper. I like to hang out at the coffee house because I see many of my friends. I usually meet Ron, Aldona and Jennifer there. We spend our time doing homework, gossiping, or just hanging out. We tend to laugh a lot. This usually draws a lot of attention to us because Ron has a loud hearty laugh. I love spending time with my friends at the coffee house. It's like spending time in a special secret club.

COMMAS WITH INTRODUCTORY WORDS

Use a comma to set off an introductory word, phrase, or clause from the rest of its sentence.

If you are unsure whether to add a comma, try reading the sentence with your reader in mind. If you want your reader to pause after the introductory word or phrase, you should insert a comma.

Introductory Word:	**Yes,** that would be great.
Introductory Word:	**Actually,** the plane wasn't as late as we thought it might be.
Introductory Phrase:	**In reality,** she's the best coach in town.
Introductory Phrase:	**To make the best of a bad situation,** we all went out for frozen yogourt.
Introductory Clause:	**When the band finished,** everyone clapped.
Introductory Clause:	**As the lights dimmed,** we all began screaming.

REVIEWING COMMAS WITH INTRODUCTORY WORDS

Why use commas with introductory words, phrases, and clauses?

_____

How can you tell if a comma is needed?

_____

_____

◆ *P r a c t i c e* **3** **Identifying** In the following sentences, circle the commas that are used incorrectly and add any commas that are missing.

1. When, he was a young boy he lived in New Brunswick.
2. The next time I go to the store, I will buy some snack foods.
3. Hoping to solve, the problem Katie wrote to the school principal.
4. Honestly that was the best home-cooked meal I've had in months.
5. As the band entered, the stadium everyone stood up.

◆ *P r a c t i c e* **4** **Completing** Add the missing commas to the following paragraph.

This past weekend my sister and I took her eight-month-old daughter, Jamie, to the beach for the first time. At first Jamie was afraid of the ocean, but she soon learned to love it. When my sister would hold Jamie in the water Jamie would scream out loud and laugh uncontrollably. However Jamie was still frightened when my sister wasn't holding her. Overall we had a great time watching Jamie explore the water, sand, and seagulls for the first time. In two weeks we are going back, and I can't wait.

COMMAS WITH INDEPENDENT CLAUSES

Use a comma before *and, but, for, nor, or, so,* and *yet* when they join two independent clauses. (Remember that an independent clause must have both a subject and a verb.)

Independent Clauses: Australia is a beautiful continent, **and** it holds many surprises for tourists.

Independent Clauses: Norman went to Europe, **but** he enjoyed Australia more.

Hint: Do not use a comma when a single subject has two verbs.

no
comma

s   v   ↓   v

Australia is a beautiful country and **has** a large tourist trade.

Adding a comma when none is needed is one of the most common errors in college or university writing assignments. Only if the second verb has its own subject should you add a comma.

comma

s   v   ↓   s   v

Australia is a beautiful country, and **it has** a large tourist trade.

REVIEWING COMMAS WITH INDEPENDENT CLAUSES

Name three coordinating conjunctions.

_____   _____   _____

When should you use a comma before a coordinating conjunction?

_____

Should you use a comma before a coordinating conjunction when a single subject has two verbs?

_____

Practice 5 Identifying Underline the subjects and circle the coordinating conjunctions in the following sentences. Then cross out any commas used incorrectly, and add those that are missing.

1. I finished my paper tonight, so I will be ready for class tomorrow.
2. This maple syrup smells good, and tastes even better.
3. Watching TV made Nadir calm, and relaxed.
4. Jasmine is going to the library today and then she will go home.
5. The gardener mowed the lawn, and pruned the hedge in the front yard.

Practice 6 Completing Add the missing commas to the following paragraph.

On Valentine's Day, my boyfriend told me we would have a special day. He would pick me up at 5:00 and he would take me to a very romantic place. He told me to dress up and look my best. I wore my new red dress and spent an hour on my hair and makeup. He picked me up promptly at 5:00. I had never been so disappointed for he took me to the movies. We watched an action flick. I tried not to get angry but I just couldn't help myself. After the movie, he said he needed to pick up something from his apartment and he made me come inside. Boy, was I surprised to see the entire apartment lit up with candles and to hear music playing all around me. His table was elegantly set and his two best friends were in tuxes waiting to serve us a five-course meal. Valentine's Day was exciting and special after all.

COMMAS WITH INTERRUPTERS

Use a comma before and after a word or phrase that interrupts the flow of a sentence.

Most words that interrupt a sentence are not necessary for understanding the main point of a sentence. Setting them off makes it easier to recognize the main point.

Word:	She called her boyfriend, **Marc,** to pick us up.
Word:	I didn't hear the buzzer, **however,** because the radio was on.
Phrase:	My favourite dessert, **banana cream pie,** is on the menu.
Phrase:	The mayor, **running for a third term,** is very popular.
Phrase:	The city with the fastest growing population, **according to government figures,** is Barrie, Ontario.

A very common type of interrupter is a clause that begins with *who, whose, which, when,* or *where* and is not necessary for understanding the main point of the sentence:

Clause:	Rosemary Smith, **who is a travel agent,** was chosen jury foreman.

Because the information "who is a travel agent" is not necessary for understanding the main idea of the sentence, it is set off with commas.

Clause:	The YWCA, **which is on Central Street,** now offers daycare.

The main point here is that the YWCA offers daycare. Since the other information isn't necessary to understanding the sentence, it can be set off with commas.

Hint: Do not use commas with *who, whose, which, when,* or *where* if the information is necessary for understanding the main point of the sentence.

My friend **who is a travel agent** was chosen jury foreman.

Since I have more than one friend, we need the information after *who* to know which friend I am referring to. Do not use commas if you need this information.

Hint: Do not use commas to set off clauses beginning with *that*.

The YWCA **that is on Central Street** now offers daycare.

REVIEWING COMMAS WITH INTERRUPTERS

Why should you use commas to set off words and phrases in the middle of a sentence?

_____

When should you use commas with who, whose, which, when, *or* where?

_____

_____

When should you not *use commas before these words?*

_____

◆ *P r a c t i c e 7* **Identifying** Label each sentence C if commas are used correctly with the underlined words and phrases or X if they are not.

1. _____ My brother, <u>trying to pass the class studied</u>, for an entire week.

2. _____ The dog, <u>with a bone in his mouth ran</u>, quickly down the street.

3. _____ The best, <u>shopping mall Fashion Plaza</u>, is not open on Sundays.

4. _____ My sister's baby, <u>who is asleep in the back room</u>, is my nephew.

5. _____ Stephen Ames, <u>a golfer played in</u>, the PGA tour.

◆ *P r a c t i c e 8* **Completing** Insert commas around the interrupting words and phrases in the following paragraph.

   A rocking chair worn by years of use sits in a corner of my room. My grandmother used it when she had my mom Sarah many years ago. My mom used it with me, and I'll use it of course when I have children. I like looking at the rocker which holds so many memories for so many people because it makes me think of home. I sometimes read in the chair however so I can quietly sit in the most peaceful place and let my mind rest. This rocking chair which is simply made of wood keeps me sane while I am so far away from home.

COMMAS WITH DIRECT QUOTATIONS

Use commas to mark direct quotations. A direct quotation records a person's exact words. Commas set off the exact words from the rest of the sentence, making it easier to understand who said what.

Direct Quotation: My friends often say, **"You are so lucky."**

Direct Quotation: **"You are so lucky,"** my friends often say.

Direct Quotation: **"You are so lucky,"** says my grandmother, **"to have good friends."**

Hint: If a quotation ends with a question mark or an exclamation point, do not use a comma. Only one punctuation mark is needed.

NOT   **"What did he say?,"** she asked.

CORRECT   **"What did he say?"** she asked.

REVIEWING COMMAS WITH DIRECT QUOTATIONS

Why should you use commas with a direct quotation?

_____

_____

Should you use a comma if the quotation ends with a question mark or an exclamation point? Why or why not?

_____

_____

◆ *P r a c t i c e 9* **Identifying** In the following sentences, circle the commas that are used incorrectly and add any commas that are missing.

1. She remarked ",My favourite food is Mexican."

2. "I don't know the answer," Mark confessed "but I'll keep trying to figure it out."

3. "Are you out of your mind?," he asked.

4. "I remember," Thanh said, "when we all went camping in Banff."

5. "Get here right now!," screamed the mother.

◆ *P r a c t i c e 1 0* **Completing** Add the missing commas to the following passage.

Joey and Dawn decided to go to a movie. "What do you want to see?" he asked.

"Definitely the new *Harry Potter*" Dawn replied.

Joey was disappointed and responded "But I've already seen that one."

"If you see it again" she said "you might catch something you missed before."

"Well, I guess that's a good point" he admitted.

OTHER USES OF COMMAS

Other commas clarify information in everyday writing.

Numbers: The answer to the third problem is **12,487.**

Notice that in the metric system spaces are used instead: **12 487.** Both styles are common in Canada.

Dates: My grandmother was born **July 12, 1942,** in Chicoutimi, Quebec.

Notice that there is a comma both before and after the year.

Addresses: Bruce's new address is 1200 Dundas St., Toronto, ON M5E 1E1.

Notice that there is no comma between the province and the postal code—use a double space.

Provinces: He lives in **Vancouver, B.C.,** and she lives in **Charlottetown, P.E.I.**

Notice that there is a comma both before and after a province.

Letters: **Dear John,**
Sincerely yours,

REVIEWING OTHER USES OF COMMAS

Give one example of commas in each of the following situations:

Numbers: _____

Dates: _____

Addresses: _____

Letters: _____

Why are these commas important?

_____

◆ *Practice 11* **Identifying** In the following sentences, circle the commas that are used incorrectly and add any commas that are missing.

1. I live at 4,801 Pine Street in Nanaimo British Columbia.
2. He threw 3,847 pitches in his baseball career.
3. I need to deliver 14,00 flyers before the big sale this weekend.
4. There are more than 5,000 people with the last name of Martin in the city of, Ottawa Ontario.
5. I think he moved to Long, Point, Ontario.

◆ *Practice 12* **Completing** Add the missing commas to the following paragraph.

The world record for jump-roping is 1200 hours. The jump-roper accomplished this feat on October 12 1961 at his home in Biloxi Mississippi. Another guy who was from Ontario Canada tried to break the record in 1973, but he could only jump rope for 1070 consecutive hours.

CHAPTER REVIEW

You might want to reread your answers to the questions in all the review boxes before you do the following exercises.

◆ *Review Practice 1* **Identifying** Add the missing commas to the following sentences.

1. On the second Saturday of each month Sensei Allen holds a karate tournament.
2. Victor and Lou took the truck in to be fixed but the automotive shop was closed.
3. The boy however believed that his horse would win.
4. I stood in awe as Kelsey my beautiful golden retriever won first place in the national dog show.
5. The tall lean good-looking motorcycle cop was ticketing a speeder.

◆ *Review Practice 2* **Completing** Add the missing commas to the following paragraph.

Sometimes when I walk into the library I am immediately overwhelmed. Books magazines and newspapers are everywhere and then I think to myself "This is only the first floor!" Last Friday evening I went to the library with Ophelia who is my science lab partner to join a study group. We never made it to the study group however because we got sidetracked by the popular magazines on the first floor. Later that evening we saw the tired depressed faces of our study group members and were glad we had stayed in the magazine section taking magazine quizzes and reading for pleasure.

◆ *Review   Practice   3* **Writing Your Own** Write a paragraph about one of your neighbours. What are some identifying qualities of this person? Do you like him or her?

◆ *Review Practice   4* **Editing Through Collaboration** Exchange paragraphs from Review Practice 3 with another student, and do the following:

1. Circle any misplaced commas.
2. Suggest corrections for the incorrect commas.

Then return the paragraph to its writer, and use the information in this chapter to correct any comma errors in your own paragraph. Record your errors on the Error Log in Appendix 6.

CHAPTER 43

APOSTROPHES

☑ CHECKLIST for Using Apostrophes

> ✔Are apostrophes used correctly in contractions?
> ✔Are apostrophes used correctly to show possession?

Test Yourself

Add an apostrophe or an apostrophe and *-s* to the following sentences.

- The followers went into their leaders home.
- Its not important that you understand its every function.
- Thats not a good enough reason to believe Tracys story.
- The childrens toys were scattered around the room.
- Charles party was a lot of fun.

(Answers are in Appendix 8.)

The **apostrophe** looks like a single closing quotation mark. Its two main purposes are to indicate where letters have been left out and to show ownership.

MARKING CONTRACTIONS

Use an apostrophe to show that letters have been omitted to form a contraction. A **contraction** is the shortening of one or more words. Our everyday speech is filled with contractions.

I have	=	I've (*h* and *a* have been omitted)
you are	=	you're (*a* has been omitted)
let us	=	let's (*u* has been omitted)

Here is a list of commonly used contractions.

Some Common Contractions

I am	=	*I'm*	*we have*	=	*we've*
I would	=	*I'd*	*we will*	=	*we'll*
I will	=	*I'll*	*they are*	=	*they're*
you have	=	*you've*	*they have*	=	*they've*
you will	=	*you'll*	*do not*	=	*don't*
he is	=	*he's*	*did not*	=	*didn't*
she will	=	*she'll*	*have not*	=	*haven't*
it is	=	*it's*	*could not*	=	*couldn't*

Hint: Two words that are frequently misused are *it's* and *its*.

it's = contraction: it is (or it has)   **It's** too late to go to the movie.

its = pronoun: belonging to it   **Its** eyes are really large.

To see if you are using the correct word, say the sentence with the words *it is*. If that is what you want to say, add an apostrophe to the word.

>**?**   I think **its** boiling.
>**Test:**   I think **it is** boiling.   **YES, add an apostrophe**

This sentence makes sense with *it is*, so you should write *it's*.

>**Correct:**   I think **it's** boiling.

>**?**   The kitten drank **its** milk.
>**Test:**   The kitten drank **it is** milk.   **NO, so no apostrophe**

This sentence does not make sense with *it is*, so you should not use the apostrophe in *its*.

>**Correct:**   The kitten drank **its** milk.

REVIEWING CONTRACTIONS

What is the purpose of an apostrophe in a contraction?

_____

Write five contractions, and tell which letters have been omitted.

_____   _____

_____   _____

_____   _____

_____   _____

_____   _____

What is the difference between it's and its?

_____

◆ **P r a c t i c e   1   Identifying** In the following sentences, circle the apostrophes that are used incorrectly and add any apostrophes that are missing.

1. It's about time to get out of bed.
2. I think Ahmad should'nt join us.
3. They ve got a lot of nerve saying that.
4. If you're happy about it, then Im happy for you.
5. This is the last time shell borrow my car.

◆ **P r a c t i c e   2   Completing** Write contractions for the following words.

1. we + would   =   _____

2. they + will   =   _____

3. would + not   =   _____

4. does + not   =   _____

5. can + not   =   _____

SHOWING POSSESSION

Use an apostrophe to show **possession.**

1. For a singular word, use *'s* to indicate possession or ownership.
   You can always replace a possessive with *of* plus the noun or pronoun.

the dog's collar	=	the collar **of the dog** (the dog owns the collar)
everyone's opinion	=	the opinion **of everyone** (all the people possess a single opinion)
boss's office	=	the office **of the boss** (the boss possesses the office)
today's news	=	the news **of today** (today "owns" or "possesses" the news)

2. For plural nouns ending in -*s*, use only an apostrophe.

the dogs' collars	=	the collars **of the dogs**
the ladies' pearls	=	the pearls **of the ladies**
the owners' children	=	the children **of the owners**
the teachers' friends	=	the friends **of the teachers**
the friends' families	=	the families **of the friends**

3. For plural nouns that do not end in -*s*, add '*s*.

the men's shirts	=	the shirts **of the men**
the children's teachers	=	the teachers **of the children**
the women's savings	=	the savings **of the women**

REVIEWING POSSESSIVES

How do you mark possession or ownership for a singular word?

_____

How do you mark possession or ownership for a plural word that ends in -s?

_____

How do you mark possession or ownership for a plural word that doesn't end in -s?

_____

◆ **P r a c t i c e   3   Identifying** In the following sentences, circle the apostrophes that are used incorrectly, and add any apostrophes that are missing.

1. The kids skateboards are in the garage.
2. Serenity had to get five shot's today in compliance with her doctor's order's.

3. The mens retreat is this weekend.

4. My boyfriend's attitude is very negative today.

5. All of the babies diaper's need to be changed.

◆ *P r a c t i c e 4* **Completing** Write a possessive for each of the following phrases.

1. the parrot of Mr. Brown _____

2. the shoes of Marcus _____

3. the meal of the prison inmates _____

4. the holiday celebration of the Smith families _____

_____

5. the water level of the lake _____

COMMON APOSTROPHE ERRORS

Two common errors occur with apostrophes. The following guidelines will help you avoid these errors.

No Apostrophe with Possessive Pronouns

Do not use an apostrophe with a possessive pronoun. Possessive pronouns already show ownership, so they do not need an apostrophe.

Incorrect	Correct
his'	his
her's *or* hers'	hers
it's *or* its'	its
your's *or* yours'	yours
our's *or* ours'	ours
their's *or* theirs'	theirs

No Apostrophe to Form the Plural

Do not use an apostrophe to form a plural word. This error occurs most often with plural words ending in *-s*. An apostrophe indicates possession or contraction; it does *not* indicate the plural. Therefore, a plural word never takes an apostrophe unless it is possessive.

NOT	The **shirts'** are on the hangers.
CORRECT	The **shirts** are on the hangers.

NOT	She went to get the **groceries'** over an hour ago.
CORRECT	She went to get the **groceries** over an hour ago.

NOT	Watching old family **movies'** is a lot of fun.
CORRECT	Watching old family **movies** is a lot of fun.

REVIEWING APOSTROPHE ERRORS

List three possessive pronouns.

_____ _____ _____

Why don't possessive pronouns take apostrophes?

_____

What is wrong with the apostrophe in each of the following sentences?
The last float in the parade is ours'.

_____

There must be 100 floats' in the parade.

_____

P r a c t i c e **5** **Identifying** In the following sentences, circle the apostrophes that are used incorrectly and add any apostrophes that are missing.

1. The cat licked it's paws for 10 minutes after eating.
2. Why don't we go to the movie's?
3. If you join these two club's with me, we can take the members' pledge together.
4. I'm going to buy pant's just like your's.
5. That's my friend Amine from my computer classes'.

P r a c t i c e **6** **Completing** Write a possessive for each of the following phrases.

1. the pen of him _____

2. the car of her _____

3. the shirts of them _____

4. the sound of it _____

5. a book of yours _____

CHAPTER REVIEW

You might want to reread your answers to the questions in all the review boxes before you do the following exercises.

◆ *Review Practice 1* **Identifying** In the following sentences, circle the apostrophes that are used incorrectly and add any apostrophes that are missing.

1. Jame's dog's were jumping on the furniture.
2. I was'nt surprised that everyone admires Raymond.
3. This pencil looks like its mine.
4. The biochemist's could'nt figure out the error in the two formula's.
5. Eleanor's grandmother's look a lot alike.

◆ *Review Practice 2* **Completing** Add the missing apostrophes to the following sentences.

1. Everyones choice is pizza, but somebody has to call in the order.
2. Womens clothing has been marked down, but all childrens items are still regular price.
3. My father-in-laws job has been eliminated through downsizing.
4. There arent any more cookies in the cupboard.
5. Ronnys apartment is located just five minutes from the beach.

◆ *Review Practice 3* **Writing Your Own** Write a paragraph about your favourite birthday celebration in your life so far. Use at least six apostrophes correctly.

◆ *Review Practice 4* **Editing Through Collaboration** Exchange paragraphs from Review Practice 3 with another student, and do the following:

1. Circle any misplaced or missing apostrophes.
2. Indicate whether they mark possession (P) or contraction (C).

Then return the paragraph to its writer, and use the information in this chapter to correct any apostrophe errors in your own paragraph. Record your errors on the Error Log in Appendix 6.

QUOTATION MARKS

☑ CHECKLIST for Using Quotation Marks

✔ Are quotation marks used to indicate someone's exact words?

✔ Are all periods and commas inside quotation marks?

✔ Are words capitalized correctly in quotations?

✔ Are quotation marks used to indicate the title of a short work, such as a short story or a poem?

Test Yourself

Add quotation marks where needed in the following sentences.

- Let's have a picnic, she said.
- My mom screamed, Tom! Get this spider!
- Put ice on the muscle, said Dr. Jansen, as soon as possible.
- I read three poems, including The Groundhog.
- Derek said I'll make dinner.

(Answers are in Appendix 8.)

Quotation marks are punctuation marks that work together in pairs. Their most common use is to indicate someone's exact words. They are also used to mark the title of a short piece of writing, such as a short story or a poem.

DIRECT QUOTATIONS

Use quotation marks to indicate a **direct quotation**—someone's exact words.

Here are some examples. They show the three basic forms of a direct quotation.

Direct Quotation: "I am not leaving without you," said the spy.

In this example, the quoted words come first.

411

Direct Quotation: The spy said, "I am not leaving without you."

In this example, the quoted words come after the speaker is named.

Direct Quotation: "I am not," the spy said, "leaving without you."

In this example, the quoted words are interrupted, and the speaker is named in the middle. This form emphasizes the first few words.

INDIRECT QUOTATIONS

If you just talk about someone's words, an **indirect quotation,** you do not need quotation marks. Indirect quotations usually include the word *that*, as in *said that*. In questions, the wording is often *asked if*. Look at these examples of **indirect quotations**.

Direct Quotation: "I interviewed for a job at Magna International," said Bob.

These are Bob's exact words, so you must use quotation marks.

Indirect Quotation: Bob **said that** he interviewed for a job at Magna International.

This sentence explains what Bob said but does not use Bob's exact words. So quotation marks should not be used.

Direct Quotation: "We walked four kilometres," said Kira.
Indirect Quotation: Kira **said that** they walked four kilometres.

Direct Quotation: "Did you apply for a student loan?" Mom asked.
Indirect Quotation: Mom **asked if** I had applied for a student loan.

REVIEWING QUOTATION MARKS WITH QUOTATIONS

How do you show that you are repeating someone's exact words?

_____

What is an indirect quotation?

_____

◆ **P r a c t i c e   1   Identifying** In the following sentences, circle the quotation marks used incorrectly and add any quotation marks that are missing.

1. "Watch out! screamed the firefighter."
2. "I wish they'd stop throwing things" on the field, commented the football player.
3. He asked, How "much longer do we wait?"
4. "Go to your room, said the father, and clean it up."
5. Bojan said that "he enjoyed the game."

◆ *P r a c t i c e   2*   **Completing** Add the missing quotation marks to the following paragraph.

Yesterday my manager stuck up for me when a customer came in saying, That young man sold me a defective computer. She was really mad. Ma'am, my manager patiently replied, he sold you our top-of-the-line computer. She said, But my computer still doesn't work. After a series of questions, my manager finally asked her what was wrong with her computer. The monitor is black, she replied. After another series of questions, my manager discovered her monitor was not plugged in, but he handled the customer as if her mistake was the most logical and frequent one ever made. The customer left happy that her system would now work. No matter what, my manager said, the customer is always right . . . and smart.

CAPITALIZING AND USING OTHER PUNCTUATION MARKS WITH QUOTATION MARKS

When you are quoting someone's complete sentences, begin with a capital letter and use appropriate end punctuation—a period, a question mark, or an exclamation point.

Capitalize the first letter of the first word being quoted, and put a period at the end of the sentence if it is a statement. Separate the spoken words from the rest of the sentence with a comma.

"**S**he doesn't really love me," he said.
She replied, "**T**ie your shoelaces."

If the quotation ends with a question mark or an exclamation point, use that punctuation instead of a comma or a period.

He yelled, "**T**urn off that music!"
"**W**hy do you want to know?" she asked.

In a quotation that is interrupted, capitalize the first word being quoted, but do not capitalize words in the middle of the sentence. Use a comma both before and after the interruption. End with a period if it is a statement.

"**N**o," said the student, "this seat isn't taken."

You do not need to capitalize the first word of a quotation that is only part of a sentence.

I don't think that he will ever **"find himself."**

Hint: Look at the examples again. Notice that periods and commas always go inside the quotation marks.

NOT	"Yes", she said, "please sit here".
CORRECT	"Yes," she said, "please sit here."

REVIEWING CAPITALIZATION AND PUNCTUATION
WITH QUOTATION MARKS

When you quote someone's exact words, why should you begin with a capital letter?

_____

Where do commas go in relation to quotation marks? Where do periods go?

_____

◆ **P r a c t i c e 3 Identifying** In the following sentences, circle the quotation marks, capital letters, and other punctuation marks that are used incorrectly, and add any missing quotation marks and punctuation.

1. "How are the Knights doing this season"? she asked her boyfriend.
2. I need a new job" said Stan.
3. Victor wondered "How will they ever make it without me?"
4. "If you want to meet me", he said "just come to the concert tonight."
5. "I can't be there," Callum explained ", unless I get time off work.

◆ **P r a c t i c e 4 Completing** Add the missing quotation marks and punctuation to the following paragraph.

I have always said that I love the snow, but I hate the cold. I'm not sure how this works actually. My best friend asked How can you hate the cold so much when you are constantly out skiing or making a snowman I replied, I'm just weird that way, I guess I have always been like this. My mom never had to say Put on your jacket It was more like, Why are you wearing a jacket in 30-degree weather No one understands this weird quirk in me. I'll say Yes to skiing any day. Maybe someone will invent snow skiing in Jamaica. Then I'd be set.

QUOTATION MARKS AROUND TITLES

Put quotation marks around the titles of short works that are parts of larger works. The titles of longer works are put in italics (or underlined).

Quotation Marks	Italics/Underlining
"The Black Cat" (short story)	*Harry Potter and the Goblet of Fire* (book)
"The Emperor of Ice Cream" (poem)	*An Introduction to Literature* (book)
"Rainy Day Woman" (song)	*Bob Dylan's Greatest Hits* (album)
"Florida Keys Beckon Tourists" (magazine article)	*Travel and Leisure* (magazine)
"Ferbey's Foursome Rock Solid in Final" (newspaper article)	The *Ottawa Citizen* (newspaper)
"Must Be a Night for Fires" (episode on TV series)	*DaVinci's Inquest* (TV series)

REVIEWING QUOTATION MARKS WITH TITLES

When do you put quotation marks around a title?

_____

When do you italicize (or underline) a title?

_____

◆ *P r a c t i c e   5*   **Identifying** Put an X in front of each sentence with errors in quotation marks or italics/underlining. Add any missing quotation marks and italics or underlining.

1. _____ I really like the song <u>Complicated</u> by Avril Lavigne.

2. _____ Did you read Keats's poem *Ode to a Nightingale?*

3. _____ My favourite short story is Alice Munro's Walker Brothers Cowboy.

4. _____ The best entry in the poetry contest was "Trial" by Evelyn Main.

5. _____ If you want to come over, we're watching the *I Love Lucy* episode called <u>Grape Smashing</u>.

◆ *P r a c t i c e 6* **Completing** Place quotation marks around the titles of short works, and underline the titles of long works in the following paragraph.

When Terrance was in high school, he was in a literature club. They read the short stories Araby, Mrs. Turner Cutting the Grass, and Stranger than Fiction. They also read several poems by Margaret Atwood. Terrance's favourite poem was Postcard and Variations on the Word *Sleep*. Every week the club wrote a book review for the school newspaper, The Northbrook News. One particular article was called Finding Bliss. It was about Edith Wharton's novel, The House of Mirth. These articles really encouraged other students to read for pleasure.

CHAPTER REVIEW

You might want to reread your answers to the questions in all the review boxes before you do the following exercises.

◆ *Review   P r a c t i c e 1* **Identifying** Add the missing quotation marks and punctuation to the following sentences.

1. Priscilla's favourite song is Smooth by Carlos Santana and Rob Thomas.
2. The short story The Almond Tree is my son's favourite.
3. I hate to break the news to you Louis said but I've found someone new
4. Did she ever answer her cellphone? I asked.
5. The news writer titled his article Somewhere in the Devil's Domain.

◆ *Review P r a c t i c e 2* **Completing** Add the missing quotation marks, commas, and underlining for italics to the following dialogue.

Hey, Elena I called let's go to Chapters.
We were just there she answered.
Well, let's go again. I have to get a novel for English I said.
Which novel do you need? asked Elena.
It's called Waiting by Her Jinn I said.
Oh, I read that. It's great. You'll love it she said as she waved good bye.

◆ *Review   Practice   3*   **Writing Your Own** In paragraph form, record a conversation from your day. What did you talk about? What was the point of this conversation? What were your exact words?

◆ *Review   Practice   4*   **Editing Through Collaboration** Exchange paragraphs from Review Practice 3 with another student, and do the following:

1. Circle any incorrect or missing quotation marks.

2. Underline any faulty punctuation.

3. Put an X over any incorrect use of italics/underlining.

Then return the paragraph to its writer, and use the information in this chapter to correct any errors with quotation marks and italics/underlining in your own paragraph. Record your errors on the Error Log in Appendix 6.

CHAPTER 45

OTHER PUNCTUATION MARKS

☑ CHECKLIST for Using Semicolons, Colons, Dashes, and Parentheses

> ✔ Are semicolons used to join two closely related complete sentences?
> ✔ Are long items in a series that already contain commas separated by semicolons?
> ✔ Are colons used correctly to introduce a list?
> ✔ Are dashes used to emphasize or further explain a point?
> ✔ Are parentheses used to include additional, but not necessary, information?

Test Yourself

Add semicolons, colons, dashes, or parentheses to the following sentences.

- Matthew turned his paper in early Erica decided not to turn in a paper at all.
- Dave felt sorry for the defendant however, he had to vote for a conviction.
- Aaron needed several items for his dorm room a comforter, new sheets, a lamp, and a rug.
- Amanda had only two words to say about bungee jumping "Never again."
- The recipe says to fold gently mix the berries into the batter.

(Answers are in Appendix 8.)

This chapter explains the uses of the **semicolon, colon, dash,** and **parentheses.** We'll look at these punctuation marks one by one.

SEMICOLONS

Semicolons are used to separate equal parts of a sentence. They are also used to avoid confusion when listing items in a series.

1. Use a semicolon to separate two closely related independent clauses.

   An independent clause is a group of words with a subject and a verb that can stand alone as a sentence. You might use a semicolon instead of a coordinating conjunction (*and, but, for, nor, or, so, yet*) or a period. Any one of the three options would be correct.

	Independent	Independent

   Semicolon: Henry never took a lunch break; he was too busy at his job.

   Conjunction: Henry never took a lunch break, **for** he was too busy at his job.

   Period: Henry never took a lunch break. **He** was too busy at his job.

2. Use a semicolon to join two independent clauses that are connected by such words as *however, therefore, furthermore, moreover, for example*, or *consequently*. Put a comma after the connecting word.

	Independent	Independent

   Semicolon: Shrimp is expensive; **nevertheless**, it's always worth the money.

   Semicolon: Hiroko is very talented musically; **for example**, she can play the piano and the flute.

   Semicolon: She has always worked hard; **in fact**, she put herself through university.

3. Use a semicolon to separate items in a series when any of the items contain commas.

   NOT At the party, Lily drank some tasty red punch, ate some delicious chicken with garlic, herbs, and lemon, and danced with several old boyfriends.

   CORRECT At the party, Lily drank some tasty red punch; ate some delicious chicken with garlic, herbs, and lemon; and danced with several old boyfriends.

REVIEWING SEMICOLONS

How are semicolons used between two independent clauses?

_____

How are semicolons used with items in a series?

_____

◆ **P r a c t i c e   1   Identifying** In the following sentences, circle the semicolons that are used incorrectly and add any commas and semicolons that are missing.

1. Baking homemade bread is very easy however; it's faster to use a bread maker.
2. I walked my dog to the park; ran into Mike; Zoe, and Christine; and invited them over for dinner.
3. She's allergic to chocolate and honey she rarely eats other sweets either.
4. I'm a horrible cook for example, I burned the toast at breakfast today.
5. This trip cost us a fortune we'll be paying off the credit card for a year.

◆ **P r a c t i c e 2 Completing** Add semicolons to the following paragraph.

   One day I went fishing with Uncle Peter it was the last day I would spend with him before he left for university. When we arrived at the lake, we realized that we forgot the bait nevertheless, we knew where we could buy more nearby. Inside the store were racks and racks of things for sale, but we were interested in only three of them. One rack displayed bait, tackle, and fishing line one shelved candy and snack foods and the other held cigarettes and chewing tobacco. The bait gave us about fourteen fish, and the candy gave me a cavity however, that can of Copenhagen gave us grief from our moms every time they caught us chewing.

COLONS

Colons introduce a list or idea that follows them.

1. The main use of the colon is to introduce a list or thought. Here are some examples:

   Colon: Bring the following supplies to class: sketch pad, India ink, pen tips, and a charcoal pencil.

   Colon: I noticed several fire hazards: old paint cans and rags, curtains near the stove, and lit candles with no one present.

Colon: The decision was easy: return the favour.

The most common error with colons is using one where it isn't needed.

2. Do not use a colon after the words *such as* or *including*. A complete sentence must come before a colon.

NOT	Use good packing materials, **such as:** bubble wrap, styro pellets, and foam.
CORRECT	Use good packing materials, **such as** bubble wrap, styro pellets, and foam.
NOT	We saw many sights, **including:** Lake Louise, Banff Springs, and Cascade Mountain.
CORRECT	We saw many sights, **including** Lake Louise, Banff Springs, and Cascade Mountain.

3. In addition, you should not use a colon after a verb or after a preposition. Remember that a complete sentence must come before a colon.

NOT	The topics to be discussed **are:** memory, hard drive, and new software.
CORRECT	The topics to be discussed **are** memory, hard drive, and software.
NOT	The program consisted **of:** a lecture, a Powerpoint presentation, and lunch.
CORRECT	The program consisted **of** a lecture, a Powerpoint presentation, and lunch.

REVIEWING COLONS

What is the main use of a colon?

_____

Why should you not use a colon after such words as is *or* of?

_____

◆ *P r a c t i c e   3*   **Identifying** In the following sentences, circle the colons that are used incorrectly and add any colons that are missing.

1. You should take: hiking boots, cotton socks, and sunscreen.
2. Mark still has to take the following classes biology, chemistry, political science, and geometry.
3. I have a lot to do today wash the car, pick up Theo at the airport, and finish my English paper.

4. The aerobics class consisted of: step exercises, line dancing, and the stairmaster.

5. I like: the fireplace, the gardens, and the vaulted ceilings.

6. The presentation covered many topics, including: company goals, stock options, and benefits.

◆ *P r a c t i c e   5* **Completing** Add colons to the following paragraph.

People can learn a lot from visiting museums they can learn about history, psychology, and sociology for numerous cultures. Many museums have enormous collections of various types of art ancient, Renaissance, Victorian, modern, and so on. I particularly like ancient art. Two museums have tremendous ancient art exhibits the J. Paul Getty Museum and the British Museum. I can spend hours looking at all the statuary and pottery. Museums are just loaded with fabulous cultural information.

DASHES AND PARENTHESES

Dashes and parentheses set ideas off from the rest of their sentence.

Dashes

Dashes emphasize ideas.

1. Use dashes to emphasize or draw attention to a point.

   Dash: I know what I want out of life—happiness.

   In this example, the beginning of the sentence introduces an idea, and the dash then sets off the answer.

   Dash: Peace, love, and good health—these are my words for the new year.

   In this example, the key words are set off at the beginning, and the explanation follows. Beginning this way adds some suspense to the sentence.

   Dashes: I know what I want in a roommate—thoughtfulness— and I plan to get it.

   The dashes divide this sentence into three distinct parts, which makes the reader pause and think about each part.

Parentheses

Whereas dashes set off material that the writer wants to emphasize, **parentheses** do just the opposite.

2. Use parentheses to set off information that is interesting or helpful but not necessary for understanding the sentence.

Parentheses: Their oldest son left his family at age 18 (**never to return again).**

Parentheses: The handbook put out by the MLA (**Modern Language Association)** is the best guideline.

3. Parentheses are also used to mark a person's lifespan and to number items in a sentence. They are always used in pairs. Here are some examples.

Parentheses: Mordecai Richler (**1931–2001)** is one of Canada's great writers.

Parentheses: Follow these steps in writing a paragraph: (**1)** brainstorm for ideas, (**2)** choose a topic, and (**3)** formulate a topic sentence.

REVIEWING DASHES AND PARENTHESES

What is the difference between dashes and parentheses?

_____

_____

When do you use dashes?

_____

When do you use parentheses?

_____

◆ *P r a c t i c e 5* **Identifying** Use dashes or parentheses with the underlined words in the following sentences.

1. I met the new neighbours   the ones at the end of the block   and brought them cookies.
2. My wife is going out with her friends tomorrow and taking the kids so I can watch the big fight on TV.
3. My neighbours   the Parkers   are nice people, but they're awful housekeepers.
4. There is one kind of food that everyone likes   barbecue.
5. While you are house-sitting for us, please don't forget to   1   feed the cats,   2   check the mail, and   3   water the houseplants.

◆ *P r a c t i c e* **6**   **Completing**   Add dashes and parentheses to the following paragraph.

Reiko and I became best friends 10 years ago in university at UWO. Our British literature teacher an enormously tall and bald man who enjoyed playing pranks on other faculty members made us senior seminar partners. Ever since then, we've been best friends. We've been through a lot together ex-husbands, self-doubt, and other trying issues but we've never abandoned each other. I hope as I'm sure she does that we never lose contact with one another.

CHAPTER REVIEW

You might want to reread your answers to the questions in all the review boxes before you do the following exercises.

◆ *Review*   *P r a c t i c e*   **1**   **Identifying** Add semicolons, colons, dashes, and parentheses to the following sentences.

1. She never lost her money she forgot to take the cheque out of her pocket.
2. She never listens she always asks questions that were already answered.
3. Hand me a pencil the yellow one so I can make up a grocery list.
4. There are several reasons I refuse to go out with you you tend to ignore what I say, you treat your girlfriends disrespectfully, and I am dating your brother.
5. The impatient people in line at the bank the rude ones are usually the ones who take the longest at the counter.

◆ *Review*   *P r a c t i c e*   **2**   **Completing** Add semicolons, colons, dashes, and parentheses to the following paragraph.

Our house is affectionately known as the "Gibson Zoo." Outside we have two very large dogs inside we have a smaller dog and two cats. The bird population is also recognized in our house since we have two love birds Dorris and Pierre. All of our animals the ones we have purchased and the ones we found as strays have been given appropriate names. Our favourite names are from literature and Greek mythology Zeus, Apollo, Beowulf, Romeo, Juliet, and Macbeth. We're still thinking about adding one more pet it will be either an iguana or a hamster. And we have only one requirement for the new addition it must be able to get along with the rest of the family.

◆ *Review   Practice   3*   **Writing Your Own** Write a paragraph explaining to someone how to do something that you do well.

◆ *Review   Practice   4*   **Editing Through Collaboration** Exchange paragraphs from Review Practice 3 with another student, and do the following:

1. Circle any incorrect or missing semicolons.
2. Circle any incorrect or missing colons.
3. Circle any incorrect or missing dashes.
4. Circle any incorrect or missing parentheses.

Then return the paragraph to its writer, and use the information in this chapter to correct any punctuation errors in your own paragraph. Record your errors on the Error Log in Appendix 6.

UNIT TESTS

Here are some exercises that test your understanding of all the material in this unit: Commas, Apostrophes, Quotation Marks, Semicolons, Colons, Dashes, and Parentheses.

Unit Test I

Correct the punctuation errors in the following sentences.

1. My girlfriend wants me to visit her in college but I can't get off work.
2. Gabi's dentist has an office on 3rd.St by the drugstore.
3. Don't you think you've studied, hard enough?
4. Did you see the "Third Watch" episode last night, The Edge?
5. We left our two dog's toys all over the yard.
6. The test will be given on September 28 2005.
7. The Ramparts, Battlefield Park and, the Martello Tower were full of pushy irritable people this afternoon.
8. What I like best about Mike is what he's most shy about his beautiful poetry.
9. "Don't waste my time!" he exclaimed.
10. Ted's flag was red, white, and blue, Millie's was orange, green, and gold, and Ivan's was just black and white.

11. The four things left in my refrigerator are: a can of Pepsi, a slice of left-over pizza, an ice cream sandwich, and a candy bar.

12. Mark Thomas is divorcing, his wife Martha, after several years of marriage.

13. If I wanted your advice; I would ask for it.

14. Too much sun is coming through the front window's and I can't tell if his' computer screen is on.

15. Martina asked, "Have you read that book" yet.

16. Yesterdays weather was very warm.

17. "If you buy this today" the clerk said, "you can save 20 per cent."

18. Quite frankly I always thought I was in over my head.

19. Could you imagine how awful, being homeless would be?

20. I cant believe they won.

Unit Test II

Correct the punctuation errors in the following paragraph.

Once when I was in high school my friends and I organized something together (a protest of Valentines' Day). Im pretty sure the idea started as a silly conversation at lunch but it became something much bigger than any of us imagined. The high school in my hometown of Roberts Creek B.C. was very small with a population of about 300 students (therefore, most ideas traveled very quickly). My friends and I started discussing our protest of Valentine's Day the last week of January. We had decided to dress in all black instead of the normal colour combinations for Valentine's Day; red, white, and pink, all red, all pink, or pink and white. By February 14 2001, over 50 students' had joined our "crusade." In fact, we made the front page of the student newspaper the next week. The article, just Say no to Love, featured student quotes', such as: I hate this holiday! and "i was wondering why all those kids were dressed in black last week". Looking back on it now, I wonder, why so many of my fellow students wanted to join in our protest of this holiday. I think there were three reasons (1) most people like to be part of something bigger than themselves, 2 we were all looking for something to rally against, and (3) we were all single and a little bitter about romance. Whatever my classmates' reasons were, I know that I had fun that day.

CAPITALIZATION

✔ CHECKLIST for Editing Capitalization

> ✔ Are all proper nouns capitalized?
> ✔ Are all words in titles capitalized correctly?
> ✔ Have you followed the other rules for capitalizing correctly?

Test Yourself

Correct the capitalization errors in the following sentences.

- The smith family lives on laurier avenue.
- we fly into trudeau airport and then get a taxi to mcGill university.
- This term I'm taking spanish, biology 200, history, and english.
- In june, I drove to british columbia in my honda civic.
- We read several plays by shakespeare, including *hamlet*.

(Answers are in Appendix 8.)

Because every sentence begins with a capital letter, **capitalization** is the best place to start discussing the mechanics of good writing. Capital letters signal where sentences begin. They also call attention to certain kinds of words, making sentences easier to read and understand.

Correct capitalization coupled with correct punctuation adds up to good, clear writing. Here are some guidelines to help you capitalize correctly.

1. Capitalize the first word of every sentence, including the first word of a quotation that forms a sentence.

> **T**he best route is down Alpine Street.
> "**T**he best route is down Alpine Street," he said.
> **H**e said, "**T**he best route is down Alpine Street."

Do not capitalize the second part of a quotation that is split.

> "**T**he best route," he said, "is down Alpine Street."

2. Capitalize all proper nouns. Do not capitalize common nouns.

Common Nouns	Proper Nouns
person	John Doe
city	Winnipeg
building	Edmonton Mall
lake	Lake Huron
spacecraft	*Apollo 11*

3. Capitalize titles used with people's names or in place of their names.

> **M**r. John W. Cooper, **M**s. Gladys Reynolds, **D**r. Kayla Robinson
> **A**unt Judy, **G**randpa John, **C**ousin Larry

Do not capitalize words that identify family relationships.

NOT	I will ask my Mother.
CORRECT	I will ask **my** mother.
CORRECT	I will ask **M**other.

4. Capitalize the titles of creative works.

Books:	*I Know Why the Caged Bird Sings*
Short Stories:	"The Lottery"
Plays:	*The Rez Sisters*
Poems:	"Song of Myself"
Articles:	"Hockey Strike Finally Over"
Magazines:	*Maclean's*
Songs:	"Jailhouse Rock"
Albums or CDs:	*Metallica Live*
Films:	*War of the Worlds*
TV Series:	*The Eleventh Hour*
Works of Art:	*The Scream*
Computer Programs:	*Microsoft Word*

Do not capitalize *a*, *an*, *the*, or short prepositions unless they are the first or last word in a title.

5. Capitalize days of the week, months, holidays, and special events.

> **F**riday, **A**ugust, **C**anada **D**ay, **T**hanksgiving, **L**abour **D**ay, **M**ardi **G**ras

Do not capitalize the names of seasons: *summer, fall, winter, spring*.

6. Capitalize the names of historical events, periods, and documents.

> Stone Age, Renaissance Period, Seventies, Battle of Hastings, World War II

7. Capitalize specific course titles and the names of language courses.

> History 201, Psychology 101, English 200

Do not capitalize a course or subject you are referring to in a general way unless the course is a language.

> my economics course, my philosophy course, my Spanish course, my history course

8. Capitalize references to regions of the country but not words that merely indicate direction.

> If you travel due south from Ohio, eventually you will end up in the South, probably in Kentucky or Tennessee.

9. Capitalize the opening of a letter and the first word of the closing.

> Dear Liza, Dear Sir,
> Best wishes, Sincerely,

Notice that a comma comes after the opening and closing.

REVIEWING CAPITALIZATION

Why is capitalization important in your writing?

_____

_____

What is the difference between a proper noun and a common noun?

_____

_____

◆ *P r a c t i c e   1* **Identifying** Correct the capitalization errors in the following sentences.

1. My Dad bought a new ford mustang last saturday.
2. Lake street is where the pastor of the local Church resides.

3. Jim Morrison's Song "the End" was used as the opening music for *Apocalypse Now,* a Movie by Francis ford Copolla.

4. The editors' association of canada will participate in word on the street in several major cities in september.

5. My family—all my brothers, sisters, cousins, Aunts, and Uncles—love to watch the santa claus parade.

◀ *P r a c t i c e* **2** **Completing** Fill in each blank with words that complete the sentence. Be sure to capitalize words correctly. (You can make up titles if necessary.)

1. Last week I went to see _____ in concert.

2. Shelley will graduate from _____ University.

3. I signed up to take _____ because _____ is such a popular teacher.

4. My favorite holiday is _____ because I get to see my favourite relative, _____.

5. The _____ is sponsoring a barbecue this weekend.

CHAPTER REVIEW

You might want to reread your answers to the questions in the review box before you do the following exercises.

◀ *Review   P r a c t i c e* **1** **Identifying** Correct the capitalization errors in the following sentences.

1. Even though my zenith television has only a 13-inch screen, I still enjoy watching *canadian idol*.

2. Didn't Hamlet say, "to be or not to be"?

3. If you turn South at lover's lane, you'll run directly into my Sister's Ranch, affectionately named lovers' ranch.

4. My Uncle Conrad would like to hire mrs. Chandra Smith for the Department of english and communications.

5. My favourite Novel by Jane Austen is *emma*.

◀ *Review   P r a c t i c e* **2** **Completing** Fill in each blank with words that complete the sentence. Be sure to capitalize words correctly.

1. My mother joined _____, and the work she does helps save lives.

2. It's possible to climb Mt. _____, but not Mt. _____.

3. We have to read _____ for my _____ literature class.

4. Travel _____ to get to _____, and _____ to get to _____.

5. The injured man was taken to _____, where he received treatment from _____.

◀ *Review   Practice   3*   **Writing Your Own** Write a paragraph about a province, famous person, or course you find particularly interesting.

◀ *Review   Practice   4*   **Editing Through Collaboration** Exchange paragraphs from Review Practice 3 with another student, and do the following tasks:

1. Circle any capital letters that don't follow the capitalization rules.
2. Write the rule number next to the error for the writer to refer to.

Then return the paragraph to its writer, and use the information in this chapter to correct any capitalization errors in your own paragraph. Record your errors on the Error Log in Appendix 6.

CHAPTER 47

ABBREVIATIONS AND NUMBERS

✔ CHECKLIST for Using Abbreviations and Numbers

> ✔ Are titles before and after proper names abbreviated correctly?
>
> ✔ Are government agencies and other organizations abbreviated correctly?
>
> ✔ Are numbers *zero* through *nine* spelled out?
>
> ✔ Are numbers 10 and over written as figures (10, 25, 1–20, 324)?

Test Yourself

Correct the abbreviation and number errors in these sentences.

- Lt. Gen. Dallaire wrote a book on his experiences in Rwanda.
- My dog had 4 puppies.
- Over one thousand two hundred and twelve people attended.
- After I'm laid off, I hope to apply for emp. ins.
- Crystal just moved to the U.S. from Canada.

(Answers are in Appendix 8.)

Like capitalization, abbreviations and numbers are also mechanical features of writing that help us communicate what we want to say. Following the rules that govern their use will make your writing as precise as possible.

ABBREVIATIONS

Abbreviations help us move communication along. They follow a set of rules when used in writing.

1. Abbreviate titles before proper names.

   Mr. Mrs. Ms. Dr. Rev. Sen. Sgt.

Abbreviate religious, governmental, and military titles when used with an entire name. Do not abbreviate them when used only with a last name.

NOT We thought that **Sen.** Pepin would speak first.
CORRECT We thought that **Senator** Pepin would speak first.
CORRECT We thought that **Sen.** Lucy Pepin would speak first.

Professor is not usually abbreviated: Professor Sandra Cole is here.

2. Abbreviate academic degrees.

 B.S. (Bachelor of Science)
 R.N. (Registered Nurse)
 D.V.M. (Doctor of Veterinary Medicine)

3. Use the following abbreviations with numbers.

 A.M. *or* **a.m.** (ante meridiem)
 P.M. *or* **p.m.** (post meridiem)
 kph (kilometres per hour)

4. Abbreviate the names of certain government agencies, businesses, and educational institutions by using their initials without periods.

 CBC (Canadian Broadcasting Corporation)
 IBM (International Business Machines)
 CSIS (Canadian Security Intelligence Service)
 CPP (Canada Pension Plan)
 UBC (University of British Columbia)

5. Abbreviate names of provinces when addressing mail or writing out the postal address. Otherwise, spell out the names in full.

 Tamara's new address is 451 Kingston St., St. John's, **NL**.
 Tamara has moved to St. John's, **Newfoundland.**

REVIEWING ABBREVIATIONS

When you write, are you free to abbreviate any words you want?

◆ *P r a c t i c e 1* **Identifying** Correct the underlined words in each of the following sentences.

1. The <u>Rev.</u> Jackson gave a wonderful sermon.

2. The letter was addressed to <u>Mister</u> Clark Reynolds, 758 First Avenue, Smiths Falls, <u>Ontario</u>.

3. Former <u>TX</u> Governor George W. Bush became a <u>United States</u> president.

4. When the police clocked Beth on Ridgeland Highway, she was going 140 <u>kilometres per hour</u>.

5. My favourite show has been picked up by the <u>C.B.C.</u>

◆ *P r a c t i c e   2*   **Completing**   In each sentence, write either an abbreviation or the complete word, whichever is correct.

1. The _____ (U.S./United States) will send two representatives to Ottawa.

2. I have _____ (Prof./Professor) Perry for English this term.

3. For years, J. Edgar Hoover was head of the _____ (FBI/F.B.I./ Federal Bureau of Investigation).

4. She was introduced to _____ (Rev./Reverend) Barbara Shaw.

5. Matt has lived in _____ (BC/British Columbia) and _____ (NB/New Brunswick).

NUMBERS

Most writers ask the same question about using **numbers:** When should a number be spelled out, and when is it all right to use numerals? The following simple rules will help you make this decision.

1. Spell out numbers from *zero* to *nine*. Use figures for numbers 10 and over.

> I have **four** brothers.
> My mom has **12** nieces and nephews and **43** cousins.

Do not mix spelled-out numbers and figures in a sentence if they refer to the same types of items. Use numerals for all numbers in that case.

> **NOT**   I have **four** brothers, **12** nieces and nephews, and **43** cousins.
>
> **CORRECT** I have **4** brothers, **12** nieces and nephews, and **43** cousins.

2. For very large numbers, use a combination of figures and words.

> The athletic department's yearly budget is **$4.6 million.**
> Sales last year totaled approximately **$1.2 billion.**

3. Always spell out a number that begins a sentence. If this becomes awkward, reword the sentence. (See p. 401 for spaces in numbers.)

> **Twenty-two** people were injured in the train accident.
> Approximately **250 000** people live in Saskatoon.

4. Use figures for dates, addresses, telephone numbers, identification numbers, and time.

> My new telephone number is **(555) 877-1420.**
> My Social Insurance Number is **123-456-789.**
> My alarm went off at **6:37** a.m.

5. Use figures for fractions, decimals, and percentages.

> The recipe calls for **3/4** cup of milk and **1/2** cup of sugar.
> He registered **.03** on the Breathalyzer test.
> Almost **15** per cent of the city's inhabitants are graduates of the community college.

Notice that *per cent* is written out; it can be either one word (*percent*) or two (*per cent*).

6. Use figures for exact measurements, including amounts of money. Use a dollar sign for amounts over $1.

> The room is **4** metres wide and **5.2** metres long.
> I made **$34.60** in tips today.

7. Use figures for the parts of a book.

> Chapter **10**   page **20**   Exercise **5**   questions **4** and **6**

Notice that *Chapter* and *Exercise* are capitalized.

REVIEWING NUMBERS

What is the general rule for spelling out numbers as opposed to using numerals?

_____

◆ *P r a c t i c e* **3** **Identifying** Correct any errors with numbers in each of the following sentences.

1. The university's 2005 budget is approximately $75 000 000.

2. The committee will choose 6 finalists for the thousand-dollar scholarship.

3. Nearly half of a cup of chocolate went into this recipe.
4. The hotel manager agreed to give us a twenty % discount since we had fourteen people in our group.
5. 292 people voted in the school election; there were fifteen candidates.

◄ *P r a c t i c e   4*   **Completing** Fill in each blank in the following sentences with numbers in the proper form.

1. With _____ billion dollars in the bank, he is the richest man I know.
2. _____ fireworks were set off for our annual charity drive.
3. Five minus two is _____.
4. To review the comma rules, do Exercise _____ on page _____.
5. You will need _____ cups of flour, _____ cup of water, and _____ eggs to make fried bread.

CHAPTER REVIEW

You might want to reread your answers to the questions in all the review boxes before you do the following exercises.

◄ *Review   Practice   1*   **Identifying** Circle the abbreviation errors and underline the number errors in each of the following sentences. Some sentences contain more than one error.

1. We must leave at ten a.m., or we will miss Sen. Breven's speech.
2. 25 candidates showed up for the one job opening.
3. I am going to college to receive a Registered Nurse degree.
4. Last week, Christy earned fifty-five dollars babysitting.
5. If you had 7 puppies, and you gave away 3, then you would have 4 puppies.

◄ *Review   Practice   2*   **Completing** Correct the errors in Review Practice 1 by rewriting the sentences.

◄ *Review   Practice   3*   **Writing Your Own** Write a paragraph giving directions to a place near your college. Use numbers and abbreviations in your paragraph.

◆ *Review   P r a c t i c e   4*   **Editing Through Collaboration** Exchange paragraphs from Review Practice 3 with another student, and do the following:

1. Underline all abbreviations, numbers, and figures.

2. Circle any abbreviations, numbers, or figures that are not in their correct form.

Then return the paragraph to its writer, and use the information in this chapter to correct any abbreviation and number errors in your own paragraph. Record your errors on the Error Log in Appendix 6.

UNIT TESTS

Here are some exercises that test your understanding of all the material in this unit: Capitalization, Abbreviations, and Numbers.

Unit Test I

A. Underline the errors in capitalization, abbreviations, and numbers in the following sentences.

1. I gave you 6 tulips, and you gave me 3 roses; then we had a bouquet of 9 flowers.

2. I love paintings from the renaissance period.

3. My Mom bought a new chevy trailblazer last saturday.

4. A copy of the defendant's phone bill shows that at six fifteen ante meridiem he called 601-555-4251 and talked for ten minutes.

5. Bob Gainey of the Montreal canadiens was the first Player to be awarded the national Hockey League's Selke trophy.

6. The shopping mall will be one hundred seventy-five thousand square feet and cost two point three billion dollars.

7. Have you signed up for humanities 201, or have you decided to take a psychology or Sociology course instead?

8. Last month, Ravi earned three hundred dollars in his teaching assistant job.

9. Terry was born on August tenth, 1976.

10. We got up at 5:30 ante meridiem to watch the sun rise on the lake, and then had cheese and wine at 7:30 post meridiem on the same lake, so we could watch the sun set.

11. Did you say that Doctor Reynolds told you to lose 10 kilos?

12. In Chapter ten, Exercise five, do questions 4 through 7.

13. The store manager gave us a twenty % discount since we bought sixteen items.

14. my good friend is going south for the summer, staying with relatives in the Southern parts of ontario.

15. Prof. Turner gave a very enlightening lecture on the writing process today.

16. Most geologists estimate that the world is between 4 and 5 000 000 000 years old.

17. Having lived in many countries, I prefer Canada.

18. In order to join the canadian security intelligence service, I had to first get my Bachelor of Science degree.

19. My 1998 zenith tv still works great, and i've never had to get it serviced.

20. In *the merchant of venice* by william shakespeare, portia says, "the quality of mercy is not strained."

B. Correct the errors in capitalization, abbreviations, and numbers in Part A by rewriting each incorrect sentence.

Unit Test II

A. Underline the errors in capitalization, abbreviations, and numbers in the following paragraph.

When I graduated from High School last year, I moved from north bay, ON to London, ON. I was a little nervous about moving out on my own right after high school, but I was excited to start my new life as a Psychology Major at huron university college. Since I could not afford more than two hundred dollars per month for rent, I decided to rent a room instead of an entire apartment. My university is a small school, so my psychology 101 professor, Dr. smith, was able to spend time helping me find a room to rent. We met in may to discuss my big move on august twentieth two thousand two. He recommended misses Berry, a registered nurse with a basement room to rent on Franklin Boulevard. I was so nervous the first time I arrived at thirty-five Grey way, but it only took me 5 minutes to feel at home. Mrs. berry is a wonderful landlady, and she treats me more like her granddaughter than a tenant. Renting a room for one hundred fifty dollars per month has helped me save a lot of money. Living with misses berry has also made the transition to college easier. Sometimes having less money to spend at age Eighteen is better!

B. Correct the errors in capitalization, abbreviations, and numbers in Part A by rewriting the paragraph.

Varying Sentence Structure

✅ CHECKLIST for Varying Sentence Patterns

> ✔ Do you add introductory material to vary your sentence patterns?
>
> ✔ Do you occasionally reverse the order of some subjects and verbs?
>
> ✔ Do you move sentence parts to add variety to your sentences?
>
> ✔ Do you sometimes use questions and exclamations to vary your sentence structure?

Test Yourself

Turn each of the following pairs of sentences into one sentence that is more interesting.

- I live in an old house. I have lived here my whole life.
- I am too busy. I need to work less.
- I love cheeseburgers and fries. I love fast-food places.
- My dog sleeps 14 hours every day. She is overweight.
- I enjoy writing. I keep a notebook for jotting down my thoughts.

(Answers are in Appendix 8.)

Reading the same sentence pattern sentence after sentence can become very monotonous for your readers. This chapter will help you solve this problem in your writing. Look at the following example.

> I have never lived away from home. I am about to start my second year of college. I think I am ready to be on my own. I am excited about this new phase of my life. I have student loans and a part-time job. I can't wait to feel true independence.

This paragraph has some terrific ideas, but they are expressed in such a monotonous way that the readers might doze off. What this paragraph needs is variety in its sentence structure. Here are some ideas for keeping your readers awake and ready to hear your good thoughts.

ADD INTRODUCTORY WORDS

Add some introductory words to your sentences so that they don't all start the same way.

In my lifetime, I have never lived away from home. **Now** I am about to start my second year of college. I think I am ready to be on my own. I am excited about this new phase of my life. **To pay for life away from home,** I have student loans and a part-time job. I can't wait to feel true independence.

◆ **P r a c t i c e 1 Identifying** Underline the sentence in each pair that could be turned into an introductory word, phrase, or clause.

1. It was early morning. Jay had a throbbing headache.
2. We stripped the paper from the walls. We started in the kitchen.
3. I'm shocked. The Blue Rodeo concert sold out in one day.
4. We want fast delivery. We must place our order this week.
5. We got centre row tickets for the concert. I can't believe it.

◆ **P r a c t i c e 2 Completing** Rewrite the sentences in Practice 1 by turning each sentence you underlined into an introductory word, phrase, or clause.

MOVE SENTENCE PARTS

Move some parts of the sentence around. Experiment to see which order works best.

In my lifetime, I have never lived away from home. Now I am about to start my second year of college. I think I am ready to be on my own. Am I ever excited about this new phase in my life. **Student loans and a part-time job can pay for a life away from home.** I can't wait to feel true independence.

◆ **P r a c t i c e 3 Identifying** Underline any parts of the following sentences that can be moved around.

1. I was incredibly hungry after breakfast.
2. Some experts say that computers increase isolation among people.
3. Your outfit is lovely today.
4. There is a great deal we don't know about the common cold.
5. I absolutely love chocolate, not surprisingly.

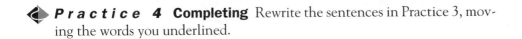 ***Practice 4* Completing** Rewrite the sentences in Practice 3, moving the words you underlined.

VARY SENTENCE TYPE

Use a question, a command, or an exclamation occasionally.

   In my lifetime, I have never lived away from home. **Have you?** Now I am about to start my second year of college. I think I am ready to be on my own. **Boy, am I ever excited about this new phase in my life!** Student loans and a part-time job can pay for a life away from home. I can't wait to feel true independence.

***Practice 5* Identifying** Identify each of the following sentences as a statement (S), a question (Q), a command (C), or an exclamation (E).

1. _____ Look over there at the elephant

2. _____ How does she do that

3. _____ My mom always asked herself why she never finished graduate school

4. _____ Whatever you decide is fine with me

5. _____ Look out for that falling rock

***Practice 6* Completing** Complete the following sentences, making them into questions, commands, or exclamations. Then supply the correct punctuation.

1. Will there ever _____

2. You should not have taken _____

3. Do you know if _____

4. At the first stoplight _____

5. Don't you ever _____

REVIEWING WAYS TO VARY SENTENCE PATTERNS

Why is varying sentence patterns important in your writing?

_____

Name four ways to vary your sentence patterns.

_____

_____

_____

_____

What other kinds of sentences besides statements can you use for variety?

_____   _____   _____

CHAPTER REVIEW

You might want to reread your answers to the questions in the review box before you do the following exercises.

◆ *Review   P r a c t i c e   1*   **Identifying** Underline the words or groups of words that have been added or moved in each revised sentence. Then use the following key to tell which rule was applied to the sentence:

1. Add introductory words.
2. Move parts of the sentence around.
3. Use a question, a command, or an exclamation occasionally.

   a. She does that very well.

   _____ How does she do that so well?

   b. I must call Jarrett in an emergency. Can anyone tell me Jarrett's phone number?

   _____ In case of an emergency, can anyone tell me Jarrett's phone number?

   c. You can't play now. Finish your homework first.

   _____ Before you can play, you must finish your homework.

   d. He is an optimist. He always believes everything will turn out all right.

   _____ An optimist, he always believes everything will turn out all right.

   e. Call our store, send a fax, or visit our website to order.

   _____ To order, call our store, send a fax, or visit our website.

◆ *Review   Practice   2*   **Completing** Vary the structure of the following sentences with at least three of the four ideas you just learned.

The local teen centre has a problem. It cannot afford to stay open, so it might be shut down this weekend. It can't make its monthly dues any higher because most of its members cannot afford increased fees. Government funding and donations aren't enough to keep the centre open. A solution has to exist.

◆ *Review   Practice   3*   **Writing Your Own** Write a paragraph about a historical event. Try to use each of the three ways you have learned to make sentences interesting.

◆ *Review   Practice   4*   **Editing Through Collaboration** Exchange paragraphs from Review Practice 3 with another student, and do the following:

1. Put brackets around any sentences that sound monotonous.
2. Suggest a way to vary each of these sentences.

Then return the paragraph to its writer, and use the information in this chapter to vary the sentence structure in your own paragraph. Record your errors on the Error Log in Appendix 6.

CHAPTER 49

PARALLELISM

✅ CHECKLIST for Using Parallelism

> ✔ Can you use parallelism to add coherence to your sentences and paragraphs?
>
> ✔ Are all items in a series grammatically balanced?

Test Yourself

Underline the parts in each of the following sentences that seem awkward or unbalanced.

- We decided to forget about the lawsuit and then moving on with our lives.
- Last year, I graduated from college, moved from Toronto to Charlottetown, and have been married.
- My sister and brother raise money to feed the homeless and for building a new shelter.
- Exercising, eating right, and water will improve a person's health.
- Jack went back to school because he wanted to get a better job and because of the girls on campus.

(Answers are in Appendix 8.)

When sentences are **parallel,** they are balanced. That is, words, phrases, or clauses in a series start with the same grammatical form. Parallel structures make your sentences interesting and clear.

The following is a paragraph that could be greatly improved with parallel structures.

> My teenaged sister, Amanda, was not thrilled when she learned the family was going to drive to Ottawa for the May 24 weekend. She has been looking forward to her time at home. She was planning on reading romance novels, to hang out with her friends, and was going to organize her schoolwork. Instead, she will be touring the Houses of Parliament, seeing the Rideau Canal, and will visit many art galleries.

Words and phrases in a series should be parallel, which means they should start with the same type of word. Parallelism makes your sentence structure smoother and more interesting. Look at this sentence, for example.

NOT   She was planning on **reading** romance novels,
      to hang out with her friends, and
      was going to organize her
      schoolwork.

CORRECT   She was planning on **reading** romance novels,
      hanging out with her friends, and
      organizing her schoolwork.

CORRECT   She was planning to **read** romance novels,
      hang out with her friends, and
      organize her schoolwork.

Here is another sentence that would read better if the parts were parallel:

NOT   Instead, she will be **touring** the Houses of Parliament,
      seeing the Rideau Canal, and
      will visit many art galleries.

CORRECT   Instead, she will be **touring** the Houses of Parliament,
      seeing the Rideau Canal, and
      visiting many art galleries.

CORRECT   Instead, she will tour **the Houses of Parliament,**
      the Rideau Canal, and
      many art galleries.

Now read the paragraph with these two sentences made parallel or balanced.

  My teenaged sister, Amanda, was not thrilled when she learned the family was going to drive to Ottawa for the May 24 weekend. She has been looking forward to her time at home. She was planning on reading romance novels, hanging out with her friends, and organizing her schoolwork. Instead, she will be touring the Houses of Parliament, seeing the Rideau Canal, and visiting many art galleries.

REVIEWING PARALLELISM

What is parallelism?

_____

_____

> *Why should you use parallelism in your writing?*
>
> _____

◆ *P r a c t i c e   1*   **Identifying** Underline the parallel structures in each of the following sentences.

1. We never expected the girls to start buying alcohol and bringing it into the residence.
2. She often prepares recipes that she finds in her fancy cooking magazines or that she sees on the Food Network.
3. He would start skipping class and sleeping late.
4. One day when I was 10 years old, my dad revealed that there was no Santa Claus and that babies did not come from storks.
5. I baked cookies, cleaned the house, and paid the bills.

◆ *P r a c t i c e   2*   **Completing** Make the underlined elements parallel in each of the following sentences.

1. Jessica likes skiing, cooking, and to do crossword puzzles in her spare time.

   _____

2. On our trip to Vancouver, we have many things to do, people to visit, and sights that should be seen.

   _____

3. Carmella went to the picnic because she wanted to support her co-workers and because of the massive fireworks show.

   _____

4. In 1950, my mom and dad moved out of the city, bought land in the country, and have become self-sufficient.

   _____

5. Fighting, cheating, and to use drugs will get you kicked out immediately.

   _____

CHAPTER REVIEW

You might want to reread your answers to the questions in the review box before you do the following exercises.

◆ *Review   Practice   1*   **Identifying** Underline the parallel struc-tures in each of the following sentences.

1. Kristi will make deviled eggs, bring baked beans, and order the cake.
2. To stay healthy, do not smoke, stay out of the sun, and don't abuse alco-hol.
3. Students should learn to manage their time, to study efficiently, and to have a social life.
4. Biking, swimming, and hiking are all good sports to build endurance, stamina, and flexibility.
5. Please wake up the baby, give her a bath, and feed her.

◆ *Review   Practice   2*   **Completing** Complete each of the follow-ing sentences with parallel structures.

1. My favourite hobbies are ——————, ——————, and ——————.
2. Because —————— and because ——————, I decided to stay home.
3. You could have ——————, ——————, and —————— if you had truly wanted to pass that test.
4. ——————, ——————, and —————— are essential items at the beach.
5. Sam and Tabitha enjoy ——————, ——————, and ——————.

◆ *Review   Practice   3*   **Writing Your Own** Write a paragraph about your favourite movie. What is the movie? Why is it your favourite? Use two examples of parallelism in your paragraph.

◆ *Review   Practice   4*   **Editing Through Collaboration** Exchange paragraphs from Review Practice 3 with another student, and do the following:

1. Underline any items in a series.
2. Put brackets around any of these items that are not grammatically parallel.

Then return the paragraph to its writer, and use the information in this chapter to correct any parallelism errors in your own paragraph. Record your errors on the Error Log in Appendix 6.

CHAPTER 50

COMBINING SENTENCES

☑ CHECKLIST for Combining Sentences

> ✔ Do you combine sentences to avoid too many short, choppy sentences in a row?
>
> ✔ Do you use different types of sentences?

Test Yourself

Combine each set of sentences into one sentence.

- My mother is taking ballet lessons. She takes her lessons at the YWCA.
- We love to swim. It's just too hot to be outside.
- Robin lives in Edmonton. Andy lives in Winnipeg.
- We lived on the beach. We were there for two weeks.
- I am going to study hard. I want to get a good grade on my final.
- I love to travel. I love the strange animals in Australia. I want to go to Australia.

(Answers are in Appendix 8.)

Still another way to add variety to your writing is to combine short, choppy sentences into longer sentences. You can combine simple sentences to make compound or complex sentences. You can also combine compound and complex sentences.

SIMPLE SENTENCES

A **simple sentence** consists of one independent clause. Remember that a clause has a subject and a main verb.

In the following examples, notice that a simple sentence can have more than one subject and more than one verb. (For more on compound subjects and compound verbs, see Chapter 30.)

s   v

I have several very good friends.

s   s   v

Martin and Louis are good friends.

s   s   v   v

Martin and I do interesting things and go to interesting places.

REVIEWING SIMPLE SENTENCES

What does a simple sentence consist of?

_____

Write a simple sentence.

_____

◆ **P r a c t i c e 1 Identifying** Underline the subjects once and the verbs twice in each of the following sentences. Then label the simple sentences SS.

1. _____ Every day I went to the bagel shop and bought a newspaper.
2. _____ Sinya and I knew the answer, even though we didn't study.
3. _____ Before the last show begins, I'll get some popcorn.
4. _____ They're flying to Newfoundland on Thursday.
5. _____ Going to the movies alone is peaceful.

◆ **P r a c t i c e 2 Completing** Make simple sentences out of the sentences in Practice 1 that are not simple.

COMPOUND SENTENCES

A **compound sentence** consists of two or more independent clauses joined by a coordinating conjunction (*and, but, for, nor, or, so,* or *yet*). In other words, you can create a compound sentence from two (or more) simple sentences.

Simple: I can add quickly in my head.
Simple: I am very good at math.

s   v   s v
Compound: I can add quickly in my head, **and** I am very good at math.

Simple: He leads a very busy life.

Simple: His family always comes first.

                    s   v   s
Compound: He leads a very busy life, **but** his family always

                    v
              comes first.

Simple: Mike and Diana are running a 10K on Saturday.

Simple: They will not go with us Friday night.

                    s   s   v
Compound: Mike and Diana are running a 10K Saturday, **so**

                s   v   v
              they will not be going with us Friday night.

Hint: As the examples show, a comma comes before the coordinating conjunction in a compound sentence.

REVIEWING COMPOUND SENTENCES

What does a compound sentence consist of?

_____

Write a compound sentence.

_____

◆ *P r a c t i c e   3* **Identifying** Underline the independent clauses in the following sentences, and circle the coordinating conjunctions.

1. I hate to repeat myself, but I will.

2. Just beyond that sign is a highway patrol cop waiting to ticket someone, yet he won't catch me.

3. Harry began the race, and he never looked back.

4. She's been in these kinds of predicaments before, yet each time she's come out ahead.

5. You are not allowed to bring food or drinks into this room, nor are you allowed to move the desks.

◆ *P r a c t i c e 4* **Completing** Combine each pair of simple sentences into a compound sentence.

1. Mom and Dad love to play golf.   They never seem to have enough time for it.
2. Our backyard faces the highway.   It's always noisy.
3. My Uncle Simon and Aunt Jean always take a month-long vacation. They are always relieved to return home.
4. Our phone rings day and night.   It is very annoying.
5. My favourite meal is barbecued salmon and rice.   My favourite dessert is peach cobbler.

COMPLEX SENTENCES

A **complex sentence** is composed of one independent clause and at least one dependent clause. A **dependent clause** begins with either a subordinating conjunction or a relative pronoun.

Subordinating Conjunctions

after	because	since	until
although	before	so	when
as	even if	so that	whenever
as if	even though	than	where
as long as	how	that	wherever
as soon as	if	though	whether
as though	in order that	unless	while

Relative Pronouns

who	whom	whose	which	that

You can use subordinating conjunctions and relative pronouns to make a simple sentence (an independent clause) into a dependent clause. Then you can add the new dependent clause to an independent clause to produce a complex sentence that adds interest and variety to your writing.

How do you know which simple sentence should be independent and which should be dependent? The idea that you think is more important should be the independent clause. The less important idea will then be the dependent clause.

The following are some examples of how to combine simple sentences to make a complex sentence.

Simple: Shawna has a big collection of video games.
Simple: Shawna plays the same games over and over.

                                                    Dep
Complex: **Even though** Shawna has a big collection of video

                        Ind
games, she plays the same ones over and over.

This complex sentence stresses that Shawna plays the same games over and over. The size of her collection is of secondary importance.

                        Ind
Complex: Shawna has a big collection of video games, **though**

                        Dep
she plays the same ones over and over.

In this complex sentence, the size of the collection is most important, so it is the independent clause.

Simple: The winner of the 5K race was Torrie.
Simple: Torrie is my roommate.

                        Ind   Dep
Complex: The winner of the 5K race was Torrie, **who** is my
               roommate.

This complex sentence answers the question "Who won the 5K race?" The information about Torrie being the roommate is secondary in importance.

                    Ind   Dep
Complex: My roommate is Torrie, **who** won the 5K race.

This complex sentence answers the question "Who is your roommate?" The information that she won the race is secondary.

REVIEWING COMPLEX SENTENCES

What does a complex sentence consist of?

_____

Write a complex sentence.

_____

◆ *P r a c t i c e   5* **Identifying** Label the underlined part of each sentence as either an independent (I) or a dependent (D) clause.

1. _____ <u>Although I was exhausted</u>, I still went to work.

2. _____ If someone scores 50, <u>the game is over</u>.

3. _____ Trisha is majoring in marine biology <u>since she loves working with sea life</u>.

4. _____ Brittany, <u>whom I've known for years</u>, decided to move to the Yukon.

5. _____ While people in third world countries starve, <u>people in Canada eat too much and waste food</u>.

◆ *P r a c t i c e   6* **Completing** Finish each sentence, and label the new clause either dependent (D) or independent (I).

1. _____ _____, call your mother.

2. _____ When you signed up for this class, _____?

3. _____ Mrs. Benson, _____, won the lottery and moved to Florida.

4. _____ Whenever Diane's face turns red, _____.

5. _____ If Mark is cold, _____.

COMPOUND-COMPLEX SENTENCES

If you combine a compound sentence with a complex sentence, you produce a **compound-complex sentence.** That means your sentence has at least two independent clauses (to make it compound) and at least one dependent clause (to make it complex). Here are some examples.

Simple: We both love warm weather.

Simple: We will go to Jamaica for our honeymoon.

Simple: We plan to have a good time.

Ind

Compound-Complex: We will go to Jamaica for our honeymoon,

Ind

and we plan to have a good time **since**

Dep

we both love warm weather.

Simple: She bought a used car.

Simple: It has 50 000 kilometres on it.

Simple: It runs like a dream.

                                            Ind

Compound-Complex: She bought a used car, **which** has

                                  Dep   Ind

        50 000 kilometres on it, **but** it runs like a dream.

Simple: Rush-hour traffic is very bad.

Simple: You could miss your flight.

Simple: You should leave soon.

                                            Ind

Compound-Complex: Rush-hour traffic is very bad, **and** you could

                               Ind   Dep

      miss your flight **if** you don't leave soon.

Hint: Notice in these examples that we occasionally had to change words in the combined sentences so they make sense.

REVIEWING COMPOUND-COMPLEX SENTENCES

What does a compound-complex sentence consist of?

_____

Write a compound-complex sentence.

_____

◀ **P r a c t i c e   7   Identifying** Underline the clauses in each of the following compound-complex sentences. Then identify each clause as either independent (I) or dependent (D).

1. We cannot host the meeting, nor can we attend because we will be out of town.

2. Professor Shilling said that I couldn't turn in my essay late because I had three months to write it, so I decided to turn it in on time.

3. Because we were out of money, we begged our guide to take us to the bank, yet our guide said that he didn't have enough gas in the bus.

4. Even though Marcy doesn't like the water and even though she can't swim, she should go fishing with us, for she will have a good time.

5. After all the fuss died down, the boys decided to shake hands and let bygones be bygones; then, they took each other out for pizza.

◄ *P r a c t i c e   8*   **Completing** Make each sentence below into a compound-complex sentence. You may have to change some of the wording.

1. Gina believes in ghosts.

_____

2. Edward collects rare books.

_____

3. The contestants were nervous.

_____

4. Motorcycles can be dangerous.

_____

5. Jack says that he will eat liver and onions "when pigs fly."

_____

CHAPTER REVIEW

You might want to reread your answers to the questions in all the review boxes before you do the following exercises.

◄ *R e v i e w   P r a c t i c e   1*   **Identifying** Underline the independent clauses in each sentence. Then label the sentence simple (SS), compound (C), complex (X), or compound-complex (CX). The following definitions might help you.

Simple	=	one independent clause
Compound	=	two or more independent clauses joined by *and, but, for, nor, or, so,* or *yet*

| Complex | = | one independent clause and at least one dependent clause |
| Compound-complex | = | at least two independent clauses and one or more dependent clauses |

1. _____ DVD players are becoming more popular than VCRs.

2. _____ Bananas are a nutritious part of Leo's breakfast each morning.

3. _____ The grandparents' house, which sits at the edge of the woods, was built around the turn of the century.

4. _____ Sheila says that music is her passion, but she has little time to pursue her interests since she took on a part-time job.

5. _____ I like the feel of sand between my toes when I walk along the beach.

◆ *Review Practice 2* **Completing** Combine each set of sentences to make the sentence pattern indicated in parentheses. You may need to change some wording in the sentences so they make sense. The list of sentence types in Review Practice 1 may help you with this exercise.

1. My best friend, Tina, and I always have a great time together.   We share all of our secrets. (compound)

2. I have so much energy.   I'm going to clean my closet. (complex)

3. You should never leave an iron on unattended.   You should never use an iron on clothes you are wearing.   You may be injured. (compound-complex)

4. I know you don't like pears.   Try some of this pastry anyway. (complex)

5. I'm sorry.   I can't lend you any money.   I am broke. (compound-complex)

◆ *Review Practice 3* **Writing Your Own** Write a paragraph about your fondest teenage memory. What are the details of this memory? Why do you remember this event?

◆ *Review Practice 4* **Editing Through Collaboration** Exchange paragraphs from Review Practice 3 with another student, and do the following:

1. Put brackets around any sentences that you think should be combined.

2. Underline sentences that are incorrectly combined (for example, ones that have a weak connecting word or no connecting word).

Then return the paragraph to its writer, and use the information in this chapter to combine sentences in your own paragraph. Record your errors on the Error Log in Appendix 6.

UNIT TESTS

Here are some exercises that test your understanding of all the material in this unit: Varying Sentence Structure, Parallelism, and Combining Sentences.

Unit Test I

A. In each of the following sentences, underline and label the errors in variety, parallelism, and sentence combining.

1. The turn-off will be hard to see. I will be driving at night.

2. She lived like a queen and to enjoy her lifestyle.

3. We stopped to get lunch, fill up on gas, and stretching our legs.

4. John and Martin always invite my brother and me to swim in their pool. They never invite our neighbours. Our neighbours really want to come.

5. I listen to the radio in the car. I listen to station CJAD.

6. We took Yolanda to Long Beach. We let Yolanda feed the seagulls.

7. We had a family reunion. Josh fell out of a tree there and broke his wrist.

8. We decided to scuba dive for five days, explore the jungle for three days, and climbed the Mayan ruins for two days.

9. They had been building this database. They collected it for over three years.

10. Tuesday is today. My paper is due on Tuesday.

11. Working for CSIS comes with many perks. I take advantage of them all.

12. Being my friend will make you happy. You will never have to be alone.

13. His birthday is on Thursday. We're celebrating it on Friday.

14. Training for the marathon means eating right, running hard, and will be getting plenty of sleep.

15. The martial arts instructor is a professional. The martial arts instructor said that Cole could compete as long as he practised hard.

16. Trimming, weeding, and to plant flowers always make a yard look better.

17. It's best to wait for my mom. My mom will be home soon.

18. The mouse chewed through the wire. I had to pay to replace it.

19. I used to dance in puddles. I used to squish my toes in the mud. Now I am an adult with a job and family. I don't have time for these simple pleasures.

20. Skydiving is great. You need to know what you are doing when you skydive. Skydiving can be a very dangerous sport.

B. Correct the errors you identified in Part A by rewriting each incorrect sentence.

Unit Test II

A. In the following paragraph, underline and label the errors in variety, parallelism, and sentence combining.

Entering high school is scary at first. Entering high school is fun once students get used to their new environment. Entering high school and to deal with all the stress of being a teenager is the first step to adulthood. In high school, students have to learn to manage their time to get good grades, a social life, and get involved in hobbies. Some students are really afraid of high school. They just want to stay kids forever. They need to give high school a chance. They will see that it is a lot of fun. They will see that growing up is exciting.

B. Correct the errors you identified in Part A by rewriting the paragraph.

Standard and Nonstandard English

✅ CHECKLIST for Standard and Nonstandard English

- ✔ Do you consistently use standard English in your paper?
- ✔ Is your paper free of nonstandard, ungrammatical words?
- ✔ Have you changed any slang to standard English?

Test Yourself

Label the following sentences as correct, incorrect, or slang.

- So she goes, can't I meet you at the theatre? _____
- Will u be there b4 me? _____
- We were totally grossed out. _____
- They changed the tire theirselves. _____
- We're jamming in the morning. _____

(Answers are in Appendix 8.)

Choosing the right words for what you want to say is an important part of effective communication. This chapter will help you find the right words and phrases for the audience you are trying to reach.

Look, for example, at the following sentences. They all have a similar message, expressed in different words.

I want to do good in college, the reason being that I can get a good job.

I'm going to hit the books so I can rake in the bucks.

I want to go to college, graduate, and get a good job.

Which of these sentences would you probably say to a friend or to someone in your family? Which would you most likely say in a job interview? Which would be good for a college or university paper?

The first two sentences are nonstandard English. They might be said or written to a friend or family member, but they would not be appropriate in an academic setting or in a job situation. Only the third sentence would be appropriate in an academic paper or in a job interview.

STANDARD AND NONSTANDARD ENGLISH

Most of the English language falls into one of two categories—either *standard* or *nonstandard*. **Standard English** is the language of college and university, business, and the media. It is used by reporters on television, by newspapers, in most magazines, and on websites created by schools, government, business, and organizations. Standard English is always grammatically correct and free of slang.

Nonstandard English does not follow all the rules of grammar and often includes slang. Recently, the language of instant messaging has also crept into regular writing. Nonstandard English is not necessarily wrong, but it is more appropriate in some settings (with friends and family) than others. It is not appropriate in college and university or business writing. To understand the difference between standard and nonstandard English, compare the following paragraphs.

Nonstandard English

My buddy, Tyler, doesn't get why people go to college. He thinks that college is a waste of time and dough. He's like, my parents didn't go to school, and they aren't exactly broke. But lotsa people go to college for other reasons than making more bucks. Irregardless of whether college gets you ready for a career or not, it helps a person find hisself and meet others who are basically kinda like you. I definitely think that a college education is worth the money and the time.

Standard English

My friend Tyler can't understand why people go to college. He believes that in terms of money and time, higher education is wasteful. He likes to point out that both of his parents have high-paying jobs and never went to college. However, he doesn't realize that many people go to college for other reasons than increasing their earning power. They also hope to discover what they would enjoy doing for the rest of their lives. College not only prepares people for a career, it helps them learn more about themselves and meet others with similar interests. I strongly believe that the money and time invested in a college education are justified.

In the rest of this chapter, you will learn how to recognize and correct ungrammatical English and how to avoid slang in your writing.

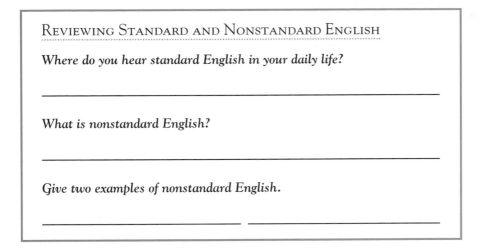

REVIEWING STANDARD AND NONSTANDARD ENGLISH

Where do you hear standard English in your daily life?

_____

What is nonstandard English?

_____

Give two examples of nonstandard English.

_____   _____

NONSTANDARD ENGLISH

Nonstandard English is ungrammatical. It does not follow the rules of standard English that are required in college or university writing. The academic and business worlds expect you to be able to recognize and avoid nonstandard English. This is not always easy because some nonstandard terms are used so often in speech that many people think they are acceptable in writing. The following list might help you choose the correct words in your own writing.

anywheres

NOT	Jake makes himself at home **anywheres** he goes.
CORRECT	Jakes makes himself at home **anywhere** he goes.

being as, being that

NOT	**Being as** Rhonda is late, we can't start the party.
CORRECT	**Because** Rhonda is late, we can't start the party.

coulda/could of, shoulda/should of

NOT	My brother **could of** played basketball in college. He **should of** stuck with it.
CORRECT	My brother **could have** (or **could've**) played basketball in college. He **should have** (or **should've**) stuck with it.

different than

NOT	I am no **different than** all your other friends.
CORRECT	I am no **different from** all your other friends.

enthused

NOT	Jay was **enthused** about his trip to Hawaii.
CORRECT	Jay was **enthusiastic** about his trip to Hawaii.

goes

NOT	Then he **goes,** I'll wait for you downstairs.
CORRECT	Then he **says,** "I'll wait for you downstairs."
CORRECT	Then he **said** he would wait for me downstairs.

hisself

NOT	Marshall made **hisself** a budget for the next month.
CORRECT	Marshall made **himself** a budget for the next month.

in regards to

NOT	**In regards to** your proposal, we have decided to consider it.
CORRECT	**In regard to** your proposal, we have decided to consider it.

irregardless

NOT	**Irregardless** of how much time you spent on your paper, it still needs work.
CORRECT	**Regardless** of the time you spent on your paper, it still needs work.

kinda/kind of, sorta/sort of

NOT	Abby's perfume smells **kinda** sweet, **sorta** like vanilla.
CORRECT	Abby's perfume smells **rather** sweet, **much** like vanilla.

most

NOT	**Most** everyone we invited will come to the party.
CORRECT	**Almost** everyone we invited will come to the party.

must of

NOT	I **must of** left my gloves in the car.
CORRECT	I **must have** left my gloves in the car.

off of

NOT	Jim accidentally knocked the vase **off of** the coffee table.
CORRECT	Jim accidentally knocked the vase **off** the coffee table.

oughta

NOT	Sometimes I think I **oughta** try out for the swim team.
CORRECT	Sometimes I think I **ought to** try out for the swim team.

real

NOT	My mom was **real** upset when I came in at 4 a.m.
CORRECT	My mom was **really** upset when I came in at 4 a.m.

theirselves

NOT	My grandfather thinks people should help **theirselves** instead of waiting for a handout.
CORRECT	My grandfather thinks people should help **themselves** instead of waiting for a handout.

use to

NOT	Nassar **use to** live in Egypt.
CORRECT	Nassar **used to** live in Egypt.

ways

NOT	Both sides say they are a long **ways** from agreement.
CORRECT	Both sides say they are a long **way** from agreement.

where . . . at

NOT	Do you know **where** your keys are **at**?
CORRECT	Do you know **where** your keys **are**?

REVIEWING NONSTANDARD ENGLISH

What is one reason using nonstandard English in written work is easy to do?

_____

Give four examples of nonstandard English; then correct them.

_____   _____

_____   _____

_____   _____

_____   _____

◆ *P r a c t i c e   1 A* **Identifying** Underline the ungrammatical words or phrases in each of the following sentences.

1. I shoulda went to class yesterday.

2. I was real excited to see my new baby brother.

3. Sometimes people should keep their thoughts to theirselves.

4. Being as my brother has more money than I, he should pay for dinner.

5. We use to go to the lake every summer.

◆ *P r a c t i c e* **1 B** **Correcting** Correct the ungrammatical words and expressions in Practice 1A by rewriting the incorrect sentences.

◆ *P r a c t i c e* **2** **Completing** Change the underlined ungrammatical words and phrases to standard English.

1. <u>where am I at</u> _____

2. How are <u>yous</u> doing today? _____

3. She <u>goes</u>, "Sure." _____

4. <u>kinda</u> _____

5. Email me if <u>ur</u> coming to the party. _____

SLANG

Another example of nonstandard English is **slang,** popular words and expressions that come and go, much like the latest fashions. For example, in the 1950s, someone might call his or her special someone a *dreamboat*. In the 1960s, you might hear a boyfriend or girlfriend described as *groovy,* and in the 1990s, *sweet* was the popular slang term. Today your significant other might be *hot* or *dope*. In recent years, as instant messaging has become more common, certain abbreviations have started to turn up in student writing. Avoid using expressions like *ur* (you are), *plz* (please), *nbd* (no big deal), *l8r* (later), *b4* (before), or *wu* (what's up?) in any place other than instant or text messaging, including email. Once you begin to use these abbreviations in email, they will begin to slip into your more formal writing.

These expressions are slang because they are part of the spoken (and written) language that changes from generation to generation and from place to place. As you might suspect, slang communicates to a limited audience who share common interests and experiences. Some slang words, such as *cool* and *neat*, have become part of our language, but most slang is temporary. What's in today may be out tomorrow, so the best advice is to avoid slang in your writing.

R EVIEWING S LANG

What is slang?

_____

Give two examples of slang terms that were popular but aren't any longer.

_____ _____

> *Give two examples of slang terms that you and your friends use today.*
>
> _____   _____

◈ **P r a c t i c e 3 Identifying** Underline the slang words and expressions in each of the following sentences.

1. Just because she's pretty doesn't mean she's all that.
2. We were just hangin with our homies.
3. My sister and I are tight.
4. That guy is hot.
5. Give it up for Dave Matthews.

◈ **P r a c t i c e 4 Completing** Translate the following slang expressions into standard English.

1. That rocks. _____

2. Say what? _____

3. Keep it real, man. _____

4. What up? _____

5. We're just kickin' it. _____

CHAPTER REVIEW

You might want to reread your answers to the questions in all the review boxes before you do the following exercises.

◈ **Review P r a c t i c e 1 Identifying** Underline the ungrammatical or slang words in the following sentences.

1. In regards to your recent request we are not able to give you an answer.
2. The music got louder and faster, and then we were really rolling.
3. Hey, that's real cool.
4. Do you know where my sunglasses are at?
5. She's very enthused about the trip.

◆ *Review   Practice   2*   **Completing** Correct any nonstandard English in each of the following sentences by rewriting the sentences.

1. You really need to chill out.
2. I'm so sorry that I knocked your picture off of the wall.
3. Hey man, do you think you can make room for one more person?
4. You could of always asked for help.
5. Whatcha doin' in the basement?

◆ *Review   Practice   3*   **Writing Your Own** Write a paragraph on a community problem. What are the details? What is the problem? What solution do you propose?

◆ *Review   Practice   4*   **Editing Through Collaboration** Exchange paragraphs from Review Practice 3 with another student, and do the following:

1. Underline any ungrammatical language.
2. Circle any slang.

Then return the paragraph to its writer, and use the information in this chapter to correct any nonstandard or slang expressions in your own paragraph. Record your errors on the Error Log in Appendix 6.

EASILY CONFUSED WORDS

52

✅ CHECKLIST for Easily Confused Words

> ✔ Is the correct word chosen from the easily confused words?
>
> ✔ Are the following words used correctly: *its/it's, their/there/they're, to/too/two, who's/whose, your/you're?*

Test Yourself

Choose the correct word in parentheses.

- I have to (accept, except) that I won't be graduating this spring.
- (Who's, Whose) bike is this?
- I'm not saying (it's, its) Johnny's fault.
- We are going to need (their, there, they're) help.
- (Wear, Where, Were) did you say your parents lived?

(Answers are in Appendix 8.)

Some words are easily confused. They may look alike, sound alike, or have similar meanings. But they all play different roles in the English language. This chapter will help you choose the right words for your sentences.

EASILY CONFUSED WORDS, PART I

a/an: Use *a* before words that begin with a consonant. Use *an* before words that begin with a *vowel* (*a, e, i, o, u*).

> **a** party, **a** dollar, **a** car
> **an** apple, **an** elephant, **an** opportunity

accept/except: *Accept* means "receive." *Except* means "other than."
> Yolanda says she will not **accept** my apology.
> I answered every question **except** the last one.

advice/advise: *Advice* means "helpful information." *Advise* means "give advice or help."

> Whenever I need **advice,** I call my older brother Greg.
>
> Greg usually **advises** me to make a list before taking action.

affect/effect: *Affect* (verb) means "influence." *Effect* means "bring about" (verb) or "a result" (noun).

> Omar hopes his new job won't **affect** his study time.
>
> The governor of the Bank of Canada believes higher taxes will **effect** positive economic changes.
>
> The pill produced a calming **effect.**

already/all ready: *Already* means "in the past." *All ready* means "completely prepared."

> Hope has **already** registered for the spring semester.
>
> We were **all ready** to go when the phone rang.

among/between: Use *among* when referring to three or more people or things. Use *between* when referring to only two people or things.

> **Among** all the students in our class, Nadine is the most mature.
>
> I can't decide **between** cheesecake and apple pie for dessert.

bad/badly: *Bad* means "not good." *Badly* means "not well."

> That milk is **bad,** so don't drink it.
>
> The team played **badly** in the first half but came back to win.
>
> Kiki felt **bad** that she could not go.

beside/besides: *Beside* means "next to." *Besides* means "in addition (to)."

> Burt stood **beside** Kevin in the team photo.
>
> She's a very calm person. **Besides,** she has nothing to worry about.

brake/break: *Brake* means "stop" or "the parts that stop a moving vehicle." *Break* means "shatter, come apart" or "a rest between work periods."

> My car needs new **brakes.**
>
> Esther wants to **break** up with Stan.

breath/breathe: *Breath* means "air." *Breathe* means "taking in air."

> Take several big **breaths** as you cool down.
>
> To cure hiccups, **breathe** into a paper bag.

choose/chose: *Choose* means "select." *Chose* is the past tense of *choose*.

> Please **choose** something from the menu.
>
> Andy **chose** the trip to Paris as his prize.

REVIEWING WORDS THAT ARE EASILY CONFUSED, PART I

Do you understand the differences in the sets of words in Part I of the list of easily confused words?

_____

Have you ever confused any of these words? If so, which ones?

_____

◆ **P r a c t i c e 1 Identifying** Underline the correct word in each of the following sentences.

1. You should try to (choose, chose) a computer that will meet your needs.
2. When I mixed vinegar with baking soda, the (affect, effect) was astounding.
3. (Beside, Besides) being cold, I was also hungry.
4. I'll call you when I'm on my (brake, break) at work.
5. Your car keys are (among, between) the two books on the fireplace mantel.

◆ **P r a c t i c e 2 Completing** Complete the following sentences with a correct word from Part I of the list of easily confused words.

1. I was so shocked I couldn't catch my _____.
2. I decided to take your _____.
3. Elaine will _____ your invitation to the prom if you will only ask her.
4. I feel _____ that I arrived late.
5. Thank you for the invitation to lunch, but I have _____ eaten.

EASILY CONFUSED WORDS, PART II

coarse/course: *Coarse* refers to something that is rough. *Course* refers to a class.

> Sandpaper can be very fine or very **coarse.**
> My computer science **course** is really interesting.

desert/dessert: *Desert* refers to dry, sandy land or means "abandon." *Dessert* refers to the last course of a meal.

> Las Vegas was once nothing but a **desert.**
> The main character in the short story **deserted** his family.
> We had strawberry shortcake for **dessert.**

Hint: You can remember that *dessert* has two s's if you think of *strawberry shortcake*.

fewer/less: *Fewer* refers to things that can be counted. *Less* refers to things that cannot be counted.

> There are **fewer** cookies in the jar since Joey has been home.
> Because my mom is working another job, she has **less** time to spend with us.

good/well: *Good* modifies nouns. *Well* modifies verbs, adjectives, and adverbs. *Well* also refers to a state of health.

> Barbie looks **good** in her new outfit.
> Dave looks as if he doesn't feel **well.**
> Karen didn't do **well** on the typing test because she was nervous.

hear/here: *Hear* refers to the act of listening. *Here* means "in this place."

> I can't **hear** you because the music is too loud.
> You dropped some food **here** on the carpet.

it's/its: *It's* is the contraction for *it is* or *it has*. *Its* is a possessive pronoun.

> The forecasters say **it's** going to snow this afternoon.
> The cat ate breakfast and then washed **its** face.

knew/new: *Knew* is the past tense of *know*. *New* means "recent."

> I thought you **knew** I had a **new** car.

lay/lie: *Lay* means "set down." (Its principal parts are *lay, laid, laid*.) *Lie* means "recline." (Its principal parts are *lie, lay, lain*.)

> The train crew **lays** about a mile of track a day.
> He **laid** down his burden.
> Morrie **lies** down and takes a short nap every afternoon.
> I **lay** on the beach until the sun set.

loose/lose: *Loose* means "free" or "unattached." *Lose* means "misplace" or "not win."

> I tightened the **loose** screws on the door hinge.
> If the Rough Riders **lose** this game, they will be out of the playoffs.

passed/past: *Passed* is the past tense of *pass*. *Past* refers to an earlier time or means "beyond."

>   Mei **passed** the exam with an "A."
>   Having survived four husbands, Aunt Jane has an interesting **past.**
>   He ran **past** Ginger and into Reba's outstretched arms.

REVIEWING WORDS THAT ARE EASILY CONFUSED, PART II

Do you understand the differences in the sets of words in Part II of the list of easily confused words?

_____

Have you ever confused any of these words? If so, which ones?

_____

◆ **Practice 3 Identifying** Underline the correct word in each of the following sentences.

1. Sandy, will you please come (hear, here) so I can show you how to set the VCR?

2. Now that I have eaten dinner, I feel (good, well).

3. The outdoor shutters came (loose, lose) during the storm.

4. (It's, Its) going to be a very long day.

5. My go-cart blew a tire, and so Jed (passed, past) me on the third lap.

◆ **Practice 4 Completing** Complete the following sentences with a correct word from Part II of the list of easily confused words.

1. I need to take only one more _____ to complete my degree.

2. Would you please _____ those clean clothes on the bed?

3. The doctor told my mom that he _____ what was making her ill.

4. Camels can live in the _____ because they store water in their humps.

5. Since Judy has _____ cookies, you should share with her.

EASILY CONFUSED WORDS, PART III

principal/principle: *Principal* means "main, most important," "a school official," or "a sum of money." A *principle* is a rule. (Think of *principle* and *rule*—both end in *-le.*)

> My **principal** reason for moving is to be nearer my family.
> Mr. Kobler is the **principal** at Westside Elementary School.
> He lives by certain **principles,** including honesty and fairness.

quiet/quite: *Quiet* means "without noise." *Quite* means "very."

> It was a warm, **quiet** night.
> Vanessa said she was **quite** satisfied with her grade.

raise/rise: *Raise* means "increase" or "lift up." *Rise* means "get up from a sitting or reclining position."

> The premier does not plan to **raise** taxes.
> Ernie **rises** at 5 a.m. every morning to go to the health club.

set/sit: *Set* means "put down." *Sit* means "take a seated position."

> Mohammed, you can **set** the packages over there.
> If I **sit** for a long period of time, my back starts hurting.

(For additional help with *sit* and *set*, see Chapter 33, "Regular and Irregular Verbs.")

than/then: *Than* is used in making comparisons. *Then* means "next."

> Louise is younger **than** her sister Linda.
> The ball rolled around the hoop, **then** dropped through the net.

their/there/they're: *Their* is possessive. *There* indicates location. *They're* is the contraction of *they are.*

> **Their** car broke down in the middle of the freeway.
> Too much trash is over **there** by the riverbank.
> **They're** not coming to the party because **they're** tired.

threw/through: *Threw,* the past tense of *throw,* means "tossed." *Through* means "finished" or "passing from one point to another."

> Beth **threw** the ball to Wes, who easily caught it.
> Allen is **through** with his lunch, so he will leave soon.
> Rico went **through** his closet searching for his G.I. Joes.

to/too/two: *To* means "toward" or is used with a verb. *Too* means "also" or "very." *Two* is a number.

> Tori went **to** Johnny's house **to** return his ring.
> Tori returned Johnny's photo albums, **too.**
> Mariel thinks **two** is her lucky number.

wear/were/where: *Wear* means "have on one's body." *Were* is the past tense of *be*. *Where* refers to a place.

> **Where were** you going when I saw you?
> Can you **wear** jeans to that restaurant?

weather/whether: *Weather* refers to outdoor conditions. *Whether* expresses possibility.

> **Whether** the **weather** will improve or not is a good question.

who's/whose: *Who's* is a contraction of *who is* or *who has*. *Whose* is a possessive pronoun.

> We wonder **who's** going to decide **whose** opinion is correct.

your/you're: *Your* means "belonging to you." *You're* is the contraction of *you are*.

> **Your** appointment will be canceled if **you're** not on time.

REVIEWING WORDS THAT ARE EASILY CONFUSED, PART III

Do you understand the differences in the sets of words in Part III of the list of easily confused words?

_____

Have you ever confused any of these words? If so, which ones?

_____

◆ **P r a c t i c e   5   Identifying** Underline the correct word in each of the following sentences.

1. There are (to, too, two) many swimmers in the pool.
2. (Were, Wear, Where) were you going in such a hurry?

3. For extra income, we (raise, rise) hamsters and sell them on the Internet.

4. If you don't mow the lawn, (your, you're) mom is going to get upset.

5. (Who's, Whose) that girl with Bob?

◆ *P r a c t i c e* **6 Completing** Complete the following sentences with a correct word from Part III of the list of easily confused words.

1. Haythem has a better sense of humour _____ his sister.

2. If the firefighters can't put out the blaze, _____ going to call for reinforcements.

3. Much to our surprise, the bird flew _____ our car window.

4. The _____ of our school is very strict.

5. Could you please be _____ so I can hear the speaker?

CHAPTER REVIEW

You might want to reread your answers to the questions in all the review boxes before you do the following exercises.

◆ *Review P r a c t i c e* **1 Identifying** Underline the correct word in each of the following sentences.

1. Simone had (fewer, less) mistakes on her quiz this time.

2. I got all the answers right (accept, except) two.

3. Every time Mel goes (to, too, two) the beach, he gets sunburned.

4. (Their, There, They're) are too many people in this room to be comfortable.

5. That smell (affects, effects) me in strange ways.

◆ *Review P r a c t i c e* **2 Completing** Complete the following sentences with a correct word from all three parts of the list of easily confused words.

1. The nurse told Wilbur to _____ down and try to relax.

2. The _____ should be just fine for our picnic today.

3. The proudest day of Ricky's life was when he _____ the big test.

4. Whenever you get anxious, _____ deeply.

5. Yoshi should _____ those books down before he hurts himself.

◈ *Review   P r a c t i c e   3*   **Writing Your Own** Write a paragraph about a recent decision you had to make, explaining what the problem was and why you made the decision you did. Try to use some of the easily confused words from this chapter.

◈ *Review   P r a c t i c e   4*   **Editing Through Collaboration** Exchange paragraphs from Review Practice 3 with another student, and do the following:

1. Circle any words used incorrectly.
2. Write the correct form of the word above the error.

Then return the paragraph to its writer, and use the information in this chapter to correct any confused words in your own paragraph. Record your errors on the Error Log in Appendix 6.

CHAPTER **53**

SPELLING

✅ CHECKLIST for Identifying Misspelled Words

> ✔ Do you follow the basic spelling rules?
> ✔ Are all words spelled correctly?

Test Yourself

Correct the misspelled words in the following sentences.

- My cousin just moved to a forign country.
- Your grandmother makes delishous chicken and dumplings.
- Dennis is trying to persuaid me to join his fraternity.
- Winning two years in a row is quite an achievment.
- Eat your vegtables.

(Answers are in Appendix 8.)

If you think back over your education, you will realize that teachers believe spelling is important. There is a good reason they feel that way: Spelling errors send negative messages. Misspellings seem to leap out at readers, creating serious doubts about the writer's abilities in general. Because you will not always have access to spell-checkers—and because spell-checkers do not catch all spelling errors—improving your spelling skills is important.

SPELLING HINTS

The spelling rules in this chapter will help you become a better speller. But first, here are some practical hints that will also help you improve your spelling.

1. Start a personal spelling list of your own. Use the list of commonly misspelled words on pages 480–484 as your starting point.
2. Study the lists of easily confused words in Chapter 52.

3. Avoid all nonstandard expressions (see Chapter 51).

4. Use a dictionary when you run across words you don't know.

5. Run the spell-check program if you are writing on a computer. Keep in mind, however, that spell-check cannot tell if you have incorrectly used one word in place of another (such as *to, too,* or *two*).

REVIEWING HINTS FOR BECOMING A BETTER SPELLER

Name two things you can do immediately to become a better speller.

_____

Why can't you depend on a spell-check program to find every misspelled word?

_____

Practice 1A Identifying Underline the misspelled words in each of the following sentences. Refer to the list of easily confused words in Chapter 52 and to the spelling list in this chapter as necessary.

1. Maria is a beatiful person.

2. Hugo is familar with these math formulas.

3. My mother says there are many different kinds of intelligance.

4. Would you please acompany me to the store?

5. This is a new developement.

Practice 1B Correcting Correct the spelling errors in Practice 1A by rewriting the incorrect sentences.

Practice 2 Completing Fill in each blank in the following sentences with hints that help with spelling.

1. Use a _____ to look up words you don't know.

2. Start a _____ to help you remember words you commonly misspell.

3. You can always use the _____ on your computer, but you should remember that it cannot correct easily confused words, only misspelled words.

4. Try to avoid all _____ English.

5. Study the list of _____ in Chapter _____.

SPELLING RULES

Four basic spelling rules can help you avoid many misspellings. It pays to spend a little time learning them now.

1. **Words that end in -e:** When adding a suffix beginning with a vowel (*a, e, i, o, u*), drop the final *-e*.

believe + -ing	=	believing
include + -ed	=	included (*-e* is from the *-ed*)
value + -able	=	valuable

    When adding a suffix beginning with a consonant, keep the final *-e*.

aware + -ness	=	awareness
improve + -ment	=	improvement
leisure + -ly	=	leisurely

2. **Words with *ie* and *ei*:** Put *i* before *e* except after *c* or when sounded like *ay* as in *neighbour* and *weigh*.

c + *ei*	(no *c*) + *ie*	Exceptions
receive	grieve	height
conceive	niece	leisure
deceive	friend	foreign
perceive	relief	science

3. **Words that end in -y:** When adding a suffix to a word that ends in a consonant plus *-y*, change the *y* to *i*.

funny + -er	=	funnier
try + -ed	=	tried
easy + -er	=	easier

4. **Words that double the final consonant:** When adding a suffix starting with a vowel to a one-syllable word, double the final consonant.

big + -est	=	biggest
quit + -er	=	quitter
get + -ing	=	getting

    With words of more than one syllable, double the final consonant if (1) the final syllable is stressed and (2) the word ends in a single vowel plus a single consonant.

begin + -ing	=	beginning
admit + -ed	=	admitted
rebel + -ious	=	rebellious

REVIEWING FOUR BASIC SPELLING RULES

What is the rule for adding a suffix to words ending in -e (such as date + -ing)?

_____

_____

What is the rule for spelling ie *and* ei *words (such as* receive, neighbour, *and* friend)?

_____

_____

When do you change -y to i before a suffix (such as sunny + -est)?

_____

_____

When do you double the final consonant of a word before adding a suffix (such as cut or begin)?

_____

_____

_____

P r a c t i c e   3 A   Identifying Underline the spelling errors in each of the following sentences.

1. The secretarys went out to lunch together.
2. Your encouragment helped me get through a tough time.
3. Sarah percieved that Fernando was upset.
4. The reason should have occured to you.
5. In winter, Frances likes going on sliegh rides.

P r a c t i c e   3 B   Correcting Correct the spelling errors in Practice 3A by rewriting the incorrect sentences.

◆ **P r a c t i c e 4 Completing** Complete the following spelling rules.

1. With words that end with -e, _____ when adding a suffix beginning with a vowel.

2. -I comes before -e except after _____ or when sounded as _____ as in _____ .

3. Change the _____ to an _____ when adding a suffix to a word that ends in a consonant plus -y.

4. When adding a suffix that begins with a _____ to a one-syllable word, _____ the final consonant.

5. With words that are more than one syllable, _____ the final consonant if (1) the last syllable is stressed and (2) the word ends in a single vowel plus a single consonant.

COMMONLY MISSPELLED WORDS

Use the following list of commonly misspelled words to check your spelling when you write.

abbreviate	advertisement	assassin
absence	afraid	athletic
accelerate	aggravate	attach
accessible	aisle	audience
accidentally	although	authority
accommodate	aluminum	autumn
accompany	amateur	auxiliary
accomplish	ambulance	avenue
accumulate	ancient	awkward
accurate	anonymous	baggage
ache	anxiety	balloon
achievement	anxious	banana
acknowledgment *or*	appreciate	bankrupt
acknowledgement	appropriate	banquet
acre	approximate	beautiful
actual	architect	beggar
address	arithmetic	beginning
adequate	artificial	behaviour

benefited

bicycle

biscuit

bought

boundary

brilliant

brought

buoyant

bureau

burglar

business

cabbage

cafeteria

calendar

campaign

canoe

canyon

captain

career

carriage

cashier

catastrophe

caterpillar

ceiling

cemetery

census

certain

certificate

challenge

champion

character

chief

children

chimney

coffee

collar

college

column

commit

committee

communicate

community

comparison

competent

competition

complexion

conceive

concession

concrete

condemn

conference

congratulate

conscience

consensus

continuous

convenience

cooperate *or*
   co-operate

corporation

correspond

cough

counterfeit

courageous

courteous

cozy

criticize

curiosity

curious

curriculum

cylinder

dairy

dangerous

dealt

deceive

decision

definition

delicious

descend

describe

description

deteriorate

determine

development

dictionary

difficulty

diploma

disappear

disastrous

discipline

disease

dissatisfied

divisional

dormitory

economy

efficiency

eighth

elaborate

electricity

eligible

embarrass

emphasize

employee

encourage

enormous

enough

enthusiastic

envelope

environment

equipment

equivalent

especially

essential

establish

exaggerate

excellent
exceptionally
excessive
exhaust
exhilarating
existence
explanation
extinct
extraordinary
familiar
famous
fascinate
fashion
fatigue
faucet
February
fiery
financial
foreign
forfeit
fortunate
forty
freight
friend
fundamental
gauge
genius
genuine
geography
gnaw
government
graduation
grammar
grief
grocery
gruesome
guarantee
guess

guidance
handkerchief
handsome
haphazard
happiness
harass
height
hesitate
hoping
humorous
hygiene
hymn
icicle
illustrate
imaginary
immediately
immortal
impossible
incidentally
incredible
independence
indispensable
individual
inferior
infinite
influential
initial
initiation
innocence
installation
intelligence
interfere
interrupt
invitation
irrelevant
irrigate
issue
jealous

jewellery or
   jewelry
journalism
judgment *or*
   judgement
kindergarten
knife
knowledge
knuckles
laboratory
laborious
language
laugh
laundry
league
legible
legislature
leisure
length
library
licence (n)
license (v)
lieutenant
lightning
likable *or* likeable
liquid
listen
literature
machinery
magazine
magnificent
majority
manufacture
marriage
material
mathematics
maximum
mayor

meant	partial	rhyme
medicine	particular	rhythm
message	pastime	salary
mileage	patience	satisfactory
miniature	peculiar	scarcity
minimum	permanent	scenery
minute	persistent	schedule
mirror	personnel	science
miscellaneous	persuade	scissors
mischievous	physician	secretary
miserable	pitcher	seize
misspell	pneumonia	separate
monotonous	politician	significant
mortgage	possess	similar
mysterious	prairie	skiing
necessary	precede	soldier
neighbourhood	precious	souvenir
niece	preferred	sovereign
nineteen	prejudice	spaghetti
ninety	previous	squirrel
noticeable	privilege	statue
nuisance	procedure	stomach
obedience	proceed	strength
obstacle	pronounce	subtle
occasion	psychology	succeed
occurred	publicly	success
official	questionnaire	sufficient
omission	quotient	surprise
omitted	realize	syllable
opponent	receipt	symptom
opportunity	recipe	technique
opposite	recommend	temperature
original	reign	temporary
outrageous	religious	terrible
pamphlet	representative	theatre
paragraph	reservoir	thief
parallel	responsibility	thorough
parentheses	restaurant	tobacco

tomorrow	valuable	whose
tongue	various	width
tournament	vegetable	worst
tragedy	vehicle	wreckage
truly	vicinity	writing
unanimous	villain	yacht
undoubtedly	visible	yearn
unique	volunteer	yield
university	weather	zealous
usable *or* useable	Wednesday	zoology
usually	weigh	
vacuum	weird	

REVIEWING COMMONLY MISSPELLED WORDS

Why is spelling important in your writing?

_____

Start a personal spelling log of your most commonly misspelled words.

_____   _____   _____

_____   _____   _____

_____   _____   _____

◄ *P r a c t i c e   5 A* **Identifying** Underline any words that are misspelled in the following sentences.

1. My best freind has a tendency to exagerate.
2. If Justin stays on scheduele, he'll be a sophomore next year.
3. My third-grader gets perfect arithmatic scores.
4. She is a very sucessful lawyer.
5. The restarant is undoutedly the finest in town.

◄ *P r a c t i c e   5 B* **Correcting** Correct any spelling errors that you identified in Practice 5A by rewriting the incorrect sentences.

◄ *P r a c t i c e   6* **Completing** Correct the spelling errors in the following paragraph.

This past Febuary, an anonimous tip was called into the police station. Apparently, a provincial politition was having severe finantial difficulties, so he started making counterfit money. There was really no noticible difference between his funny money and real money. He passed the money through his wife's retail company. It was only when the politition became overly enthusiastick about his scam that he got caught. He revealed his scam to another politition, one who did not want the whole goverment to take the fall for one man. So, he called the police and left the anonimous tip. Now the only londry the dirty politition is doing is in jail.

CHAPTER REVIEW

You might want to reread your answers to the questions in all the review boxes before you do the following exercises.

◆ *Review Practice 1* **Identifying** Underline the misspelled words in each of the following sentences.

1. My parents have truely had a good marriege.
2. The new restraunt will offer incredably delishious deserts.
3. The recommended salery for a professer is not what it should be these days.
4. Professor Barton is an extrordinary teacher.
5. Rafael's parents perfered that he pursue a career in psycology.

◆ *Review Practice 2* **Completing** Correct the spelling errors in Review Practice 1 by rewriting the incorrect sentences.

◆ *Review Practice 3* **Writing Your Own** Write a paragraph explaining how you might go about becoming a better speller. Can you learn how to spell in college or university? Before college or university?

◆ *Review Practice 4* **Editing Through Collaboration** Exchange paragraphs from Review Practice 3 with another student, and do the following:

1. Underline any words that are used incorrectly.
2. Circle any misspelled words.

Then return the paragraph to its writer, and use the information in this chapter to correct any spelling errors in your own paragraph. Record your errors on the Spelling Log in Appendix 7.

UNIT TESTS

Here are some exercises that test your understanding of all the material in this unit: Standard and Nonstandard English, Easily Confused Words, and Spelling.

Unit Test I

A. Underline the word choice and spelling errors in the following sentences.

1. You shoulda seen the show; it was fantastic.
2. This coat is so big that it feels akward.
3. Dean was embarased by her rude behavior.
4. Many of us live by our principals.
5. Incidentaly, I met someone who says she works with you.
6. I gave the fern fewer water since its soil is still moist.
7. I would love some desert after dinner.
8. Marco felt badly that he'd broken the dish.
9. He prefered to eat at the coffee shop on campus.
10. Could you please advice me on the best course of action?
11. The sackcloth we had to wear in the play was course and itchy.
12. The Tragically Hip are playing at the arena tommorow night.
13. My mom freaked out when I came in at 5 a.m.
14. Finish your homework, and than you can go to the movies.
15. No exchanges will be made without a reciept.
16. Let's cut class and go catch some rays.
17. My 1968 Corvette is very different than your 1968 Mustang.
18. The children are already to go to the park.
19. Irregardless of the time change, I slept late and was tardy getting to work.
20. I believe you've had quiet enough cake for today.

B. Correct the errors in Part A by rewriting each incorrect sentence.

Unit Test II

A. Underline the word choice and spelling errors in the following paragraph.

The number of teenagers and young adults suffering from depression is growing each year. The medical and sikological communities have worked together to try to determine the cause of depresion and to develop treatment options. So far, it is unclear as to weather deppression is caused by genetics or enviurnment or both. Whatever. Irregardless of these dissagreements, most profesionals now beleive that the best treatment option is a combination of therapy and medication. Most people who suffer from depression are able to live healthy, productive lives with litle or no medisin and some kinda therapy. Even so, they're are some people who are a risk to theirselves or others. These folks oughta be hospitlized for a spell. No matter how severe there problems are, people should not be embarrassed about getting help. Anybody who says differently is messed up.

B. Correct the word choice and spelling errors in Part A by rewriting the paragraph.

APPENDIX 1

Use the following questions to help you find editing errors in your partner's paragraph. Mark the errors directly on your partner's paper using the Editing Symbols on the inside back cover. For more editing sheets, see the Companion Website.

Writer: _____   **Peer:** _____

Sentences

1. Does each sentence have a subject and verb?

    Mark any fragments you find with **frag.**

    Put a slash (/) between any fused sentences and comma splices.

2. Do all subjects and verbs agree?

    Mark any subject-verb agreement errors you find with **sv.**

3. Do all pronouns agree with their nouns?

    Mark any pronoun errors you find with **pro agr.**

4. Are all modifiers as close as possible to the words they modify?

    Mark any modifier errors you find with **ad** (adjective or adverb problem), **mm** (misplaced modifier), or **dm** (dangling modifier).

Punctuation and Mechanics

5. Are sentences punctuated correctly?

    Mark any punctuation errors you find with the appropriate symbol under Unit 5 of the Editing Symbols (inside back cover).

6. Are words capitalized properly?

    Mark any capitalization errors you find with **lc** (lowercase) or **cap** (capital).

Word Choice and Spelling

7. Are words used correctly?

    Mark any words that are used incorrectly with **wc** (word choice) or **ww** (wrong word).

8. Are words spelled correctly?

    Mark any misspelled words you find with **sp.**

APPENDIX 2A

Use the following questions to evaluate your partner's paragraph. Direct your comments to your partner.

Writer: _____ **Peer:** _____

Describing

1. Is the dominant impression clearly communicated? If not, how can the writer make it clearer?

2. Does the paragraph *show* rather than *tell?* Explain your answer.

Topic Sentence

3. Does the topic sentence convey the paragraph's controlling idea? Explain your answer.

Development

4. Does the paragraph contain enough specific details to develop the topic sentence? Explain your answer.

Unity

5. Do all the sentences in the paragraph support the topic sentence? Explain your answer.

Organization

6. Is the paragraph organized so that readers can easily follow it? Explain your answer.

Coherence

7. Do the sentences move smoothly and logically from one to the next? Explain your answer.

Use the following questions to evaluate your partner's paragraph. Direct your comments to your partner.

Writer: _____   **Peer:** _____

Narrating

1. What is the paragraph's main point? If you're not sure, show the writer how he or she can make the main point clearer.

2. Does the writer use the five W's and one H to construct the paragraph? Where does the paragraph need more information?

3. Does the writer use vivid descriptive details in the paragraph? Where can more details be added?

Topic Sentence

4. Does the topic sentence convey the paragraph's controlling idea? Explain your answer.

Development

5. Does the paragraph contain enough specific details to develop the topic sentence? Explain your answer.

Unity

6. Do all the sentences in the paragraph support the topic sentence? Explain your answer.

Organization

7. Is the paragraph organized so that readers can easily follow it? Explain your answer.

Coherence

8. Do the sentences move smoothly and logically from one to the next? Explain your answer.

APPENDIX 2C

Use the following questions to evaluate your partner's paragraph. Direct your comments to your partner.

Writer: _____   **Peer:** _____

Illustrating

1. What is the paragraph's main point? If you're not sure, show the writer how he or she can make the main point clearer.

2. Did the writer choose examples that focus on the main point? If not, which examples need to be changed?

3. Does the writer use a sufficient number of examples to make his or her point? Where can more examples be added?

Topic Sentence

4. Does the topic sentence convey the paragraph's controlling idea? Explain your answer.

Development

5. Does the paragraph contain enough specific details to develop the topic sentence? Explain your answer.

Unity

6. Do all the sentences in the paragraph support the topic sentence? Explain your answer.

Organization

7. Is the paragraph organized so that readers can easily follow it? Explain your answer.

Coherence

8. Do the sentences move smoothly and logically from one to the next? Explain your answer.

APPENDIX 2D

Use the following questions to evaluate your partner's paragraph. Direct your comments to your partner.

Writer: _____ **Peer:** _____

Analyzing a Process

1. Does the writer state in the topic sentence what the reader should be able to do or understand by the end of the paragraph? If not, what information does the topic sentence need to be clearer?

2. Does the remainder of the paragraph explain the rest of the process? If not, what seems to be missing?

Topic Sentence

3. Does the topic sentence convey the paragraph's controlling idea? Explain your answer.

Development

4. Does the paragraph contain enough specific details to develop the topic sentence? Explain your answer.

Unity

5. Do all the sentences in the paragraph support the topic sentence? Explain your answer.

Organization

6. Is the paragraph organized in chronological order? Explain your answer.

Coherence

7. Do the sentences move smoothly and logically from one to the next? Explain your answer.

Use the following questions to evaluate your partner's paragraph. Direct your comments to your partner.

Writer: _____   **Peer:** _____

Comparing and Contrasting

1. Does the paragraph state the point the writer is trying to make with a comparison in the topic sentence? If not, what part of the comparison does the writer need to focus on?

2. Does the writer choose items to compare and contrast that will make his or her point most effectively? What details need to be added to make the comparison more effective?

Topic Sentence

3. Does the topic sentence convey the paragraph's controlling idea? Explain your answer.

Development

4. Does the paragraph contain enough specific details to develop the topic sentence? Explain your answer.

Unity

5. Do all the sentences in the paragraph support the topic sentence? Explain your answer.

Organization

6. Is the paragraph organized either by topics or by points of comparison? Explain your answer.

Coherence

7. Do the sentences move smoothly and logically from one to the next? Explain your answer.

APPENDIX 2F

Use the following questions to evaluate your partner's paragraph. Direct your comments to your partner.

Writer: _____ **Peer:** _____

Dividing and Classifying

1. What is the overall purpose for the paragraph, and is it stated in the topic sentence? If not, where does the paragraph need clarification?

2. Does the writer divide the topic into categories (division) and explain each category with details and examples (classification)? If not, where is more division or classification needed?

Topic Sentence

3. Does the topic sentence convey the paragraph's controlling idea? Explain your answer.

Development

4. Does the paragraph contain enough specific details to develop the topic sentence? Explain your answer.

Unity

5. Do all the sentences in the paragraph support the topic sentence? Explain your answer.

Organization

6. Is the paragraph organized so that the categories communicate the meaning clearly? Explain your answer.

Coherence

7. Do the sentences move smoothly and logically from one to the next? Explain your answer.

Use the following questions to evaluate your partner's paragraph. Direct your comments to your partner.

Writer: _____ **Peer:** _____

Defining

1. Does the paragraph have a clear audience and purpose? What are they? If you are not sure, how can the writer make them clearer?

2. Does the writer define his or her term or idea by synonym, category, or negation? Is this approach effective? Why or why not?

3. Does the writer use examples to expand on his or her definition of the term or idea? Where does the definition need more information?

Topic Sentence

4. Does the topic sentence convey the paragraph's controlling idea? Explain your answer.

Development

5. Does the paragraph contain enough specific details to develop the topic sentence? Explain your answer.

Unity

6. Do all the sentences in the paragraph support the topic sentence? Explain your answer.

Organization

7. Is the paragraph organized so that it communicates the definition as clearly as possible? Explain your answer.

Coherence

8. Do the sentences move smoothly and logically from one to the next? Explain your answer.

Use the following questions to evaluate your partner's paragraph. Direct your comments to your partner.

Writer: _____   **Peer:** _____

Analyzing Causes and Effects

1. Does the topic sentence make a clear statement about what is being analyzed? If not, what information does it need to be clearer?

2. Does the writer use facts and details to support the topic sentence? What details need to be added?

3. Does the writer include the *real* causes and effects for his or her topic? What details are unnecessary?

Topic Sentence

4. Does the topic sentence convey the paragraph's controlling idea? Explain your answer.

Development

5. Does the paragraph contain enough specific details to develop the topic sentence? Explain your answer.

Unity

6. Do all the sentences in the paragraph support the topic sentence? Explain your answer.

Organization

7. Is the paragraph organized so that it communicates the message as clearly as possible? Explain your answer.

Coherence

8. Do the sentences move smoothly and logically from one to the next? Explain your answer.

APPENDIX 21

Use the following questions to evaluate your partner's paragraph. Direct your comments to your partner.

Writer: _____   **Peer:** _____

Arguing

1. Does the writer state his or her opinion on the subject matter in the topic sentence? What information is missing?

2. Who is the intended audience for this paragraph? Does the writer adequately persuade this audience? Why or why not?

3. Does the writer choose appropriate evidence to support the topic sentence? What evidence is needed? What evidence is unnecessary?

Topic Sentence

4. Does the topic sentence convey the paragraph's controlling idea? Explain your answer.

Development

5. Does the paragraph contain enough specific details to develop the topic sentence? Explain your answer.

Unity

6. Do all the sentences in the paragraph support the topic sentence? Explain your answer.

Organization

7. Is the paragraph organized so that the evidence supports the argument as effectively as possible? Explain your answer.

Coherence

8. Do the sentences move smoothly and logically from one to the next? Explain your answer.

Use the following questions to evaluate your partner's essay. Direct your comments to your partner.

Writer: _____   **Peer:** _____

Thesis Statement

1. Does the thesis statement contain the essay's controlling idea and appear as the first or last sentence in the introduction? Explain your answer.

Basic Elements

2. Does the writer include effective basic elements (title, introduction, single-topic paragraphs, conclusion)? Explain your answer.

Development

3. Is the essay adequately developed (thesis, specific and enough details)? Explain your answer.

Unity

4. Is the essay unified (topics relate to thesis and sentences in paragraphs relate to topic sentences)? Explain your answer.

Organization

5. Is the essay organized logically (including the paragraphs within the essay)? Explain your answer.

Coherence

6. Do the paragraphs and sentences move smoothly and logically from one to the next? Explain your answer.

Use the following questions to help you find editing errors in your partner's essay. Mark the errors directly on your partner's paper using the Editing Symbols on the inside back cover.

Writer: _____ **Peer:** _____

Sentences

1. Does each sentence have a subject and verb?

    Mark any fragments you find with *frag.*

    Put a slash (/) between any fused sentences or comma splices.

2. Do all subjects and verbs agree?

    Mark any subject-verb agreement errors you find with *sv.*

3. Do all pronouns agree with their nouns?

    Mark any pronoun errors you find with *pro agr.*

4. Are all modifiers as close as possible to the words they modify?

    Mark any modifier errors you find with *ad* (adjective or adverb problem), *mm* (misplaced modifier), or *dm* (dangling modifier).

Punctuation and Mechanics

5. Are sentences punctuated correctly?

    Mark any punctuation errors you find with the appropriate symbol under Unit 5 of the Editing Symbols (inside back cover).

6. Are words capitalized properly?

    Mark any capitalization errors you find with *lc* (lowercase) or *cap* (capital).

Word Choice and Spelling

7. Are words used correctly?

    Mark any words that are used incorrectly with *wc* (word choice) or *ww* (wrong word).

8. Are words spelled correctly?

    Mark any misspelled words you find with *sp.*

Put an X in the square that corresponds to each question that you missed.

	a	b	c	d	e	f
1						
2						
3						
4						
5						
6						
7						
8						
9						
10						

Then record your errors in the categories below to find out where you might need help.

Fragments

1a _____ 1b _____ 2c _____ 2e _____ 3d _____

4a _____ 6b _____ 7e _____ 8b _____ 9e _____

10a _____ 10c _____

Run-ons

1c _____ 1d _____ 2a _____ 3b _____ 4f _____

5a _____ 5d _____ 6d _____ 7b _____ 7c _____

8d _____ 9b _____ 10b _____

Subject-verb agreement

2b _____ 2d _____ 9d _____

Verb forms

3a _____ 3e _____

Pronoun agreement

4b _____ 4c _____ 4d _____ 4e _____ 10f _____

Modifiers

5b _____ 5c _____

End punctuation

6e _____

Commas	6c _____	9f _____	10e _____
Capitalization	6a _____	9a _____	
Abbreviations	7d _____		
Numbers	3c _____	7a _____	
Confused words	8e _____	9c _____	
Spelling	8a _____	8c _____	10d _____

APPENDIX **6** Error Log

List any grammar, punctuation, and mechanics errors you make in your writing on the following chart. Then, on the lines provided, record (1) the actual error from your writing, (2) the rule for correcting this error, and (3) your correction.

Error	
	Example I went to the new seafood restaurant and I ordered the lobster.
Comma	**Rule** Always use a comma before a coordinating conjunction when joining two independent clauses.
	Correction I went to the new seafood restaurant, and I ordered the lobster.
Error	Example
	Rule
	Correction
Error	Example
	Rule
	Correction
Error	Example
	Rule
	Correction
Error	Example
	Rule
	Correction
Error	Example
	Rule
	Correction
Error	Example
	Rule
	Correction
Error	Example
	Rule
	Correction

Error	Example
	Rule
	Correction
Error	Example
	Rule
	Correction
Error	Example
	Rule
	Correction
Error	Example
	Rule
	Correction
Error	Example
	Rule
	Correction
Error	Example
	Rule
	Correction
Error	Example
	Rule
	Correction
Error	Example
	Rule
	Correction

APPENDIX 7 Spelling Log

On this chart, record any words you misspell, and write the correct spelling in the space next to the misspelled word. In the right column, write a note to yourself to help you remember the correct spelling. (See the first line for an example.) Refer to this chart as often as necessary to avoid misspelling the same words again.

Misspelled Word	Correct Spelling	Definition/Notes
there	their	there = place; their = pronoun; they're = "they are"

APPENDIX 8 Test Yourself Answers Handbook

Here are the answers to the Test Yourself questions from the Introduction to and beginning of each chapter in the Handbook (Part V). Where are your strengths? Where are your weaknesses?

Introduction: Parts of Speech (p. 271)

The personality trait that I **like** (v) best about myself is my **healthy** (adj) sense of humour. No matter **how** (adv) bad a **situation** (n) is, I can usually find something funny to say to cheer everyone up. **When** (conj) Toby's ancient **car** (n) **was stolen,** (v) I told him it was a piece of junk anyway, **and** (conj) I felt sorry for the **foolish** (adj) person who stole it. **Man,** (int) **we** (pro) laughed so hard, imagining the car thief broken down **on** (prep) the side of the road **somewhere** (prep) in town. **Oh,** (int) there are some things that **I** (pro) don't even try to joke about, like death and diseases. A person would have to be **extremely** (adv) insensitive to joke about those situations.

Introduction: Phrases (p. 285)

After the concert, to get some food

To get a good grade on the test to study

in the brick house at the end of the block behind the park

am going to get a job this year

Do you want to see a movie with us

Introduction: Clauses (p. 286)

Mallory will get what she wants out of life because she is assertive

Since you don't have time to go to dinner I'll bring you some food

If Rachel is going to leave first she needs a map

We finished painting then we celebrated

I enjoyed the book the most when Harry Potter got the sorcerer's stone

Chapter 30: Subjects and Verbs (p. 290)

(We) really **liked** the movie.

Melissa and (Brian) **left** early.

(She) **is** in class.

Clean your room. (implied (You))

The **Masons have** never **remodeled** their kitchen.

She **checked** the oil and **put** air in the tires.

Chapter 31: Fragments (p. 297)

_____   We were hoping that the test would be easy.

___X___   Which he did not see at first.

_____   She wanted to become a musician.

___X___   Running to catch the plane, with her suitcase flying.

___X___   Since the newspaper had reported it.

Chapter 32: Fused Sentences and Comma Splices (p. 310)

Jennifer was elected Academic President, / I voted for her.

The beach is a great getaway / we're fortunate it's only 45 minutes away.

He wanted to participate, but he wasn't sure of the rules.

Casey is hard to get to know / she hides her thoughts and feelings well.

I hope I get into Dr. Jones's class, / I hear he's the best teacher to get.

Chapter 33: Regular and Irregular Verbs (p. 318)

___X___   We **brang** our new neighbour a pizza for dinner.

_____   My brother **married** on February 14—Valentine's Day.

___X___   He **drug** the heavy suitcase down the street.

___X___   This CD **costed** $15.

___X___   My roommate's waterbed **has sprang** a leak.

Chapter 34: Subject-Verb Agreement (p. 328)

___X___   **Ben** and **Tess** ~~has become~~ become great friends.

___X___   **Each** of the nurses **are** with a patient.

___X___   **Macaroni and cheese** **are** my favourite food.

_____   There **are** two **trains** to Moncton in the morning.

___X___   **Everyone** **are** ready to leave.

Chapter 35: Verb Tense (p. 339)

___I___   When my brother won the gold medal, my father looks very proud.

___P___   All new employees are trained by a professional.

___P___   The child was saved by the firefighters.

___I___   My friend got home early, so we go to the movies.

___P___   The student was given the answers in advance.

Chapter 36: Pronoun Problems (p. 345)

The toy was ~~her's~~ hers to begin with.

Bradley told Megan and ~~I~~ me the funniest story.

He can run a lot faster than ~~me~~ I.

Those ~~there~~ ballet shoes are Laura's.

Ted and ~~me~~ I are going to the game tonight.

Chapter 37: Pronoun Reference and Point of View (p. 354)

Emily and Grace decided that s̲h̲e̲ would try out for the team.

T̲h̲e̲y̲ say y̲o̲u̲ should drink eight glasses of water a day.

I̲ take the bus because y̲o̲u̲ can save a lot of money that way.

The reporter did not check h̲e̲r̲ facts or talk to the main witness, which s̲h̲e̲ regretted.

I̲t̲ says to notify the dean if y̲o̲u̲ are dropping a class.

Chapter 38: Pronoun Agreement (p. 360)

Harriett and Maureen walked <u>their</u> dogs in the park.

Each person is responsible for <u>their</u> own transportation.

Although the **pieces** of furniture were used, <u>it</u> looked new.

Someone left <u>their</u> dirty dishes in the sink.

Everyone contributed <u>his</u> work to the assignment.

Chapter 39: Adjectives (p. 367)

The <u>grey</u> stingrays were very <u>beautiful.</u>

We were <u>more happier</u> when the rain cooled the <u>hot</u> day.

This is the <u>worstest</u> cold I've ever had.

<u>This</u> textbook is <u>more better</u> than <u>that</u> one.

She is the <u>oldest</u> of the <u>two</u> sisters.

Chapter 40: Adverbs (p. 375)

We were led <u>quickly</u> out the back door.

He hugged her <u>tight</u> when he saw her.

Tina left <u>early</u> because she was<u>n't</u> feeling <u>good.</u>

She feels <u>badly</u> that she could<u>n't</u> stay.

I ca<u>n't never</u> meet on Tuesdays because I work that night.

Chapter 41: Modifier Errors (p. 386)

When we arrived at the concert, Sandy told her mother <u>**that she should call home**</u>.

<u>**Before going to the store**</u>, the car needed gas.

The teacher told the students their grades would be posted <u>**before she dismissed them**</u>.

<u>**To enter the contest**</u>, the application must be submitted by Friday.

We found the magazine and put it in a safe place <u>**that had an article about saving money**</u>.

Chapter 42: Commas (p. 393)

We went to the mall, and we saw a great movie.

When we get really tired, we act really silly.

"He's taking flying lessons," said Steven.

The job market, however, is starting to look better.

On Saturday, we went hiking, fishing, and camping.

He was born August 5, 1987, in St. Thomas, Ontario.

Chapter 43: Apostrophes (p. 404)

The followers went into their leader's home.

It's not important that you understand its every function.

That's not a good enough reason to believe Tracy's story.

The children's toys were scattered around the room.

Charles's party was a lot of fun.

Chapter 44: Quotation Marks (p. 411)

"Let's have a picnic," she said.

My mom screamed, "Tom! Get this spider!"

"Put ice on the muscle," said Dr. Jansen, "as soon as possible."

I read three poems, including "The Groundhog."

Derek said, "I'll make dinner."

Chapter 45: Other Punctuation Marks (p. 418)

Matthew turned his paper in early; Erica decided not to turn in a paper at all.

Dave felt sorry for the defendant; however, he had to vote for a conviction.

Aaron needed several items for his dorm room: a comforter, new sheets, a lamp, and a rug.

Amanda had only two words to say about bungee jumping— "Never again."

The recipe says to fold (gently mix) the berries into the batter.

Chapter 46: Capitalization (p. 427)

The Smith family lives on Laurier Avenue.

We fly into Trudeau Airport and then get a taxi to McGill University.

This term I'm taking Spanish, Biology 200, history, and English.

In June, I drove to British Columbia in my Honda Civic.

We read several plays by Shakespeare, including *Hamlet*.

Chapter 47: Abbreviations and Numbers (p. 432)

Lieutenant General Dallaire wrote a book on his experiences in Rwanda.

My dog had **four** puppies.

Over **1 212** people attended.

After I'm laid off, I hope to apply for **EI.**

Crystal just moved to the **United States** from Canada.

Chapter 48: Varying Sentence Structure (p. 439)

Answers will vary.

Chapter 49: Parallelism (p. 444)

We decided <u>to forget about the lawsuit</u> and then <u>moving on with our lives</u>.

Last year, I <u>graduated from college</u>, <u>moved from Toronto to Charlottetown</u>, and <u>have been married</u>.

My sister and brother raise money <u>to feed the homeless</u> and <u>for building a new shelter</u>.

<u>Exercising</u>, <u>eating right</u>, and <u>water</u> will improve a person's health.

Jack went back to school <u>because he wanted to get a better job</u> and <u>because of the girls on campus</u>.

Chapter 50: Combining Sentences (p. 448)

Answers will vary.

Chapter 51: Standard and Nonstandard English (p. 459)

So she <u>goes</u>, can't I meet you at the theatre? **(slang)**

Will you <u>u</u> be there <u>b4</u> me? **(slang)**

We were totally <u>grossed out</u>. **(slang)**

They changed the tire <u>theirselves</u>. **(incorrect)**

We're <u>jamming</u> in the morning. **(slang)**

Chapter 52: Easily Confused Words (p. 467)

I have to <u>accept</u> that I won't be graduating this spring.

<u>Whose</u> bike is this?

I'm not saying <u>it's</u> Johnny's fault.

We are going to need <u>their</u> help.

<u>Where</u> did you say your parents lived?

Chapter 53: Spelling (p. 476)

My cousin just moved to a ~~forign~~ **foreign** country.

Your grandmother makes ~~delishous~~ **delicious** chicken and dumplings.

Dennis is trying to ~~persuaid~~ **persuade** me to join his fraternity.

Winning two years in a row is quite an ~~achievment~~ **achievement.**

Eat your ~~vegtables~~ **vegetables.**

CREDITS ❖

INDEX ❖